Kirsten,

Xmas 2006

If you dream about it, try for it!
We will be behind you and
cheering you on. XOXO Mom & Dad

Directors Close Up

Interviews with Directors Nominated for
Best Film by the Directors Guild of America

Second Edition

Moderated and Edited by
Jeremy Kagan

The Scarecrow Press, Inc.
Lanham, Maryland • Toronto • Oxford
2006

SCARECROW PRESS, INC.

Published in the United States of America
by Scarecrow Press, Inc.
A wholly owned subsidary of
The Rowman & Littlefield Publishing Group, Inc.
4501 Forbes Boulevard, Suite 200, Lanham, Maryland 20706
www.scarecrowpress.com

PO Box 317
Oxford
OX2 9RU, UK

British Library Cataloguing in Publication Information Available

Library of Congress Cataloging-in-Publication Data

Directors close up : interviews with directors nominated for best film by the Directors Guild
of America / edited by Jeremy Kagan.—2nd ed.
p. cm.
Includes index.
ISBN 0–8108–5712–X (pbk. : alk. paper)
1. Motion pictures—Production and direction.   2. Motion picture producers
and directors—United States—Interviews.   I. Kagan, Jeremy Paul.
PN1995.9.P7D543   2006
791.43′0233092273—dc22

2005025790

♾ ™ The paper used in this publication meets the minimum requirements of American National
Standard for Information Sciences—Permanence of Paper for Printed Library Materials, ANSI/NISO
Z39.48–1992. Manufactured in the United States of America.

Contents

Introduction

If we want to discuss the art of filmmaking, we are going to be talking about the work of the great directors. For it is their visions that have expanded the form and content of the movies. Though cinema is certainly a collaborative medium, just mention the names of the finest directors, and we are immediately reminded of the indelible films they have made.

Yet the question is often asked: What does a director do? It might be better phrased: What doesn't a director do? For it is the responsibility of the director to supervise, if not to initiate, all the creative aspects of a movie.

Of course, it is the films themselves that reveal the innovative contributions of these directors. It is on the screen where you will find what they truly do. And to intimately know how they do it, we would have to be in their minds, hearts, and souls during the myriad private moments and public meetings with their team of artists and associates. We would want to be on the sets as they deal with the countless daily challenges of performance and production, and in the editing rooms as they rediscover their stories and combine images and sound to complete their expressions. Since these voyages are often individual ones, we tend to learn about their work more through reflective discussions. And on this quest, we have asked some of the most successful directors of our times a number of questions to hear them talk about their process. And even if words are sometimes limiting, they still give us a taste of the variety of methods these directors employ. With all this in mind, the following are edited selections from interviews that began in 1992 when The Directors Guild of America started a series of yearly seminars with the Nominees for Outstanding Feature Film Directing.

The structure of each of these discussions followed the stages of filmmaking that the director oversees. Facetiously it has been observed that the order of these steps starts with inspiration and enthusiasm, moving to entanglements and panic, leading to a search for the guilty ones, punishment of the innocents, and ending up with rewards to the nonparticipants! Though there is some truth to the above, these symposia were more concerned with exploring creative and pragmatic issues.

Filmmaking is an evolutionary journey. Along the path, the movie goes through four metamorphoses. The first stage usually begins with guiding the development of the script. The second period deals with all the challenges of preproduction that include casting the actors and assembling the crew and its key personnel including the cinematographer, the production designer, the assistant director, the wardrobe designer, the editor, the composer, and many other highly skilled technicians. With these other artists comes the development of the design of the picture: where and how it will be staged and photographed. This process encompasses scouting locations, the construction of sets, the making of costumes and props, the preparation of special effects and stunts, and the countless choices that must be made before the first day of photography. During this time there is often a rehearsal period where the director works with the actors to explore the script and the characters. The shoot is the third phase and many adjustments now arise, both practical and creative, that bring the movie to another level, as the director daily leads the often hundreds of people to deliver their best under the pressures of time and money. And the fourth stage is postproduction. Here the director is in charge of the editing team, supervising the assembling of image, sound, and visual effects. Music now becomes another affective element of the work. And finally, the director oversees all the aural elements as they are mixed together and then he/she approves of the final visual look of the film. Throughout, the work of the director is aesthetically, emotionally, psychologically, and physically challenging. What you will read here are masters of the media explaining their approaches to all these aspects of directing.

The design of this book is to allow you to either read it straight through or dip in anywhere, where you will discover fascinating and sometimes contradictory methods of confronting the intricate directorial process.

As to the language in these selections, we tried to retain the unique speech patterns of each of these directors, so sometimes, the grammar and the vocabulary "ain't the King's English," but it is how these artists talked at these symposia.

We have also included in an appendix a lecture given by Elia Kazan entitled "On What Makes a Director" that was delivered in 1973 at Wesleyan University. Though it reflects the pronoun gender predilections of the time, it remains one of the most elegant declarations of the qualities a director should possess.

To complete this book, I am indebted to many people. My thanks and personal admiration to Robert Wise, master director and cofounder of the Special Projects Committee of the Directors Guild, and to former Guild President Gene Reynolds who initiated these seminars; to persevering Jay Roth, National Executive Director of the Guild, who pressed to have this collection made public; to the devoted National Executive in Charge of Special Projects, Gina Blumenfeld, and the hardworking staff, especially Suzy Dyer and Pamela Kile, who organized all the transcriptions; and to Norm Anderson who turned computer chaos into order. I also want to acknowledge the contribution of Stephen Ryan and Scarecrow Press for being so helpful and expedient in producing this book. But most of all, I want to thank the directors themselves who so generously shared their knowledge and experiences.

I hope you enjoy these encounters and learn from them as I have.

Jeremy Kagan
Moderator and Editor

Nominees in Attendance, 1992–2005

1992

Barry Levinson, *Bugsy*
Oliver Stone, *JFK*
Barbra Streisand, *The Prince of Tides*

1993

Clint Eastwood, *Unforgiven*
Neil Jordan, *The Crying Game*
Rob Reiner, *A Few Good Men*

1994

Andrew Davis, *The Fugitive*

1995

Frank Darabont, *The Shawshank Redemption*
Mike Newell, *Four Weddings and a Funeral*
Quentin Tarantino, *Pulp Fiction*
Robert Zemeckis, *Forrest Gump*

1996

Mel Gibson, *Braveheart*
Michael Radford, *Il Postino*

1997

Cameron Crowe, *Jerry Maguire*
Scott Hicks, *Shine*
Mike Leigh, *Secrets & Lies*
Anthony Minghella, *The English Patient*
Steven Spielberg, *Amistad*

1998

James L. Brooks, *As Good As It Gets*
James Cameron, *Titanic*
Curtis Hanson, *L.A. Confidential*
Gus Van Sant, *Good Will Hunting*

1999

Roberto Benigni, *Life Is Beautiful*
John Madden, *Shakespeare in Love*
Steven Spielberg, *Saving Private Ryan*
Peter Weir, *The Truman Show*

2000

Frank Darabont, *The Green Mile*
Spike Jonze, *Being John Malkovich*
Michael Mann, *The Insider*
Sam Mendes, *American Beauty*
M. Night Shyamalan, *The Sixth Sense*

2001

Ang Lee, *Crouching Tiger, Hidden Dragon*
Steven Soderbergh, *Erin Brockovich* and *Traffic*

2002

Ron Howard, *A Beautiful Mind*
Peter Jackson, *The Lord of the Rings: The Fellowship of the Ring*
Baz Luhrmann, *Moulin Rouge*
Christopher Nolan, *Memento*
Ridley Scott, *Black Hawk Down*

2003

Stephen Daldry, *The Hours*
Peter Jackson, *The Lord of the Rings: The Two Towers*
Rob Marshall, *Chicago*
Roman Polanski, *The Pianist*
Martin Scorsese, *Gangs of New York*

2004

Sofia Coppola, *Lost in Translation*
Clint Eastwood, *Mystic River*
Peter Jackson, *The Lord of the Rings: The Return of the King*
Gary Ross, *Seabiscuit*
Peter Weir, *Master and Commander: The Far Side of the World*

2005

Clint Eastwood, *Million Dollar Baby*
Marc Forster, *Finding Neverland*
Taylor Hackford, *Ray*
Alexander Payne, *Sideways*
Martin Scorsese, *The Aviator*

"How I Got Here"

Robert Zemeckis, *Forrest Gump*

I grew up watching a lot of television and going to the movies when I was a kid to see horror movies and fantasy movies and action movies and war movies. I was entertained by movies and tried to figure out how they did things because it was an awesome power: the idea that millions of strangers are moved by your work. I found out there was a college that had a course in filmmaking. It was USC Film School and I've been doing movies ever since.

By the time I got to film school, I understood it was a director's medium. I'm actually not sure that filmmaking can be taught. They can teach what to do—what not to do. They give you the tools, but they can't make you a filmmaker, there's no way. You have to have that fire inside.

When I was in film school, it was a very exciting time because [George] Lucas and [Francis Ford] Coppola were just about to crack in the industry. We had a sense that something was going to happen, because all we did was think about movies all the time. And the first year in film school, *The Godfather* came out and the second year I was in film school *American Graffiti* came out and it was this big explosion. I mean George Lucas was our hero 'cause he made it happen. And we were all in that kind of campaign to have film students be able to get into mainstream moviemaking at the time.

I think the same exact problems that I had when I was making my little student films are the exact same problems that I have making features. Everything just gets bigger and more expensive.

I have a long list of directors who have had a tremendous influence on me, but I think if I really broke it down, the director who had the most influence probably more than any was Jules White. Jules White directed almost every episode of *The Three Stooges*. Seriously, I think that I have memorized every one of those episodes.

Quentin Tarantino, *Pulp Fiction*

I don't ever remember a time in my life where, like, movies weren't my favorite thing. I didn't have a ton of varied interests as far as like what I wanted to do in my free time. I wasn't into sports, wasn't into building models, and wasn't into all that other boy stuff. I was into movies. I mean, it was, like, it's my birthday or something and if an uncle said to me, "Okay, Quentin, you could go to Disneyland, Knott's Berry Farm, or to any movie you want to see," I'd always pick a movie. When I was a little kid, you'd look at movies and television and go, "I want to do that. I wanna be a part of that." And who you see are the actors. That's who you identify with. So all through my childhood, I wanted to be an actor. I quit ninth grade, I quit junior high, to become an actor.

I studied for years as an actor and that's when I really started kind of understanding how the film medium works. I realized that I just loved movies too much to appear in them. I wanted them to be my movies.

I wanted to be this student of film. This film historian of my own mind, you know. Nobody was hiring me to do it. I just did it. I believe that Jules White is the first director credit that I ever remember seeing, 'cause I watched the Three Stooges every single solitary day, all right? "Directed by Jules White." At the end I thought it was Jules Verne!

When I was a little kid, my favorite kinds of movies in the world were horror films and comedies. I remember I saw *Abbott and Costello Meet Frankenstein,* then I saw *Abbott and Costello Meet the Mummy,* and I remember thinking these are the greatest movies ever made because the funny stuff is really funny and the scary stuff is really scary! Two movies for the price of one!

When I was a teenager, I really had a love and a passion for exploitation films because they were naughty.

In Los Angeles they used to have Filmex, where they would have these fifty-two-hour marathons. They would pick a genre and just show them. I was there all fifty-two hours. Man, it was really kind of cool because you'd just fall asleep and you'd wake up in the middle of *My Fair Lady* or a comedy marathon, and it was there the very first time I saw *His Girl Friday* and I just thought, in a life of laughing I had never laughed so hard consecutively in a movie in my life. I always knew who Howard Hawks was, but it was like, gosh, I've got to see everything he's done! And after a year, I did. And it was really interesting because he taught me storytelling. He taught me how to be entertaining or try to make it an entertaining experience for an audience. When I see *Rio Bravo*, which is one of my favorite three movies of all time, the script is just a masterpiece of storytelling, all right, and it's all tight and confined and there's really wonderful stories going on. But as you're watching the movie, little by little, the characters become such great company. You know, you just really like hanging out with them. And at one point in the middle of this tense situation, four, five, six scenes happen where the bad guys are around and they're kinda laughing and joking. And you forget about, like, the drama and you just get into hanging out with these guys. You just want to hang out with your friends and there's this one moment in it when John Wayne is visiting Angie Dickinson and the bad guys are there and they don't know and they're going to lay this rope down the stairs and they're going to trip him and get him. You know, it's like they're your friends; you want the bad guys to go away. You just want to see these people just having a good time for the rest of the movie and that got me.

Then I discovered Godard and he taught me experimentation. He taught me how to try to make the medium bend in on itself, entertain the audience, but challenge them. You know, give them an uncomfortable experience.

In the movie *The Misfits*, there's a line that Clark Gable has where Marilyn Monroe is complaining about their sorry state of life and he goes, "Hey! That's the way it goes, but it goes the other way, too." And I've been told by seems like everyone on the planet about what a ridiculously lucky guy I am, okay? The thing is though, I went through my entire twenties with the worst luck in the world! For ten years everything that could go wrong went wrong, all right? Now, it's funny, but at the same time when you've donated your twenties, which are your "topsoil years," you, you don't piss your twenties away! If you're going to have a harvest, then you'd better start planting! I had nothing to show for my twenties except hopes, dreams, and my own aspirations. I had even tried to make a movie, at twenty-three, just paying for it myself, getting the equipment on the weekends, shooting in 16mm film and I worked on it for four years and it ended up becoming guitar picks. The single number one thing of my whole life that I am the proudest of that I've done is that I didn't give up then.

M. Night Shyamalan, *The Sixth Sense*

My parents—they're both doctors and everybody in the family is a doctor, and I was supposed to be a doctor. I think how they influenced me was their work ethic. The sixteen-hour days that we do in production, they do all the time. I think that even that they just allowed me to follow this dream was a big, big vote of confidence from them.

When I made my first film, which was in India, it was called *Praying with Anger,* and it was totally just a bomb. When it came out, my dad saw it, and one of the things he advised was put white people in it. So I did that and . . . $650 million! I did my post [the editing of the film] in New York at Sound One, and I used to hear stories about Jonathan Demme coming into an editing room and seeing young filmmakers work and saying, "I'll produce your stuff, this is great," and all this. So I used to keep my editing room open—but nobody came by.

I am inspired by filmmakers that honor both gods: the critical and the kind of intellectual, but also the mass audience. And it's tough to find them. There's an audience IQ, but there's an emotional IQ as well and that is very, very high around the world for everybody. And that's what I try to serve when I make more films and try to find those filmmakers that are making very, very smart movies for a mass audience.

Ridley Scott, *Black Hawk Down*

I was stuck up in the northeast of England, so I wasn't introduced to the full range of cinema in those days. I'd been brought up on Hollywood movies and was passionate about Westerns, to the extent that my parents began to think I was retarded.

I was looking at, you know, the main guys were really John Ford. I think I wanted to be a cowboy till I was eighteen. That's seriously late. I was still riding on the rocking horse, you know. I had since I was five years old. That's really dodgy. So when my dad said, you know, "It's really time you thought about paying attention to what you're gonna do," I was very bad academically at school, since I simply wasn't interested. So I went to art school, and that's where the world opened up for me and in there I had a very good mentor. He said, "You draw well." He said, "There's money in commercial art." He said, "There's money in posters."

I had no formal training in terms of preparing myself as a director. One day I was a pretty good designer, actually, and doing big plays for BBC and things like that. And I was such a nuisance because I was criticizing directors, they finally gave me a production job.

Frank Darabont, *The Green Mile*

My parents' advice about filmmaking was "Don't." Particularly from my father. It was not highly encouraged—quite discouraged in fact. He also wanted me to be a doctor!

On our account, it's just sort of the immigrant dream. We came from Hungary and he said, "Oh be a doctor! You'll put food on the table." And I thought, I don't want to put food on the table. I want to express whatever it is I have in me to express.

Influences, I guess every movie that I ever saw that was great that moved me, that touched my heart, every book I ever read that told me a story that sucked me in. Specifically in terms of directors, oh gosh, starting with Buster Keaton. He was a filmmaker of tremendous heart. I had a high school drama teacher, Jerry Melton, who was terrific. And for three years in high school that's all I did. I don't think I ever left that auditorium. In my adulthood, I've had enormous encouragement from George Lucas, who I've been privileged to work with. And Steven Spielberg, who gave me the wear-comfortable-shoes advice!

Frank Darabont, *The Shawshank Redemption*

For me, seeing George Lucas's *THX 1138* when I was twelve, I remember thinking that if I could stick my head into the screen, through the screen, and like look off to the side of the camera frame, I'd see whoever the hell it was telling me the story. I always wanted to be a storyteller.

These were my gods: David Lean, John Ford, Kubrick, Buster Keaton*, The General*, one of the greatest movies ever, Carol Reed's *The Third Man*. It really comes down to every movie that kind of rocked you back in your seat. When you're sitting in the theater and in the back of your mind there's a little voice saying, "Holy shit!" There's something about a film when it grabs you on some sort of visceral emotion level and just pulls you into that world. That's irreplaceable. The filmmakers I've admired the most are the most versatile ones. Robert Wise was sort of amazing: *The Day the Earth Stood Still* and *The Sound of Music, West Side Story*.

The delightful thing I've discovered in working in this business is that, if you put out the effort, if you really care about what you do, you will find people along the way who lend you a helping hand and that's lovely. It's just a kindness I think that is motivated by shared enthusiasm for what you love—in this case, movies.

Sometimes bad luck comes along and I think that the people who are able to weather that or think their way through it, rather than be consumed by it, are the people to admire.

I've been writing professionally ten years now. I'm stunned to realize it's been going on that long and I've been given the opportunity to now direct as well. I feel damn fortunate. But I also think that you make your own luck by expending the effort. There's a persistence I think that one needs in order to get lucky. And I think one needs to apply the elbow grease of determination and have faith in oneself in order to get lucky. I think you manufacture your opportunities as you go along. Knowing lessens the luck of it. It just heightens your chances of seizing that luck. Somebody once pointed out to me that it took Thomas Edison a thousand attempts using various methods and materials before the damn lightbulb turned on. So what I always keep planted in my head is, "What if he'd gotten really discouraged after nine hundred and ninety-nine times?"

Christopher Nolan, *Memento*

My older brother and I, when we were seven years old, decided to get into filmmaking, and my dad very kindly lent us his very expensive Super 8 camera, and we, you know, started making little war movies using Action Man, which is this sort of G.I. Joe thing, in stop-motion. And then, when I was in my seventh year, I saw *Star Wars,* and everything changed. The world completely changed. And than all my films were called "Space Wars," and I didn't quite know where that title came from. Lucas hasn't sued yet. My dad worked in advertising. He's a very creative guy, and he encouraged me to look at the work of the directors who he kind of knew through that circuit, like Ridley [Scott] and Alan Parker and Hugh Hudson. And I carried on making my own films, just kind of playing around, but my filmmaking could only sustain you for a couple of minutes. Then you had to start thinking about "Well, what's the story? What are you trying to tell?" And so I went to university and studied English literature and the way stories are told.

Steven Soderbergh, *Erin Brockovich* **and** *Traffic*

I had a mentor when I was going to high school in Baton Rouge. I was hanging out with some college students on the LSU campus who were in a film class and it was being taught by a gentleman named Michael McCallan, who was a documentary filmmaker. And I met him when I was thirteen, a time when things imprint very strongly. And he was someone who had certain attitudes about how you work and how you treat people and that you're the audience and that you never speak down to the audience and anything you can understand, they can understand. And he believed in a chain of command but not a chain of respect.

Sometimes a bad movie has a huge impact. I mean in a good way. The ease with which you can make something bad is terrifying. It's like this shadow movie that's running in parallel, you know? All the time. And you're just stepping over land mines every day. Every film I've made has some element about it that scared me before I started.

Oliver Stone, *JFK*

My dad didn't like to go to movies that much, and it was a big thing on a Saturday afternoon if he'd take me to a movie. And I just remember being struck by [Stanley] Kubrick because he liked him. And then [David] Lean, my dad liked and respected David. That made a real impression on me. And a little later—I remember when *La Dolce Vita* came: this was something very intimate and about life, urban life, contemporary life.

Then in film school I was nuts about Godard. That was again a breakthrough because everything was disassociated. There was no narrative line.

Of course, the big breakthrough was when Scorsese did *Taxi Driver*, which we thought was like the world's end. It was like the first American film. It was the first one that really hit me between the eyes and said, "We can do what the Europeans have been doing." Marty [Scorsese] had a lot of passion. He loved movies. That's all he talked about. There was no video in those days so he'd stay up till four in the morning, five in the morning, to watch a Von Sternberg picture. He had these bags under his eyes, his hair down to here. Believe me, it was hard before VCRs to see pictures. It was a hotbed, a ferment of new ideas. A very radical time. People were stealing cameras, taking over universities, or trying to make films into collectives. That didn't work. You can't make a collective movie.

I learned a lot from [Brian] DePalma too. He goes out there and he just says, Well, nothing is going to stop me, no matter how insane the idea is.

When I got out of film school, I thought I was as good as Godard. Nobody else agreed with me. It took me fifteen years to convince anybody.

I did two horror films that flopped and that was a really tough experience. On *Salvador*, I bit the bullet: This is the line no one is going to cross. I'm going to make this movie. We mortgaged the house; my wife agreed. We went down to Salvador and tried to con them into giving us all their helicopters. We said we want to portray the government as the good guys. We gave them a dummy script and we almost pulled it off. We came within that close of doing it, and our adviser got killed. Unfortunately, he got shot by the communists on a tennis court, so that ended that escapade.

I went up to Mexico and shot the film there, and we ran out of money. They closed us down and threw us out of Mexico on the forty-second day. But I hadn't shot the beginning or the end, which was a brilliant move on my part. I just shot the middle and I told John Daly at Hemdale, I said, "Look, you can't release this film. You can't release just the middle of the picture; you need a beginning and an end." He gave me nine more days and another million dollars, I think, to finish it in Las Vegas. That's how the first one got made.

Rob Reiner, *A Few Good Men*

I think basically for me, I'm better at giving orders than taking them! While I was acting, and particularly in shows that were done in front of a live audience, I did the worst possible thing you could do as an actor. I was aware constantly of what the audience was doing every second. I was aware of every camera. I was always more aware of the overall than I was of my part. So I think that was my natural instinct, to go in that direction. And I always said that a director was somebody who's the worst at any job on the set. He stinks at everything, basically. He's not as good an actor as the actors, he can't light like the cameraman, he's not a good prop guy, he can't do a stunt like a stunt man, he can't do anything basically, but he kind of knows a little bit about everything. And so I figured I know a little bit about music, I know a little bit about putting furniture in the right place, I know a little bit about acting, I know a little bit . . . and this is a job where I can put all those little bits of knowledge into something, and the sum total hopefully would be better than just those little things.

I spent most of my youth hanging around *The Dick Van Dyke Show*, watching how my father [Carl Reiner] worked. And I saw how each week a play got created from nothing. And then I had firsthand experience when I did *All in the Family*. I got to see what an audience responded to every single week for two hundred shows.

Elia Kazan was always somebody I looked towards as a great storyteller and also somebody whose pictures had a lot of humanity in them. They were character-driven pieces.

John Madden, *Shakespeare in Love*

I kind of backed into it. I started out as an actor. I was a mimic as a kid and a lot of people mistake that for acting. And I found myself onstage in quite a lot of Shakespeare and thinking not ever about what I was doing in the scene. I wasn't playing very interesting parts I have to admit, but always thinking about everybody else on the stage. And it kind of dawned on me rather late that perhaps I was in the wrong position, that I should be outside looking in. But even then, I took awhile to get to it. I was sort of a director in my social life, I suppose. In the sense that I had a kind of fascistic tendency to want to make people see the world the way I saw it. And I thought that was probably unhealthy. You can ask my wife about that. But and then I decided that maybe there was a way that I could channel this professionally. But it all happened kind of accidentally.

Barry Levinson, *Bugsy*

I'm not sure how you learn what we do. And I'm not exactly sure how we really do what we do. There doesn't seem to be this one book that explains it. I think probably it goes back to watching movies and being in awe of what you see on the screen.

I've always been impressed with John Ford's movies. I find it extraordinary how he made it work. There's a great simplicity to the way he did it. Obviously Orson Welles's *Citizen Kane, Magnificent Ambersons, Touch of Evil,* and *Chimes at Midnight,* you look at some of his movies and you see an incredibly brilliant mind at work. Although he never had a large body of work and many of his films got butchered along the way, I think you're looking at true genius.

I had not intended to be a director. But I'll never forget I went onto the set of the film that I cowrote, and there was a barroom. Interior, barroom, I looked at it, and as soon as I saw the set, I knew it was a totally different movie. It was a square room, and the people at the table were very close to the bar. And in my head I thought it was a very long room and sort of dark, and the people sat very far away from the bar. What it does is it changes the relationship of those people as outcasts in terms of the position to the bar. It makes them more friendly or more disenfranchised by their position to the bar. And making it long to me made it more kind of a lonelier situation. And I think that was the first time that I began to think about—well maybe, how would I do it?

Then I wrote *Diner,* really by accident, and I thought I ought to do this because I know these people and I've lived this life and I don't know who would do it in the way that I see it. And all of sudden you say, here's the script and I want to direct it. And if we can't make the script with me directing it, then let's not make the movie.

Ang Lee, *Crouching Tiger, Hidden Dragon*

I grew up in Taiwan and back then I saw [Ingmar] Bergman's *Virgin Spring.* I just got knocked out. Life is different from then on, and when I came to the States, in theater department every weekend I'd get to see a lot of the films, the nonmainstream films. I think film school does a lot of good. You get to develop as a filmmaker. You get to try something you want to do and then get a response from your classmates. Most of them are pretty brutal. And then when I started to professionally make movies I think step-by-step, it's really about facing the embarrassment, facing the deepest fear you have both in life and in filmmaking and facing audience, being scrutinized.

I can name a whole lot of masters that influenced me. I probably copied them. Probably I took something and tried to make it different, such as the bamboo scene, which a lot of Chinese masters have done sword fighting in bamboo. But nobody ever get up there, so let me try that.

I have very short attention span in following a lecture or reading. That's why I'm a filmmaker, you know. I fail in college exam in Taiwan. That's how I get into drama school and I discover that's what I wanted to do.

Michael Radford, *Il Postino*

I fell in love with the cinema when I was sixteen. When I was a kid, I went to an English public school where the cinema wasn't considered to be a cultural activity. But, when I was sixteen, I was allowed to go to the Bedford Cinemagraphical Society to watch movies with subtitles, which somehow were considered to be superior in some kind of way. You could smoke quietly in the back of the cinema and nobody would notice. And I remember the first movie that I saw was [François] Truffaut's *Shoot the Piano Player*, and it was amazing. I was just kind of knocked out by it. And as I sat entranced every Sunday afternoon, I thought to myself, "Gee whiz . . . I'd like to do that."

I went to film school and made a little film. I don't say that everybody has to go to film school to become a director, but for me it was very good because I found myself able just to concentrate on my own heart's desire without any economic pressures. I was able to just soak up the cinema and soak up the great directors. In my early formation it was in European cinema, it was Godard and Antonioni, and we all tried to make films like Godard and we all failed miserably, because he was always one jump ahead of you. And then I started to study Hollywood cinema, American cinema, and I began to see the fabulous techniques that directors could use with sometimes incredibly shoddy material. I saw these movies which were theoretically run-of-the-mill movies, made by guys like Nicholas Ray and Raoul Walsh and other great moviemakers in Hollywood, and I was amazed how this voice would come through.

But the thing about directing, finally, is that you have to do it yourself. I mean, there's no substitute.

Peter Weir, *The Truman Show*

Well, from my background, from Australia, and making short films and acting in reviews and so on in the '60s, there was no film industry. I was drawn to the life of the theater, of show business. It was something that was distant from me. So I got into university reviews and began to make film clips. Australia was in great upheaval: we were of course in the war too, the Vietnam War, and it was the year of, you know, do your own thing. And there was a feeling that you could, as it were, do anything. You could break from the life that your parents hoped for you, university and so on, and that was my own case. A lot of heartache with my family because I was going into something that they had no idea, you know, "What's this acting?" and so on. And slowly by making the film clips I began to think I was far better at doing this than the acting, and continued writing. So again, it was something that happened to me. It was a case of finding which part to play in this wonderful theatrical life. I never planned it. One day somebody said, "You are a director, not a producer" because on a little short film I had put down that I was the producer. They said, "No, no," and I said, "Well, what does it matter?" The screen was your teacher as you went along. And sometimes I craved those elders that you knew existed in Europe and America. But on the other hand we were free. In as much you didn't get advice, you were free to do anything. You were blazing trails. It was terribly exciting just to get an image up on the screen.

Sam Mendes, *American Beauty*

I didn't go to film school. I learned through the theater really doing play after play after play and sitting with an audience and letting them tell me when it was bad and when it was good.

   The movies made in this country between 1967 approximately and 1975, particularly [Stanley] Kubrick, also Robert Altman—and [Roman] Polanski and [François] Truffaut—those people came into my head more than anyone else when I was making the film, so I suppose I classify them as my main influences.

Peter Jackson, *The Lord of the Rings: The Fellowship of the Ring*

I grew up in New Zealand, a time where there was no film industry. *Thunderbirds*, which was this amazing English children's puppet show, was the first real big influence in my life when I was about five years old. And I then grew up wanting to get into special effects, I think because *Thunderbirds* had all these amazing spaceships, and I started to build models. And I was an only child, so I was by myself a lot of the time and I used to play in my parents' back garden with like little, you know, cars and trucks and toys and make little adventures and carve roads into the bank and have little rescue missions when trucks went over the edge of the bank, and kind of the fact that you can now do that as a grown-up is fantastic.

   I'd start to dream up little stories. And then around about the time I was seven, my mom and dad got given a Super 8 movie camera for a Christmas present. And I immediately grabbed this camera. And another big influence was *King Kong*, the original 1933 *King Kong*, which I saw on TV when I was about nine years old. The day after I saw the movie, it was a Saturday and I was due to go on a hike with my local Scout group. And I took my Super 8 camera along to film some of this hiking, and I insisted that the Scouts, instead of me filming them walking along the trail with their pack, that I did it in stop-motion. So I got them to just move a frame at a time, and it was a stop-motion hike. Which probably turned the entire journey into a pretty painful experience for all of the other scouts. I wanted to be a stop-motion animator for a while.

Ray Harryhausen [famed fantasy filmmaker] was a huge influence. I came to realize, though, that if you were an animator or a special effects guy, it was ultimately gonna be frustrating, because you were gonna have to do what other people told you to do. And I kind of realized that my real love was the stories, was telling the stories, not just doing the effects. So I started to realize that the guy who tells the stories is the director. I couldn't get a job in the film industry when I left school, so I became a photoengraver at a newspaper. And I worked there for seven years. I saved up my money, I bought a 16mm camera, I made a little film, which I started out as a short film during the weekends with friends of mine, and that grew into a feature film, which we shot on Sundays, basically, over four years called *Bad Taste.* And then that film got sold at the Cannes Film Festival, and that sort of kicked things off for me. I'm really a child of commercial cinema, I guess. I love making movies because I love seeing movies.

Baz Luhrmann, *Moulin Rouge*

I grew up in the . . . in the middle of absolutely nowhere. I mean we lived on a gas station that was on this sort of vast highway, and we had a farm and I'm realizing more and more what a great influence my father was on me. The thing is that the man who sold the petrol to us, to the gas station, owned the cinema. And at a certain point, he died, and because my father had been in the Vietnam War, and he knew how to thread some 16mm footage through a gate, he took over the cinema for a short time, and that allowed me to see, you know, adult films, and indeed, I saw my first adult film, which, like, really was a Western, except people sang. It was called *Paint Your Wagon,* you know. And actually, when I saw my second Western, I was like, you know, like, "Where's the singing?" So that kinda screwed with my head a bit, you know. Then we got what we call cheap television. Cheap rubbish, things that studios would dump down, like *Citizen Kane* or *Red Shoes* or *Singin' in the Rain* or *Top Hat,* and really obscure things that had subtitles on them, right? So I grew up in that. My father, he had a Straight 8 camera and we would make films and do magic shows. So it was always, just this really rich kind of fantasy world. And with my father, it wasn't enough just to have an idea, and then to invent a way of it happening, but he also had to change the world around us so that it would accept the idea, which, you know, is a little wearying, I've gotta tell you. Then my folks split up, and I found myself in drama school. And it was there that I continued this thing of telling story, making what I would call shows. And there was, however, a true mentor for me. He really made opportunity happen to me, and he's a recluse now. And he only ever made one motion picture. And his name was Jim Sharman. It was called *The Rocky Horror Picture Show.* And he created that piece, you know. And then I was mentored to Peter Brook, who's an English theater director did a piece called *The Mahabharata,* of which I seconded, and he gave me great advice, which was "What are you wasting your time here? Go and do it yourself." And then I went to make a film of a play I did called *Strictly Ballroom.* So I reached back into this kind of love of musicals, but I have to say that directors like Peter Weir and Jane Campion and a lot of the Aussie directors just came out of the woodwork for absolutely no reason, and came to me and said, you know, like "This is a camera, and you look in this end, and you know." Like fundamental lessons about making a film. And they were incredibly supportive. That exchange among directors is something that I feel very, very appreciative of.

Spike Jonze, *Being John Malkovich*

There's a lot of directors that I've sort of worked along with through music videos and commercials. We all influence each other. Michel Gondry, who's a French video director and commercial director—just being able to talk, show each other our new things and talk about stuff or ask questions, has been a big thing.

Clint Eastwood, *Unforgiven*

Well, I'd been an actor for quite a few years. I was figuring one day it might not be a thing I'd like to do or else I'd look up there and say, "That's the end of that kid. You'd better get lost." I started getting interested in directing in the 1960s especially working with European directors. And then in 1970 I found a little script I liked, which I could do for a very modest price and so I decided to dive in. They said you're welcome to direct the film, no problem, as long as you're in it. So I had that little bit of leverage to get me started.

   The thing that kills you about directing is the amount of questions that are asked per day and how can you possibly come up with the answers. And you have to get to a point in your psyche, where you say, "I'm gonna answer this even if it's wrong. I've got to come up with something." But then after a while, after you've been with it quite a few years, I think you build a routine and some of the questions you can answer.

   I grew up on John Ford movies, and Howard Hawks I like very much. *His Girl Friday* still knocks me out. I like Preston Sturges a lot. Later I became a fan of Kurosawa. On the *Rawhide* days I got to work with a lot of directors and you see ideas that they do, you see the way they operate and you get opinions, and even directors you don't care for sometimes, you say, "Well that's great but this isn't the way I would do it." Of course, Sergio Leone in the 1960s was a very big influence on me, and the whole different approach of European filmmakers at that particular time. Don Siegel, I'd say, was on the top of the list for me because he was a close friend and he was a terribly efficient filmmaker, very underrated because he came up through the ranks.

Andrew Davis, *The Fugitive*

I was always interested in reality. My degree is in journalism, and I was drawn to films that had a certain kind of honesty. I was not one of those filmmakers who studied Hitchcock, for example. I was more interested in films by the Italian realists. Fellini, Bertolucci, Stanley Kubrick, Sidney Lumet, Bill Friedkin's early work, these were all filmmakers that did things that inspired me. My parents had a big role in my getting involved. My father and mother were friends with a man named Haskell Wexler, a great filmmaker and cinematographer, and a role model for me. And I actually was very lucky because when I was twenty-one, I got to shoot a commercial and I became a camera-man. And then I came to California and I couldn't get in the union because they had these restrictive policies. I said, "You know, it's easier to be a director." I was fortunate to have worked with young directors, and we struggled together and I said, "Well, I'll do a film about my kid brother." And I made a movie called *Stony Island*, which was very autobiographical. So I did that film, and it led to another film, but eventually, through very strange circumstances, and sort of falling out of windows and landing on my feet, I was offered a film called *Code of Silence*, which I desperately needed because I thought I'd never work again. And the film was fairly successful, so I became an action director.

Mike Newell, *Four Weddings and a Funeral*

The first film that I remember seeing was a film called *Bad Day at Black Rock,* which was a Spencer Tracy movie, and it was on my tenth birthday and my mother gave us all half a crown and sent us off to the local cinema. And then we came back and played the film out in the field afterwards. I remember *Grand Illusion*, a Renoir film about the First World War. There was an extraordinary sequence with a German aristocrat and a French aristocrat. The German being the commander of the prison camp in which the Frenchman is talking about their common aristocracy rather than their being on opposite sides. And I found that a lot of my expectations were overturned by that. It's sort of humanist stuff that was the stuff that got me.

The films which made me laugh were obvious. There is a wonderful film called *Kind Hearts and Coronets*, which is a blinding piece of storytelling apart from anything else. But then there's Billy Wilder, and you used to go and see everything that Billy Wilder ever made.

I wanted to become an actor, because clearly they had fun and I thought I was very beautiful. But then as a student, I did an audition in front of another student and looked up after doing my piece of Hamlet, and he said, "Thank you." And so I stopped being an actor and became a stagehand. And then I went into television because I couldn't get a job in the theater, and they showed me the instruments of torture and I was hooked and that's where I stayed.

When I started there weren't film schools in England. You started out working. If there were mentors, they tended to be people who worked along side you. And there were wonderful television directors. I started in television because that's where you started work.

Ron Howard, *A Beautiful Mind*

A significant part of my childhood was spent on a set. And some of the first directors that I really remember, when I was working on *The Andy Griffith Show,* had been also actors. Bob Sweeney and later Lee Phillips and Richard Crenna directed a bunch of episodes. These were guys who had made this transition. And I was also fascinated by what was going on behind the camera. Mostly because I liked the guys, and back then it was all guys. And they'd show me the difference between lenses. I acted for Vincente

Minnelli in a movie. And that was really the first time that I was aware of the difference between what I was doing as a kid actor on a TV show and what happened on one of those big stages at MGM.

When people would say when I was eight years old, they'd say, "What do you wanna be when you grow up?" I didn't say cowboy; I said, "I want to be an actor/ writer/producer/director/cameraman." And baseball player. Thinking it could be sort of a seasonal deal. And when I was about fifteen, there was a director that I worked for named Robert Totten. It was a Disney film and what I found early on was he had directed his first film at twenty-one. Now, this is 1969. At that time, it was very hard to get movies going, you know, coming out of film school. When I talked to him, he said, "Well, what do you want to do?" And I said, "Well, maybe I wanna direct some-day." His answer was "What are you waiting for?" And that was the first time that that sort of comment was ever met with that sort of response. And a couple years later, I was acting in a TV series with Henry Fonda. And it was a pretty dreadful show, and I began showing him some of the Super 8 movies that I was making, and asking him to read some of the scripts that I was writing, and he said, you know, "If you love movies as much as I can see that you do, you oughtta become a director. Because it's a director's medium." And it was that boost that meant a lot.

And I learned a lot from George Lucas. Working on *American Graffiti*. Because it was a totally revolutionary kind of approach, and suddenly, that was all about detail. To George, the cars in the background were as important as what the actors were doing in the foreground. And that was weird to me as an actor, but when I saw the movie, I understood.

Steven Spielberg, *Saving Private Ryan*

I was always looking for a way to act out and I found that the best way to act out was to get a movie camera and let that do it for you. I also got in less trouble because they'd blame the film, not the filmmaker.

When I first started out making movies, it was just simply a matter of taking a camera and trying to make ends meet, if you know what I mean. The best advice, not the best advice, but I remember the advice of Fellini, gave me. I met Fellini when I brought *Duel* over to Europe for the first time in 1971 or '72. And I met the master. I was waiting for some sage advice from him. I kept asking him, "Help me be a better director. What can I do?" and he said, "When you talk to the press, lie." He said because you'll bore yourself, you'll tell the same story which is the truth over and over again. You have forty interviews today, right? I said yeah. He says, "Lie to each one; tell each one a different story."

Roberto Benigni, *Life Is Beautiful*

I think that making movies is, and we know I'm saying now a very idiotic thing, that it is the most wonderful way to tell a story. Nothing is more beautiful. Directors they are dreaming for us, they are the benefactors. So I would like to thank every director.

And the advice I had, for example Fellini told me, "Robertino, remember, always tell the truth." Now I understand, he was lying to me. Wonderful advice!

Mel Gibson, *Braveheart*

One of my most favorite things to do is tell a story and have it work, just in a room. That to me is one of the greatest sources of pleasure you can give other people and you feel pretty good doing it yourself. And it just seemed the natural progression from where I was. And I was frightened and terrified to do it. But I worked with a director, who shall remain nameless, and I thought, if he can do it, anybody can. It sort of creeps into your dreams a little bit.

I was a TV junkie in the '60s, and they put everything on television then. So I had a lot of things to watch and analyze and reenact. But surely the people that I worked with were the strongest influence, directors like George Miller and Peter Weir.

Neil Jordan, *The Crying Game*

I was in Ireland and there had never been any directors in Ireland as far as I knew, and I was very interested in films and I thought movies were made from creatures from the United States or from Italy. Irish people what they did was write books, or they got very black and dark and said they were writing a book. But I started writing scripts. I was very interested in movies since I was a kid, and the books I was writing were so overlaid with visual description for some reason, probably because my mother was a painter. After a certain stage it became redundant for me to write them as books anymore so I began to write screenplays. And I would have been perfectly happy writing scripts forever if I could have found someone who would do exactly what I wanted them to do as a director. Honestly, because I had no idea what directing entailed. So if I said, "Exterior day, rather dark, but not too dark," or something like that, and "the guy comes through the door and he coughs," if somebody would have done exactly that, I would have been perfectly happy to be a writer for the rest of my life but that person was not around of course. So I decided to do it myself. I got a friend of mine, John Boorman [director of *Deliverance* and *The Emerald Forest*], who I'd written a screenplay with, and I'd written part of the screenplay for *Excalibur*, and he agreed to produce for me. So that was the first film I did. But I really didn't know anything. I just knew about the pictures that I wanted to see in my mind really.

I'd made two kinds of Hollywood films and I was kind of exhausted because there they didn't do very well, neither of them. They were a bit both wearying experiences and they didn't perform at the box office. And you get exhausted. You get depressed. You feel rejected.

Mike Leigh, *Secrets & Lies*

I grew up in the '40s and '50s in Manchester. It was a period where there were movie houses on every street corner and I spent a huge amount of time going to the "pictures," as we all called it. So I kind of had an early passion for the movies. I think that I wanted to be a film director from quite an early age because it was very exciting really. I got to London in the '60s and started to discover the international cinema of every kind. And it really took off from there. I trained as an actor and went to art school and did a film course and really moved in the direction of filmmaking.

Michael Mann, *The Insider*

In terms of influences, it shifts, and it still shifts. I was very taken with [Stanley] Kubrick, because *Dr. Strangelove* came out in '63 just when I decided I wanted to make film. But also Eisenstein and concepts of montage, not the graphic, more the montage in *Lawrence [of Arabia]*, the match becoming the sun over the Sahara, that kind of juxtapositions of meaning and content. And Murnau and in a different vein some of the early [directors]—Pabst's *The Joyless Street*, that kind of film.

Barbra Streisand, *The Prince of Tides*

I think directing comes from the instinct. I did have the great fortune and privilege to have my first director be William Wyler, whom I adored. He is one of the greatest directors of all time—a great storyteller. It was interesting because he wasn't a man of many words. In fact sometimes he couldn't tell you what he really wanted, but he knew when it was right. And you knew that he knew. So he was the best audience that you could have—the best director I could have learned from. He gave me a silver megaphone at the end of shooting and encouraged me to direct.

Scott Hicks, *Shine*

I heard somebody say in Australia that everybody who can't play the piano wants to become a director. Which has sort of taken on a whole new resonance for me because I wanted to play the piano but I never did. I didn't grow up as a child of film. I grew up in Kenya. There was no cinema. There was no television. And I didn't discover film until quite later when I was at a university. And I set about acquiring an education in film, which really for me was looking at the great masters of European cinema of the '60s. There was Bergman and Fellini. And Orson Welles was an enormous sort of pal to me, as a teenager, when I was on this discovery voyage.

People often ask me how your career sort of develops and I remind them that if you look up the word *career* in the *Oxford English Dictionary*, it's defined as something like an uncontrolled lurch downhill. You know it is a series of accidents in a way and it depends on how you seize certain moments.

Anthony Minghella, *The English Patient*

Well, I am a pianist and that's what I wanted. I wanted to be a musician. I remember driving my father's ice cream van on the Isle of Wight thinking, "I promise myself, I'll never have anything to do with selling anything. I'll be a writer or a musician or a director." And then I find myself here a few years ago with my ice cream trying to sell it to somebody.

You know, I'm a wop, so all of the Italian cinema appeals to me: Fellini, Visconti, Taviani brothers, Olmi. I mean those are the films that I cherished when I was growing up.

I think that the gift you have as a director is that if your interest is in music and in painting, as mine was as a student, then it's the one activity that you can do which calls into play all of your passions and enthusiasm.

• 2 •

The Script

Oliver Stone, *JFK*

I do not worship the script as a sacred thing at all. I sometimes just get rid of it and say let's go without it. I like to keep that improvisatory nature on the set. It has to be spontaneous; it has to be felt. If it's not working, rip it up and change it right then and there. The writing process is—like writing. You sit there. Ass plus seat equals writing.

It takes a long time. I'd read all the books I could that are credible, and I hired a very brainy young researcher. She read everything: three hundred of the credible books and every article. We joined the network of research buffs. We got a lot of information, the usual witnesses that came into the office and said they were there, that they killed so and so. And we got all the theories. We listened to everybody. It was the longest research job I've ever been involved with.

We refined the script, Zack Sklar and I, over a period of a year. There were six drafts. The first of which of course was notoriously stolen from the Warner Xerox room. There were approximately two thousand facts that we wanted to have in the original draft. I think we dropped it down—there are twelve hundred facts in this movie at this stage. We simplified. We had to. We had to condense characters. We had to redistribute events to a certain degree because the Kennedy killing is so mosaic: the fragments have come out over eighteen to twenty years and they're all in different places.

It's a 180-page script, 2,000 camera setups at least, and probably 2,500 cuts in the movie.

The hardest part of the writing was refining the facts to where somebody could understand them. How can you say it in a simpler way? Two sentences instead of three. You're down to counting words. Literally, with a stopwatch, because you want to move the thing along.

Themes change. This was a tricky one because it started out as a microcosm of Jim Garrison investigating a small police report that leads to the macrocosmic, global crime of the murder of a president. I didn't see all the themes that were coming. I never saw the linkage of Kennedy's murder to the differences in policy in Vietnam. It was not just about some ancient history. It's about whether we have a democracy in this country, whether the state is keeping the secrets. Who owns reality? That's certainly a philosophical theme of the movie. It comes up again and again in the style of the movie, because

17

(Rev.4/1/91)   90

②

FRANK
You've got nothin' Bill. I'm talking as a friend now. You're riding on the Titanic. Time to jump off before you get destroyed along with Garrison...

BOXLEY
Frank, I don't want to hear it.

FRANK
Senator Long set your boss up, my friend...

This gets Boxley's attention.

FRANK
Who do you think fed him that information? Garrison's going down. We're talking about your career here Bill, your life. You're a young guy...we know you're working that Castro thing.

BOXLEY
No I'm not...

FRANK
Yes you are. Look we know Oswald didn't pull that trigger. Castro did. But if that comes out, there's gonna be a war boy -- millions of people are gonna die. That's a hell of a lot more important than Jim Garrison. (suddenly) Goddammit, look at me when I talk to you! You're goddamn too self-opinionated, now shut up. If you got a brain in that thick skull of yours, listen to me. Listen real hard.

③ Boxley, taken aback, listens.

63. EXT. WASHINGTON D.C. PARK - DAY (1967)   SC.63

JIM walks down from the Lincoln Memorial, where he is met unobtrusively by a military MAN in his 50's in casual civilian clothing, hat on his head, an erect posture. They walk towards the Mall, with the Capital building looming in the background.

                        X
Jim Garrison?

                    JIM
Yes.

                    X (shakes hands)
I'm glad you came. I'm sorry about the precautions.

                    JIM
Well, I just hope it was worth my while, Mr....

The man doesn't answer. Jim, after his meeting with Miller and loss of Ferrie, is testy and suspicious.

Rewrites by Oliver Stone for JFK. (Excerpts from JFK granted courtesy of Warner Bros. Entertainment Inc. and Oliver Stone.)

it's fractured. It's disassociated, like Godard. You can never get into a conventional linear pattern because there's no conventional linear pattern to the history of that period. The media owns reality. The government owns reality. It's so fractured, and the camera and the style really tries to reflect the *Rashômon* truth to that story.

Salvador was about a small theme. At the beginning it was a journalist I knew who was a rascal who got hooked by a woman and a boy, and a family. And all of the sudden he's a less selfish individual at the end of the movie. I thought that was a nice transcendent theme.

Frank Darabont, *The Green Mile*

To me the script is always my life preserver. I'm not the "oh, let's improv a scene" kind of guy. That would absolutely horrify me. Because my process of invention, I think, is much slower, which is why I started out as a writer. So aside from, literally, minor little dialogue tweaks between finishing the script and actually shooting the script, there's really not that much evolution that goes on for me.

I'm learning to recognize shoe leather. It's amazing how many shots of people walking you wind up with in a movie and if it doesn't mean something that they're walking, you shouldn't even write it if possible.

Frank Darabont, *The Shawshank Redemption*

I'm a big believer in walking onto a set with a script that I feel is pretty much the movie you're gonna make. I know there's some folks in the world, Woody Allen and Robert Altman, who kind of get in and want to discover this as they're shooting. I can't think of anything more terrifying than not knowing at the end of the day I have a scene that works, that I can put on film. Within the contents of that, certainly, any given day of shooting an actor will maybe modify dialogue a little bit here and there. I mean, you do want to be flexible. The writer does somewhat come off and the director goes, "Well, okay, let's see if we can improve on what the writer did."

I always write for the director, at least in my screenplays. I find I have a projector running in my head. I feel that my job is to visualize the movie on paper as closely as possible, so that when the reader goes to the script, they see the movie the same way I do. So I really try to replicate it in that sense. Oftentimes things get lost in the translation. I discovered as a writer that there was, in the making of *Shawshank*, a real advantage in having the director working towards the same goal.

This came from a Stephen King novella and it just goes to show what you can do with a good source material. The technique of telling most of the story in flashback and then clicking into sort of real time in the last, say, ten, fifteen minutes of the movie, was a direct lift from King's structure. There was a certain amount of invention on my part as the screenwriter, but even when I was inventing or changing something, I always tried very hard to bear in mind what King's intent was. Because he just told such a good story that I didn't want to mess with too much. But it was such a sort of amicable, rambling kind of first-person narrative that there was a certain level of mechanical screen structure that I had to bring to it.

Ridley Scott, *Black Hawk Down*

This script was in a constant state of evolution—it's becoming the norm, actually, isn't it? And I don't mind that. I think what's dangerous in having a very prepared script is that you relax. And you must never take your eye off the ball. Whereas if you're going where the script is in flux, you're constantly paying attention.

I like to study people on the edge of some form, of event or cutting edge of society, because that's where you see human behavior most stretched and most challenged.

It's really my job to take you into a zone that you normally wouldn't experience. I'm gonna transport you like a good piece of music. I think more films in the mainstream should provoke discussion and not be simply entertainment.

There are no good guys and bad guys in this story other than the person you're trying to arrest, which is very similar to what's happening today.

Stephen Daldry, *The Hours*

I suppose I spend most of my life working with writers, mostly in the theater, particularly at the Royal Court Theatre, so the process of developing something from commission through to realization is something I'm incredibly used to. David Hare is a very old collaborator of mine, and we were working on a piece of theater when this project came up and we're very close. He is my core collaborator in a sense, and David stayed with me not just in the writing but he would stay through the shoot and through post-production and through to final mix. So he's my sort of . . . my lynch pin. People always said Michael Cunningham's book was very difficult, and David and I never really felt that. It seemed that there was an incredibly strong internal dramatic mechanism to it, you know, a writer, a reader, and a character, and there was inevitably going to be the relationship between the three women, not just thematically but literally, narratively. And once those narrative strands start combining, there was always going to be a cinematic rush to it. David explored the idea of voiceover and then that was ditched quite early 'cause, quite simply, there would have to be three voiceovers. We pretty much knew exactly what we were doing and how the cutting pattern was going to work before we started shooting. The architecture was entirely in place. David writes in an elliptical way. I always used to get him to read the scenes so I could actually understand exactly what he was saying.

What I always loved about the material, both Michael Cunningham's book and David Hare's screenplay, was it charted very brilliantly the very difficult choices that people have to make in their lives and, more importantly perhaps, the cost of those choices. So that I always felt that the three women got somewhere, that they were actually moving and needing and in the end managing to find a means by which they can live. In terms of Virginia Woolf, knowing that there was going to be a cost involved and the cost was going to be the demons were potentially going to come and probably would come, but in the intervening years she wrote probably some of the greatest works of the twentieth century. So that she'd managed to do what she wanted.

Mike Newell, *Four Weddings and a Funeral*

The script, and it isn't always, should be questionable. You should have the right to work on the script and change things. Sometimes that can be very harmonious and sometimes that can be very distressing. An unharmonious relationship with a writer will never produce anything. And I suppose one of the lessons that I also learned was to make harmony no matter what. Then I guess what you do is follow your nose; you tend not to follow logic.

When I started work in television in the middle to late '60s, you'd do shows with a six-week turnaround. So you could do eight, ten, twelve shows a year. And you'd get to learn the writing process from the ground up. A lot of the time I remember spending in preparation for the television shows with scripts spread out on the floor of an office and actually cutting and pasting with the producer who would say, "No, no put that there, put that there." What you were learning was structure and editing. And it was a very simple unmysterious process. You could actually take scene 3 and put it next to scene 18 and then put that next to scene 25 and fiddle about and watch it be different and that was tremendous: a pair of scissors and a pot of glue.

Four Weddings was a very good script and it was very funny, but it was too funny. There wasn't anything lying through it. It was simply a succession of very well honed jokes. But also it didn't work—there wasn't an arc in the character properly. We did a dozen drafts. We would just play a theme: commitment or the lack of commitment.

I don't like writing during shooting, and I try to have it all done. Of course it's going to happen, little bits and pieces are going to happen. I have also found myself in the situation where things are much looser than that because people have asked for them to be looser or you've lost control of it or whatever and it's always a nightmare.

You'd better use the script process for finding out what it's about. I mean, it's a long three-month, four-month process of understanding what's on the page. So to start to visualize is irrelevant to me. That has it's own time.

And part of the director's job is to say in a very large overall way, "I won't have it like that. I will have it like that."

James L. Brooks, *As Good As It Gets*

I had a funny journey because this was a wonderful script by Mark Andrus that I took on first as a producer. And as such, I really just was bringing it along, and then at some point I got involved where I knew I was going to direct it, and then I just wanted to work with the script. Then a year later I was still working with the script and we formed some alchemy. We didn't know each other well, and we're very different men, but somehow each of us got very personally invested and we were this writing team that came out with something where we each feel very together on it. So I think that gave me a less secure footing than I've had in the past, because I was trying to represent some very deep feelings that weren't from me, and the tone changed. Tone was up for grabs. It was never an absolute tone that I started the movie from the script that I knew that I would follow.

James Cameron, *Titanic*

Well as a director I was constantly cursing that son of a bitch the writer every day for getting me into this mess! There was the evolution of the script certainly from a pretty nebulous first idea, which was, "Wouldn't it be cool to make a movie about the Titanic?!" So how do you deal with that subject? How do you treat it respectfully? How do you do something new, carve out your own territory? And I pretty quickly hit on the idea of doing a love story.

I wanted to do something with great passion so that the interior power of the story was as strong as the exterior. And I couldn't find any true story that had actually transpired from history that had that kind of passionate energy to it, so I thought it was better to do it with fictitious characters.

I start with images because I started as an illustrator and production designer and so for me it always becomes a number of visual set pieces. I sort of collect a few and then I'll start at the very beginning and build the character and really start to tell the story from the character standpoint, with those set pieces in the back of my mind.

I had written an early version of the script, which I euphemistically call "a scriptment." Because if I can't think of the exact dialogue for a scene, I don't bog down. I just write, "And then they have an argument and the argument is about this." It drops into a novelistic default kind of form and then it goes back into script form when I can actually think of what the people might be saying, so it oscillates back and forth. It's kind of a bastard document but it's a great starting point. And we went and dove the ship and coming back from that experience, it colored the directing process after that quite a bit. I had wanted suspense thriller elements in the story to kind of energize it and keep it moving, and I found those becoming increasingly less necessary as I went along.

Anthony Minghella, *The English Patient*

I can't imagine wanting to write a film and not direct because they're such an organic activity, and I think that the pen continues to work all the way through filmmaking and in a sense that I think that you begin with ink, and you write on paper, and then you swap that instrument for a camera and that continues to write. And I'm incredibly alert to the fact that you're writing all the way through the filmmaking process. And then you get to the cutting room and again you become another kind of writer. And I felt that I was directing on the very first day that I was writing, and writing literally about a week before I finished the film. Literally writing new material. I have the advantage in the sense that there was a novel that provided the source for this film. In many ways that became as much a curse as a blessing because it's an incredible novel but it's got nothing to do with the movie.

I remember somebody calling me and saying, "I like it. Where's the third act?" And I said, "Where's the second act of this screenplay?" I mean one thing about Hollywood is that it's become more Aristotelian than Aristotle about this notion about what a screenplay has to be like. I didn't share that belief, but I do very much think that our job is to tell stories. The two years that I was working on the screenplay were very much about how to transport the audience in the way that I had been transported as a reader. I felt in a way that I couldn't adapt the book. I could only respond to it. I felt as if I were the only person allowed to read this novel, and then my job was to try and find a way to communicate it to an audience who knew nothing about it.

I think you need architecture in films. Architecture in the sense that I think there needs to be a guiding idea. There needs to be a sense that there's a phrasing. The shape of the journey is stated very early so that the audience feels in safe hands.

I had this image that I brought out from Japan where they were telling us how the samurai sword is made. They bang out a piece of metal until it's very sharp and then they shove it in the furnace and fold it over and bang it out again until it's really sharp.

And when it's as sharp as it can be, then they put it back in the furnace. With my screenplay, I'd bring it out, bang it very hard, and lots of my favorite bits would drop off. That process was an incredible time for me, meticulous and rigorous. I think that the film finds itself. I don't think that I woke up on the first day of this project and knew what this film was going to be.

When I'm writing, I like to work by myself for long periods of time. And so I enjoy the process of imagining what a film would be like and imagining how it might play.

Spike Jonze, *Being John Malkovich*

Charlie Kaufman wrote the script, and when I read it, I was amazed by it and loved it. But probably it took a while to get it going, and we worked on it a lot together and went through it scene by scene, just sat in a room for a few weeks and just talked about what parts we thought worked and didn't work, and why they didn't work.

Charlie's writing has a lot to it in terms of having humor, but also in having complex characters and absurd ideas. And as far as tone goes, it was just walking that fine line of not trying too hard and not going for jokes too much.

Martin Scorsese, *Gangs of New York*

The Gangs of New York I had in my head for many, many years. I was seven years old when I first heard the story about the Catholic church about to be attacked by the Know Nothings, the Anglos who felt they were the real Americans. It takes place in the neighborhood I grew up. I'm interested in the breakdown of a civilization and how does an individual survive and then groups of people survive. And ultimately who will wind up killing for food to survive. It's tribal. And fathers and sons, blood oaths, blood rituals, and using religion as a faith to bind them all, but basically religion is used as a weapon. That was the idea. Through all this turmoil and struggle and people living, loving, dying, re-creating, all kinds of things, you know, civilization seems to go on. But the struggles are so primal and the world we're in now is so small that ultimately, yeah, we're facing a very serious threat of total extinction. But I'm a fatalist. I'm Sicilian.

Usually it's gotta be on the page even to the extent for me usually of dissolves, tracking, camera angles, colors, that sort of thing 'cause I've come out of a situation where I used to have to work very quickly and I wanted everything drawn incorporating room for improvisation, depending on the type of film you're doing. Like *Mean Streets*, for example, there's a scene with De Niro and Harvey Keitel in the back room of the bar, which goes on for about five minutes which is a total improv and which we squeezed into the last day of shooting. Jay Cocks [the writer] is my closest friend. I told him about this book *Gangs of New York*. Basically, all those stories were in my head already. My father had told me certain things about the Irish gangs because Sicilians and the Irish didn't get along in the Lower East Side. We started talking about this underworld in New York, and by 1977 he had pulled together a first draft, about 180 pages, 190 pages. It was like a novel. It was quite beautiful. I had this concept of something about use of voiceover narration, which I happen to like. And then when we decided to write it, we went to a—I was living in an apartment on Fifty-seventh Street—we did it, everything, line by line together, shot by shot, color, movement, dissolves, in two and a half weeks. The beginning is still the same. You don't know where you are. The gangs come up through from the inferno below and fight it out in the streets. Then you see New York City 1846. By that point we never heard about the draft riots. It was never talked about in America and never taught in school: New York City being almost a Southern sympathizer, really. It's just that Jay and I had such a feeling about it over the years. He had worked by himself on it. And by '79, 1980, I was doing *Raging Bull*. *Heaven's Gate* [a big period picture that was financially unsuccessful] came out and the industry changed, and the type of picture we were talking about would not get funded. It was put away and eventually, every few years we brought it out and we started working on it together. And when we heard this new digital thing was happening: oh, is this going to be great. We could do the draft riots all on a computer. Didn't work. I couldn't do it; I don't even know how to work the computer. It stayed in my head for so many years, and ultimately by 1990, after we did *Goodfellas* and it was released at Warner Bros., we got together and rewrote the script for me again, and at that point we decided on the element of the revenge motor. Over the years my interests kind of changed as to what I wanted to tell. I was afraid of doing it in a way. My interest had more to do with the anthropology of the time. What it would be like to go to a theater at the time where people—the working class and the lower classes and the underworld—used the theater to express themselves politically. To deal with the rich people coming downtown to check out the poor and help them. A couple of the characters are based on real people. Bill the Butcher is based on a real guy

And Jay and I felt we were so close to the project and I wouldn't let go of certain things in the script, I said, "Look, we need new blood." At that point Steven Zaillian came in, and Steve was going to come in for about five weeks or so. He stayed like six months! Ultimately Steve had to leave. He had his own life. Then I get to Rome and the sets are all built: the whole lower part of Manhattan, two or three miles. And ultimately at that point Kenny Lonergan was visiting Rome on his honeymoon so we called him in. And he's a friend of mine. He's a wonderful writer, playwright. And he stayed with us for a few months and worked developing characters as we shot but then ultimately improvising with the actors but within the language of the period, which was very hard to do.

There is a book that's out, written by an ex–police chief in 1859 called *The Rogue's Lexicon*, so we kept playing around with that. I wanted it to be alive and I was afraid of doing something that had been in my head for twenty-some-odd, thirty years and that it would be stale. So I kept changing it.

M. Night Shyamalan, *The Sixth Sense*

I was kind of surprised when I got into preproduction and looking at people saying the dialogue in casting sessions that I felt like the beginning of the movie, the first forty minutes of the movie, that so many dialogue pieces were adding up to a lot of talking heads, so there was a lot of killing scenes. In a literary form, looking at the screenplay, it was wonderful to read those and understand the characters deeper and deeper, but as a director and understanding the pace and where everything goes. I feel, ironically, like the audience will take more of that towards the end of the movie when they're invested in the characters. I can do my big dialogue scene with no cuts towards the three-quarter point because they're invested in the words. In the beginning it's kind of like when they sense there's going to be a long dialogue scene, everybody starts shifting in the theater. You do the establishing shot of the two people on the bench, and it's all she wrote because everybody's like, okay, here we go.

And so kind of trying to remember it's a visual medium. It was interesting, when I did location scouting, that if I couldn't find the location, it was like, no this isn't right, this isn't right, I realized that the scene was written improperly.

Taylor Hackford, *Ray*

When you get a script it's a literary form. You've got to sell it to a studio. They've got to read it; they've got to feel, "Oh, gee, this holds together," as you would in a novel. But of course we're not making a novel. We move in and one look from an actor can say half a page of dialogue, and, boom, what was vital in that script is no longer vital.

Barbra Streisand, *The Prince of Tides*

I read the book at least four times. And every time I kind of paired it down to what jumped out at me, what was the essence of the story for me, what was the story I wanted to tell. I even took it on a trip to Greece because I wanted to visit the ancient sites of myths, because I believe in the archetypal nature of stories, and then all of the sudden it was there for me.

We worked on the script for two years. The original script had no flashbacks, had no rape. It was very important to me to show [the hero's] background and what affected his present-day nature, what gave him the problems he had. And that's how I saw it and that's how I did it.

I constantly worked with the novel. I said there has to be a way to put in narration to remind people this is a novel and to respect this form. I couldn't quite figure it out but I had Nick Nolte read passages from the book into a tape recorder, and I ended up using them in the film. I had a wonderful time with Pat Conroy [the author of the book] listening to the stories of his childhood.

I had Becky Johnston [the screenwriter] move into my house with me for three weeks and we just worked morning till night. I had to put down first the structure I saw in my head. And then we would flesh out the dialogue. She would go away and write for a couple of hours, or I would write for a couple of hours, then come together, talk it out, and read it. That was the process. The script had to serve the story that I wanted to tell. The story I felt was relevant to today, the theme of this man's journey, this man's growth, this theme of transformation through love.

I guess I'm a little obsessed with the notion that people should be all that they can be. The theme in *Yentl* is that women should be able to live the full range of their capacity. I guess it's striving towards wholeness, that we can accept the masculine and feminine within us.

The Prince of Tides has a lot of themes. It's about forgiveness, about acceptance,

handwritten note: You once said I was withholding... well I was [?] I didn't want to have to dredge up the past - what's done is done

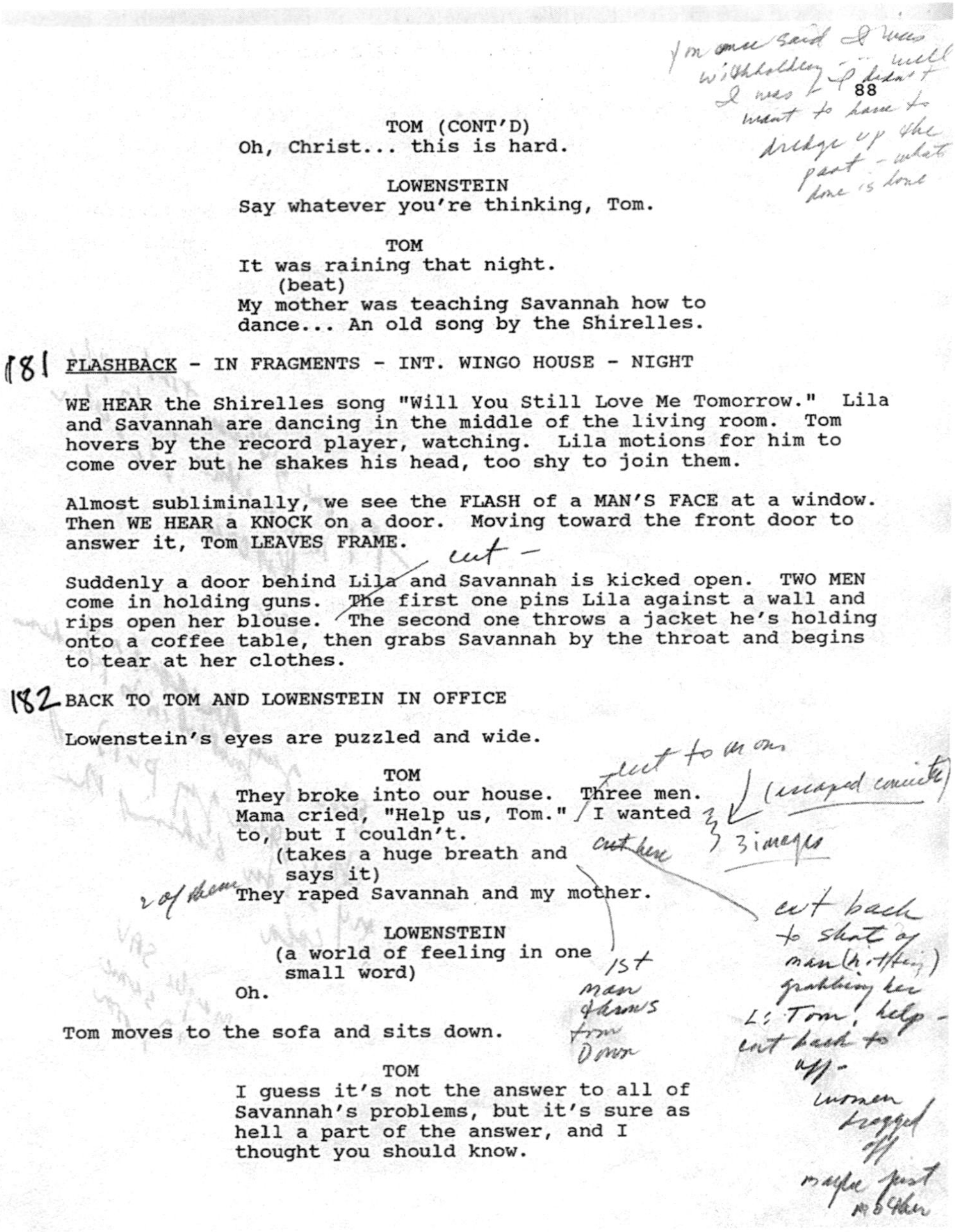

88

TOM (CONT'D)
Oh, Christ... this is hard.

LOWENSTEIN
Say whatever you're thinking, Tom.

TOM
It was raining that night.
   (beat)
My mother was teaching Savannah how to
dance... An old song by the Shirelles.

181 FLASHBACK - IN FRAGMENTS - INT. WINGO HOUSE - NIGHT

WE HEAR the Shirelles song "Will You Still Love Me Tomorrow." Lila
and Savannah are dancing in the middle of the living room. Tom
hovers by the record player, watching. Lila motions for him to
come over but he shakes his head, too shy to join them.

Almost subliminally, we see the FLASH of a MAN'S FACE at a window.
Then WE HEAR a KNOCK on a door. Moving toward the front door to
answer it, Tom LEAVES FRAME. *cut -*

Suddenly a door behind Lila and Savannah is kicked open. TWO MEN
come in holding guns. The first one pins Lila against a wall and
rips open her blouse. The second one throws a jacket he's holding
onto a coffee table, then grabs Savannah by the throat and begins
to tear at her clothes.

182 BACK TO TOM AND LOWENSTEIN IN OFFICE

Lowenstein's eyes are puzzled and wide.

TOM
They broke into our house. Three men.
Mama cried, "Help us, Tom." I wanted
to, but I couldn't.
   (takes a huge breath and
   says it)
They raped Savannah and my mother.

LOWENSTEIN
   (a world of feeling in one
   small word)
Oh.

Tom moves to the sofa and sits down.

TOM
I guess it's not the answer to all of
Savannah's problems, but it's sure as
hell a part of the answer, and I
thought you should know.

handwritten margin notes: cut to m ons / (escaped convicts) / cut here / 3 images / 2 of them / cut back to shot of man (hitting) grabbing her / L: Tom! help - cut back to off - women dragged off / maybe just mother / VAR / 1st / man & arms from Door

Barbra Streisand's notes to herself for The Prince of Tides. *(Courtesy of Sony Pictures and Barbra Streisand.)*

about consciousness, how fear and oppression come in the way of being the most loving human being you can be.

John Madden, *Shakespeare in Love*

There were two writers on the script, Marc Norman and Tom Stoppard. It was Marc Norman's idea originally. It was his concept. He wrote a script, which had very much the kind of basic concrete of the movie that you now see. Tom came in to work on it fairly early on. The movie was going to be made at that point with Julia Roberts and nobody definitely playing Will. And I think that's the reason it floundered in its first incarnation. They got a fair way into preproduction so they had started building sets and certainly had done some casting. But it ground to a halt because they couldn't cast Will, and then the project went belly up and remained in a kind of dormant state for about the next five years. During that time, Harvey Weinstein [executive producer and cofounder of Miramax] became aware of the script and fell in love with it. I'd just done a movie for Harvey and I was the lap that was in the way when the script was dropped, as it were. And as a matter of fact, when I read the script, I remember distinctly not being in any way sure that I was being offered it. Which I suspect means that I wasn't. So I read it actually without that kind of normal fear that one has when one reads a script, thinking, "Is this going to be as good as I think it's going to be?" Or "Will I be up to it?" I just read it as a script, which was a pretty astonishing experience. I mean, I've never read a script that so astonished. Literally halfway through the first page I thought there's such an amazing mind at work here. It was the most astounding script. And I remember waking up the night after I'd said I'd do it, rather the way Violet does in the movie, a couple of times sitting bolt upright thinking, "What the fuck have I done?" Because there's a girl playing a boy in this movie and you will never get away with it. That was just the first kind of assaults on my consciousness. I thought there were just so many things in this script that don't seem doable. It was just stupid, of course. You should trust your first instincts when you read it.

I'm dealing with story and character and emotional tone, emotional texture. And I have to get those kind of shifts and weights right before going to the next step. I mean, the trouble is, it doesn't really fall into stages like that. You find your way towards telling the story that you think needs to be told. And images pop up at certain moments and certain ideas come fully formed into your head that then find their way onto the screen and certain others don't. It felt to me like it was a movie that I absolutely had to have nailed down as far as possible at script level before we would go into it. Because it was so complex and working at so many levels and dealing with so many kinds of kaleidoscopic tonal shifts all the time.

I love making movies where you make it and then you discover it's a different kind of film in the editing room. But I didn't think this movie was going to be that. And when you're working with a mind like that frankly, and somebody who writes with extraordinary economy and yet with total freedom, you know, you can pluck an idea from anywhere and of course you don't. You think twice about saying, "Uh, Tom, I don't think this line works terribly well," given the man you're working with. But he is an extraordinary gentleman and totally open. He's directed himself as you know and he understands that it has to be the director's film. And so he went wherever I wanted him to go. The main work on the script was in the last third. It had to do with the resolution of the Will and Violet relationship in terms of the play and how the barriers eventually break down completely between the play and their life so there's no distinction between one or the other. That process went right the way through the filming as well. We rewrote and reshot the ending during the filming.

Marc Forster, *Finding Neverland*

It was a real challenge when the wall lifts and Kate walks into Neverland. In the script it wasn't that the wall lifts, and I didn't tell the studio either because I thought they would be nuts if suddenly the living room wall lifts and they think he's marrying reality with fantasy. Because originally in the script they walk through the door and then there's a garden which turned into Neverland. But I thought, the whole concept of the wall lifting was much more interesting, like marrying in that moment reality and fantasy. But I thought if I tell the studio and it costs a lot of money, so the producer really made sure nobody knows. And like the writer didn't know.

Ron Howard, *A Beautiful Mind*

The screenplay offered insight into this disorder in a very personal way, in a way that would fool the audience. I hope to offer insight into both the creative mind and his delusional mind because for Nash it was very difficult for him to come to terms with his disease because he relied very much on epiphany, sort of bursts of creative insight in his mathematics. I thought, "All right, well how do you not sort of give this away too quickly, and how do you establish a set of rules that actually may hold water?" You know, when you watch the movie a second time, I don't want there to have been a lot of tricks. So I simply decided to present as much of the movie as possible from Nash's point of view. All the delusional characters were heard before they were seen particularly in the first half or so of the film. And then, of course, we take the delusional character out of the shot, and we really say, "No, there really is no one there, trust me."

Michael Radford, *Il Postino*

Burning Patience was a Chilean novel about a seventeen-year-old boy and the death of Pablo Neruda [Nobel-prize-winning Chilean poet] and it was a beautiful book. When I first looked at it, I thought, "Well, why would you want to change this in any kind of way?" You could just shoot it straight as it is and make a Chilean movie. But I couldn't make a Chilean movie because I had an Italian star, so although I speak Italian, I didn't feel confident to write the movie myself, so we handed it over to one of the great Italian writers, and he came back about three months later with the biggest piece of garbage I'd ever read in my life.

And one day, I said to Massimo [the star of *Il Postino*], "You and your cowriter have written five screenplays together. I've written four. Why don't we just write it ourselves?" Unfortunately, in Italy, you get a credit even if you brush past somebody who's tapping away at a typewriter. There's a vast number of people credited for this movie who never actually wrote a word of it.

I normally work very closely and often I write a draft myself. Obviously I can't write in Italian, so what happened was, Massimo and I came to Los Angeles. He used to like to come to Los Angeles because nobody knew who he was, so he could walk around. Often we would go to an Italian restaurant just to remind him he was a star. Generally speaking we sat in a hotel room and I wrote in English and then he spoke in Italian and I kind of copied it down. So we had this screenplay, which was kind of half in English and half in Italian. And then we just structured a screenplay, literally, in about two weeks.

The theme of the book was the theme of revolution and how two people got

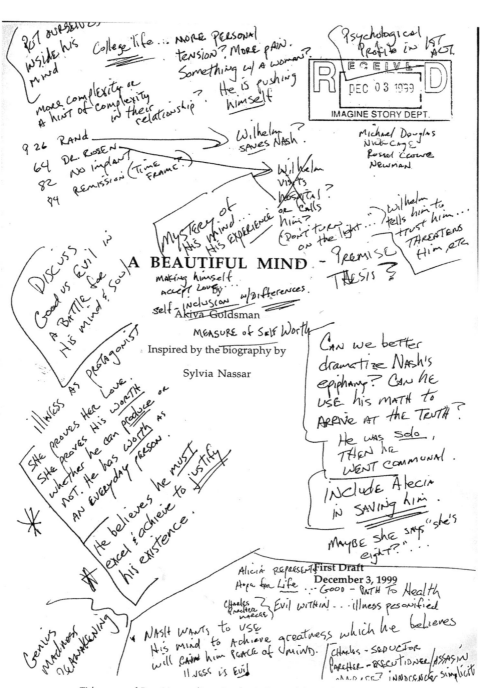

Title page of Ron Howard's script for A Beautiful Mind. (Courtesy of Universal Studios Licensing LLLP and Ron Howard.)

caught up in a revolution and started to need each other. I knew that I couldn't make that film. So I had to change the theme of the book. And it's very interesting, about ten years ago I made a film called *Another Time, Another Place*, which was the story of three Italians in the north of Scotland. One actor I picked up, literally, off the street, and it turned out that he was a gangster. I took him to Scotland and years later we met again in Rome and he confessed to me that I had completely changed his life. As he talked to me, I saw the theme of this screenplay. I remembered all those times when you've been on holiday and you've met somebody and you've wanted to communicate with them and you didn't. And it was there that the true line of this piece was born.

Curtis Hanson, *L.A. Confidential*

I can't separate from myself the process of writing and directing. It's all part of the same thing; it's all part of the storytelling.

With *L.A. Confidential*, I read James Ellroy's wonderful book and just became captivated by the characters, and my reaction to them, much more than the plot. Ellroy's novel is in fact very interior. Much of it takes place in the people's heads. In our script, we tried to keep description to a minimum, and to try to make it as visual as possible.

I think the first shot that I actually sort of conceptualized during the writing process summed up the theme of the movie, which is the difference between image and reality and how things and people appear and how they really are. And it was a shot where Kim Basinger's character, Lynn Bracken, who looks like Veronica Lake and she sells that resemblance to her customers, she's created a scene where she is projecting on the wall of her home a clip from a picture called *This Gun for Hire*. And we are seeing the real Veronica Lake and Alan Ladd, and then with a camera move, Kim's head comes in and literally moves into the old movie and blocks it, and the audience is allowed to see she does look like Veronica Lake. Thematically and stylistically, we're saying, classic film noir with its black-and-white lighting is artificial, and she knows it's artificial. Her customer knows it's artificial. And that's the game. He's paying to make love with this icon from the screen. But here in the foreground is our character, Kim, who is leading her own existence. I'm trying to say, I do not want this movie to be an homage to film noir; I wanted it to have its own life.

During the writing process, I think about the shooting of the scenes. I see the scenes, as they are being written. I'm not somebody who does sketches and storyboards and so forth, but I very much visualize it and try to actually indicate that on the page with the choice of language, to give the script a directorial point of view.

Ang Lee, *Crouching Tiger, Hidden Dragon*

There has to be enough ingredients for you to play around or develop. So when I feel that, have a gut feeling, whether it's emotional or intellectually it's inspiring, or [there are] just elements or a combination of elements that interest me. For this one, I see the Freudian approach into repressed Chinese society. A different way of looking at the genre which really is inspiring and the last image of the girl flying down, I just, you know, that won't go out of my head. So I decided to develop it.

We work on the last image and then backtrack it. Count backwards. What does it take to get the final feeling? It sounds easy, but when you're dealing with day-to-day life, that's very difficult. It's kind of scary. And martial arts! So you're dealing with gravity and human body contact. It could be dangerous. Could be not really workable. And aesthetically, it might not be in balance. It could be laughable. And then when it's out in Asia, I don't know if there's enough fight for them, maybe too much talk. And when that film has to hit Western art house, will they laugh? I don't know. It's a constant fear.

Sam Mendes, *American Beauty*

It was always a fantastic script. It just blew me away when I read it, but the thing is Alan had written it while he was a staff writer on a sitcom, and he wasn't very happy during this period. But I think one of the things I loved about the script was there was this kind of joyous rage in the script. He was so angry, but at given points in the script, he had actually made Lester [the part played by Kevin Spacey] too angry and too aggressive, and there were two key changes, which looking back now changed the whole movie. The first one was the biggest, really, which was that Lester at the end of the original script slept with Angela [the young girl played by Mena Suvari]. He had sex with the young girl and, as I remember, sat down and made himself a sandwich and was sitting really contentedly, kind of postcoital, in the kitchen and got his brains blown out. To me, there was no redemption in this journey, and I thought that the movie was moving towards the possibility of redemption. And so I insisted—I discussed it with Alan—and said, what you've written is this one man's journey towards a better place, an unexpected state of grace. Now you have to write the scene where he achieves that. And Alan then came back, literally two days later, with a three-page scene. I didn't change a word; it was absolutely perfect. And the other one was the character of the colonel. He made it obvious that the colonel was gay, and I said, that's profoundly wrong, because clearly there was this huge scene begging to be played at the end, which we then did, where you don't know that that's the case. I love improvisation, but I would never encourage it in front of the cameras, I mean. I rehearse for two weeks, and because I am from the theater, I loved having the writer around and we kind of formed a partnership, and that was really a happy one and he wrote lines occasionally. I would turn around and say, "This doesn't feel right. Can we have an extra line here?"

Steven Soderbergh, *Erin Brockovich*

I think there are filmmakers with an aesthetic that they then try and find a piece of material to fit with that aesthetic. And then there are filmmakers who look for material and then try and come up with the right aesthetic for that material. And I tend to be the latter. So I'm only looking for something that engages me emotionally that I want to see. I was told about *Erin Brockovich* by Jersey Films when I was finishing *Out of Sight* and I remember being on the set and they pitched me this story. And they gave me the five-minute version. I said, "That just sounds awful," you know? And I went off and did *The Limey,* and then in the middle of trying to put that together, I picked up the script, which they'd sent me anyway, and suddenly it seemed like the perfect thing to do.

The first step is research, is sort of steeping yourself in the material that's available to tell that story. In the case of *Erin Brockovich*, I interviewed at length Erin and Ed Masry, transcribed those interviews, highlighted things that I thought were interesting, researched the case, and then sort of sat in the room with the writer over a series of drafts and went through it piece by piece.

I remember specifically just before I went off to shoot *Erin Brockovich* sitting with Steve Gaghan in my apartment and in a series of tricolored index cards mapping out the structure for the entire film on the floor. We'd lock ourselves in a hotel room for three or four days, wouldn't tell anybody where we were, and wouldn't leave until we had a new draft. We did that three times. We'd talk through stuff. You know about why this section of the film's not moving forward. Why is that? Or shouldn't somebody articulate this idea? Or are too many people articulating ideas? It's all potential and it's really exciting.

I have to respect all the characters. And I believe you should never sell out a character, even the antagonist. There's that line from *Rules of the Game*: "The trouble with life is that everyone has their own reasons." And so I look at them as just somebody with a very different belief system than mine, but in their minds legitimate. And so I think it's, it's important to try and identify with them in some way. Otherwise, you are constantly selling them out for the sake of the narrative or to get a laugh or to get a rise out of somebody. And I hate to do that.

One of the difficulties in *Erin Brockovich* was there's no antagonist. It's a company, who you never meet. There were some people who said there needs to be a villain. She needs to meet them. You know, four guys in a black town car. And I said, no, that's the point: You can't reach them. There're too many layers. The emotional closure for the people involved is just taken off the table because they never get to confront who did this, the people who did this to them, and that's part of the story. I managed to talk everybody into that, but there were a lot of discussions about it. There was material in the version of the script I read where she was being chased, you know. And I asked Erin Brockovich, "Did you ever feel like your life was in danger? Did you ever feel physically threatened?" She said, "No, I knew I was being watched and I knew they were listening to my phones, but I never felt in danger." I said, "Well then, can't do that."

Roman Polanski, *The Pianist*

I believe that writing the script it's really making the movie. Script for me, it's like a manual. It's so all you have to do is just to shoot it.

To me, the script is the inherent part of the moviemaking and I really believe more and more in the saying that what's not on the paper will not be on the screen. And in the case of this picture we had no pink pages at all. No yellow pages, no blue pages. They were all white until the bitter end. I could not afford experimentation. I had to have it all written so the crew and all people involved would be well informed of what is needed. I just could not come to the actor's trailer in the morning saying, "Hey, we have a new scene here." That just didn't happen. First of all, when Ronald Harwood read the book, he said that "I don't know how to start it," and I told him, "Just write it down; don't think of anybody else but us. It's for our eyes only. Just write straight and don't worry about anything. Just translate it into a film language because, in fact, the book consists of recollections." It's like a journal of somebody who went through all these six years of misery and a few months later decided to put it down. And that's what he did. He just wrote down that first draft, which nobody beside him and myself knew, and then we started working. We went to a country house near Paris. We locked ourselves up there and we worked like fourteen hours a day for about, I'd say a month and a half. And that was the script.

I would be improvising dialogue. Ronnie would come up in the morning with new pages. He would read it and I would read it and we would make the corrections. I used a lot of my own recollections to illustrate certain things, which in the book were only ideas. Also we went through a tremendous amount of archives. We were constantly in liaison with coproducers in Warsaw who would send us either the cassettes or the photographs. There's masses of archive material. Germans loved filming their work, and we would use this also. So it was quite painful. And I must say that, strangely enough, we had a lot of fun during this script that must have been some kind of defense mechanism. But we would laugh a lot, you know. We would end up the day and we would say, "So how many Jews we kill today?" There was Ronnie writing in the evening or toward the end of the morning coming back to lunch and reading pages before and then going through it again, rewriting it, adding scenes and me acting away. I love acting away.

However, when I'm working on a script with the writer, I don't ask myself questions about how I am going to achieve it. I just try to imagine the scene as it's going to be presented in the film. I think that any kind of technical questions would sort of cramp our style and maybe limit ourselves in the description of it. So that comes later when we start preparing the picture.

The whole film is about survival and it was the preponderant theme of my childhood. The film is about the survival and is also about the victory of those positive forces that surround us. In fact, in this case, the music and art which helps someone to go through difficult, sometimes the greatest, adversities.

Peter Weir, *The Truman Show*

I was looking for something different. I was kind of wanting to explore an area I'd never done before. The material I was getting was sometimes good, but it was more conventional, a lot of biographies, a lot of true stories and things. I felt like something different. So here it was, *The Truman Show.* It was a startling read. Very different in tone to what the film became, which you might expect. In other words, it has become my sensibility.

I don't think I'd have got working on this without a lead actor. This was such dangerous material it could just destroy you. It was never going to be halfway right. It was never going to be a "good try" because it was too expensive, so you could never in all good conscience take it on without saying, "I've got a pretty good idea I can get people along to this show." And that's how Jim Carrey got involved. He read it too, and he was looking for a change. Jim and I got on. And Andrew Niccol [the writer] and I worked on the draft. Jim wasn't available; I didn't realize this, for a year. But it turned out to be very, very fortunate because we then had a year to take what was already a good read, and . . . . the odd thing was, I'd never had a situation where there was something working that you then took apart. Like a beautiful mechanism, we took it all to pieces, just so I could see how Andrew had. He could get to know me and we could rebuild it through my sensibility. And he was very willing to do that. He wasn't defensive of his material. And he had boundless energy. He wasn't written out. So for a year, sometimes I'd come over, sometimes we'd just exchange the material through the mail, but we went through an excessive number of drafts. Like an excessive number of cuts, I've never had a film where we'd done so many passes at both stages. Fourteen drafts, often minute changes.

I do say to a writer, as a kind of a joke, that I have to eat this script. It has to become organic; it has to become part of me. I mean in order to follow the analogy to its full. It in a way has to be as if I did write it. It's not always to the same extent: I mean that wasn't quite the case with *Witness* in which I came on much more as a hired gun. I mean I did a couple of passes on that, strong, strong changes to the extent where the writers objected strongly to those changes!

I'll record the script usually myself and then play it in the car. I think it's great, particularly driving along in traffic and hear your own screenplay coming back and you do the voices. You learn a lot about the characters by speaking their lines.

Peter Weir, *Master and Commander: The Far Side of the World*

The books from which I was working—there's twenty in the series by the late Patrick O'Brian—they are extremely well researched, and that was my starting point. Then I went beyond that. I did go sailing on the *Endeavor*. I thought it was right to spend a little time as a crew. You sign your life away when you come on board because you go up top and that was a bit of a struggle and you do sleep in hammocks and live somewhat the life of the eighteenth century. I like a kind of tactile research, and then, of course, there's just books and books and books. I tried to stick, the writer, John Collee, and I, to the language of the time as much as we could. I did think this is a rare chance to record life in this period in one location. So I thought I'd rather go further by not compromising, by the uniforms and details including language, so that it would be as close as possible to how it was.

Peter Jackson, *The Lord of the Rings: The Fellowship of the Ring*

We were developing this project for about four years, but it went through various permutations with Miramax, and then with New Line, and at one stage, it was gonna be two movies, and we'd written that script, spent a lot of time on that. Then New Line wanted to do three movies, so we had to rewrite the script from page one, and the result of that was, by the time we started shooting, our three-movie version had only gone through a couple of drafts of screenwriting, so we weren't very happy with the scripts. So we got into a situation where we'd be writing as we were shooting and we'd be slipping scenes under the actors' doors, like the night before they were due to start shooting the scene.

What we did during the four years of preproduction that we had before the actors even arrived—I'd did something which I'd never done before. Once we had a draft of our screenplay, and this was an early draft that ultimately doesn't bear much relationship to the film, but I got a group of actors in New Zealand and we went into a studio and we recorded an audio version of the script, like a radio play. And at the same time I was storyboarding the script. And then we cut the storyboards together against the audio track and we put a temp music score with it, even put some sound effects with it, actually. And we ended up with like, I'd say like a two-and-a-half-hour version of the movie, early version, where you could sit and watch it. I ultimately thought I was doing it because it would help me shoot the movie, but what it proved to be was much more useful as a script tool. Because you could literally watch the film and say, "Oh my God, this is terrible." Or "This bit's really boring." Or "That scene doesn't work." Or "We hear this information twice." So it ultimately turned out to be a really useful script tool. Then we took that animatic, we called it, and we kept updating when the script had changed.

I always felt very comfortable with the story and the characters. Mind you, if it was me, I'd probably, several times on the journey, I would have turned around and run back home again, but with Frodo, he doesn't really have that choice. We took a lot of Tolkien and his life, and the First World War had severely impacted him personally, 'cause he fought and he saw most of his school class die around him. And he felt, I think, very strong feelings about having to do something that you don't understand, how to be part of some greater conflict that you don't really understand. You're not making judgments on the good versus evil, but you know that you have a job to do. What I was very concerned about, I guess, with *Lord of the Rings* was that I wanted our different characters to be making their decision on-screen in a way that we could understand: that, because Gandalf is a wizard, I wanted still to be able to understand what he was feeling, and why he was making a decision. I wanted everything, all of his emotions to be on a human level. Regardless of what race or culture these people were. I thought if we made it too fantastical, it wouldn't work.

Peter Jackson, *The Lord of the Rings: The Two Towers*

We felt making the middle chapter of three, sort of upping the ante, was very important because the first film introduces everybody and gets the mission sort of established and sets the characters on the road. And then the second chapter of the trilogy really the screws have to tighten and so their survival does have to become in question and the survival of the values that they're fighting for. The script writing on *The Lord of the Rings* has been a very strange evolution. We entered the shoot not really having what I would regard as being a totally locked-off script. Which became an interesting process and it's something that I think we used to our advantage because it became very collaborative. You know, you can always obviously shoot the scene that you've written and that's there, but I always believe that nothing's ever perfect and just keep working at it and working at it. And that's really my philosophy with script writing, that unless you're prepared to sit back at one point in time and say it's perfect, don't change a thing—

which I don't believe that moment ever actually exists—then take advantage of every second of the day that you have to improve it. We have a strong philosophy in believing in pick-up shooting, and in each of the *Lord of the Rings* movies during the postproduction period we've had two or three weeks of shooting pick-ups. And these aren't pick-ups because we have previewed the film and the scores are bad and everyone's got this knee-jerk reaction, oh my God, we have to fix it, because we've never actually previewed the films. These have never been seen by an audience. But we preview them for ourselves. I mean, we're just like, we cut the movie together, we look at it, and basically the filmmakers sit there as their own preview audience and just feel what we like about the film, feel what we don't like, what's working, what can be improved. We then write some more script to fix the things that we want to fix, to improve the things. The actors come back down to New Zealand and we shoot for two or three more weeks. And for every film that I make in the future I'm always going to build in that period of additional shooting because it's such a valuable tool to filmmaking. And you just organically develop the thing right the way through to the very end.

Peter Jackson, *The Lord of the Rings: The Return of the King*

You know, we were shooting the three movies at the same time for about fifteen months and we were writing. We had Phillippa Boyens and Fran Walsh writing continuously; continuously every single day during that fifteen months, they would be working on scenes. And obviously, we started with a script, but we would just keep working on it because I never want to get to a moment where you say the script's perfect. I always believe that the longer you spend on something, the better it's going to get and it's all just about running out of time at the end of the day and you eventually have to stop because I need to release the movie.

Baz Luhrmann, *Moulin Rouge*

You know, the journey of making *Moulin Rouge,* it's part of ten-year process, really. It began with *Strictly Ballroom* and *Romeo + Juliet*, and again, they all had the same basic mechanics. They're based on a primary myth, a shape, so that no matter who you are in the audience, you know how it's going to end when it begins, the first ten minutes of it. You go, "Okay, the boy's gonna get with the girl." And this is a fundamental rule with all musical form, be it opera or music on stages and so forth. So we began with a very intense investigation into musical form and taking some basic rules we felt we had to deal. There's quite an old idea to have contemporary music in a period setting, you know? Judy Garland sings, "Clang, clang, clang went the trolley" in *Meet Me in St. Louis.* The film's set in 1900, the same year of *Moulin Rouge*, but she's singing, you know, big band 1940s radio music, and the audience had a preexisting relationship with the music. I mean, trailers in the old days used to have things like "with five new songs." Presumably, ten were really old sing-alongs, you know, and the audience was going along going, "Oh, here comes that number I love." So we had to find a way of getting that into the text. It all came to fruition when we came up with a story problem. First of all, we took the Orpheus myth, we went to Paris, we researched it meticulously, and we grafted onto the myth, basically, Emil Zola's *Nana*, Dumas's *Camille,* and *La Vie Boheme.* It was about making a thin plot very recognizable for complex execution, okay? So now we've got the plot, right? And Christian, the character, the poet, had to be a genius poet. So we started writing genius poetry. And it became really clear, quickly, as we read it to people, that it wasn't, you know? And people would say, "We don't believe he's a genius," you know? So what we thought—to solve all these problems, what if every time he opened his mouth, one of the great iconic songs of the last hundred years came out. And so basically, you know, whatever you think of *Sound of Music,* the moment he says, "The hills are alive with the sound of music," you go, "Oh, my God, he's a genius!" And it's comic, but you move on, right? And so then came the telling of the story through classic songs. We did treatment after treatment after treatment. And then we began to write the text. And we would break it down; I mean, every beat is allocated. We'd get to each beat, and then we'd scan—my music department would scan literally thousands of songs—to find the right piece that would tell that piece of story.

That myth is about the transition from youthful idealism. Orpheus goes into the underworld with youthful idealism, tries to rescue perfect love, he makes a human mistake, he loses that love forever, is scarred by the experience, and returns to the upper world having grown internally, spiritually from the experience. So that's the shape of the story I wanted to deal with. I guess the thing was that it was coming to the realization in your journeys that there comes a time where there are things outside of your control. People die, relationships that can't be, World War III breaks out, you can't control that. That happens to you in your prime journey. And your ego can be destroyed by that—when you see that happening. And Christian could have been destroyed by the loss of his perfect ideal love. When you are going to go on and grow internally, spiritually, from the experience. And he says at the beginning of the film, "The woman I love is dead." And by telling the story, he goes through that journey and he's brought back to life so he can go on having brand-new experience.

Rob Marshall, *Chicago*

I brought to Bill [Condon, the screenwriter] this idea of these two parallel worlds, you know, the vaudeville world and then the sort of realistic world of the '20s in Chicago. I knew that these numbers need to take place on a stage, but coming up with how we go back and forth or why, and the catalyst into that whole conceptual idea was something that we had to work out first. So we just thought for a long time about, Can it be through Roxie's mind? Should it be a flashback? So we sort of came up with the big idea first, which was that it will all take place through Roxie's eyes and that's how we'll move in and out of these numbers. And then, you know, the painful thing about sitting down with a musical that's so beautifully done, I don't think you can really do a three-and-a-half-hour musical and that's what it would have been if we had fleshed out the story plus kept all the numbers in there. So we had to eliminate numbers. We had the big bulletin board with all the numbers. And the first draft of this had every number in it. And then the story starts telling you this can't stay 'cause it doesn't forward the plot or forward the characters. So we started piece by piece eliminating numbers. We spent a lot of time on an outline. I think we had like a twenty- or twenty-five-page outline that we actually brought to everybody—the producers and the studio—and read it to them and it sort of made sense to them, and then we started writing. And probably out of total fear on my part, I really wanted it structured in the script exactly how we were going to shoot it. Bill Condon actually came to rehearsals with my choreographic team and we'd say, "Well, here at this moment we'll cut. She'll hit her thigh onstage and then we'll cut to Fred Casely hitting Roxie's thigh." It was all that kind of stuff—very, very specific. It wasn't something that I sort of found in the editing room. So I'd say 90 percent of what's on the screen is in the script.

It's a satire, you know. And the great thing about Bob Fosse and the original creators, John Kander and Fred Ebb, when they began this, it was, you know, written in the '20s by Maurine Dallas Watkins. She was a cub reporter in Chicago and was witnessing all this happening around her. I think it's sort of a deluded sense of survival for these ladies. I mean, it's a survival wrapped up in celebrity and fame. The quest for fame and the line drawn between celebrity and criminal and all that is so blurred, you know? It's around us everywhere. It's on the entertainment channel every night. Things haven't changed. I hope it's a warning to people.

Christopher Nolan, *Memento*

I think the source is a person who has something removed from them that we all have, and take for granted completely, which is the ability to make memories. And I was fascinated by the idea that this is something so small and simple that does happen in real life. And when that ability is damaged or taken away, your life changes completely and what's represented on-screen and in the story becomes unimaginably horrific for somebody to contemplate outside that character. The other main idea of suffering that enters the story very strongly is it's a revenge drama. But it's intended as a subversive revenge drama. And that fascination with the way that cinema can put you in a character's point of view, tweak that moral balance, and make the horrendous act totally palatable and, indeed, admirable.

Mike Leigh, *Secrets & Lies*

With all of my films, and *Secrets & Lies* is my sixteenth, the job has been to discover what the film is by making it. There's always a feeling, a notion, a conception on the go, that varies in its vagueness. For me, one of the first ingredients is to get the backing for the film without the backers having any idea what the film is going to be. Because it is about embarking on a journey through which the film, characters, the whole thing comes into existence. And so with some notions on the go, we always agree to make the film on budget, in time, and not beyond a certain length. Beyond that there is carte blanche. Now that then leaves me free to explore possibilities and to discover things and for things to happen which I didn't necessarily or I certainly didn't know were going to happen.

The only actual piece of writing that I do is a document which is usually no longer than three or four pages long which I write at the end of the rehearsal period just before we shoot which literally says, "Scene One—Cemetery—Day—Funeral; Scene Two—

House; Scene Three—Maurice and Monica—House." That's all it says. To me my job as writer-director of a potential film is to push and pull and bully and cajole and massage and generally direct the whole thing into existence.

The thing that concerns everybody is how is it that what you see on the screen in my films, with the tiniest of exceptions, is very highly structured, very written, very thoroughly disciplined in the style of the storytelling and the shooting. That's really a matter of taking those one-line scenes, scene by scene, and going to the location for each one of them. And starting with improvising and building up the thing. And writing through rehearsal and structuring through rehearsal. And finally it's a question of "you say that and you say this, and you move there," and it winds up being finished.

And in the case of all my films, and *Secrets & Lies* being no exception, there's a very long period of what is not very accurately described as rehearsal. Which is that period of a lot of discussion of inventing characters, doing a lot of research, and a huge amount of improvisation work through which the characters come into existence and the whole world of the film is really created in a tangible three-dimensional way. Out of which I'm then about to distill and structure a film. So what we do in the preliminary period is to create, if you like, the premise for the film, but not the film itself. The truth is, I could talk about this for a month and never mention the word *script*.

There's a scene towards the end of *Secrets & Lies* where they all come to the house where Monica shows two of the other women around the house. And she puts down the toilet lid in each of a number of different toilets. I mean you can't sit home and think of that.

Gus Van Sant, *Good Will Hunting*

When I read a screenplay, I'm looking for a number of things: character and setting, dialogue, and a good first act, second act, third act, and then an ending. And all these things are really crucial when I'm reading a screenplay. And they don't have to just be there; they have to be good ones! It's very easy to find a screenplay that has great character and setting. And you get through the first act and you find out that there's not really a second act or there's not really a third act or not really a great ending. Dialogue is important as well. This screenplay, as I was reading, this often happens, you read along, you say, well, this is a great setting and great characters and great dialogue, but I bet there's not gonna be a great second act. And lo and behold, there's a second act! And you go, "Oh, this is great, second act, but I'll bet there's not like development third act," and you read along and you go, "Oh my God, there's actually this, ya know, all these elements," and you go, "But there can't be an ending." And there's actually an ending! And so when I read *Good Will Hunting*, all these things were there in place. My reaction was to just call the writers [Ben Affleck and Matt Damon] immediately and just say, this is fantastic and I'd be on board, because you just don't find that a lot—all in one screenplay.

There was a problem in *Good Will Hunting* that the script had early on. Will was in his apartment, and he was reading very fast from a book, inhumanly fast. And you got the idea that this guy could absorb information and he could retain it. And you understood in the script stage that this guy was a very brilliant character but somehow the film needed to spend more time with him absorbing information, how his mind worked. It came down to him writing equations on the wall. And working on the problems that the professor had put up on the board in the hallway. When you are describing somebody like that, who you are saying is a genius character, you sort of need some visual representation of that.

Quentin Tarantino, *Pulp Fiction*

There's the writing process and then, in a way, when I'm making the movie, I'm writing it with actors. You know they're like a collaborator, and then when I'm editing it, that's writing too.

But the script is your safety net. I actually feel better about the fact that I can take more risks and walk the tightwire, because I know at the end of the day I have a script to catch me. If I just have to shoot it like bad television, I've still got a scene.

One of the first things that always goes after I do my first draft, that only I see, is I write down every shot, but then I always have a tremendous problem with page length.

In the case of *Reservoir Dogs*, where I had never done anything before, I went to a Sundance workshop [a creative lab developing film and filmmakers originated by Robert Redford] and I drafted a couple of the scenes there. I had a meeting with a bunch of the resource directors that were there, and they started asking me certain questions and they were saying, "Did you do your subtext work?" And "What do you mean?" And they go, "Hhh . . . see you think you know everything because you wrote it, but you've just done the writer's work. You haven't done the director's work." So I took a scene, one of the first scenes—when Mr. White brings Mr. Orange, shot, into the warehouse and he's trying to calm him down, and what I did was, my approach as an actor: "Okay, I'm Mr. White. All right, what do I want from this more than anything else? I'm Mr. Orange—what does Mr. Orange want from this scene more than anyone else?" And fifteen things start popping out and everything; it was growing. And then I wrote as a director—what do I want the audience to take away from this scene more than anything else?

Roberto Benigni, *Life Is Beautiful*

During the screenwriting. Oh, this is my favorite moment. I can say I am directing the movie twice. Now you may say, "Twice?" Because when we are writing, this is really my favorite moment. The world is in your hand now. You can do what you want. What a wonderful moment. This really is imagination, the body is exploding in the brain. And during the writing, I am directing. I like to improvise, but not to leave an open door because this isn't very healthy. I like to prepare the improvisation. It takes me as much as a week to prepare a good improvisation. Because your improvisation you can fly very, very high. But sometimes it's very dangerous. You are possessed by an angel who is improvising; they can improvise something very bad. So during the script, I am playing all the characters and trying to do everything. I remember, it was René Clair who said, "There are three important things to make a good movie: the script, the script, the script."

Andrew Davis, *The Fugitive*

The Fugitive had been in development for many years. There were lots of permutations of different drafts. The question was, "How could you say no to working with Harrison Ford?" Because you knew it would open these doors, and all of the sudden you would become acceptable as a director in every area. But there were certain key things that were critical, to me, to change, to make the script work.

The basic story is great drama, the unjustly accused man on the run. It's a great story line, it's got great empathy and simpatico, so there was a great spine to work with. I never saw the television show, Harrison never saw the television show during the '60s; we just were not watching *The Fugitive*.

In the original story I think that the marriage wasn't so healthy, and there were problems between him and his wife. I felt that you had to be invested in the life of this doctor, and to see his loss, his fall from grace. So we tried to create a prologue, which is the beginning of the movie, in the flashbacks. You really got to believe that they had a wonderful life together, and there was a great sense of loss. I also felt that the reason that Mrs. Kimble was killed could not be about a bungled burglary. It had to be about something more substantial than that, so that the movie had a soul, and a content.

There were at least five other writers working on it before I got involved. And every time we'd talk about a scene, it's "Oh yeah, in draft three we did that."

But the process of working on the script—and anything I say is not to demean the work of the writers who worked very hard—but this is a film that had a release date before the script was done. There was enough there for Harrison to commit to in terms of character. But I would say 60 to 70 percent of the dialogue was written on the set. I would say that 40 percent of the movie was hardly scripted at all. There were ideas for scenes that at the end of the day we would say, "Quickly, let's see, can we grab this? Can we put this scene in? Can we improvise this?" What I've learned is I'm scared to put myself in a situation where I won't experiment. I think that, especially working with actors. You can sit in a room and you can conceive a scene, and you can say, "This is a gem. We shouldn't touch a word." But then when you get there, and you see how the light is, and you see what the clothes are like, and somebody had garlic the night before and they're burping, and you take all these elements and you put it together and you say, "Let's think of it in a different way."

I would love to have a great script that I could shoot with my eyes closed. At the same time, I think the magic of moviemaking is making it happen while you're shooting the picture.

Clint Eastwood, *Unforgiven*

I had read it and liked it immediately, and thought it was one of the better scripts. I liked the fact that you never quite could guess where it was taking you. And then I sat on it. I bought it in 1984 and I thought, it needs to be done down the line. I felt that maybe I could even age into it a little more. It had certain things in the story, certain moralities, that I thought would be a nice wrap up for me in the genre.

You kind of read it as an entertainment piece, and then afterward you start digesting the various aspects of it, and it just kind of takes you over and eventually you say I'd like to present this and see if I could successfully transfer this onto the screen.

It's a constantly evolving process for me. You get a first impression, then you get a second impression, and many impressions along the way, and I think as you get into it, it starts taking on a life of its own.

Sometimes you get committees at studios who will have input and they decide the input is important because they have a little idea that they want to inject into it, and maybe the idea is a good one, and maybe it's so far out in left field, it has nothing to do with this particular story. The big thing you have to do is either forcefully, or diplomatically, or however you chose to do so, is to try to make sure you carry on the line and be true to the story.

I change things quite often because I feel actors must be comfortable. A lot of times the lines won't fit. I'm not afraid to change the dialogue, as long as the intent is good. Sometimes you find that the actor will come up with a suggestion that might even improve some of it. That's not to say that he or she is changing the direction of the story line or main points you are trying to make. You always must be flexible.

I made few suggestions, and the more I would fool with these suggestions, the more I realized I was unraveling some of the key points to the script. And so I had to go back to my own adage of "Let's not kill this with improvements."

One of the things that can make any film uninteresting is if you kind of assume what's gonna happen most the way.

Sometimes a writer will dry up or for some reason, maybe they just plain run out of steam. By and large I've been lucky, though. In fact, I did one picture where I shot the first draft of it, and the writer was incensed. He said, "I can do another draft. I can do another draft. I've never had a picture shot with the first draft." And I said, "Well, I like this draft." It was the film about Charlie Parker [*Bird*].

Rob Reiner, *A Few Good Men*

Aside from good writing and well-developed characters and a good story and a theme that has something to say, I try to look to the main character and see if it's somebody I can identify with that's either experiencing something that I've gone through, or that I am going through, so that I can connect up with the main character and put myself in that character. Even though I'm not playing the part, I'll know how to tell that story.

A Few Good Men with Tom's character [Kaffee]—this one is close to me, in that he is the son of an accomplished father who was in the same business, and he's living in the shadow of a famous father, and he's frightened to test himself. And eventually has to find his way, as opposed to his father's. I went through that when I was making *Stand by Me*. I realized, that's a film that my father [Carl Reiner] never would have made. It was very close to my personality, and as I was making it, I was very conscious of the fact that, if the audience was accepting this, then the audience was accepting who I was and my sensibility, separate and apart from my father's, because I'd always thought of myself as an adjunct to my father.

I had seen the play and I was very bowled over by it. It was a very emotional play, and it had an enormous amount of holes, plot holes, which you can get away with on stage a lot of the times, because you get wrapped up in the emotion of seeing live

109

MARKINSON (continued)
(beat)
And Putting me on the stand isn't gonna
make him step on one. ~~either~~.

KAFFEE stares at him.

Then shakes his head, sighs, and picks the log book up off the
table, and heads for the door.

KAFFEE
You're taking the stand. Thursday.

KAFFEE leaves.

HOLD on MARKINSON.

CUT TO

72 Int. KAFFEE'S APARTMENT - NIGHT

It's later that night and SAM and JO have just heard the report
from KAFFEE.

JO
There's gotta be someone who can   member·
testify to the flight. A ground crew, someone·

KAFFEE
~~We'll~~ Forget ~~about~~ the flight. We'll
put ~~him~~ on the stand and we'll deal
with Jessep's refusal to transfer
Santiago and he'll testify to the
forged tranfer order. That'll be
enough. That and Downey's testimony
really oughta be enough.

CUT TO

73 Int. THE HOLDING ROOM - DAY

JO is working with DOWNEY. He sits on a mock witness stand. *SAM*

JO
Private Downey, why did you go
into Santiago's room on the night
of the 6th?

DOWNEY
To give Private Santiago a Code
Red, ma'am.

JO
And why did you give him a Code
Red?

Page from Rob Reiner's script for A Few Good Men. *(Courtesy of Sony Pictures and Rob Reiner.)*

theater and you don't notice that "Hey, wait a minute, that doesn't make any sense."
When you put it on film, those things become much more apparent.

So I worked pretty closely in restructuring it and filling in those plot holes. It
wasn't—we weren't making a bad play into something good—I mean it was already a
good play, but the screenplay was way better than the play, and the national touring
company, *A Few Good Men*, reflected the work we did on the screenplay, which to my

knowledge, I don't think has ever been done with a successful Broadway play, that the writer has completely rewritten the play for the national touring company.

I'm very respectful of writers. I mean, if you've got a good solid screenplay, you're 80 percent home. If you've got a good solid story and good characters—Hitchcock used to say that once he's finished the script, the film was done.

You collaborate with a writer—I act out the parts, we change the lines, I open the hood and get in there. Hopefully the writers are not too upset because they see that it's not a director trying to make it into his film and ruin their material, but it's really trying to shore up what they already have. I worked with Bill Goldman on *Misery*, and it even got to the point where the last couple of drafts, I wrote without Bill. To where he would say, "Go ahead, you know what you are doing here." And it doesn't take anything from him, his name's there, and everybody knows, he worked on it, and Stephen King wrote the novel, and it's his story, it's not mine. But if everybody understands the process is collaborative and there is no ownership on it, then you get in there and do whatever it takes. Once I have the script then obviously there are problems with locations that don't work, and because you can't get things there, you alter things slightly to fit what's there. A particular actor may have a problem with a certain kind of emotion so you alter it to help him, but always never to destroy what your main plan is to begin with.

Barry Levinson, *Bugsy*

I read the 260-page screenplay, and I was intrigued by it. I basically said to Warren [Beatty] that I was interested in making a movie if we basically go into preproduction now and fix the script, just to accelerate the process.

We kept whittling the script down and changing things radically as we went along, and kept evolving it throughout the preproduction period and during the shooting period, finding new things and exploring other aspects of it rather than sitting with a writer and working and ultimately then going into preproduction.

So everything was happening simultaneously. Which I think was probably a good way to do it, because Jimmy [Toback, the screenwriter] was writing the script for six years before that. And I think that if we would've continued that way, it might've been another five or six. Since we had a set date to start production, it forced everything to come alive.

I think what you want to do is improve character and relationships. Ultimately we had to condense the story. We threw out some characters. We telescoped it somewhat. At the same time we were able to heighten the characters and the relationships. Because as you work with structure it'll affect character, and you don't want to give up character for structure, because then you're just going A, B, C, D, and you're not depicting life and all the idiosyncrasies that can come with character. I'm always fascinated by character behavior. And I don't want to give that up just to propel the story along to some kind of conclusion. I think *Bugsy* has a very strong story line and at the same time the characters have their own kind of idiosyncrasies and certain strange and peculiar behavior that's functioning throughout the piece.

Ideas create other ideas. Rather than looking at the problem and just staring at it, sometimes you just start trying things and it's just like a chain reaction. Things kick off other ideas and all of a sudden it opens up new doors. So rather than be afraid to explore, you chase it and see where it'll take you.

It still ended up a very long screenplay. I think we shot about 165 pages plus. And we only lost one scene, so what it is, is people are talking much faster than they normally would.

I think *Diner* only was able to happen when I began to realize that everything that I had talked about was about male-female relationship. So even if these guys hanging out, what it was all based on was the problems with women. When I understood that, then I could write it.

When I read *Bugsy*, it was fascinating. We always say Hollywood is infatuated with gangsters, but here was a gangster who was infatuated with Hollywood. He basically invented Las Vegas by saying, "Well, I'll take all the entertainment and I'll put it in the desert and I'll use all of the things that I know about gambling and invent some crazy city." That kind of lunatic sensibility and that kind of collision of a gangster in Hollywood was an idea that was real intriguing.

I think every time you do a movie, there's a strong theme and an idea that motivates you.

Sofia Coppola, *Lost in Translation*

It was kind of all accidents. It was scripted, but a lot of it was just kind of running around Tokyo and seeing what we would find. Certain scenes were more improvised. I wanted the audience to feel like the main characters, who had no idea what was going on, so it's through their point of view. But I remember being in Japan for *Virgin Suicides* and doing interviews and the translator, you know, answering shortly and the translator going on and on and I thought, "Is she adding her ideas about filmmaking?" And then to find out that the language is much longer and there's more formality to it, so we just sort of exaggerated that.

Neil Jordan, *The Crying Game*

I wrote the basic situation of the kidnapping of a black soldier by an IRA activist who basically was troubled about what he's doing, because terrorism is a very troubling and horrible thing.

I just wrote out the brief story about three pages and I didn't proceed with it. Over the years I'd been thinking about it and saying maybe if I did this, maybe if I did that. I came back to it, and I said, okay, I'll write the script now, and it became very exciting. But I don't know why I could finish the script last year as opposed to eight years ago. It's hard to explain. Maybe because what it says about the world we live in now is somehow more relevant than it was then. It's kind of a bit mysterious. When it happens at its best, you're a participant rather than a manipulator.

I like stories about characters who exist in situations of moral unease, who feel the need to make a moral choice, but the moral choice they're presented with is unclear. In other words, where they're kind of in a world where there should be marks between good and evil and there actually are none. And I like stories about fallen characters, probably because I'm from a Catholic background!

I think there's nothing like the pleasure of a well-constructed story. It's like a piece of music or a piece of architecture. The pleasure of putting the shape on a script is a wonderful pleasure, whether you are the director doing it with the writer or the writer doing it yourself.

I have to get the story solved before I start the film; otherwise I would get into trouble with directing it. And I've been in one situation where the script has been a movable feast, which was pretty horrible, because basically if you take a script, and you get fifteen different voices saying we could do this, or we could do that, I mean the choices are endless, and there should be one choice really. If there are twenty solutions, there's something wrong. Maybe one writer cannot find it. I just finished doing a screenplay for this book, *Interview with the Vampire*, which is an interesting, very tangled book. And there have been a whole series of scripts written and I realized that nobody had actually told a story from beginning to end. And when you do that, it's absolutely fascinating. If you just tell the story pure and simple. It sometimes puzzles me, the way that people who are neither directors nor writers have input into screenplays—that confuses me; I don't understand.

Robert Zemeckis, *Forrest Gump*

I've never found a screenplay yet that didn't need massive amounts of what we call rewriting. For me the writing never stops, whether we admit it or not; film directors are writing and they're writing with film. Maybe the more appropriate word is *storytellers*, and I think what we are doing with the writer is, both telling the same story and it's separated by our guilds [the Directors Guild of America and the Writers Guild of America]. But in what I do, the writer has got to be there with me all the time. The first thing I do is just lock myself in a room with the writer on the first day. It's not in the ugly "director making the writer rewrite the script" sense. It's just we gotta hone this movie into something. As every department starts to warm up, all that has to be fed back into the screenplay. And I think the final writing that I do is color timing the negative and the final sound mix.

I believe that in the classic dramatic sense that your character arc is what proves the ultimate premise for the movie, and you have to try to see if that fits into that classic dramatic structure in Western entertainment.

The major structural thing that changed when I got on board was the idea that the movie would start off being narrated in a flashback and then we would catch up to real time. You were able to invest the audience for three-quarters of the movie in the character; then all of the sudden, nobody knew—even Forrest—didn't know what was going to happen. It took me awhile to figure out that the love story between Forrest and Jenny in actuality is the suspense that holds the film together.

Mel Gibson, *Braveheart*

There was a theme—it was the idea of freedom as something you can't buy—and it's something to be prized above things, and that we take it for granted and that there are people who have given everything, their last drop of blood, for something that we all possibly take for granted.

The script from sparse history, legend, and imagination was not bad. I shied away from it for a year—it was kind of unwieldy and larger than what we ended up with. There were twice as many castles and ten times as many battles. I didn't change writers because I thought that he really caught the essence of something that stirred me up and kept me building these images in my head before I'd go to sleep at night. Gradually we married scenes together—we [he and screenwriter Randall Wallace] would sort of sit down and wander in and out of character, just us talking, so you had to be there, you had to be in our mind-sets; otherwise you were just looking at two lunatics in a room.

We were writing some of these scenes as we were shooting too; they were last-minute things. If you come across a problem, you find every means at your disposal to fix it. And sometimes a lot changes the whole tone of a scene.

Some things you really can't write: the relationship between Wallace and the Robert the Bruce character. The Bruce's journey through the story was like the worst bastard you've ever seen on a page. But you had to be with him somehow.

Scott Hicks, *Shine*

I learned a very powerful lesson on the first feature film that I directed, which for reasons best known to himself, the producer decided since he had a first-time director and a first-time writer that we would not meet and discuss in case we sort of ran amuck. Which is really what you want people to do in a sense, is run amuck. So I vowed never again: I've been involved as a writer on all of the documentary projects which I've made. The second feature film that I made, I wrote, directed, and produced. With *Shine* it started out as an idea which I researched and developed for about four years while I was making other projects. I'd written a number of treatments and I wrote a first draft of the screenplay, which was called *Flight of the Bumble Bee*. I always had in my mind the structure of how I wanted to tell the story, where I wanted to begin and how.

I saw a little story in the newspaper. I went to see a concert. I was fascinated. And from that moment I knew I wanted to make a film. And really the first year or so we [Hicks and David Helfgott, the subject of the film] spent getting to form a friendship so that I could actually understand and come to the details of the story. Because nobody sits down and reveals their most intimate details of their past on first meeting.

After four or five years of working on arriving at this point, I had the structure, I had the characters, and I had made a large amount of David's dialogue because it was drawn from David's mouth. Then I wanted to bring in a new sensibility and someone who I could collaborate with as writer and director because I sensed that this was a film that was going to take every bit of my concentration as a director to execute. And Jan Sardi had worked with me as a script editor on the previous feature film that I had written. We had a very good relationship and so I said to him, "Let's do this." And he took it on and began to make it his own. We kept the structural architecture of the piece and Jan took it into some new direction, some of which I liked, some of which I didn't. It was a very collaborative process but with Jan as writer and me as director. And I enjoy the process of collaboration. I don't have a love of sitting down to write. I write in order to direct.

My draft was sort of a vast sprawling, embracing everything that I knew about David and his life and family. There were many, many stories that were bubbling out in it. So what we set about doing was essentially finding key turning points in David's life, which started to dictate the selection of material. In a way it was like starting with a vast and sprawling novel. If you are adapting a novel, you have to pick which story you're telling out of those hundreds of pages.

Cameron Crowe, *Jerry Maguire*

I originally wanted to do a movie that was about how you would arrive at your greatest success through incredible failure. Success being an emotional success really. And it sort of began with a picture in the newspaper, of a sports agent or sports manager and his client. They were two guys of very different sizes and loud shirts. But they were clearly two guys against the world. And from there the whole story of *Jerry Maguire* over a number of years of research became a very personal story for me. The journey of a man to complete himself. And basically what I ended up with was a movie much more emotional than any of us thought when we entered into it.

I worked on the script for a long time, about three and a half years, and I felt like I directed it a number of times while I was writing it. A couple of different movies were directed along the way.

Originally the movie was written with Tom Hanks in mind. And it was Miles Davis music that I heard. Particularly this one live version of the song called "So What," which had many different changes to it. But it was a really adrenalized, hyped-up live version of that song from a concert in Stockholm. But as I kept working, another song kept coming to mind, which was a track called "Magic Bus," from The Who's album *Live at Leeds*, and it was a younger man's story. I think the idea of writing for a star probably added more time to the process.

Steven Spielberg, *Amistad*

I feel that I'm really not a writer. I'm an illustrator trying to find ways to illustrate the story, with just a brevity of dialogue when necessary.

My involvement with this screenplay was minimal compared to my involvement with other screenplays of films I've directed. I had a wonderful script. My only real contribution I think to the screenplay was to try and find visual metaphors to take the place of dialogue. It was necessarily a wordy film because it was a courtroom drama. So my first idea was that I wanted all the Africans to speak in their native dialects and not speak English, which I thought would contemporize the film too much and make it very much like a Hollywood picture about a period.

Steven Spielberg, *Saving Private Ryan*

Well, let me start by saying that it's one of the only times in my entire film career where someone actually, at an agency, gave me a script that I committed to direct. Even

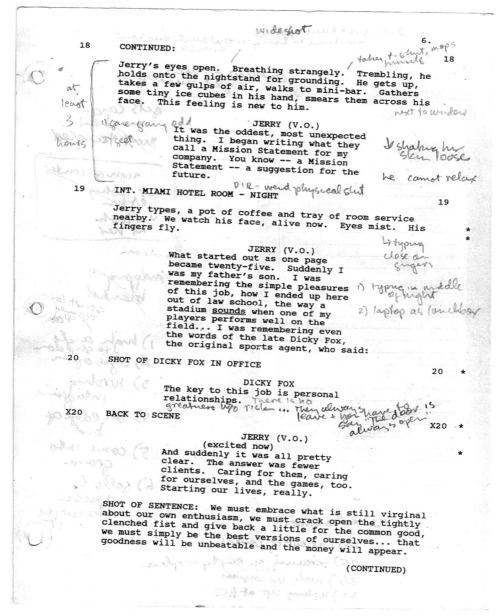

Cameron Crowe's notes on script page from Jerry Maguire. (Courtesy of Sony Pictures and Cameron Crowe.)

though the screenplay wasn't the intense experience that the film became, the screenplay was much more a morality play about the kind of trading of lives for another life. So the screenplay really grappled with those issues of—do you really sacrifice eight people to save one—and it was really much more focused on that. But I had experienced a lot with my father who fought in Burma in WWII. I discovered post–*Saving Private Ryan* that so many of the actual veterans didn't speak about their experiences, if they in fact saw intense action, not unlike the Holocaust survivors who never speak of the actions taken against them because they're afraid they're going to taint the lives of their children and the grandchildren. But my father spoke openly about it and got me very interested in it. There were a couple of moments at home when I was growing up in Arizona that my dad used to have reunions with his bomber squadron. Every three, four years, they'd come over to the house and they'd have a reunion. It always perplexed me why they would start out laughing and then start drinking and then end up crying. Because when you're a kid and you hear eight or nine guys in a room, adults, your father's age crying, it's kind of a disconcerting moment. And in putting all that together, and having learned a lot from *Schindler's List* about docudrama, about creating a reality that is conducive for the screen but not so much that you wouldn't really allow yourself to even watch it, that kind of fine line between what's tolerable and what's intolerable, I really wanted to bring to [*Saving*] *Private Ryan* an experience that would be the experience of a soldier, not the experience of a filmmaker. And to that end I talked to a lot of soldiers who saw a lot of combat. And that informed me to inform Robert Rodat [the screenwriter] and to begin the rewrite process. Which was to essentially create an experience that would be very first person.

I began directing the movie before I began directing the movie. I began directing the movie on paper. Although I didn't storyboard and I didn't really know how to help tell that story except to sort of say to Robert Rodat and to a few of the others who helped me with the screenplay, "Let's get to location and see what happens." So here was one situation where I really went to location with a screenplay that all of us thought was going to change, but we didn't quite know how it was going to change. And the experience I allowed myself to have on this, which I'm really happy I did because it transformed what the film would have been had I not done this.

I knew that a lot of who these characters were going to be was going to happen on location, not really in rehearsal or in the casting process. For instance, the character that Jeremy Davies plays, who some people think is a coward, at the very end of the story that entire story was manufactured on location. None of that was in the screenplay. His trying to defend Mellish on the staircase and losing his nerve and dropping to the steps, not going through with saving his comrade's life, none of that was in the script. And that was just the evolution of being able to sit with these people and dealing with them like they were real people. And talking to them, "What would you do in a situation like this? Who would you come through for? Who would you fail for?" and a lot of that was done just talking to the actors from day to day.

Preproduction

Clint Eastwood, *Unforgiven*

A director is like a platoon leader. You kind of get everybody encouraged to charge the hill with some enthusiasm.

Ridley Scott, *Black Hawk Down*

You're thinking of all the reasons why you don't wanna make the movie and looking at only the negatives. And I think the thing I've learned to do is just not address the problems, only address "When's the start date?" 'Cause as the problems come at you, you'll deal with them on a daily basis.

Christopher Nolan, *Memento*

Well, for me, preproduction on *Memento* was a very new and frightening experience, 'cause I'd never been in that situation before. All my other films had been me and a bunch of friends just figuring out what to do and, you know, really having fun.

All the departments, when they got the script and when we had that thing of "okay, open up the office and get everyone the script," just lost their minds. And I'd forbidden anyone to reorder the script, because I felt that as soon as you open that door, you know, it would be a very dangerous road, but my wife and producer on the sly reordered the script and gave it to the department.

I had to figure out how I was going to shift my directing to accommodate. You know, you're there with a camera and you turn and you say, "Oh, I'd like to shoot this thing instead," and you look behind you there's a hundred people with cars just getting out of the way, which for an independent filmmaker is a very peculiar hindrance. And you have to learn to rethink things. And it becomes more a process of being prepared, where you need all the departments to really understand.

Roman Polanski, *The Pianist*

I think that for a director the most difficult part of the filmmaking is to stick to his initial imagination. When you start a film, you have a model of the picture in your mind, and gradually as you work on the picture, this model is being somehow overshadowed by the reality, because the reality, even if you're very precise in your planning, it's not exactly the way you have imagined. It's much richer, much more complex. That model is sort of disappearing. The new reality superimposes itself over it.

Anthony Minghella, *The English Patient*

Whatever you think you're gonna do never quite happens the way that you imagine it's going to. I think that everything that you do before the day of filming pays off, even if it seems to be abandoned in every day of filming.

The extraordinary gift of filmmaking is that you're all trying to make this painting, and you've got 150 or 200 people also holding the brush with you and guiding the brush. And somehow, out of that, something coherent emerges. And that comes from talking and planning. We were in different countries, with different languages. I dread to think how many languages were spoken on our set but certainly into double figures at certain points. All the time trying to pursue your vision like a madman and like a bull, just get to where you want to go. At the same time, you need all these people to be coming with you and pushing you and pulling you and supporting you, and how that quite works I don't know.

You call in favors wherever you can when you are making a film.

Saul [Zaentz, the producer] has a mantra which sounds in public, like many of his things—a loud and ludicrous statement but, in fact in life, is a wonderful mantra which is "No me, no you, just the movie."

Peter Jackson, *The Lord of the Rings: The Fellowship of the Ring*

We had designed some sets so I had the art department build me some twelve-inch scale cardboard models of our sets. And I got little Barbie dolls and a DV camera. So I was able to go around my little cardboard sets with the Barbie dolls and actually shoot angles which were a lot more accurate to what the film was gonna be. And the actors arrived in New Zealand about five or six weeks before the shoot. And I actually insisted that they sit down and watch this movie even though Ian McKellen saw his role being played by a Barbie doll at the time. I had to apologize. But what I thought was important, that everybody got to see the film that was kind of floating around in my mind. It was very important that the actors all knew that we were all working on the same movie.

Mike Newell, *Four Weddings and a Funeral*

We were a little movie and we were a junk movie and a throwaway which got incredibly lucky. And so we were going to make it a year before it was finally made. And we couldn't make it that year because it was going to cost about four to five hundred thousand dollars more than it eventually cost. And we had to fight the budget down.

The thing has to have a life beyond what you've planned, and beyond what is on the page, beyond what anybody expects of it. It's got to have a kind of an eternal life. Somewhere along the line you have to legislate for independence and unexpectedness, changeability and unquantifiableness.

Mike Leigh, *Secrets & Lies*

We'll sit down at a planning meeting before the shoot. And they'll say, "Okay, scene 29, Johnny in office meets night security guard. Now is that a long scene or a short scene?" And I'll say that I think that's a long scene, I feel there's some length. Because don't forget the scene doesn't exist. So I've got to say instinctively that we'll need some time in there to rehearse and it will take us awhile to shoot. There's other scenes and it's the same one line there and I'll say that's an instant thing or that's just a narrative scene that I know will be quick. We can knock it out. We don't need to rehearse it. I can rehearse it on the day. We can invent it on the spot, write it as we go, whatever. And it's a balancing act.

Baz Luhrmann, *Moulin Rouge*

It's been this absolutely consistent feeling of responsibility of having led a lot of people down a road of trust that we could make the musical work again, and through a sort of forest of "That will never happen. It is foolhardy. You will be destroyed. Do not go there. Anything can happen and will." And you're having to find your way out of the forest. One of the hardest things around a musical form is that we don't have the mechanisms anymore to sustain what we need. You know, there isn't a dance chorus that MGM's got on standby that actually sleeps on the set. Or that you ring up and go "Bring the dance chorus down. We need to do a new number." And in Australia, I can guarantee you there isn't a dance chorus like that, all right? So we had to find a dance chorus, and all my collaborators [who] are longtime collaborators, had to build a dance chorus, and we had to keep them enthusiastic. And of course, the schedule would keep changing. They've been working on the cancan, these girls, and it is so physically hard to do. Like, it used to kill people at the turn of the century. It was quite common to die from doing the cancan, you know, whatever, you know. It made break dancing look positively safe, right? And eventually, the tension on the film got to such an extraordinary level. People weren't going, "I'm leaving." It was just, you know, "Where are we? Are we all gonna be incinerated, you know? When will this hell end, you know?"

The process of this giant, this artifice, this big lie in which to reveal the big truth—everyone has to be in a very specific philosophy about, How are we going to tell this story? And what are the rules? So that they were free to be spontaneous within that mechanism, you know.

What I'm trying to say is that actually the production designer, the editor, the photographer were actually involved in the process of text development. We evolved the text with them.

Cameron Crowe, *Jerry Maguire*

It was an L.A. movie and the challenge was to make it not look like the L.A. you see in movies everywhere, all the time. I have big scrapbooks and I'm always pulling stuff from magazines. There's also a great device that Sony made that allows you to take still photos from movies and videotapes and stills from commercials. There were two stills that I took from *Woman of the Year* that I had in the front page of my script, and it was Spencer Tracy looking at Katharine Hepburn and then Katharine Hepburn returning that look and I kept those two photos with me all the time. I would always flip open this first page and Tom would be like, okay, I got it, I got it. It was amazing how much those little blasts of inspiration help when you're tired, when it's late. You can open up one of your scrapbooks and see what the soul of the scene should be.

Gary Ross, *Seabiscuit*

I'm ashamed to say that I'd done a lot of research at racetracks long before I ever found the material. That's not something I'm necessarily proud of, you know. At that point I was on the deficit end of the project. But there's a lot of very specific period detail, and the first place you really start is with the source material. I was suddenly entering a world of horse racing in the '30s at a time when it was very, very different and there was a whole world to explore. I spent a lot of time at Santa Anita just wandering the backstretch, talking to jocks, being in the stables, being around the horses, stuff like that just so you can feel it, and if you haven't sort of done enough homework, you're not going to have it inside you on the day when there are thirty other things going on. So I got versed in that and then I read a lot of books about the Depression just to understand what it was like. I found it to be a very uninvestigated period of history, certainly compared to World War II or a lot of things that came after it. I think we viscerally feel it through things like the photographs of Dorothea Lange. But what was going on culturally, what was going on with the individuals, what it felt like to be in the Depression—I'd heard stories from my father, but I wasn't really that aware of it. If you're a migrant worker from another country or you're coming here to try to get a job, these conditions exist right now. If you're working in a sweatshop in East L.A., these conditions exist right now. So it's not outside of our experience. I think the difference with the Depression was it was so pervasive.

Horse racing has the highest mortality rate per capita of any sport in the world. More people die horse racing than in auto racing, for the amount of people who do it. So the only way to really do this was we would have a race meeting every day in my office for three months. We only had three months to prep the movie, which we could have used a lot more. I shot listed everything. And then once we did the shot list, we would sort of do like big military chalk talk. I'd map out the thing and all the people would be there. We would have everybody involved in this gather together and we would talk through every shot in the movie so that by the time we got there, it was rote. It was like football plays almost.

Martin Scorsese, *The Aviator*

When I received the script—John Logan's script—it was 190 pages and I realized it would have to be cut down. But there's something that I guess they call the director's disease that's "Hey, yeah, let's do this. This is great. It's like about, you know, flying like a god and at the same time it's a doorknob." And then as you start to do the pre-pro[duction—you are] cutting the script down.

Andrew Davis, *The Fugitive*

I've been lucky to sort of create a family, a little repertory company of technicians and actors, that just really like being together. And they're very supportive. I'll take recommendations from everybody, and I actually love it. I've gotten some of my best ideas from teamsters and craft service people [who supply food on set].

Neil Jordan, *The Crying Game*

It's extraordinary but you see how this kind of big rather vulgar and noisy machine can be accessible, or can be molded, by the spirit of one person, and that fascinated me.

• 4 •

The Cast

Peter Weir, *The Truman Show*

I love the process. I mean, it is exhausting, there's no question of it and you know it's sort of difficult when you do find yourself opposite somebody and sense their tension and nervousness in the casting. But I love to read all the parts. I'll tend to, at least in the final sessions, play the part off camera unless the actor objects. It's the most mysterious business. I sometimes think it's like a missing person's search. You're like a detective trying to find this person that exists on paper and you're meeting people who claim to be the person. I think there's another mysterious side, some sort of other than verbal connection with the person, you feel you get on with them, and you're going to direct them, and you know you need that rapport. That's the most mysterious side of it.

I tend not to say much. I shoot a video. I love to shoot that wonderful system of recording and taking it home with you. Make it very informal, camera running all the time. I'll improvise sometimes. If I find somebody's interesting, but the lines are getting stuck, I'll interview them. I've done that a bit. I'll say, "Okay, you're playing the mother whose husband's just left. Let me talk to you as if I was a journalist." That sort of frees it up. I mean, "What sort of life did you have or why did this happen or whatever." Sometimes I'll do that. Sometimes I'll ask them if they've got a scene in a church or something and I'll get some music, put some music on.

The whole thing is you're trying to take the dialogue down as much as you can and tell the story with the camera. I'll say let's put some music on here, let's just have a quiet moment where you are just thinking to yourself, or if it was a church scene that you're praying or something. And then I'll move even that little camera myself and get some interesting angles. Try and break the formality of it—get them less tense.

In *The Truman Show*, the part of Christof, the Ed Harris part, somebody else was cast that didn't work out. So that was only the second time of my career in which a mistake was made, on my part. Differences arose, which can be very painful. That part wasn't fully realized. I think it's really fair to say this: the part of the villain as it were, in the story, was really a kind of stock character. It worked because the plot was moving at such a pace at this point that in a way, as long as the actor was competent and so forth, it would work. But I began to realize as we shot because the villain, Christof's stuff was to be done at the end of the shoot, that there hadn't been enough thought about this character. I began to make decisions on his behalf: Christof wouldn't do this. In meetings I used to say in preproduction, the first half hour we'll do it as if it were

The Truman Show, and I'll be Christof. You know we'd laugh and then get on with it. So we'd do half an hour as if I was Christof and then I began to see, and of course the man's got an aesthetic and once we'd chosen the town, it was a man who wanted a town that looked like this. Now I'd cast the part but the character emerging through the shoot, via myself in a sense, at one stage I thought maybe I should play this. It was a joke you know, but I sort of knew this man. You know I knew his obsessiveness and so I ended up with a part that really was very different to the part offered to the actor. I needed another, some other type of person. It was an awful situation.

Mike Newell, *Four Weddings and a Funeral*

When you cast, there's all sorts of practical things to take into account, like the money. Who will do the trick for you and who won't? And that obviously affects the top two or three [roles]. The thing that's most depressing is that there's a package before you even start. Nobody says, "Did you see that tracking shot?" It's like the Bill Wilder line about "Let's go see this picture; I heard it came in under budget." People don't go and see a script; they do go and see actors. Somewhere in the casting, you try to find actors who will give you more than you put in. I see them a lot and I talk to them a lot, and it's one of the arrogances of our jobs, that you reckon that you judge people to an extent, and you hope that their selves will reveal themselves. But then simply they have to be able to play it. They have to be able to do it—whether they are educated or not educated, whether experienced or inexperienced.

There comes a point at which you do have to be able to say, "I back you, it's yours—I want what you are."

Peter Weir with Ed Harris on the set of The Truman Show. *(Courtesy of Paramount Pictures.)*

Every script requires different techniques and different sorts of actors and there are all sorts of actors. I mean, they do fall into categories. The writer, who was a man whom I greatly valued and worked with immensely, happily, said right at the beginning that he intended not to write anything that wasn't in the medium of jokes. We all know a joke will fall off its pedestal very quickly if you get it even slightly wrong. So it has to be very precise and had to be spoken precisely, and Hugh had the ability to speak it precisely and at the same time be believable.

There are an awful lot of actors screaming for love and you can see it. You can see that kind—they're looking for the lens the whole time, and when they find it, they start to make up to it. They start to kind of flirt with it. It's not particularly lovable, but it has to be lived with.

I talk to them to sort of get a sense of whether I'm going to be able to work with this person or not, but if someone's really going to be trouble, I think you can get a sense of that by bringing them in and meeting with them.

Ron Howard, *A Beautiful Mind*

Casting, well, it's a phase of the process that I really, really despise. I just hate everything about it. I mean, once in a while you have a friendly conversation with somebody, but I just feel that, you know, I mean, I relate to the tension of the people who are coming in and that. And I find it very, very challenging. I mean, sometimes somebody comes in and you know that's what you had in mind, that's what you were looking for, and they've got it. Paul Bettany in our movie was that way. Here's this guy who comes in—character's not written British—but seeing a little footage with Paul Bettany, having one conversation with him—I didn't ask him to read or anything—I was completely convinced. And I even decided it's okay that he's British, because Nash is from a Southern aristocratic family, or at least wannabe aristocracy, and there's always an inferiority complex that many Southerners have. And if he was going to imagine a best friend, you know, he probably would like to imagine him being British.

I do audition actors. I do callbacks. Sometimes a person comes in and it's just spot on, and you sort of say, "Well, they understand." Sometimes they completely turn you around. That's exciting. An actor will come in—I always try to tell actors, don't try to do anything except your best work, because you can't begin to imagine what anyone's really looking for beyond, you know, your interpretation of the scene. I tend to look for someone who I think is going to be able to do something that I hadn't particularly thought of. For me it's a very thorough process.

When I was cast as an actor in *American Graffiti*, it was six callbacks over a period of, you know, like, five months. And each time you'd figure that you didn't get the job, and then you'd get another callback. And it was really frustrating. I was kind of pissed off about it. But when I saw, you know, again, what Lucas had done in terms of really thoughtfully putting together a group, the chemistry was the most important thing.

Sometimes with really key supporting characters, I'm interested in what their sort of creative instincts might be, in hopes that they're going to fill in the gaps in interesting ways.

If somebody says something and you say, "Well, that's interesting." It's not even about them improvising in the audition, necessarily. And you maybe have them try the scene again, you throw something out, or they'll say something. You say, "Well, try it that way." See what it is when they take their own idea and begin to experiment with it. Then take it away from them and see if now they're lost. Are they hurt or something, you know? So I try to see how flexible they're going to be, how inventive they're going to be, and whether they're going to be a big pain in the ass or not. And you can sort of tell in a meeting, if you stick with it for more than ten or fifteen minutes.

Jennifer Connelly really won the role. When I began to talk to her about this particular movie, her own academic background was an interest to me. She went to Yale and Stanford. She sort of understood the world. Then I saw her in *Requiem for a Dream*, a very courageous performance, even though that character has nothing to do with Alicia Nash, and then an audition with Russell and Jennifer, and it was decided that day.

Steven Spielberg, *Amistad*

I had sort of built in for myself a golden parachute. I was a little nuts to have decided to make three movies in twelve months. After I had committed to *Amistad* and I had everyone to move over from one production to the other, I realized that perhaps I was making a mistake. So I set a very high watermark and I basically said that if I don't find the right power for Cinque, there's no reason to make the picture. Just when I decided I was not making the picture, along came this young man, Djimon Hounsou. He was homeless on the streets of Paris for a number of years and then was discovered by Herb Ritts, the fashion photographer. Then he found his way to New York and then found his way to Los Angeles, and he answered an open casting call, which often happens. I wasn't looking for well-known actors to play the Africans. I wanted people who spoke all the different dialects. So the thing to do was to have open casting calls where you actually put ads in papers in Atlanta, Boston, San Francisco, Los Angeles, Chicago. And all the different African communities would come to those casting calls and they would be put on videotape. So Vickie Thomas, the casting lady, and I looked at hundreds and hundreds of hours of videotape.

What I do when I have an actor read a scene is, I never give them the scene out of the movie, because I get sick and tired of hearing the scene thirty times a day. I don't want to hear the scenes two months in advance and then have to hear them again on the day [of shooting]. So instead, we'll just write a mock scene that has all the emotional beats of the scene that's in the picture.

This tape went into the player, and there were twenty actors on the tape, all reading for Cinque, and he came on the tape. It was a wake-up call. It was probably the most phenomenal awakening I've ever had. Next to maybe discovering Ralph Fiennes for *Schindler's List*, which really woke me up. When Djimon came on the tape, it was the power of what he didn't say that made me say to Vickie, I pray he's in L.A., because I want to see him today. And he was, and he came in the day I saw the tape. And I interviewed him, or spoke with him for a while. The problem that I've had sometimes in the past is, certain actors that aren't actors per se, they're aspiring actors, they get in a room with me, and they get all clammed up, and I do a lot of work to relax them. And Djimon came into the room, and he was not intimidated by anybody. And it was really one of those things where after he left the meeting, the entire office was a buzz. He had left a real scent and a charisma behind him.

I had not worked with Anthony Hopkins before. I had always wanted to work with him, and one day I was presenting at the Academy Awards one year and I met him for the first time in the green room, and we were both rehearsing our presentation speeches, and we did that thing that you always do in Hollywood, you always hear done—you say, "Gee, I really wanna work with you someday." That happens all the time, actors and directors are always saying, "I love your work; I wanna work with you someday," and I really meant it. But I didn't think of him as my first choice for John Quincy Adams. I had five other actors turn me down. I had five actors that I thought I wanted say no to the part for various reasons. Paul Scofield felt that he had touched on the tone of that character in *The Crucible*. Paul Newman just didn't want to work in that window [a specific time available for production]. I had one talk with Anthony Hopkins on the telephone, and he talked to me in the voice of John Quincy Adams. And it was a telephone interview—that was all we had together—and that was all it took for me to say, if he wants to still do it after my hesitating so much, I'd love to do it with him.

Steven Spielberg, *Saving Private Ryan*

I got Tom [Hanks] involved from the moment I read the script. But the rest of the cast was a little more problematic because I have a different kind of process for casting. And that is, I spend a lot of time looking at actors' reels, television, movies, whatever they've done. I find it more valuable for me to see someone's work before I meet them and often I won't even meet them. I will just cast them based on something I've seen of theirs or reading they've done on videotape for me. I don't like to read actors on video-tape based on the screenplay I'm directing. Because in my early films when I did that I'd get so sick of the scene. You hear it 120 times and then you really throw out the baby with the bathwater. Because you go back to the writer and say I'm sick of this scene, write me a new one because it's a test scene. So I usually write sides [a few pages of the script] or have the writer construct sides that are completely different than the screenplay but still reflect the character. And I judge that way. In the case of *Ryan*, I didn't meet any of the actors until we got to Ireland. I just didn't want to. I had a couple of criteria for myself: I'm a big collector of *Life* magazine. Because I've made so many movies that take place in the 1940s and it's very hard to find faces today that look like the faces of twenty-, twenty-two-year-olds back in 1944. So I was really in a face hunt before I was in a talent hunt. And when my casting [person] had brought me some sensational people, most of them I said they don't look like 1940s kids. They look like modern kids. So right away that just brought down the possibilities to a select few, and then of that select few I was very fortunate that—with the exception of Jeremy Davies, who plays Corporal Upham, whom I'd met through my wife, who was co-starring with him in a movie—I met him on a location in Texas and cast him right there in Texas— aside from him, it was really an interesting experiment, which I had never done before in that way.

Steven Spielberg and Tom Hanks on the set of Saving Private Ryan. *(© 1998 Dreamworks reprinted with permission by Dreamworks, LLC. Photograph by David James.)*

Peter Weir, *Master and Commander: The Far Side of the World*

I think you can get by with a great concept and a good cast and the rest of the things can suffer, including the script strangely. That's why some first films people make are so great, because they have this sort of burning, bright idea and they get the right people, often friends, you know. You've got a description of a character and a lot of people are going to come along and pretend to be this person and you've got to weed them out. You've got to get the fakes out and find that one. It's a very mysterious business because it's not just that they fit the thing and they've got the right kind of qualifications, but that there's some rapport. I think it's an unconscious, unknown thing. And it doesn't mean that they're going to be friends or something. You don't need that. But it just means there's some connection. And if you cast the thing right, you don't really have to say much to the actors.

We knew we'd have to go to what they call the public schools, you know, to Eton and so forth. Max Pirkis is now at Eton and because I knew they had a hierarchy, they had a structure, probably had parents who'd brought them up with a very definite kind of code of behavior. And so these young fellows came in. And we didn't have a large pool to choose from, naturally. We're going to Mexico for six months, breaking school, and so on. And in came Max. I tested them on video the normal way and whittled it down to the four we used. I had no idea that this young boy would be as good as he was. In the video test he always had a little smile on his face, and I'd say, "Max, I know this is funny. I know you're pretending you're on a ship and I'm standing here with a digital camera, but just try, don't smile." And he said, "I'm not smiling." I said, "You are, you know." So as with amateurs, I thought, well, you take potluck.

Oliver Stone, *JFK*

An actor cannot resemble a look or wear the same clothes or have the same voice as the person that is actually historically accurate. Therefore a film is a fiction to begin with.

With this kind of movie, because we had to stay on the realistic side of the equation, we were trying to be believable. I tried to go against type with Ed Asner. I mean, he's the sweetest man in the world, in person, but I wanted to make him as mean as he can be, and he did it. I tried to reveal something new each time with the actors.

I love Kevin Costner. I like his small ears that kind of go back to his face. He's so cute. Let's be honest, you can watch that guy for three hours. It's a three-hour movie and, well, for me he anchors the movie. And he is so generous because there are so many wonderful supporting actors in the movie, that he allows them each to have that moment. People think he has integrity and honesty because he does, and it comes across.

Gary Oldman, everybody thinks that's Lee Oswald. They don't know that it's Gary Oldman. He just vanishes, you know. He's the most self-effacing actor I know. Amazing. He learned Russian for the film. Unfortunately I ended up cutting out most of his Russian.

It's nice to hang out with people. It's nice not to have a formal structure, to take them to Las Vegas, or just to go to a movie. Talk to them as you're walking or doing

Oliver Stone and Kevin Costner on the set of JFK. (JFK © 1991 Warner Bros. Inc., Regency Enterprises V.O.F. and Le Studio Canal +. All rights reserved.)

other things, because then you get their real-life reaction. Take them out on the street, walk them around. Do other things, just don't make it a formal head on. But alas, if you have 180 roles to cast, you do get into a formalized situation. And you do read [where an actor reads the lines from the script in a formal casting procedure]. And they come in, sometimes they come in five times. And I've learned a lot from the reading process. I have a casting [professional] generally, and maybe a second party to read or another actor who comes back and helps with the reading.

Scott Hicks, *Shine*

Everybody said, "Look, it's a wonderful script and terrific, but who's going to play this so off the wall?" At the top of the list was Geoffrey Rush, who I had seen in the early '80s in theater. I'd seen him many times and I was dazzled by him even back then. I started to look at tapes of other more recent performances, and it was just astonishing. So I met with Geoffrey, and he's so different from the characters that he plays. He's calm and very centered and very intelligent and humorous. I was actually dazzled by these incredible hands that he has, which were marvelous because I was thinking that he's going to have to look like he's a pianist. We just talked for I suppose an hour. And at the end of it I offered him the role. The casting person was saying, "Don't you want to sort of test him or audition him or read?" I said, "Well, no." In a sense his whole body of work was his audition. And I said this is a part which will never test or audition right until all the work has been done to create this character. And you can't expect an actor to fully fashion this incredibly complicated character in order to do a screen test. And I felt it would inevitably be a disappointment and then cause me to doubt my own judgment.

Scott Hicks lining up shot of Geoffrey Rush. (Courtesy of Scott Hicks.)

Once I'd cast Geoffrey, it became the stumbling block. Who the hell is he?! Literally, someone said to me, "He's forty, he's made no films, what sort of failure is this guy?!" And everybody has their own agenda when they are getting involved with you on a film—there were these attempts to sort of shuffle Geoffrey out of the pack.

This process of casting is incredibly fraught with tension and your sense of the other person's vulnerability. They only get this little time to make some sort of an impression on you, and I find it utterly exhausting. And I'm still figuring out how it all works.

[And there is] that ghastly process where you have dozens and dozens of children brought into you by parents. And each one of them thinks their child is a magical child. And indeed they all are, even when you can hear them tap dancing down the corridor on their way in. And most of the children had the worst thing of all, which is some experience of being coached or taught. We [with Alex Rafalowicz, who played David as a little boy in *Shine*] set up a chessboard and we played a few games with it. I would get him to close his eyes and I would shift pieces around on the board and say, "Tell me what move I've done." What I was looking for was his ability to play a game with me, first of all. Secondly, to focus on something that really mattered. And so I started to get a glimpse of just what kind of concentration he had and how he could keep the focus.

The approach to Sir John Gielgud got completely muddied, where I had a real sort of altercation with this particular agent who was determined to replace Geoffrey with a client of his. And I said, "We've come to talk about the part of Gielgud." And

Scott Hicks, Noah Taylor, and Sir John Gielgud on the set of Shine. *(Courtesy of Scott Hicks.)*

we left, leaving the script for Gielgud there. And then learned two days later that he had passed, Gielgud had passed on the script, and I said that was a terrible shame. And months go past in which we look for someone else. All these desperate attempts to find some great theatrical knight! We came to a point where I sent the casting lady to London and she went to see someone else in the agency and told him what this role was and he said, "Well, this sounds perfect for Sir John Gielgud!" And she said, "Well, sadly, he passed," and he said, "I beg your pardon? Let me just tell you that everything that Sir John reads goes through me, so let's just start this conversation again." And within twenty-four hours he had accepted the role!

Alexander Payne, *Sideways*

Paul [Giamatti, who plays the lead, Miles] read once and he was I think in the middle of shooting something else and his agent said, you know, "please go to this audition." And the way he picked up the pages, the sides [printed specific scenes from the script], and read it was so good that I thought what could he do with preparation! I could see he could make even bad dialogue work. And you're always just looking for casting choices that are gonna make your job easier, people that you don't really have to say anything to if you don't have to.

Thomas Haden Church first read the scene halfway through the movie where he's in the bar. And when I asked him to come for a callback, I had him do the breakdown scene. And he actually took off all of his clothes except for his underwear. Which was kind of showy. But it worked.

And the guy who runs naked is the great M. C. Gainey, whom I had worked with previously in *Citizen Ruth*, and I called him up and said, "Hey, M.C., how ya doin'?" "Doctuh Payne, how are you?" "Fine, fine, fine. Hey, I'm making a new movie." "Whatevah you want, doctor, whatevah you want." "I need you to run naked on camera." And then a silence. And then hoots of laughter. And then he said, "I'll do it."

For smaller parts, for one-line parts, I cast real people. So I have a casting [person] who kind of specializes in seeking those people out and putting them on tape, and I pour through all the tapes and then see how bulletproof they are in a comeback, in a callback.

Mel Gibson, *Braveheart*

Even a small role can really screw you up sometimes if you don't make a very careful choice. It took a good three months of almost on a daily basis for half a day, just looking. So I was very vigilant about going through that whole process with a very gifted casting lady who brought a smorgasbord of talent from the British Isles, and the decisions became so difficult because there were so many wonderful actors. I didn't read them or any of that kind of stuff in front of cameras. You just kind of sit down and talk to them for half an hour and just talk about anything. Talk about the story. And you didn't even know where you were going to place them. The guy that played Robert the Bruce came in, and I sensed in him an angst. He wasn't quite sure who he was. And I said, "Wow, that's kind of like what I want there." Later on, when we were talking, he told me that he'd only found out a couple of years before that he was adopted. So that there was this sense he didn't have a belonging—he was wandering. In the script, the king and the king's son were a little bit like some kind of goofy comedy team that they just put on the bozo wigs and come in, and I wanted to have kind of intelligence and authority. Then someone suggested [Patrick McGoohan] and I thought, he's got this tremendous presence and he hasn't worked in forever. So I invited him to lunch and he did it to me over the lunch table. I could hardly talk to him, he was just staring at me. I said, "I know you haven't worked in a long time, Mr. McGoohan, sir. Does this idea even—would you have any interest—would you do this?" and like that—and he just looked at me and went, "Baaaahhahahahaha!" And I sat there and all the neurotransmitters were going, "What does that mean?" But it meant that he wanted to do it, I guess.

If my career had been dependent on reading, I wouldn't have gone anywhere. And sometimes when people come in and they give a great reading, they never progress from there. You can tell from talking to someone whether they're capable. There's something in their eyes. The guy who played the Irishman, for instance, he came in and I said, "This is the most lawless bastard I have ever met in my life." He didn't know what a chair was for! You could've lit matches in front of his breath. And he just didn't give a fuck about anything, and I said, "This guy is just the kind of maniac I want."

Kid actors are tough—I mean, you meet the ones who have something natural going on and then you meet a whole other bunch, they're okay, but somebody got to them and gave them a bunch of bad habits. It's a tragedy that they start so young and get the wrong information from someone. Some drama coach that totally destroys them so that they're like a bunch of little parrots.

This lady had a boy who wasn't the young Wallace, but he was in a theater group there and he was a very precocious young kid and we used him. He played the other kid. And he was funny and we thought, "He's a good kid for that part there," and we asked—she actually went up and said, "Do you know anyone—I'll give you a twenty—if you dig someone up that looks like Mel Gibson." And he says, "I got your man." And he took her through the bowels of all these places and came to this kid's house and got him out from breakfast and said, "Here he is." And they brought him in and he was wonderful. He was wonderful.

Anthony Minghella, *The English Patient*

It came to the point of casting and Saul [Zaentz, the producer] said, "Where do we begin?" And what I said to him was that this is one thing that I want to do by myself. I think it was a great index to his generosity in the sense that he has been in every casting session of every film he's worked on and this was the first time that he didn't come. I don't like to read with actors. It's a mysterious thing and most of it has to do with the horrible, excruciating intimacy that you're trying to collect in a room with them. So I sit in a basement meeting actors for hours and hours and hours. Juliette Binoche was the first. Juliette Binoche was dancing through the pages of that book when I read it. And I had no idea why but as soon as I talked to Saul, the way I got him interested in the project was, I said, "There's a part for Juliette Binoche in it."

I use a casting person who's always worked with me as a writer and a director in London, Michelle Guish.

The interesting thing about casting this film is that the danger of being the writer as well as the director is that you have completed something too soon. You've got in your mind, particularly with me, the sound of a character. And then you can become overproprietorial of each moment. The odd thing for me is that Kristin Scott-Thomas is so far from the idea I had in my head when I was writing. And the reason it took me so long to cast that part was, the Katherine I had in mind was as far away from Kristin Scott-Thomas as could be imagined. The first time I met her I think we both wanted to leave the room after about five or ten minutes. But we were locked into having dinner together and it was an unhappy event. It wasn't because I didn't think she was a good actor; I thought she was a fantastic actor. It's just the music in her was so far away from the music that I had heard when I was writing. When I went back to the screenplay, every time I tried to find an actor, her noise infiltrated my thinking. What happens is the list gradually gets smaller and smaller until there's only one name there. Then what happens is that your evangelism for that person knows no bounds.

One of the things I did do, and this was a surprise to me I think, Saul prompted me to do this, I'm in his debt to this, he said, "Why don't you start to put people in a room together?" I did have a day working with Ralph [Fiennes] with the various possible people. Now I found that actually one of the most uncomfortable days, since I'm terrible at saying no and I hate feeling I've disappointed anybody. The reading that we did was really an excuse to see what alchemy there might be, and I think that it became very evident immediately to me once we did that process, who was right. The danger is that while you're watching as a director trying to work out what's going on, the actor too is responding. And I made a pact with Ralph at the beginning of the day, which was don't say anything to me until the end of the day, then we'll trade our feelings. And there were lots of very glamorous actresses in this room and they all were ravishing and Ralph seemed very interested in being ravished by them. And all I thought was "Oh no, he thinks of them as so beautiful, he's bound to say he likes her," and it was so manifest to me instantly that Kristin was the right person. And he said at the end of the day, "I know exactly who it should be," before I'd even opened my mouth, which disconcerted me. And thank God he felt as passionately [about Kristin] as I did.

Baz Luhrmann, *Moulin Rouge*

I really always come down on the side of the actor. And I'd worked with John [Leguizamo] before. He was in *Romeo + Juliet.* And you're thinking Toulouse-Lautrec, he was French aristocracy, so he has to speak with a lisp like Daffy Duck on speed or something; the last thing you think of is John Leguizamo. But in that particular case John said, "Look, you know, I want to play, actually, the unconscious Argentinean," which was the character who did the tango sequence, who, by the way, is a Polish chap who can't dance or sing, right? Which gives you an idea of the power of acting, because, really, he acts that role. Then John came to me and said, "I really don't want to play the unconscious Argentinean, right, and be in Australia for like a year playing something that isn't a challenge. I really want to try out Toulouse-Lautrec." And he came up to the Chateau Marmont, and he got on his knees and chased me around the kitchen.

With Nicole, who had this ability—I remember I worked with her years ago and we were shooting—I was guest editor at *Vogue* magazine in Australia and I shot her—and I remember the first time I met her I thought, "God, she's such a kooky, crazy, wacky, funny person, have we ever seen that before? You know, wouldn't that be great to get on-screen?"

I see all the actors and instead of making them audition I do these things called workshops. And you know, they go on for a whole year. And I try and get so involved with the work with the actor that they're forgetting that they're auditioning. When we did finally cast the company, they would come to Australia.

Rob Marshall, *Chicago*

It was very difficult because musicals are so few and far between. It was really like detective work finding out who had done that in their background. Catherine [Zeta-Jones] I had heard about. She was the most obvious choice because I had heard that she had done work. We found a tape of her doing a street scene jitterbug called "Moonfaced and Starry-Eyed" in Kurt Weill's *Street Scene* when she was nineteen or something, but I could tell then right there that she could dance and she could sing. It was clear from the folks at Miramax that this was a risky project. I could have cast it from the theater. But it was something that they weren't interested in. So I said, "I'll go and look at film stars, but if we can't find them, we're going to have to, you know, go to the theater." So I began the whole process and a lot of the superstars or whatever you might say aren't interested in auditioning. But this wasn't something I could just sort of say, "Do you sing and dance?" and "Oh you do? Great, let's do it." So we actually came up with this wonderful thing. We basically said, "Listen, if you want to be considered for this, you have to go through a work session with me." And I really sort of stayed away from the word *audition* 'cause I really didn't want them to feel like they were going to be coming in and I was going to be sitting behind a desk with my arms folded and they get up and sing and dance. They came in and it was almost like it was the first day of rehearsal. I worked with them. And it was a long process. It was over two or three hours of working with them to really get a sense of what they could do. It was great.

This happened specifically for the role of Roxie, which is the part that Renée [Zellweger] plays, because we couldn't find anybody. I actually had a wonderful time during that casting process because I found how brave actors are, so extraordinary to me. Actors want to be challenged. That's what I find. They want to try something different. And I saw these major women come in one at a time, scared to death. And it's very important to me also that people don't feel judged. I hate auditions for that reason. So the fact that I was up there working with them I think helped them. And I like them to feel protected and so that they feel comfortable to try things that they wouldn't normally try. We had a rehearsal studio, the WestBeth Theatre Center, down in lower Manhattan. And it was a great big room. Each woman came in and did "Funny Honey," and then they did the song "Roxie" and danced a little. They were coming in completely cold except that they had had the material and had the song. We filmed it, so I have serious blackmail material! But you know, I was really surprised. Some people that you would never know can really dance and some can really sing and that was extraordinary. Renée was funny because she came and she kind of dips her toe in very gingerly. She wanted to sort of suss it out and she sat and we were sort of showing her what kinds of stuff we were doing. And she watched and I thought, "She's not getting up. She's not gonna get up and do this. She's just watching." And so, um, it was over and we were like walking out the door and I said, "Well, that's that. I guess she'll, you know, she's not interested." We were walking out and she pulled me aside, shut the door—everybody had left including the pianist and the drummer and everything, everybody had gone—and she said, "Show me that step you were working on." She really wanted to do it privately with just me. And as soon as she began—you know, Renée is an athlete and was a gymnast and a cheerleader—as soon as she started I knew literally within a minute that she could dance it. She had natural line; she had natural stamina. And I was praying to God that Renée could because I knew I needed somebody with that range and that vulnerability and that likability because of what she ultimately ends up doing in the film.

John C. Reilly had done musicals in high school. He actually auditioned on videotape. He did "Mr. Cellophane." Little bowtie, he's all dressed, in his voice teacher's living room. And he did a version and before it was even over, he said, "Now, I'm going to do it again a completely different way, which was crazy 'cause after literally the first two notes I thought this is it, perfect. What he told me later, which was so sweet, is that he had actually done thirteen different versions but only sent me two. I've worked with Neil Simon before and he says to me, "You know, some actors come in and claim their roles." And I like to feel when I'm in an audition situation that the next person through the door you want to be the person. They claim it and [Queen] Latifah said, "This is mine. This, I want to do this," and it just felt right.

Rob Marshall directing Renée Zellweger on the set of Chicago. *(Chicago © used under license from Miramax Film Corp. All rights reserved.)*

Cameron Crowe, *Jerry Maguire*

When Hanks chose to direct his own movie rather than be in *Jerry Maguire*, I immediately wanted it to go to Tom Cruise. He was the "Magic Bus" to me. Tom Cruise read it and called me and said, "This is a part I'm very interested in playing; it's different." He said, "I'm coming to L.A. in a few weeks; let me read it out loud for you to see if I'm right for it," which was great. I did have friends who said, "He'll never play a loser." And in fact he was dying to play someone who was on the ropes. And it all blossomed from there.

Once I had the actor, I wanted to surround him with fresh faces—you feel like you're glimpsing real life. That's the greatest gift of all, and so it was also rewarding to find newcomers and put them next to Cruise. And you start to forget that it's Tom Cruise. You start to believe that you're in another world.

I had a casting lady I really loved, Gail Levin. She was tireless and we basically saw as many people as we could. And Tom was very available to us. So he read with many, many actors from bit parts to, of course, his leading lady. And Renée [Zellweger] was the one that came in and kind of punctured everything that you expect to see in a movie starring Tom. She came in a number of times. The first time she came in, she had read the script and didn't really have a strong take on it. But this seemed like the type of person a character like Jerry Maguire would see around the office and not take that seriously, and her beauty or her depth would appear later. Then she came back and everything that was great about her the day before was sort of gone. She'd had a problem with her dog. She was in pieces and unable to really connect. Sort of an awful

Cameron Crowe with Tom Cruise on the set of Jerry Maguire. *(*Jerry Maguire *© 1996 Pictures, Inc. All rights reserved. Courtesy of Columbia Pictures.)*

moment, when an actor leaves the room and hasn't quite lived up to the advance hype. And so for about a month we didn't speak to Renée. And then Gail brought her name up again, and she came in and nailed it. Tom was there. I actually had a video camera going. She flies into the room in all of her "Renée-ness," and she's kind of spinning around and talking about things that happened to her that day. In the background you see Tom regarding her in that great way that Spencer Tracy regards Katharine Hepburn. Just someone watching this person who, as it happens, was going to play a big part in his future life. And it was all there in the first moment. She had the qualities that set him off both personally and in the character, and you just die for that.

The little boy was tough. The little boy was written to be a joyous little guy, but I sort of fell in love with this young kid who was quiet and sad. And I thought, well, this brings out a different aspect of the script. This is a kid who has truly lost his dad. This is a sad kid. And what if Jerry Maguire sees himself in that kid and gives that kid a relationship that he hadn't had? And so I hired him. So I was trying to adapt to this sad kid and it wasn't working. He did not want to be an actor and wasn't an actor. And so three weeks in, we replaced him. And it was a very odd and terrible thing. Not to the kid—I think the kid was happy. A kid was found by one of our producers. And he was in fact everything that I didn't want in the kid that was going to be in the movie. His one experience was a McDonald's commercial. And to me that's the hellish version of kids in movies. So I kind of, in an exhausted state, went into the hotel room where the kid and his parents were staying. And I was really tired. I said, "Hi, how are you doing?" The guy said, "We think our child is a magical child." I said, "Great, great, great, great, where is he?" So out of the bathroom comes trotting this little kid [Jonathan Lipnicki]. His hair is exactly as it is in the movie. His glasses are the same as in the movie. I would never make up those glasses and that look. That was him. The kid was on fire. Knew the lines, and said, "I've wanted to be an actor my whole life." He's five! He's great. And we took him to a set and put him in the room with Tom. And Tom started doing some scenes and Tom looked over to me like "Whoa, this kid's pretty good." So we finished our little audition, and then the kid said, "I just want to tell you that my favorite movie is *Top Gun* and I've seen it twenty times." And at that point Tom turned into perfect profile and said, "I feel the need—the need for speed." And the kid just exploded and never came down. We hired him, and everything you see in the movie is his ride. That was a lucky break.

Roberto Benigni, *Life Is Beautiful*

When I'm casting the process in Italy, preparing movies is much different than the United States, much different because we don't have studios. Me, I am an independent so I'm preparing when I am casting the movie. There is something very a mystery. How to choose? Something very mysterical because you don't understand exactly what happened with the face. I am thinking or dreaming one face. Things change and it's like the movie is choosing, really. Like something happens, something strange, inexpressible, unspeakable, inexplicable that I cannot to understand why I choose. But something happens and this is really very mysterical thing. And this is very wonderful. For example, the little boy [Giorgio Cantarini], I was testing and he comes with an overcoat like a really little clown. And he told me, "I dreamt of you last night, Roberto." Because it was the movie like grabbing him. And sometimes it's so hard because in Italy we don't have such an amount of actors. I like actors very, very much. For example, Danco [Giustino Durano, who plays the uncle], he is a theater actor, very old, and never did movies before, but what an elegance, what a man. He's such a wonderful actor, the face, and he could be the grandfather of the little boy and really my uncle. This was by accident. There is the Italian writer, Machiavelli, who said, "There are people who know everything but that's all they know." Is very good because when I learn that "everything," I am missing something.

For the female protagonist I chose Nicoletta Braschi [his wife] because "mama mia," I love so much! I respect her as an actress because in my mind when I'm thinking about something feminine, her face comes up immediately!

Another example, my friend in the movie is very important because we are both together all the first part of the movie. He was bigger and taller than me. I shoot a lot with someone small, tall, and fat, skinny, like we call that "August and white, no cloud." They have to work together. And also there is some chemical that happen. Chemistry and this also is so difficult to understand. Because I called him and I said, "No, sorry, but you are not the right person; it's terrible." Then I shoot with some other actor and then at the end by accident I put in the wrong cassette and I see again him! And it was momentous; it was the first one! And I called him and said, "You are wonderful, wonderful!" And he couldn't believe!

Clint Eastwood, *Unforgiven*

Well, the unfortunate thing about being an actor first, and then being a director later on in life, is that you've gone through the acting process. You've gone through the

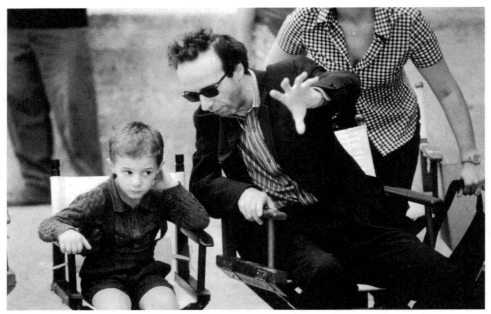

Roberto Benigni and Giorgio Cantarini on the set of Life Is Beautiful. *(*Life Is Beautiful *© 1997 used under license from Miramax Film Corp. All rights reserved. Photograph by Sergio Strizzi.)*

cattle calls. You've beaten your head against the door many times. So it's very difficult for me to meet actors. I'd hire everybody that came in the room! But fortunately now with the videotape, and I have a casting lady now who is very sensitive to actors' feelings, so she will put people on tape so I can look at them without encouraging them falsely. Then when I've made up my mind, when I'm 90 percent there, then I like to meet them maybe and say hello.

I don't like readings a lot of times because a lot of very good actors are not very good readers.

If I have the person come in, it's just to meet them, to feel how at ease they are. I'll maybe go into the philosophy about the part a little bit, but I'll try not to intellectualize it to death.

If you've seen the actor's work and know what they can do and they seem to be in line with the understanding of the character you're gonna ask them to portray, there's really no reason to beat it to death and beat them to death and make everybody all nervous and upset. Sometimes you go through many, many actors. If you're in doubt then maybe you should look further. But if you see something, you've got to say, "Okay, that's the way I want to go." I'll tell you about an experience that happened to me once in Europe. I had someone send a tape over of an actor from Munich, and I said, "This guy will be perfect, yeah, this guy, I like his face, I like everything about him, hire him." When he showed up on the set, it was another actor! And I thought, it's not the same guy! So I kind of went off in the corner and sat there. "What am I gonna do? How am I gonna handle this?" Then I looked at the guy, and he had an interesting look, and a good face, so I said, "You know, I'm not gonna tamper with this. I'm gonna go with this guy anyway!" Didn't have the heart to come up to him and say, "You know, you're not the guy," and send him all the way back home.

Pictures are very important. A lot of times people send in the pictures, and I've done that same thing myself as an actor. You submit the picture and resume and you figure, that's gonna go in the wastebasket. But it is important, because sometimes you are looking for a face that is specific because you have a certain kind of role and you feel that that role is going to be reoccurring and that face has to be very recognizable and the ability of the actor is important, but the look is very important too.

Clint Eastwood, *Mystic River*

Phyllis Huffman [casting professional] is a lady who I've worked with for many years, and she's just terrific about handling actors. She's very, very sympathetic and kind, which is very important to me. I don't sit in when she's putting them on tape. Unfortunately, coming from the actor's side of the thing you . . . and having people blow cigar smoke in your face for a lot of years . . . you get very, very sensitive to that sort of thing. So what I do is I have her—this is when I'm using unknowns—put actors on tape and then I'll look at 'em like that. And sometimes they don't have to perform well. Sometimes I'll pick somebody who's not necessarily the best performance on that particular tape. It's just you're looking for the right sound and ability. You can see if their machinery is working well and you're trying to get somebody who fits the picture because once you've cast the picture, whether it's known actors or unknown actors, once you've got all that cast together, that's where you live and die on a film. If you've miscast it, then you're fighting an uphill battle all the time. But I like to just meet the people sometimes if it's somebody I'm in doubt about, just to see the size coming in, to see what they look like. But by and large, I've cast a tremendous amount of actors without ever meeting them. The three boys I looked at on tape. Two of 'em were professional actors, had been in things before. The one who played young Sean Penn never acted before. He was in a home for kids, orphan kids, and he was terrific. He had the same attitude, that same edge that Sean has, and that's what I was looking for. When I saw him on the tape I just said there's something real about him. He doesn't look like an actor, which is the greatest compliment you can give a person. We used a wide array of actors from very experienced to two actors who had never been in a movie before, or a play even.

Clint Eastwood, *Million Dollar Baby*

I'm looking mainly just to see how they handle themselves, how they look, whether there's a tinge of something there. Then I might meet 'em if I'm down to the wire, if I'm really close, but I don't want to give a lot of false hope to somebody. Years ago, I was doing a picture called *Bird* and I was looking at some tape on various actresses and they said there's five actresses on this tape, and Diane Venora was the first one on the tape, and I said to Phyllis, "That's fine. That'll be enough." And she said, "Well, now, no, we'll run the rest of the tape." I said, "No, no. That's enough, that's the person I want." And it's just, it's all instinctive with me. It has to be, you know, right away in your mind. Now, sometimes you're disappointed, but by and large if you trust your instincts, great things happen.

I had seen the girl who plays the sister, I had seen her in a play down at Tim Robbins's theater, The Actors' Gang, and several of the referees and ring people I had seen in a play down there doing other things, and I just said, "Yeah, I'd like that guy for this, and this guy for this." I don't believe in beating people up, due to my own insecurity. I've gotta see it, and if I revisit it too many times, I figure that must not be the person. There's some little bird telling me something's wrong here.

Christopher Nolan, *Memento*

I had never done casting before. You start looking back at movies and you see there are so many films that you love—where the lead performances are great and all the secondary characters, all the tiny characters—people who come in and say a few lines—are really not very good. And you look at that and you say, "Well, why is that?" So I went into that casting process really trying to be very particular, but what I found is that there's a certain amount of luck involved. I'd chosen an actor to play the motel—you know, the innkeeper—he sort of plays quite a big part in the film. And I'd found somebody I was happy with, and then they became unavailable because our schedule shifted. And so at the last minute, I had to find another actor, and I found Mark Boone Jr. and didn't get a chance to read him, just had looked at a film he'd done. And he turned up and just does a fantastic job and was exactly what I had in mind. So a certain amount of luck involved.

I'd seen Carrie-Anne Moss in *The Matrix* and thought she had the sort of two sides to what she did that was exactly what I was looking for. I met her and we talked a lot about the way that film dealt with the nature of reality, the subjective versus the objective. And she really got that. And with me it's very important that actors, when you're sitting there in a room with them, that, that they get what you're gonna do. And on a personal level, you really, you really connect. And that was what I found with the three leads.

Sam Mendes, *American Beauty*

Kevin [Spacey] was doing a play in London and so I just said, "Look, I'm going to go and meet him." And I went and met him. Partly because I just wanted to know who he was. He's a very mysterious chap, and I think that's one of the things that's so great about him. I met him after the show and he was playing with his puppy, and he was just like a big kid. He's as vulnerable and as insecure as the next man, and that's healthy. A big influence for me on the movie was the Billy Wilder movie *The Apartment*, and I felt it needed to be an Everyman figure, a man who was ordinary but special. Who you would walk past on the street but, when you looked a little bit closer, was very intriguing. And Kevin—I don't know who coined the phrase—if there's one thing better than a great actor, it's a great actor who's hungry. And Kevin is a great actor who was hungry to play something different. You've seen him always playing the kind of Machiavellian schemer, the guy who's ten steps ahead of everybody else. And to me it was a chance to play someone who was five steps behind everyone else, and who was lost and vulnerable and funny.

Sam Mendes, Annette Bening, and Kevin Spacey on the set of American Beauty.
*(*American Beauty *courtesy of Dreamworks SKG.)*

The kids were a long, long process and I met literally hundreds of actors. And I didn't want to cast any one of them without the other two. So I needed the trio, because I needed the balance between the girl who appeared to be plain but really was, in my opinion, equally if not more beautiful than the one who appeared to be beautiful but what one discovered was plain and in many ways more ordinary. And then this extraordinary young boy. I generally believe that the actor walks in the room and you think, you make up your mind within five or ten seconds. I don't read at great length, I find it terribly boring. And it was the last day of auditions and I was about to offer the part to somebody else who I wasn't quite sure about, and Wes [Bentley] walked in and he literally opened his mouth and I just wanted to jump up and down, and you can't because you think, maybe he'll turn it down, maybe we haven't got enough money to offer, I mean all those things that go through your head. You just want to go, "That's it, that's it, you are fantastic, you've got the part," you know, and kiss him. I mean, it's just—after six months of trying—it was just a huge relief. The one thing I had to do was see them all together in the same room. So I did the last scene in the movie where they're all together. I did that several times. I originally had wanted the trump, Warren Beatty, to play the real estate king, but the idea of Annette Bening screaming, "Fuck me, your majesty," to Warren Beatty! But I think that would have had too many different meanings in there!

Robert Zemeckis, *Forrest Gump*

I've seen movies where there are two really good actors acting their butts off on a screen and you just say, "I don't believe this for a minute." And so in the case of *Forrest Gump*, it was like a rule that no actress would get the job unless she screen-tested with Tom

[Hanks]. I make actors read because I think there's a real method to the madness. I talk to them to get a sense of whether I'm going to be able to work with this person or not. But if someone is really going to be trouble, I think you can get a sense of that by bringing them in and meeting with them. I was fortunate to have Tom Hanks. He's a film actor; he knows the medium he's working in, so he's more willing to come in and read with potential actors. I'm a big believer in videotape even though I have to make deals with actors sometimes to swear to them that I won't copy the tape and I'll let them have the tape so they can burn it after. But I believe in videotape for two reasons: I believe that something happens to performers; I believe in screen presence. And while I'm sitting there at the end of the day and I'm exhausted and I've seen twenty people, an actor might be doing the greatest performance, the greatest reading, and I'm not seeing it because I just got off the phone with the head of the studio who is just screaming at me over money or something. So I like to be able to have it recorded so I can look at it again and evaluate it at a different time. I screen-tested the little kids for the movie, mainly because I wanted to make sure they weren't going to crack under the pressure of having a crew hanging around them. Once you walk on a soundstage, it's a lot more serious than videotaping somebody in your office.

There's always that time when you'll see one person and you'll just get that feeling that, wow, they've nailed it. But in some cases, I see hundreds of actors. We actually scoured the nation to find the young Forrest and found him just wading through videotapes and boom he just popped off—he went into an open call in Mississippi. And that's how we got him. His mother had never been on an airplane until we flew him out for his screen test.

Mike Leigh, *Secrets & Lies*

It's very important, the choice of actors and the influence that that has on what happens in the film. It would be quite wrong for anyone to get the idea that it doesn't really matter what actors I get because I could make the same film no matter what actors they were. The choice of actors always, in a quite specific way with my films, goes some way to defining what the film is.

I get together with a cast of people who always agree, each of them always agrees, to be in a film without having any idea what the character is going to be, any idea what the film's going to be about, or whether the character will or won't be a central character. In other words, an ensemble of actors. And it takes actors of a certain caliber to agree to embark on that risk. There is a particular kind of rapport which I like to have with each actor, because I do collaborate with each actor to create the character, and that rapport really moves in the direction of creating the character.

Marianne Jean-Baptiste, who plays Hortense, really embodies a new generation of young black actors in the United Kingdom who have the sophistication to be able to play black characters without feeling the need to act an agenda, and that is a great breakthrough. I had worked with her in a stage play a few years ago in London and I felt I just wanted to get her up there on the screen.

One of the things that motivates me is getting actors who are creative in their own right as artists and who are going to do something special.

I see a lot of actors. Because I can't say, "Well, we'll see all the heroines this week and all the old guys in the second.'' I just don't know who I'm looking for. And my worst problem is I don't want to miss anybody.

I have a couple of casting people who are able to say, "You ought to see so and so, or whatever.'' And I have an assistant. But in the end I have to sit in a room for a long time. And I see actors every twenty minutes and I just talk to them and have them talk to me. The first event is meeting people, which is to say I just get them to talk about themselves. I just find out about them and meet them a bit. And the ones that seem worth pursuing, I ask back and I spend an hour and it takes me a hell of a long time! I spend a whole hour, one to one, with every actor that I call back. I do work one to one separately with each actor to get a character going, and broadly speaking, that's done by getting the character who in the end is based on a real person. I get the actor in and ask them to talk about and do somebody, do him or her by themselves in a room not doing very much. I ask them to think about somebody and talk about the person and to do that person. And then we may do a bit more work to develop what they did. Then we talk about it. It is all about an actor going into character and sustaining—being a character in an improvisation and pretending that it's real. I'm asking you not to perform a monologue or a soliloquy, or to do an audition piece or to demonstrate. Some actors have an ability to be real, have a sense of what becoming somebody is, and others don't. The truth is that there are actors who have this natural instinct for doing real people and for what the world is about, and are turned on by that. And there are actors for whom it's all about showing off or performing in a quite obvious sort of way.

If an actor is half good, you don't need to know whether they can read. It's what they are all about which is the key.

Rob Reiner, *A Few Good Men*

I actually read everybody and I work with the actors in the readings at times. In certain films that I make, in the comedies, you have to have a certain rhythm and sense of humor, and there are certain joke constructions that only work if you perform them a certain way. You don't want to get an actor in there that isn't going to ever get that rhythm for you, because if they don't, then the joke doesn't work, then the scene doesn't work. And this is not to denigrate drama at all because that's hard to do, but comedy is way, way more difficult, and anybody who has done both will let you know that.

There are not a lot of good people who do comedy. That's why you have to see a lot of people because somebody has to come in and just hit the right notes. It's like a great studio musician. You look at a great studio musician, and he'll hit every note right, every time. And a great comedic actor will do the same thing. But you have to see whether or not they can do it. If they don't have the rhythm, you can't teach them.

We got so much bad press on using these movie stars, and I kept thinking, "Well wait a minute here, a movie star, well, where are they supposed to go except be in a movie?" It's like, that's what they do! Do you remember in the '30s, '40s, and '50s, you'd watch movies, you'd see Burt Lancaster and Kirk Douglas, or Jimmy Stewart and Henry Fonda would be in the same movie? You'd go, "Wow, isn't this great! I get to see a movie with two people I like!" Now it's like how dare you, bastard, put these people I like in a movie! You got Tom Cruise AND Jack Nicholson in the movie. What the hell is the matter with you!?

I sent Tom [Cruise] to see the play [*A Few Good Men*]. I called him and I said, "I'd be interested in you to do this," and he said, "I'll do it." And I said, "No, no, see the play. Don't say you'll do it. You don't even know what it is yet. Why don't you go and look at it, and you'll see maybe it's something you don't think you could do." But I knew he could do it, and he saw the play and said, "Okay."

Kiefer [Sutherland] I had worked with before on *Stand by Me*, so I knew I wanted him. Kevin Bacon I didn't read because I had also seen all of his work and knew. With Kevin Pollak, I did read because Kevin Pollak had never done anything like this. He was a stand-up comedian. But if you've seen an actor, you know what a guy can do. You can see it in their work, so most of the time, I don't even read. Sometimes I haven't even met the actor. I just call them up and say, "Do you want to do this?"

Roman Polanski, *The Pianist*

Well, this is a type of picture where you try to avoid well-known artists. So we were trying to find somebody who could play this role and carry the whole picture without really much experience. But that very quickly became clear, it became clear that we won't be able to find anybody like that. As a matter of fact, we tried even to reach beyond the profession and see whether somebody who doesn't have acting experience, a pianist or some upcoming actor, could do it. We asked casting [professionals] to try to look for such people in England and they gave a small ad saying what we're looking. And unexpectedly about fourteen hundred people showed up. They were not ready for it and it was a real mess. And some of them were quite interesting but nobody really enough exciting for us to try to go any further, and we just say we have to look for somebody who's done some movies before. But we couldn't afford stars. And we came upon Adrien Brody, who was making a film in Paris. I looked up his work and I met with him and I thought he was the right person.

I didn't ask him to read anything. I told him to come and talk about the picture and give us the name of his agent. As far as the German officer was concerned, I asked our German casting [person] to tape some people for me. I remember I was on vacation skiing. And in the hotel I was looking on that small screen at these tests. And I saw the guy and he was reading with a page of text from the script in a very monotonous way, and it just was absolutely clear to me that he is the right guy. Although he was in some pullover with a ring in his ear and the long hair, it felt right, and I think you just have sometimes to follow your own instincts, in spite of the studio sometimes.

I like watching readings on tape. I don't like so much meeting actors first. I prefer to meet them afterwards. Because a tape you can run back and forth many times. And that was quite a lengthy process with the family. To a certain extent, it was even more difficult than doing it with the leading parts. Basically I wanted to have English actors. I have a lot of experience with English actors and I am very fond of them and I wanted to have some kind of unity of the accent. But after having exhausted all English sources, I had to go a little bit beyond and the youngest girl, she's not English. She spoke with more of an American accent. She's an Israeli. I brought, later, a dialogue coach from the United States who worked with them extensively. I like to cast the people in the way that I have imagined them when I was working on the script. It's very important that the actors conform with my idea of the character more than anything else. If the actor has certain shortcomings, I know that I can overcome it by work on the set. It's the physical aspect, very important, and of course what goes with it. You know, there is no interior without a physique. But a physique is very important. I remember when I came to Hollywood to do *Rosemary's Baby*, and in those times they still had this very important casting department at each studio, and I tried to explain to them what I wanted and I'm lucky enough that I can draw. I drew all those characters. And they cast from my drawings.

It was a bit of a scary moment when we had the first reading, first rehearsal, to see how it works, but it was an immediate family. It was quite astonishing. I think that sometimes we're lucky in our work.

Peter Jackson, *The Lord of the Rings: The Fellowship of the Ring*

We were in an interesting situation, obviously, casting this book, because in a sense, it was more like casting an historical film because people are so familiar with the characters that you had to get them right. Because everybody has a sort of perception in their minds of who they are. And our casting really fell into two groups. It was the actors that we just sat round our lounge, you know, just brainstorming who would be a great Gandalf, who would be a great Bilbo, and thinking of people. And so we had certain actors that we, sort of, we would have loved to have gotten in the film at the very beginning, and fortunately, everybody said yes. I mean, Cate Blanchett we always wanted for Galadriel and Ian Holm and Ian McKellen for Gandalf. But then we had the other characters who we couldn't for the life of us imagine who they could be. We couldn't think of an actor for Frodo or for Sam. So then we went into this big casting process, where we had casting [people] in several countries putting people on tape for us. And we did an initial sweep on tape. But then, you know, I don't like looking at casting tapes 'cause they don't really tell me a great deal. And so we then traveled to London— Sydney, London, and Los Angeles—and did a lot of auditions. I find them very vital, but they're very awkward. The actor comes into the room, and they're nervous and they're tense, and you just know immediately that they're not right. And I look on that as a situation that's never wasted, because this particular person may be good for a future movie. We did a lot of meetings. And we ultimately cast either from the results of those meetings, or sometimes we went around slightly interesting ways. For instance, the character of Legolas, the Elf, we never met anybody that we thought was right. We were very impressed by Orlando Bloom, who came in to read for a character called Faramir, who actually appears in the second movie. And we didn't think he was very right for Faramir, but I thought, "This guy's a really good young actor. He's got a really great face." And so we gave him the Legolas role based on the fact that he'd done the audition for a completely different character. We obviously decided not to cast little people but to cast regular-sized actors that we then shrank down. Even that we thought we had to have physical constraints, because, you know, taking somebody who's a tall skinny six-foot-high guy and shrinking them down to look like a Hobbit, that just wouldn't work. And we actually did some tests where we took a bunch of our crew and we shrunk them down to see who would look good being four foot tall and who wouldn't. And tall, skinny guys didn't work. And so we made a rule that anybody auditioning for a Hobbit had to be between like five foot five inches and five foot seven. And the characters of the Elves, we wanted to cast tall, lean, skinny people. So we had all these physical constraints upon us as well, yeah.

Peter Jackson, *The Lord of the Rings: The Two Towers*

My process is better to have a first pass done by the casting person on tape because obviously you're doing a big sweep and the director shouldn't really, I don't think, spend their time being involved in meeting a hundred people in that initial sweep. But you look at the videotape and then I think it is important at that stage to meet the ten or fifteen people that you think are certainly worth meeting off that tape. You almost know immediately when somebody walks in the room that they're not right. And you've got, now you've got a twenty-minute session with them to read through two or three scenes and you kind of would love to just say, "Listen, listen, you're not right and so I don't really want to put you through this." I try to work with them anyway. I mean, we don't send anyone away. If they come in and they're not right, we still read a couple of scenes for them because, I mean, I think it's ultimately as good for them as well because these are often young actors that need some experience at doing exactly what we're doing with them. And so there's no harm to be done.

The little boy who delivered the lines about the sword is Philippa Boyens's son.

Peter Jackson and Sean Astin on the set of The Lord of the Rings. *(The Lord of the Rings: Return of the King © MMIII, New Line Productions, Inc.™ The Saul Zaentz Company d/b/c Tolkien Enterprises under license to New Line Productions, Inc. All rights reserved. Photo by Pierre Vinet.*
Photo appears courtesy of New Line Productions.)

She wrote the script and she wanted her son in the movie. It was actually the easiest bit of casting we ever did, really. He was about eleven years old, I think, when we shot that and then just this last year when we came to do the ADR [additional dialogue replacement] to replace his dialogue, his voice had broken. We had to cast somebody else to do the voice.

You like to think of the actor when you write the script. I know that for *Heavenly Creatures*, the Kate Winslet role, long before we ever met Kate and cast Kate, I know that Hayley Mills was actually our prototype for that role. I mean, she couldn't do the movie 'cause of course she was far too old. But you sort of, you tend to always want to write with somebody in mind. Except, I must admit, for *Lord of the Rings* we didn't. Ian McKellen was cast through a really weird situation because one of the problems, of course, when you're trying to cast is to get actors who are available and we really liked the idea of Ian doing Gandalf. And he was shooting *X-Men* at the time and there was a real conflict of dates. *X-Men* was falling behind schedule and we needed Ian McKellen to start on a particular date. And then an accident and they had to recast. So sort of the weirdest kind of things happen. We didn't have anything to do with the accident. And then even with somebody like Ian, you look at him and he's not, you know, he's not quite the image that you had in your mind for Gandalf and you're trying to figure out why. And you realize it's something to do with his nose. You know, because his nose was kind of soft and cute and we wanted Gandalf to have a much more of a hawklike nose. So then we come up with the idea of putting a rubber nose on him. And then you've got to break the news to the actor that you'd like him to wear a rubber nose. He was about to commit to a rubber nose for three movies, for eighteen months, and that was a difference between him getting up at five thirty in the morning and him getting up at three thirty in the morning, and you've gotta sort of try to talk him into how he'd look much better with a different nose.

The character of Smeagol or Gollum was obviously always going to be a computer-generated character, and so we thought initially that that piece of casting was going to be voice casting. And the Hubbards in London, who did our casting, our instructions to them was really, "Can we meet some English actors who are good for voices?" Andy Serkis came into the room and we videotaped even though we were just after the voice and Andy was doing this great voice sort of pulling it up out of his throat and kind of twisting himself up, and it was very, very quick, very quick decision that he was going to be right for the voice. And then when we went back to New Zealand, we were still three or four months away from starting to shoot the film, and I got into discussions with the visual-effects guys about the character of Gollum and what he should look like and what his face should be 'cause they were going to have to do him in a computer, you know. I said, "Look, I think we found the voice," and they were obviously interested. "Could we hear the voice," you know, "cause this'll be a really great lead for us as to what he should look like." And so I ran the casting tape for the computer artist, and it was really at that run-through, because I started to point out things that Andy was doing with his performance because in order to generate this voice he was doing a full acting kind of thing. And I was starting to see things in what he was doing that I really liked, and so I was talking to the animators and to the CG [computer graphics] guys and saying, "Now, see the way that he's got his shoulders there and he's twisting them? That would be great." And I suddenly realized that Andy Serkis could offer us so much more than just the voice. And at that point we realized that even though we were going to use a computer character, let's bring him down to New Zealand and have him on set when we were shooting these scenes and actually have him act the character on set. For me it was a huge advantage 'cause now I wasn't talking just to special effects guys about the creation of this character. There was actually an actor who was owning the role.

Peter Jackson, *The Lord of the Rings: The Return of the King*

We had a thing as we were casting for Elvish roles with people coming in completely serious who had gone to a Halloween store and bought big rubber pointy ears like Spock and then they come and sit down and they're ready to go. And you know that they've been working on it all night long with their mother or their partner, and you just want to tell them to take the ears off, but I was too polite.

M. Night Shyamalan, *The Sixth Sense*

I had a ton of amazing actors calling me up, saying, "I want to play Malcolm Crowe." And the level, the prestige of the actors kept rising with every phone call, and I didn't even want to hear it because I wanted to think clearly and I didn't want to hear, "Oh, Night, so and so's on line one." No, I didn't want to hear that, you know, because it's like now you have to have a conversation and then if I don't hire him, I feel like, oh, you know, it's like, "Hey, man, for another movie, but not this movie." But for Bruce [Willis] it was, we toyed with some other people before, but he was the first official submission. And he read it and immediately in a weekend said, "I'm really interested. I need to see his last film." And that's where I thought it was going to end. Because my last film was a movie about a little kid looking for God and it's pretty much Capra [Frank Capra, the director of *It Happened One Night, Mr. Smith Goes to Washington*, and *It's a Wonderful Life*] and very sweet and syrupy and makes me cry, you know. And I thought, "Oh my God, he's this action star, he was in *Armageddon*, and he was going to watch it on the set at Disney," and I was like this is all she wrote. And he went in and came out and said, "I'm in." And I thought I knew exactly that he was the right guy when he said that.

I've made movies with kids that had major parts in it, and so I had definite rules this time. [It] can't be an actor kid, it can't be a blond kid, and it can't be a kid from Los Angeles. So I ended up with an actor, blond kid, from Los Angeles. We did all the schools, the public schools, and all that stuff, and I saw all these kids and I was thinking about one beautiful kid with a lot of mystery in his face and all, but never acted before, and this is a tight movie, tight schedule and Haley Joel Osment and it was like, I don't know, some kind of miracle. He sat down and he was perfectly—first of all he was the only kid, out of maybe a thousand kids, that dressed up for the audition. Now that sounds weird, but he wore a shirt, a beautiful shirt, and he combed his hair perfectly and came like he was coming for a job interview. As opposed to kids who came in like cool with the chains and the baggy pants and the crotches near their knees. Haley came in and his hands were shaking a little and he sat down and his voice was shaking, and I said, "Did you like the scene?" He said, "Yes, you know, when I read the script for the second time . . ." I said, "What? What did you say?" And he said, "When I read the script for the second time . . ." I said, "How many times have you read it?" And he said two or three. And the way he said it, it wasn't BS; he really had read the screenplay, just for a simple audition. And already I was sensing a person working at a higher level than anybody I had come to see here. It was just me and him in the room. So I closed the door and he read the scene where Malcolm Crowe says he can't be his doctor anymore, and he just blows it away and he sits there and he's crying, and I'm like "What, what—what's going on here?" One thing with kids is sometimes when they're nervous and they come in, that by mistake translates into a good performance because their energy is up and they're nervous and it comes out so wonderfully endearing and spontaneous, and then when you get them on the set, after they know you and they're comfortable, where'd that kid go? So I tried to break him. So what I did was give him the tissues and we started to talk, and I started talking about basketball and Michael Jordan and making him laugh and all this stuff, and then, all right, let's do another scene. So he wasn't nervous and wasn't going to use that same energy. Boom, nails the second scene. What I look for is that kind of raw specific actor, that they don't know why they even did that in the scene like that. And also a certain reality in faces is something that's really important to me. Filling the movie with all real people is an important thing.

Stephen Daldry, *The Hours*

Kids are the hardest 'cause you have to spend such a lot of time over and we had to see hundreds and hundreds and hundreds of kids. And I saw all the kids. And I work with all the kids. With a six-year-old kid you're not on the whole going to talk character. You know, "Jack [Rovello, who plays the young Richie Brown], I think in this scene I think you subconsciously think your mother might be wanting to kill herself." I usually avoid kids that went to drama school. And then you have to spend time with the mothers, or it's usually the mothers, to make sure that they're not insane. I just talk to the kids. Usually try to find out about the little kid. Little Jack comes in and he's on the sofa and I ask Mum to leave. I'm filming it, but the kid wouldn't really be aware of that. And there was something about little Jack, something. And then after about twenty minutes we started talking about his parents. And I said, you know, "And where's your daddy?" And "Oh, Daddy's, Daddy died." And I said, "Well, when did Daddy die?" And it was really recent. And so there was this sort of grief in the little child that was incredibly unarticulated, which being an absolute tart, slut, I thought I could absolutely use.

Gary Ross, *Seabiscuit*

People are so nervous when they walk in the door sometimes that I at least want to give them a chance just to get by all the "mishigas" of the audition process. That's a Yiddish word meaning "craziness."

You find that somebody'll walk in the door and they're just lighting it up from the beginning and you know, I've cast a lot of parts in the room. Riddle, the guy who plays Riddle, who owned War Admiral. He was halfway through a monologue and I cast it. I stopped it and I said, "Fine, we don't have to go on. You got the part." He said, "I want to finish the monologue. I worked on this, you know." Probably halfway through the script I met Gary Stevens [who plays George Woolf the jockey] in the jock's room at Santa Anita and he kind of looks like a movie star and the point of George Woolf was that he was swaggering and confident and incredibly handsome and the best rider in the world, all of which Gary Stevens is. He has three Kentucky Derbys, three Belmonts, four Preaknesses, so I said, "Well, do you want to be in the movie?" And he said, he just lost seven races in a row, and he said, "Buddy, you don't have enough money and I don't have enough time," and he walked away. And I thought he's perfect, you know. So then I started pursuing him. And then he thought I was really crazy. So he found out this was legitimate and he came into the office and we did some improvs and I improv most of my stuff with Gary. Because if somebody hasn't acted that much, I think it's very important to get them off the lines and get them away so they can own it, because he's less experienced. So the script was very much a guideline when we would shoot with him.

I wrote the Tick-Tock character for Bill Macy, and Macy, who looks at the world like a rep company, was nice enough just to commit without reading the part. I had gotten through the first monologue and I said, "Bill, I'm writing you a great part." He goes, "Great. I'll do it." And I said, "Well, do you want to read the script?" "No, I don't." And so, all right, well, there's one down. I'll just move on.

Michael Angarano I had brought in early—he plays the young Tobey Maguire—I wasn't sure he looked enough like Tobey, so I kept sort of doing this with photographs and then torturing myself and putting up the other guys, but I liked Michael more. He's a better actor. To me, the most important thing is—are they talented, are they good at their job, are you getting somebody with chops as much as are they right for the part? Do I see that thing in them? Do they come with a lot of game? And this kid had an amazing amount of talent. It was just the physical thing. Got over that.

Gary Ross on the set of Seabiscuit. *(Seabiscuit courtesy of Universal Studios Licensing LLLP.)*

I do a lot of improvs in the session itself because I won't just kind of blow through it 'cause it's important to them and people are nervous in an audition and you want to absolutely give them a chance. And I'll look at the videotapes later. I want to explore all the nuances and stuff like that and play with the scene as much as possible. And I do that in the audition process 'cause otherwise you're not going to know how you're going to get along with them on the day and how malleable that's going to be and how do they take direction and all that stuff.

John Madden, *Shakespeare in Love*

It is a very mysterious process. What is strange is you're looking, at least you have a very strong sense or at least you think you have a strong sense about who the person should be and what the person should be. And what usually the process I have is learning that I haven't got the right idea and when the person comes along who is right, they tell me that person is right. But you have to go into it with the apparatus of certainty that this is what the part needs. And you articulate that to producers and casting [professionals] and to other people. And it's mystical in many ways because you frequently go through a very long process. I've done this and then offered the part to somebody and they say, "Well, I don't want to do it," which can be absolutely devastating because you've gone through this whole process only to find that actually you were wrong, because you are wrong if they don't want to do it. There's no point, I've made that mistake too, of forcing somebody to do a part when actually they don't want to. I made it axiomatic that I had to read everybody. It seemed to me that I was going to be doing the actor a favor because it's very, very unusual material. It's not that I wasn't necessarily able to evaluate somebody whose work I knew, but I didn't think I was going to find a Will or a Viola that way. Although I have to say Gwyneth was the first choice for that part. But she wasn't initially available. I mean I knew her from an earlier audition. But Will was incredible, that was quite a nut to crack. I opened the book as wide as I possibly could. I was certainly considering everybody from this country or from any English-speaking country. But I, in my heart of hearts I thought, he's got to be English surely, or I'll never be able to hold my head up in my own country again. But I couldn't rule out the possibility that there was going to be a male Gwyneth Paltrow somewhere. It was a very, very long process, in which certain actors simply ruled themselves out of consideration before the audition, some during the audition, some immediately after the audition. Because it's the kind of material where the demands of the actor were quite extraordinary. I mean to be able to inhabit the language, the world, the humor, just so many things at once.

I went past Joe [Fiennes] the first time. Because I still had a kind of rigid notion, and frankly, I was beginning to kind of get despairing about whether or not I would ever find this person. That was such a sort of gut terror. I mean for my own salvation however wonderful the script was, I didn't want to make the movie if we didn't have the right combination. And I think because of that I was slightly blind, looking at who I was looking at. We got way, way, way down the line and I thought, "This is crazy! This is absolutely crazy! I can't pass up this movie; it's too good." So I went back and I looked at the tapes again; I do the same thing and put everybody on tape. And I looked at Joe and I thought, this wasn't a good audition, in fairness to him. No, the opposite actually, it wasn't in fairness to me; it wasn't a good audition. But he . . . I looked at him and I thought, "He's so visually; he's so perfect for it." So I said, "Come in and don't prepare." Because Joe is an incredibly diligent and studious person who really likes to come prepared. And I said, "Don't come prepared." I said to his agent, "Have him come in tomorrow so we can just loosen up." But he wouldn't do that. And if I was going to get him back, he had to come in on his own terms and he did. So we had to spend about half a morning deconstructing and just loosening up. I had a new scene that came out of the rewrites that we were doing, which was the scene between him and Marlowe at the beginning of the movie. Where he says he hasn't written anything and Marlowe starts to spin the idea of *Romeo and Juliet* to him. And one of the things I worried about Joe was whether or not he would have the comic deftness that, of course, you can now see on the screen. And he just pulled this out of the bag. I hadn't even thought about it till just the night before and I said, "Come on, let's read this. Let's work with this a little bit," and a sort of spark started to happen. Which he then—Joe's instinct is to mistrust what he's just done and then go and do something completely different. So you kind of haul him back and I put all of this on tape. And I began to feel just that sort of tingle, thinking, "I'm sure there is something here." I found him tremendously attractive as a person, very open and vulnerable and sweet—everything that I'd been looking for but hadn't quite been able to articulate. I needed somebody who had the intelligence but also, you know, could play Romeo at the end of the movie. And the movie's about first love so you need that sort of innocence as well.

We worked on scenes, and we'd take different ways through the scenes. I'd give him different actions to play, in particular, the boat scene. You can play that scene for example, as if he knows perfectly well who he's talking to, which will reveal something

John Madden and Joseph Fiennes on the set of Shakespeare in Love. *(Shakespeare in Love © 1998 used under license from Miramax Film Corp. All rights reserved.)*

about the scene, or as if he has no idea, as if he's testing her. You shift the actions around so that different things start to come out. And in that process you begin to sense the kind of palette that he can work with and you can work with. You find out also the most crucial thing of all, which is whether you're gonna have a relationship there that you can trust.

Neil Jordan, *The Crying Game*

I had to get a guy who could be a convincing woman for thirty minutes of the film. And that was just a pure visual thing really. So I saw hundreds of people and the guy, he had to be either black or a mixed race and had to be English. So I saw hundreds of people and dressed them up basically! I sent the casting person out to all these clubs in London and in Paris and in New York. And I did video tests of everyone. And I did camera tests of everybody, a reduction of those, about thirty. And it really was finding somebody actually who could just physically carry the illusion. The thing really was to get that on a big screen and see do you notice all this stuff. You know, the shoulders, that was it really. Jaye Davidson was a very beautiful man and had never acted before and had no desire to act, but had this obviously physical beauty and could carry the illusion of it and, you know, he was the only person who could actually do it.

The problem in trying to find finance in America is, people would say, "Well, if you cast somebody that we know in one of principal roles we'll give you money to make a picture."

One thing I like to do is find experienced actors who have got technique and have worked for a long time and people who have never acted before. I've done that several

Neil Jordan with Miranda Richardson and Jaye Davidson on the set of The Crying Game. *(The Crying Game © 1992 used under license from Miramax Film Corp. All rights reserved.)*

times, putting the two together. It kind of "wrong foots" the experienced actors in some way; it stimulates them to be real, to be true, not to use technique to get them through a scene. I think, generally if you are casting a nonactor, you get somebody who is bright. If you need to cast a child and went into a school, you say to the teacher, give me the four brightest kids in your class.

Spike Jonze, *Being John Malkovich*

I got to learn a lot about the character meeting with somebody that was inappropriate for it. I'd learn as much as from somebody that might be appropriate for it. Like it made me think more what was right for the character; it made me sort of vocalize it more. So I liked reading with people a lot. And also it was good rehearsal for directing because doing mostly music videos and commercials, I haven't really worked with actors in a really in-depth way. So I used that as a way to sort of learn about just sitting with an actor reading and directing.

I would always be surprised too. When I first met Cameron [Diaz], who plays Lotte Schwartz, the puppeteer's wife, I couldn't imagine it. She just is so different from Lotte. I of course welcomed it. And she just came in and we read. And just like over an hour and a half of just working, just sort of like work sessions, where you just throw things around and try things and talk about the character. And by the end of the hour and a half I was completely sold.

Steven Soderbergh, *Erin Brockovich* and *Traffic*

I know in the back of my mind at the end of the day if we've cast properly and I've given them the right environment to do good work. That's all people care about. What they walk out of the movie with is some glance between two actors. They don't memorize scenery.

I used to read people more than I do now. If I know them at all and have seen them do work and I know that they're good, then I just want to talk to them. I just want to get a sense of how they're going to be to work with, what they're like personally. If I've never seen them in anything, then I'll have them read.

I usually talk about everything but the movie. I really want to get a sense of them so I interview them basically. Where are you from? You know, where did you go to school? What's your family like? All that stuff. I want to hear them; I want to get them as much as possible out of performance mode to see if I can get a sense of who they are. I think it's instinct. I mean, you can come up with a reason afterwards that you jam into why you pick them, but the bottom line is when they're in the room, something happens. You know, the molecules shift for you and you go, that's, that's, that's how I want it to go. For the daughter in *Traffic*, there were probably eight or nine people that were very good that we saw. The moment I saw Erika Christensen, I said, "Ah, that's it."

Quentin Tarantino, *Pulp Fiction*

Coming at casting from, like, an acting background, when I was trying to be a professional actor, I never found out a way to crack the casting process. I always knew that I

Steven Soderbergh on the set of Erin Brockovich. *(*Erin Brockovich *courtesy of Universal Studios Licensing LLLP.)*

walked out of that room and they didn't see what I had to offer. And it's like—especially when you don't go on that many of them, all right? You can go on one, the fucking weight of the world is riding on it, all right? And who can give a performance when the weight of the world is riding on the outcome? So I had to figure out how I was going to approach this. I wanted every single person to read.

It's not that I want them to come in and give a great performance—and some of them do—some of them come in and they just kick your ass. But it's like, it's more—I want to get a sense of their dynamic. What's really important is the putting of actors together. You don't cast this person and arbitrarily that person. They all have to go together. One of the reasons I cast Maria de Medeiros in the part of Bruce Willis's girlfriend in the movie was because I knew I was going to cast Bruce. If I had already cast any other actor to play Butch, Maria may or may not have gotten the part.

When you're starting the film, you've got these lists of people and everyone is considered. One of the things that I do in casting is meeting the people, just kinda getting, feeling like you get to know them a little bit and everything. And if it's a situation where it's like, I'm starting to really think and starting to narrow it down, I make everybody read with me, all right? Not with anybody else in the room, even if it means they have to get drunk before they do it! I'm just at their apartment or they're at my house or something like that, and we're just gonna read it and it's not about performance. I did that with Tim Roth on *Reservoir Dogs*. He would not read. His feeling was "I stand a better chance at getting this part, you judging my past work, than if I audition for you, because I know I won't get it if I audition." And so what happened was we

Quentin Tarantino and John Travolta on the set of Pulp Fiction. *(Pulp Fiction © 1994 used under license from Miramax Film Corp. All rights reserved.)*

just went out and had lunch, lunch turned to dinner, dinner turned into drinks in a bar, turned into two o'clock in the morning when the bar's getting ready to close, and we're both completely shit faced. And he goes, "I'll read for you now." And we read the whole damn script.

I very much believe in the idea of the director having a rep company. Most of the directors that I love have that. I wrote Pumpkin and Honey Bunny for Tim Roth and Amanda Plummer, and the reason that they're even in the film is, I bumped into the two of them one time at a party and they're friends, and I saw them together and I literally—it's one of the only times I've had it in my life—I literally had a director moment. I have got to put these two people together in a movie. In the case of Mia— she's my favorite character—I don't have the slightest idea where she came from. She's not me. She's not anybody I know. I didn't know what she looked like and I was going to find her. That was going to be my thing. I was going to find Mia and when I met her, I would know. I was very open—she could have been older, she could have been black, she could have been white, she could have been Chinese, she could have been English. I was interested in seeing all those different Mias, just knowing that when I met her I would know it. And what happened was, I ended up having dinner with Uma Thurman, and it was just in the course of having dinner with her that I realized, "She's Mia." So what happened was, I went back and just started auditioning again, but now I couldn't get Uma out of my mind. So then we got together again in New York and had dinner. We're just sitting there talking; we're talking all this subtext stuff about the character. She was very scared about reading and it was very like, "Quentin, I'm a really good actress; please don't judge me by what I'm going to do here." "It's not about being good—I don't worry about that. Let's just do it." And so I had a couple of dinners with a couple of actresses, and I felt I was cheating on her.

When it comes to casting, I'll see people, I'll see people and then at a certain point, I can't see anybody else. Okay? I don't care if it's my favorite actor in the world and they want to come in, when I get to that point, I've kind of more or less made a decision.

It was a big deal getting Ving Rhames to play Marsellus because there's a whole lot of males that will not do an anal-rape scene. That was one of the things that when the actors would come in, we had to talk about it. And one of the things that Ving said and it was really cool, not only did he come and kick everybody's ass with his wonderful reading and I've always been a fan of his, we sat and started talking and I go, "How do you feel about the rape?" And we talked and he goes, "Well, you know, that's the thing I'm attracted to as far as this part is concerned." And I said, "Well, why?" And he goes, "Because the way I look, I don't ever get the opportunity to play very many vulnerable people. And this is the most vulnerable motherfucker I'm ever gonna play."

Michael Radford, *Il Postino*

The secret of casting is once you've cast somebody, you forget all about why you've cast them and you look at that person and then you build the part around them. Because very often you don't get the person that you want; and if you don't, the secret of making them look like that was the person you wanted is to re-create the part. That's what I did with the girl. If I had actually paid attention to her reading, I'd never have chosen her. Sum total of her experience was she had been in a spaghetti commercial. I must have seen every young actress in Italy. It was terrible! Day after day these beautiful women used to come past me, and in Italy you're an actress if you wake up one morning and say, "Hey! I'd like to be an actress." And you get a photographer and you take a topless picture of yourself and that's it. You know you're in the profession. I mean, it was the most awful reading I've ever come across, but when she smiled, she lit up. So I just rewrote the part for her. She was the only person who'd come in who I thought was a real movie star.

The difficult thing was, I speak good Italian, but I don't understand the nuances of the culture. And I remember sitting in a café in the Plaza del le Coppollo, and I saw these two English girls come in and just order a cup of coffee, and I looked at them and in that one phrase when they said, "Could we have a cup of coffee?" I knew why they were in Rome, where they bought their clothes, who their boyfriends were. Being amongst the Italians I would ask Massimo [Troisi, the star, coproducer, and cowriter], I'd say, "I really like this girl or I really like this actor," and he'd say, "*Ma-es putinato.*" I went back to my assistant, I'd say, "What does *putinato* mean?" And it means he's disgraced himself. What it meant was that they'd been in a film by a rival comic.

Some people just walk in and you say, "I just want to give you this part." I mean literally, I have done that on a couple of occasions. Even though they might not look anything like you imagined when you started, you think this person has something. For instance, the guy who played the telegraph operator.

I do read people, but then I don't pay much attention to it. I read them mainly because I don't know what else to do when I'm talking, and sometimes it can tell you certain things, particularly with the character actors. I think, this is the most dangerous area of making a picture because a lot of character actors have basically done one thing all their lives and they get into terrible bad habits. I had to cast thin people in this movie, because in Italy in 1952, people didn't have enough to eat, particularly in the south of Italy. And everybody in Italy now has a lot to eat. It's a rich country. So everybody's a fat person and to find thin people was extremely difficult.

The thing about Philippe Noiret is one, he's a wonderful actor. He's made 117 movies and I never get bored of looking at him. Two, he looks exactly like Pablo Neruda. So I sent him the screenplay. He got it on Thursday morning; three o'clock on Thursday afternoon, he rang me up and said, "Don't give this part to anybody else." And I never doubted that he was the guy to play this role. We then had to deal with the fact that he had to do it in French.

Ang Lee, *Crouching Tiger, Hidden Dragon*

You know what they say about the leading man's really the better-looking version of the director. I think in the process of making the film I realize I was really dealing with my midlife crisis. I really identify with this guy. What he try to [do], preaching this young girl and make her right and how he must have feel. It's like me teaching this young actress. This is a mixed feeling and how you handle yourself. There's a certain tabooish things you're dealing with. I think the most painful part is the person walk in, the first second you just know but then you have to say the thing for twenty minutes, like he has a chance or she has a chance 'cause we're nice guys. But you have to establish your authority. You look at them and they know you're the boss.

The Chinese industry has less to choose from. Sometimes you go for the best. First round I just talk to them, just see if they have the demeanor and the look I want. God is not fair. Somebody just have the look. They don't have to do anything. The audience do the work for her. So that happens. But I think you can be very wrong about looking at a real person, especially the new faces. You don't really know until you get to screen. Down to the extras, I look at them. Make sure they look right; I handpick them. But I go for the look and I do all the makeup with them myself. I think every piece is important. Is like a note in music.

I think the face is most important. The face that sends out signal that you want to send out to the audience. I think that that's, you know, photogenic; that's very important. I think the job of casting is continuous up until the movie's done. Up to, all the way to sound mixing, you're still doing the job of casting. So many times you can be so wrong about something and you have to make it right, look like they're perfectly cast. So lot of the casting job, as far as I'm concerned, is what moviemaking is about. In that sense, the second half of the casting to me is shooting, working with actors, not only bring them to the movie but bring the movie to them. I feel like a tailor and so the movie just fit for them and try to fit everyone. Many times I feel like tailor to the actors.

Frank Darabont, *The Shawshank Redemption*

You're just cruising on instinct and hoping for the best. Pinning the 8x10s [actors' photographs] up on the wall, playing mix and match. What if this guy plays that? Certainly in *Shawshank* there was sort of an ensemble thing happening. You wind up putting those faces up on the wall and you wind up eating a lot of take-out food late at night with your casting [person]. All of our extras were local to Mansfield, Ohio, and surrounding areas, so there were a lot of unemployed steel workers that were really happy to come work for the summer. We actually did have a few guards from the new prison up the road. We had them come in and audition and there were a couple of them with speaking lines in the movie.

Sometimes the politics of things are such that you can't get certain guys to read; you have to make them an offer, so that was what we did. So we went in kind of with our fingers crossed. Our casting person would bring the actors in for specific roles and there were a few cases actually where somebody would walk out the door and I would say, "What about this guy for that guy?" Blatch—the killer, he's on-screen for like forty-five seconds in the movie—he's the one who actually did commit the murder—this guy came in to read for one of the cons and he walked out the door and I said, "I have got to see this guy read Blatch." Sometimes there's just something about an actor that just triggers something. He came back in, he read for Blatch, and I was chilled and delighted. You take everybody that walks through the door. But what you get actually on film versus videotape in an office is something else altogether. Sometimes you wind up with much more than you thought and sometimes you're watching dailies saying, "What were we thinking?" We were pretty much focused on casting for about three months.

Frank Darabont, *The Green Mile*

It's a chemistry issue. I don't think you ever really cast in a vacuum. God, the universe does provide sometimes, doesn't it? And I didn't even know going into this whether there was a person who walked the earth who fit that physical description and could break your heart. So we were beating the bushes everywhere. Bruce Willis calls us one day and says, "I think I've got your John Coffey." Bruce was a big fan of the book and heard that we were going into production on this: "You've got to read this guy." So we had him in to read. His first reading I have to confess was not great. He was incredibly nervous and somewhat inexperienced. There was something about his essence that made me keep having him back. And we got him working with an acting coach, Larry Moss, who really helped unlock whatever it was that got unlocked. Finally, we screentested three people, actually put them on film with Tom [Hanks]. I thought, if my whole movie hinges on this guy, I'm putting him on film because ultimately that's where it really lives. And he was marvelous. With those kinds of characters, by necessity a little less dimensional than say your main characters, the demands of the plot make them so—so if you can find an actor who can make these characters as dimensional as possible, you're really, you really ought to hire them. If you see something about that actor that you feel is getting close to what you're looking for, you always try to nudge them and adjust them a little bit, and if the actor adjusts well right there on the spot, that certainly reinspires your confidence. You think, "Aah, here's an actor who's really ready to duck and move a little bit." And if an actor does it the exact same way the second time, I think, "Uh-oh, this could be a problem ultimately." Because maybe there is no adjustability, maybe there is just one note that this person can play.

Curtis Hanson, *L.A. Confidential*

I got this idea in my head that I wanted to cast actors that the audience was not already familiar with, that they did not already have an emotional history, the way that we all do with movie stars. We see them, and we immediately have feelings based on past pictures. With Russell Crowe and Guy Pearce, my two leads in essence from Australia, most of the audience doesn't know these actors and consequently they don't know how they feel about them. They don't know who they like and who they don't like. This was obviously a hurdle in terms of getting the financing for the picture because normally we are all in the position of going to stars and saying, "Will you help me arrange the financing for the movie?"

Russell Crowe I had seen in an Australian picture called *Romper Stomper*, and he had just knocked me out in that movie. He plays a neo-Nazi skinhead, and I knew that he could play the brutal side of Bud White. I then brought him over here from Australia and met him and worked with him and subsequently put him on tape doing a test to convince everybody that he could play the complete character. Guy Pearce, it was sort of a Cinderella story for actors. It was on a day when I was seeing an actor every fifteen minutes and Mali Finn, my extraordinary casting lady, brought him in. He walked in the door, I had no idea who he was, and I could tell he was Australian when he said, "Hello" and he sat down and just did a great reading. And I gave him some direction and had him just make some adjustments and then worked with him and put him on tape.

The lesson that I learned is that I was then able to go to Kevin Spacey, Kim Basinger, Danny DeVito, one after the other, and say, "We're starting this picture in a few weeks and I would love you to be a part of it," rather than asking them to be the locomotive that was pulling the train. And by being able to approach them as actors instead of as say "the financing getter," they immediately jumped on board and I put that cast together actually in just a couple of weeks.

I see actors more than once and work with them and try to give them some direction, even if not the direction I want to go ultimately, but to just see how they handle the adjustments and also see how I get along with them.

And I think who would I like to see, and who can capture the essence of the character number one, but also who has the capacity to surprise me? And who can I maybe give an opportunity to that they haven't had before where they can, in a sense, blossom.

Barry Levinson, *Bugsy*

I'm always amazed at the amount of people who turn down a part because they don't see what it is that you're making. So they read something in a different way, and they don't get it. I can't think of a movie that I made that somebody who I thought was perfect for it said, "No, I don't see it." In the final analysis it's actually for the best because that person would probably be constantly trying to do another film than the movie you're doing. There are some actors always saying, "I'd really love to work with you; I love your movies. I just don't see this movie, this character." I've always sort of found that happens along the way, and then I realize that it's actually for the best.

Because then you end up with the actors that have the sensibility you have towards the work that you're trying to do. I've had cases where basically the agent will turn down the role for an actor because he'll say, "Well, you know, they don't do ensemble work."

The process is tedious because I see an enormous amount of people for a lot of the roles—I will see sometimes hundreds for a small role. I'm looking for something that seems right. You've got this whole big cast and everything has to connect. All of these people have to sort of fit, all of their different kinds of energies and rhythms, because all actors have different rhythms. You're looking for a certain rhythm that fits, and you're trying to couple that all together. It's a little bit like putting the orchestra together. You need a little of this and a little of that. Sometimes somebody may be doing some great work, but it may not be right for the movie and it can kick the movie out of balance for me.

What happens is, you're always racing that clock. In *Bugsy* we didn't have a Meyer Lansky until a week before his role actually started. I had thought of Ben Kingsley, and he happened to be in town. He came in, and it's an interesting situation. You have a man who won an Academy Award, and he's a brilliant actor. Except he's supposed to be this New York Jew—and this guy was Gandhi. I, in the politest way, I tried to say, "Ben, I think you're terrific, but what do you think?" I don't want to say, "Would you come back and read this role?" which is what I'm really kind of asking for, because if he can't deliver that accent and that kind of character, we're going to be in trouble. And he said, "Why don't I come back tomorrow and read for you?" A very proper English accent, he had. I said, "That's a terrific idea." He came back and he read like two lines, and I said, "Ben, you don't have to go on, it's terrific." That's how that happened. For him to understand the dilemma and have the confidence in himself as an actor to suggest that—I was beside myself.

If the actor is right for the role, then you're really kind of working on all of the shadings of it. You're just tuning it and you're playing it, but you know that you've got it. You're just perfecting it. If the actor is wrong for the role, you're literally fighting just to get the performance. When you cast wrong, it's not an easy day.

James Cameron, *Titanic*

We had a hundred speaking parts more or less to cast and there weren't really any star parts as written and I didn't see it that way. I think it eventually took six months or so going right into the start of photography.

I don't like to do ten or fifteen minutes with somebody, half of which is wasted talking about, you know, do you like to golf, where do you live, all that bullshit. What I like to do is, I like to prescreen on video and get an initial impact from what that person presents to the camera. I trust Mali [Finn, his casting lady] a great deal in terms of giving some initial direction in the way that I would do it, because I spend a lot of time with her on the script talking through what the characters mean to the story and who they are inside and between the lines. So I see an awful lot of tape of people because what I want to do is, when I meet people, I want to spend an hour, hour and a half, with them. I want to try the scene different ways. I'm interested in seeing if I can work with them, how they are gonna respond to me, and that sort of thing. So I see sort of a select list in person, and I work with them and I often shoot it myself on video.

I make a movie every two years approximately and it's such a narrow window to see who's out there and what's going on. It's a big opportunity for me to meet actors and get ideas about who can do what. So I like to take advantage of the casting process.

So we got down to a short list of actresses that we were considering, and rather than shoot them on tape, I decided to do a full-up film screen test, and we built a little set and lit it, and Russ Carpenter [the cinematographer] came in and lit the scene. And I wound up working with Kate Winslet during that day. I kind of was tending away from her, only because she'd done a lot of period films and because of the fact that it seemed like lazy casting in a sense. I wanted to explore other possibilities and because she was English and I wasn't sure about the accent. Then she came in and just totally won my heart and the hearts of the other people involved.

I worked with Kate for about three hours and we shot it like a scene. We did a master and a kind of two shot and I had a pretty good actor working with her and I did some close-up stuff and we did it in and out of accent. And she was actually just doing it in her English accent because she hadn't worked with a voice coach yet. Subsequently, [she] did a tremendous amount of dialogue coaching to get her Philadelphia accent just right, which is actually harder than just kind of a contemporary American accent because it's a bit Mid-Atlantic. I had five actresses that day but I spent the majority of the time with her, and as she left, I turned to the others and I said, "There's still people we need to see, but she's probably the one unless lightening strikes." A couple of weeks went by and she actually called me from England and said, "Hey, what's going on? How come you are not casting me as Rose. I'm Rose. Its obvious!" And she was very gung ho and very confident about it, and in fact, I did decide pretty quickly after that to cast her.

Leonardo DiCaprio was on a list of names. I didn't know him. I'd never met him. I think I'd only seen *Gilbert Grape* and so I didn't know really what to expect. I noticed that when he came in for the first meeting, which was not a reading, it was just a casual meeting, you know, like my female CFO of the company was there, all the female executives of the company, some of the female secretaries were all in the room, and I'm like, this is a little odd. So Leo came in and I wasn't won over right away. I saw how charming he was. I saw how he won the group very quickly and was very calm and casual and had a lot of the qualities I would have wanted in a Jack. But I wanted to see him work. So I asked him to come back and read with Kate. He came back and I got them in a room together and he said he didn't want to read. I said, "No, you have to read." He said, "No, I really don't wanna read," and I said, "You are gonna read or you are gonna go home." And he went, "Okay, let's read! " And I saw this glimpse of something totally amazing right in front of me. There was nobody else there but me and the two actors. He wouldn't let me tape it or anything and then he sort of left and so now I had to turn around to the studio and tell everybody else involved in the film and say, "I saw it! I saw it! It was great!"

Martin Scorsese, *Gangs of New York*

In the case of Cameron Diaz, Joe Roth [studio executive] mentioned her. That's when he was at Disney and so I met her. And when she auditioned with DiCaprio, something happened. She just had, I don't know, she made it very clear who the person is and she had a sense of humor and I saw something happen in him. And I said, "That definitely is the person." We had auditioned maybe twenty or thirty young women.

And in the case of Daniel Day-Lewis—would he work again? That was the key. Leo loved him and I had worked with him in *Age of Innocence*. So we brought him in and talked to him and made him feel that he'd really be a very integral part of the picture. He was not convinced but we told him basically that we loved him and loved being with him, really, wanted him to come with us on this journey. And he thought about it and said okay.

Martin Scorsese, *The Aviator*

This project was originated by Leonardo DiCaprio a number of years ago, and I've had a lotta luck with an actor coming up with a project that I could find myself somehow spending two years in it. Ellen Burstyn, De Niro, Paul Newman, a number of others. And so in a sense when I received the script obviously I knew he was involved as Howard Hughes. And having worked with Leo DiCaprio on *Gangs of New York*, which is something I generated and that he joined up with, it was almost a completion of that film in a way, working together. 'Cause I thought as an extraordinary young actor, to play a part at twenty years aging and going through a lot of psychological and emotional problems, he had the range and I thought it'd be really interesting to go through that.

The people who were based on people, each one was somewhat of a different process. In the case of Katharine Hepburn, it's a dangerous area so you have to have somebody who is not afraid of it, who has the intelligence I should say, the essence of it, because it's not going to be Katharine Hepburn. It's going to be an idea of her, an impression of her, a Northeastern person who has very strong opinions, comes from a very advanced, progressive family. And we thought of a number of people, but I was at the Golden Globes and Cate Blanchett walked out on the stage and my wife leaned over and said, "That's her." I said, "Yeah, I know." Then I saw her in this movie called *The Gift*, Sam Raimi film, and gee, I didn't know it was the same person. I could swear she was from the South. So I don't know, man, this person is amazing, I thought. And so I was all for it. I worked very closely with Ellen Lewis since 1990. And she knows the kind of people I work with and that I like. And I don't like seeing videos of sections of films the agents send. These actors should get after them because they send you a tape. You could hardly see the image. It's just dreadful.

In the case of Kate Beckinsale coming in and auditioning for Ava Gardner, she was the first audition, the first one. And we liked her yet went on for another two or three weeks. Then we videotaped them and looked at the tapes again and said we were right. It was the first one. And for Juan Trippe, Alec Baldwin. See, Alec and I had talked back 1990 on *Goodfellas* and he wasn't available. And so Alec and I over the years have always come together and want to work together. I really love his sense of humor and his timing. That slow burn. I love the idea of these two giants, titans of American industry fighting it out. Yeah, we were talking about it. I mean, through Ellen. I said first call and see if they're available 'cause I don't want to get my heart set on something and then, you know, the person can only shoot two days.

The one-liners are what gets you. The one-liner could stop you for the day, for a week unless you really read them. You know? And sometimes you read them, they're great, they get on the set, and they freeze. The first day one of the actors whom I really like, couldn't wait to work together, we're sitting there and the guy had one line, came in, and that was it. It was the wrong line. And he was a very sweet man so I went up, said, "Yeah, that's good," I said, "but actually, we need these three words, you know, too." "Yeah. Absolutely, absolutely." Take after take. Take after take. It was just movie hell, you know? Poor guy. By the end of it, we got it. And my error there was that I okayed him on video. You do have to hear them, I think. The one- or two-liners, you really gotta play it. Also, if they can improvise a little bit with the situation, that's important.

For me sometimes it's very difficult sometimes to tell the Southwest. New York, Los Angeles, Italian, Jewish, I'm very much comfortable with that. Other types that have more to do with the American landscape, I really haven't traveled that much in America. But it was very difficult for me to focus on who and what a man like Odie would be like, and luckily someone showed us some footage of the actual man. I saw it as very sweet. Had some readings and this kid Matt Ross was terrific.

Michael Mann, *The Insider*

You have a character that's preformed. And if that character's inhabited by this actor, the two collide and you get a modification to both, and then you have the combined Russell Crowe as Jeffrey Wigand. And how does that collide with the Lowell—you know, Al Pacino inhabiting Lowell Bergman? And is that going to yield the kind of oppositional—the polar oppositions that I was looking for with these two very different men who probably wouldn't even like each other if they met in a bar but are going to wind up being thrown together. So I try to think of it that way, which is method. But then method always gets thrown out the window. When I was sitting with Russell—he came down to read and he was shooting another film and he was totally distracted, which he should be. If he wasn't distracted, he wouldn't have been a good actor. And we just sat in our office, just the two of us, no one else there, and we just read dialogue back and forth to each other for about an hour. And it really wasn't going anywhere, and he had one speech and it was the moment when he learns that everything that he'd sacrificed was for naught because he was never going to see the light of day, including losing his family, his children. And Russell hit this moment, and we're about three feet apart, he hit this moment, and he went into these lines about "for my kids to have known would have been important," and he just kind of sunk into himself and I just felt this inner annihilation and I just knew and when you know, you know. I have a casting [person] I've used for a long time and she brings many people to us. I do a lot of readings. In this film, it was important to find people who had an edge too. It had to be kind of hyperreal. And then we had the difficulty of who's going to play Mike Wallace? Somebody who everybody's familiar with, you know. We see an hour of Mike Wallace fifty-two times a year. We just read a lot of actors. And I was concerned about Chris Plummer's theatricality because he'd done so much theater and I felt that that would get in the way. And then I looked at a spectacular film he did in '58, *Stage Struck* with Sidney Lumet, and it was a completely different Chris Plummer performance. So

I decided to use him. I usually have a couple of good aspiring actors who are there as part of the casting process as PAs [production assistants] and they're reading with the actors. And I do a lot of videotaping and shoot stills. I've always used a lot of real people in situations as well.

Attorney General Mike Moore plays himself. We found a homicide investigator from Mobile, Alabama, for example, who just hit this nail on the head. It's a tiny little piece, but they invest the section of the film with a certain authenticity that I think audiences react to without knowing it. The court reporter in Pascagoula, Mississippi, you could never imitate that voice or that woman. I mean, she's daunting when she asks you to take the oath.

Taylor Hackford, *Ray*

In *Ray* I had a specific thing in mind. I didn't want any known people. I wanted to get a fresh look to this. Now, with Jamie, he's ubiquitous. He's known as a comedian on television, but with Ray Charles it's not like doing a biopic on somebody who was famous at one point but has been forgotten or is not so obviously in everyone's mind. Ray Charles is in everybody's mind, whether you're a child and you see him on *Sesame Street* or you watched him in concert. We had this huge burden. I went to Jamie to begin with because of his head shape; his jawline is very similar to Ray's. Little did I know he would be able to embody him so much. But I cast from the center out. And he had not done anything of this kind of size and scope before and I was just struck with his intelligence. I found out that he went to the university on a classical piano scholarship. So you meet Jamie Foxx. He's young, he's hip, he's irreverent, he's all this stuff. You can imagine this kid from Texas who was playing classical piano. Obviously, this is a disciplined and very ambitious and a very, very prodigious talent. And I made the choice.

We have another portion of the story and that's the childhood and we knew that the children had to be from the South. You're not gonna have a young six-year-old actor who can do accents. And so we did a search through the South. And I found this boy, C. J. Sanders. Never acted before, had no tradition of acting except his father was a professional football player, a wide receiver for the Tennessee Titans. Clearly within that family there was this tradition of professionalism and achievement. His mother was a local actress in Nashville, and he looked like Jamie. That helped immensely. And when we brought him to New Orleans and I read him and he just had this . . . He listened.

The mother walked in off the street. She wasn't a member of SAG [Screen Actors Guild]. She heard they were casting the movie. I put them together as a family, and they spent a lot of time. C. J. [who plays the young Ray Charles] was fantastic and you could see him grow. When a kid gets to be about six or seven, they're able to kind of focus; they kind of understand achievement. But younger, their attention span is gone, zero. They just don't care. With the littler boy, at five, in the important scene, which had to have a certain amount of continuity for angles, we said we have to do it again. He said, "Why?" You know, I did it once and that's all I need to do. The action figures do it once. And you are stuck. The whole production stops. And everybody stops because you have a scene that's crucially involved in this character. And it was like

Taylor Hackford and Jamie Foxx on the set of Ray. *(*Ray *courtesy of Universal Studios Licensing LLLP.)*

calling the grandmother to come out. And let me tell you, the money's running, you don't have time, you can't do anything.

Marc Forster, *Finding Neverland*

I said, "Oh, I'm working with four kids." It's gonna be a nightmare. So why am I doing this? So I wanted to make sure just to see everybody. And basically we saw hundreds of kids. And I was looking for Peter constantly. Basically they came in and I wanted to be by myself in the room and just had a camera because I wanted them to feel comfortable without parents, nobody. And I just had a little bit of a conversation with them and why they were even here and why they wanted to act. Before they even read just to warm them up. And actually Freddie [Highmore, who plays Peter] had also the best story of anybody I ever heard. He said to me when he came in, he said he wanted to be a soccer player at that time. And his favorite soccer player used to do theater and was an actor when he was a kid. So he thought if he would act, he'd become a famous soccer player. And when I heard that story, I said, "Oh my God, this kid is amazing." So anyway, then he started reading and it was the scene when he tears up the little play he wrote. And he just got right into it, and it just took me by surprise and I got these chills and he almost brought me to tears there. And I thought, "Oh my God." So I thought I have to bring him back again just to make sure it wasn't an illusion, and then I was looking, the smallest one, Luke, was five at the time, and there were two final choices. And there was one kid I felt was a better actor. But he had no attention span whatsoever. He always kept on looking at the camera and I felt like he's gonna drive me nuts. And then Luke came in and he had this little lisp going on and I just thought that was so adorable and he was just so loving and sweet and he was listening and he listened to the other kids and the other kids sort of took care of him and he had just the most beautiful nature as a child.

We couldn't find for a long time someone for the producer. And suddenly we got the Dustin Hoffman call out of the blue. And I got suddenly very nervous because I only heard the Sydney Pollack stories of *Tootsie* and I started sweating profusely and I thought, "Rewrites." And I had all these sort of fears started creeping up in me. And then I met him and I had the best time with Dustin.

Sofia Coppola, *Lost in Translation*

When we went to Tokyo in the casting sessions there were a lot of the actors didn't speak English. I just remember the woman who comes to Bill Murray's door, the "rip my stockings" scene? She was in the *Chicago* cast in Tokyo. So we just met local actors. And then a lot of the characters were just real people. My friend Stephanie, who has never done casting but I've known forever, knows my taste and everything; she just went around and found the little old man in the hospital, the chess club, and the photographer in the shoot was a real photographer that we knew. We'd do casting sessions where two of the Japanese casting assistants would play Bill and Scarlett's characters, which is funny to see this Japanese man kind of being effeminate playing Scarlett's lines.

But it was different approaching actors. The managers are like the mafia there. If an actor wants to do the movie, they can't if the manager doesn't want them to. But then a lot of the characters were just people I knew and so luckily they were all comfortable being in front of the camera, but they had never been in a movie. At the time casting was a challenge, but you just forget all that after you're done. All these things

Sofia Coppola on the set of Lost in Translation. *(Courtesy of Sofia Coppola.)*

seem really hard and then when you're done, you can't remember it being any other way. Anna Faris [who plays the actress] is smart and she gets it, but she also is believable that maybe she's really kind of bubbly blonde. And we just talked about all those kind of corny clichés that you think of when you watch interviews and do press.

Andrew Davis, *The Fugitive*

It's the first time I've had an opportunity to really reach a broad audience in terms of having Harrison Ford at the center of it. And being able to reach an audience that encompassed grandmothers and their granddaughters and allowed me to play in the major leagues. It's wonderful to have the support of a huge actor and have the support of a studio that wants this movie to get out very badly.

I have sort of a team of bad guys and cops from my tough-guy movies in Chicago, and some of them are not actors. They're real policemen and real characters. And because there's such a pool of talent in Chicago now, it was very easy to say, "Okay, we're going to bring in certain people, but we'll have a core of our cast from Chicago," because we wanted people to sound and seem like they were from Chicago. I initially wanted Tommy Lee [Jones]. I went through the process of being fair to the rest of the actors in the world. And we actually did some other testing. And I just held firm and stuck with it. And the part is a much more flamboyant character. He's got all these marshals and all the buzzers and whistles around him. And at the same time, if Gerard [played by Tommy Lee Jones] was not strong enough, the movie would die.

I like to have people read. I think it's important to see how relaxed they are when they're put on the spot. And it's also important to hear their voice and just look at them. You have to remember, half the people who see this movie will not see it with the words of the people who are saying them, in terms of the world. So images and faces and textures and realities are very important. There's over a dozen actors in this movie who have never been in a movie before. The Polish lady in the basement, her son, they were people we would just meet on the streets, or people we'd meet at airports.

It's like decorating a room in a way, also. You've gotta have a balance between the different actors. The different colors and shadings, and textures of hardness and softness.

One of the joys is the strange secondary character. I love secondary characters. Because everybody goes to see the stars. And they love the stars. And yet people relate to those other characters a lot. Those are the people they can identify with. The boy, for example, who plays the young Polish boy who gets busted and then turns over Harrison to the police—he was the son of a woman we met at O'Hare when we were out scouting locations. We were going down to look for a place for the train crash. And his mother worked in an *American Graffiti*–type restaurant. It was five in the morning; she was screaming at a couple of Italian guys, calling them "spaghetti-benders." And she was a great character. We said, "Maybe she can play the woman who runs the rooming house." And then it turned out she wasn't quite right, but she had this kid who reminded us of Belushi. So he got the part.

Barbra Streisand, *The Prince of Tides*

I couldn't have gotten this picture made, I don't think, if I wasn't in it. I couldn't have gotten to direct it if I wasn't in it. I remember the argument was that it was a famous book—and that seemed to be a detriment. I thought it was a plus!

Kate Nelligan wanted to play the role of the wife. She was spectacular, fantastic in this reading. But there was something about her that was too special. I had seen her in the theater, and I was struck by her talent and her beauty. So then I thought, well, what if she plays the mother because the mother should be very strong and very beautiful. Kate is both. I had been looking for two different actresses to play the younger woman and the older woman. I could never get them—two actresses that were either that good or that looked alike. And I just thought, well, what if she plays both parts. She kind of thought I was nuts at first to suggest this. But then we did a makeup test with her. She's such a good actress from her inner sensibility, in terms of age, and the little things she did—putting a pad on her back to make a slight dowager's hump, something in her jaw, she was extraordinary. So that's how that came about.

First of all, [with Nick Nolte] I ran everything he's ever done, every film he's ever made. And I saw some interesting things, I mean. There were never any real love scenes in his movies after *Rich Man, Poor Man.* So it was an area I was really concerned with because I wanted a romantic leading man to play this part. And as a matter of fact, one studio turned us down because Nick was playing the part. They had seen him in *Q & A.* Thirty pounds heavier, a big, black mustache, and they thought that's the guy I was going to play with?! No faith, no faith. I said, "I want you to be this fantastic, romantic leading man." He'd say, "No, no, no—I'm a character, I'm a character, I'm not that." I thought he had all the potential. I mean, he had the pain behind his eyes that I needed for this guy and the sexuality. And almost a mistrust, you know, of women, which was also essential.

In casting I like to break the pattern. If somebody has a reading in their head, I like to throw it out.

Casting kids can be a difficult problem. I didn't have them read. I played with them. I talked to them. I put them on videotape to see how they would react in front of the camera. Because sometimes a kid is great in real life and then you put this thing on them and they stiffen up. Some actors do. I believe in casting people who have a quality that you want to capture for a part. Like this one kid came in and I said, "How did you get your tooth knocked out?" And he said, "Oh, I took this guy and this guy smashed me over the head with a chair and I punched him in the thing." I hired him. He couldn't act really; when I was actually directing him, he would laugh all the time. I had to get that performance from him. But he *was* that kid. I did a lot of improvisation with Nick and the children. Because even though I might've cast one girl, she had no communication with Nick.

James L. Brooks, *As Good As It Gets*

I wanted Jack Nicholson for the part and we're friends and I went to see him and our conversations tend to be very truthful with each other. It was Jack Nicholson very much as a character actor that I wanted. It was Jack Nicholson with his craft that I wanted. The movie-star part would only get in the way.

I had another actress in mind for the female lead and this was true throughout the process at the time. Every negotiation that went into the studio, it was "the check's in the mail." For months and months you never knew what would happen. There was an absolute loggerhead on the negotiation with the actress that I had offered it to, and they asked me to at least consider others. And now I'm really this many months in, maybe the movie won't happen, so it was a request that you took seriously from the studio at that time. And about the fourth person through the door was Helen Hunt and she had spoken with a mutual friend of ours who contacted me and said she'd like to come in. And very quickly, she was an actress who I really wanted to work with. The age disparity was something I had to deal with because at a certain point I just wanted her to be this character. Okay, you're four years older than you are; okay, he's four years younger.

I think it's so important that you have a casting person who, when you're into your fourth month of looking and you've looked at hundreds of people, that they not make you feel like a fool, that they stay in there with you and try, because you can start to think that you're crazy because you haven't found it and you don't know why you haven't found it. And you've already dealt with actors who you respect who under other circumstances you'd kill to work with. The part that Greg Kinnear finally got was very late in the game and his name came up and he was shooting in San Francisco, and he couldn't come down and so we went up and for what seemed like an odd choice at the time. And he'd finished shooting and it was around two o'clock in the morning, and he read beautifully and then he came down two weeks later and he read again with Jack and it was that much better.

Gus Van Sant, *Good Will Hunting*

The *Good Will Hunting* project always had Matt Damon and Ben Affleck attached as the two leads. They had cleverly put that in their contract, which was sort of a thorn in a lot of the production people's sides. A lot of other guys were interested in the parts but I knew them from previous tryouts. Matt had tried out for Jimmy in *To Die For* and he was really great. He was the best audition I'd ever seen for a part. So I knew his work and I knew he was gonna be great. I really like working with people that I've never seen before. When I met Ben and Matt, they were always expecting that their picture wasn't gonna be done. So when I first met them, talked to them, and I left, they wanted to know where the Polaroid camera was and how come why I wasn't taking their pictures, 'cause they always felt they were gonna be cheated out of these roles somewhere along the line. I've been very used to, through all my films, using a black-and-white Polaroid camera, an old camera. I take pictures that are about four by five of the characters when I first meet them and collect them and have like maybe these sixty pictures and sort of display them on the wall or use them almost like playing cards to figure out your cast. Play eight guys down and see, like, if they're working together. Like, take one out and put one in like solitaire or something. I can do that endlessly. I can sit there and mix and match for days and days. We were looking for megastars that we wanted to put into the role of Sean [the therapist] that was sort of the smallish role, kind of premiere role in the film for the star-to-be. And a couple of people looked at the part and decided not to do it. And Robin [Williams] freed up at a certain time that we were going to film, and he said he'd do it. So he was slotted in. I don't really require reading, not like the top on my list. It's mostly the visual, like what the person is like. And then I figure I can get the performance out of them in some way. I trust that I can, usually, and the visual is hugely important.

We were auditioning people for Skylar, and Minnie Driver came in one morning; it was like a Saturday morning and we'd all been out late. We showed up at my hotel room and she came over and she was presented with all these guys who had all gotten to bed at like five in the morning, had three hours sleep. She proceeded to read the lines with Matt Damon and she really blew everybody away like seriously . . . and left the room. And we just went, "Wow, how did she do that?" It was like magic; she sort of pulled this part out of a hat.

Gus Van Sant with Robin Williams and Matt Damon on the set of Good Will Hunting. *(Good Will Hunting © 1997 used under license from Miramax Film Corp. All rights reserved.)*

• 5 •

The Crew

Clint Eastwood, *Unforgiven*

*Y*ou really are only as good as the ensemble you gather. You cast the crew exactly the way you cast the cast. You try to get people whose work you respect or who you've worked with before. Some of the people I've used are brought up through the ranks, and some of them are new. I had an art director that I'd used before so I knew that a town could go up in a certain period of time. It went up in thirty-one days; that's interior and exterior. So I knew he could deliver in that fashion, but if it had been an art director I'd never worked with, that might be a little bit dodgy. You can't tell by meeting a person how they are going to be over a two-month period, but by and large you can get a feeling of a person. If I was using a cameraman for the very first time, I'd probably talk to another director who I respected who had worked with them before and ask, first, how fast he is, and secondly, does he like the mystery of it, or does he like to get right in and put it all together?

Rob Reiner, *A Few Good Men*

The most important thing is to get people that you like to see in the morning. When you come to work and you've got a long schedule and it's nice to say, "Hey, it's that guy again that I like," and "Hi, how are you?" So the most important thing is people that you can get along with, that you enjoy spending time with. The film itself is for the public; it goes out there. But what you have is your experience of actually making the film. And that's what you take with you through your life. So you want to surround yourself with people that you enjoy being with. Now, obviously, hopefully they can do their job as well, and they're not just your friends and family. Start with a group of people that you feel comfortable with and that you can communicate with. That you can talk to, that understands what you are saying. You try to build a family that way.

I find for most cinematographers, they don't understand the film because they're involved in images mostly.

Mike Leigh, *Secrets & Lies*

I'm lucky, now there is an ongoing crew who, for the most part, comes with me from one film to the next, like my cinematographer on a number of projects, a production

109

designer, the same gang of sparks [electricians], the same grips. What happens with my projects is we're in constant touch, and as soon as we get anywhere near a green light, we're calling them and they're doing their level best to juggle other offers and other films so they can be there with us. I think that's a very important part of the chemistry thing, to have a crew that was completely with it and able to be sensitive to those moments.

It's important for both the production designer and her team and the costume designer to be around way ahead of the shoot, not only to inspect the location but to be part of the creative process as the film starts to present itself.

The only thing I really think is important is the collaboration between myself, the production designer, and the cinematographer. So that in the case of *Life Is Sweet* we collaborated in a very specific way about the look and the color. It seemed to make sense to choose a particular type of stock to shoot it.

Curtis Hanson, *L.A. Confidential*

The same way I look for actors who can capture the essence of the character, I look for crew members who I think can capture the essence of the particular thing that I'm hoping to get from that particular department.

In terms of the cinematographer, I wanted somebody who could capture the lighting and style and, again, put the characters and emotions in the foreground. You start thinking of film noir, and all those great movies from that period, and I wanted to make sure that Dante Spinotti, right from the get-go, was not thinking that way. I spoke with him about a photographer named Robert Frank, and I said, "When you look at his pictures, you are struck by the emotional power of the pictures and it's only on a closer look that you see they were taken in the period." I did this little photo presentation with him of archival pictures that I had put together that represented the look and feel of the movie for me and he just got it immediately and we built from there. I used to take pictures as a still photographer, so I'm very comfortable with cameras and lenses and visualizing. I'm one of those directors who is, to some cameramen, a pain in the ass, in that I like to look through the lens at every shot. But it's a collaboration. I want them very much to understand the emotion of the scene and contribute ideas of how to shoot it.

Ang Lee, *Crouching Tiger, Hidden Dragon*

I have producer-writer-partner which start off from the first, second movie. He teaches film theory and all that in Columbia University and he is the salesman, he's the producer, he's everything for me. Everything I don't like to do, he does well. And he is the bounce of opinion for what I don't see, as the way I grow up, you know, when it comes to Western art house theater, people might laugh at this or didn't really understand that. So if I go through him, make him understand, I'm pretty much in good shape.

I like to see their [cinematographers] looks, their skills, whatever they have at that point. I'll see if I'm interest in that and then personality and also check with whoever work with them, see if they're workable. They may be the most brilliant artist but they cannot run the set, cause a lot of grief. That's not good either. But to me, their interest in drama is what interests me the most. So they're doing their visual stuff for something, not just doing to look pretty. They have to listen to my primo ideas. Then I allow myself to be inspired by them. If they talk about drama more than their own stuff, I think that's a good sign, that's a plus for me.

Neil Jordan, *The Crying Game*

I find the thing that defines the cameraman is their ability to maintain control over the look of the entire film. That's what seems to me to distinguish great ones from kind of good ones.

Frank Darabont, *The Green Mile*

The cinematographer was David Tattersall, and I knew David from the *Young Indiana Jones* TV series that I had written on. He was incredibly versatile. During three years he worked in so many different styles, with so many different directors. And he had a reputation of—that George [Lucas] not only confirmed but delighted in—for maintaining a certain pace in filming. I wanted to be able to keep a certain flow going. I saw a little movie he did for not much money, and the look that he gave that film convinced me. Because I wanted a more sort of lush, slightly romanticized period look.

M. Night Shyamalan, *The Sixth Sense*

There are lots of wonderful DPs [a phrase for the cinematographer—director of photography] that are very stylish. They'll light the hallway in their house with dark blue light and very brooding, and I'd say, my hallway does not look like that, and so it doesn't scare me and it's not real and don't give me anything that wouldn't remind me of something real that's touching me as a human being and creates fear or compassion or whatever we're going for. To do dark but be real, more natural-looking darkness, was what I was looking for. So I hired Tak [Fujimoto] for that.

Andrew Davis, *The Fugitive*

You look at their work, you find out what their schedules were like, you talk to other people. I've been very lucky to work with some wonderful cinematographers. It's all about lighting. Totally the most important part to me. Because I'm not worried about how to place the camera or what lens to use. Then it's how fast and what approach you take to get there.

Sam Mendes, *American Beauty*

With the cinematographer someone suggested Conrad Hall. And I rang up a friend who's a producer, who shall be nameless, and he said, "No, he's too old, too slow, too

M. Night Shyamalan (center) on the set of The Sixth Sense. *(The Sixth Sense courtesy of Spyglass Entertainment Group, LP.)*

cranky." I'd had another conversation with somebody who worked on a movie with him who just said he was a great man and said, "Ignore this nameless producer. If it's slow, read he is an artist and he's very precise, and for cranky, read he's passionate." I think one meets two or three people in one's lifetime you are that inspired by who believe that much in their craft. They view it almost as a child again. Conrad's a great, great figure, and a kind of talisman on the movie.

Steven Soderbergh, *Erin Brockovich* and *Traffic*

And the process of building the perfect crew is sort of a lifelong journey. You know, you pick up people on each movie. You think, they get it. They know how we like to work and they fit. And it's a jazz ensemble made up of ninety-five people, and somebody hitting a wrong note can take you somewhere you don't want to be.

With cameramen you bring them in and talk to them and you go with your instincts. You can both watch the same film in preparation and see two completely different things. I walk out of it, you know, with some visual element that sticks with me that the other person doesn't see at all. And then you know you've got a problem.

Ridley Scott, *Black Hawk Down*

I worked with Slav—dear old Slavomir [Idziak], who's a Polish—very good cameraman who I met, saying, you know, "Well, I do small personal movies with one camera, okay?" And I say, "Well, you know, that's gonna change, mate, right? " And that's what changed. It changed his life. He went off into the blue dazed—eleven cameras, you know?

Barbra Streisand, *The Prince of Tides*

I used to describe the scenes to the cameraman and sometimes he'd say to me, "I can't imagine what you're talking about until I see the actors in the room." That was really hard for me because I imagine them all in my head beforehand, but it doesn't mean he's wrong and I'm right. It's just a different way of working.

Working with cinematographers, I show pictures and paintings. Before *Yentl*, I went to Amsterdam to see the Rembrandts and discovered the paint was dark brown, not black. The edges of the faces were soft, not hard, and that affected the look of the film I did with David Watkins, who is so gifted.

Oliver Stone, *JFK*

I've done six, seven films with [cinematographer] Bob Richardson, so we talk in short-hand at this point. Basically he comes in very early, reads the early drafts, gives me his version of reality. We argue, we debate, we talk about colors, palettes, looks. He likes still photographs. I like paintings. He does his own version of shots. I do my own version of shots. There's a natural flow to a blocking that occurs and often that dictates to me the camera.

Barbra Streisand on the set of The Prince of Tides. *(The Prince of Tides © 1991 Columbia Pictures Industries, Inc. All rights reserved. Courtesy of Columbia Pictures.)*

Baz Luhrmann, *Moulin Rouge*

I need to identify my creative team, the DP, who's worked with me for two films, Jill Bilcock, who's worked on the three films, the production designer, who's my wife [Catherine Martin], you know, and has worked on all the work that I've—we've worked together on. They're all present at the very first early readings.

Anthony Minghella, *The English Patient*

You end up with the best people you can find. They become like your family. They are your family. At the same time the jarring and disturbing notion is that if *you* don't know what you want, absolutely nothing happens, and that's terrifying.

    With John Seale, the cinematographer, every Sunday in our six-day week, the seventh day we'd spend the afternoon together worrying and fretting over the next week's work and trying to work out how to achieve it.

Steven Spielberg, *Amistad*

I was very fortunate because I discovered something about the old-fashioned studio system that we don't have in place any longer, but we used to have in place forty, fifty years ago. And that is I simply took my entire crew and moved them off of *Lost World* and onto *Amistad*. I'm talking about everybody, and it was remarkable because it was as if we finished one story and we simply came to work the next day and began a new story.

James Cameron, *Titanic*

Peter Lamont had worked with me on *Aliens*. I knew him as a good kind of old-school English production designer, which means that he's the general that oversees a vast pyramid of people underneath. And it's run like the federal government, but that's what it took to do those previous pictures. We had made the decision to save money on construction and all the thousands of craftspeople that were working on the set, sculpting everything and carving everything and all the wood and all that stuff in Mexico. He knew how to use the Mexican infrastructure. And for the first time, I think in fourteen or fifteen *Titanic* projects that have been put on film over there, over the many years, for the first time Harland and Wolff actually opened their plans drawers and we got the blueprints to the damn ship! And we actually worked from the plans of the ship. And he had an interesting challenge because I would not let him diverge from what it was. If you are gonna flood the set, it has to be built to a structural integrity about four to five times normal for a set because of the mass of water. So there's a tremendous amount of engineering that went into the sets.

Cameron Crowe, *Jerry Maguire*

The main guy that I've always worked with is, he's sort of a legendary assistant director, Jerry Ziesmer. And he's retired and come back more than Sugar Ray Leonard. He's a real partner and an inspiring guy. He's also an actor and he pops up in a lot of the movies that he ADs [assistant directs]. He was AD on *Apocalypse Now* and he's the guy that says, "Terminate with extreme prejudice."

Gus Van Sant, *Good Will Hunting*

The designer was Missy Stewart, who I've worked with many times. She is a good friend and she was familiar with the locations and with Harvard and we shot half of it in Toronto, interiors were in Toronto. [Because of the value of U.S. currency and foreign tax incentives over a billion dollars a year of American film business has gone to Canada and other countries.]

James L. Brooks, *As Good As It Gets*

Bill Brzeski [the production designer], whom I'd worked with on television, had begun his feature career. When we talked for the first time, he showed me a book, and this was the most ridiculous "Eureka moment," because he showed me an old hallway with a staircase in it, which gave levels. I just embraced him.

We built everything. I wanted the picture not to be about New York, but to be about two blocks of Manhattan and three blocks in Brooklyn; that's what I wanted the picture to be about. We were having lunch at this café and suddenly you just looked around and you say, "It should be this." We built it in downtown L.A. in a welfare hotel, we took over the lobby, and one of the most difficult things were those crosses [on buildings] they have for earthquakes and how to disguise those, and how to make them look like they're in New York. But that's what we had to do; financially we had to do it there. I like being on location. I like that everybody is away from home. I think that even though it creates trials in everybody's personal life, it gives a focus and a kind of respect for what you're doing. It's less a job; it's more a calling.

I'd worked with Michael Ballhaus on two previous pictures. We've had great times working together because we each had a love of actors. We'd be in dailies, he'd be cinematographer, and he'd be talking about performance width, which is great for me. We complemented each other and I love that he operates the camera himself because when you have a picture that's going to have close-ups like this, to have your DP have his eye in there as long as yours isn't, it becomes important. He was slated to do a picture with [Robert] Redford and they were on location so he was unavailable and then the picture fell through. And on the day that it fell through, he had a friend who was doing *Air Force One*, and he had me, who had been talking to him for two years, and he had called my office, and the person who was answering the phone that day, for some reason, volunteered that I wasn't gonna be doing the picture for a while and the next phone call was *Air Force One* and I had lost Michael Ballhaus, which was a huge blow to me.

Then I began a search. The way I do it is to get a cinematographer's pictures and mix all the reels up. Usually if you do that, you can separate out the cinematographer from the director, because you're just taking odd reels with no sound and you begin to pick up a style.

Then production design was everything for me on this picture, the details of it, because we were going to be so interior, and because the problems I worried about were, I had really over forty pages in doorways.

John Madden, *Shakespeare in Love*

I took the whole production team from the last two or three films that I've made, and I felt really strongly about that. This is a $25 million dollar as opposed to £1.5 million movie. And there's a feeling of, you know, are these people up to it? And I always felt, well, if I'm up to it, then they certainly are because they've made these movies with me and they are my collaborators and they're the people on whom I depend. It's very important to have people around you who you know and who support you. You develop a language with them and I had a kind of messianic feeling that their time had come as well, and I'm so happy they've all been acknowledged because we've all done it together. Film is always collaborative, so much more so than people outside the business realize, but I've never been on a film where the collaboration was as crucial as this one.

$$\cdot 6 \cdot$$

Design

Roman Polanski, *The Pianist*

*T*he real challenge was recreating the world that I remember from my childhood. We had to confront the archive material, which is very, very difficult to watch. I actually screened the archive material to the entire crew, to our German crews, two hundred people, you know, and they saw the things that they didn't know existed. This was difficult.

Most of those streets were built, the sets. Those streets don't exist anymore. All Warsaw was leveled by the Nazis and there is only one area which the . . . on the other side of the river, which still somehow exists. But those scenes of the ghetto uprising and then the Polish uprising were made in the studio at the beginning in the first few weeks and completely out of continuity. We had very precise plans of our sets and the interiors of those apartments in which he is hiding and the windows from which he is going to be observing it. I wanted, of course, to keep this subjective narrative of the film and therefore it had to be very precise to see what you are going to see from this window.

Ridley Scott, *Black Hawk Down*

I'm a designer. Seven years at art school, I can draw. I've got a really good guy that I like to work with on the storyboards. So I will sit at a table with Sylvain [Despretz]

Roman Polanski on the set of The Pianist. *(The Pianist courtesy of Universal Studios Licensing LLLP.)*

117

with the script, and I'll start as thumbnails, 'cause I can do fast thumbnails. And usually we've got photographs of the locations. So I'm exercising what is actually gonna have to happen, which is really good. So when I walk on the set, I know exactly what I'm gonna do. Exactly.

The decision to do a film like *Black Hawk,* you stare at the problems because you can't build sets a mile long. You can only find a place to do it in. And then you've gotta go door-to-door and actually knock on the door, saying, "You're gonna have a Black Hawk over your head on, you know, April 4. I'd really like you not to be here. And how about moving to this hotel for four days because I'm gonna have this Black Hawk over your house for four days." So that had to be done on every door, every day.

M. Night Shyamalan, *The Sixth Sense*

In my first two movies I didn't even understand filmmaking that well. Just let the people do what they did and they came and the production designer said, "How about this, and I'll bring this?" And I said, "Okay, whatever," and that was that. It didn't really matter to me what somebody wore because I make contemporary movies and things like that. How does that tell stories? But I'm very different about that now, and so I'm really difficult in that respect now. If it's not telling the story, don't even think about it. What color are they wearing, all that stuff. And on *Sixth Sense* it was the process of going from not knowing how to use those elements to knowing that they're all tools. And so it was a really heavily storyboarded movie. I think you can feel that the shots were really kind of choreographed. And it all came from there, that we were making a kind of very suspenseful movie, long takes, have to earn each cut, and things like that. Every shot is storyboarded. We shot every single thing that was storyboarded. You can just flip through the book and see the final movie. It makes me feel real comfortable to come to the set, to know that we're all moving, and so when anyone asks, Bruce Willis asks, "Why am I sitting down in this take," I have a very clear answer as to why emotionally he's sitting down in the take and why the camera's over there. And if someone asks, "Aren't you doing my close-up? Aren't we doing a close-up?" And I'll say, "No, and here's why. Because of this." And so we went one by one and picked each person. I have a storyboard guy from New York and I find it one of the most important collaborations in the movie because he is kind of this very, very independent kind of guy who likes Iranian films that are silent. So when he says, "This is cheesy," he's always like my way-over-here guide in the mass-market world. He's like, who cares if they don't all get it? And I go, I do.

The entire house is built, and it's something that all the shots that were choreographed, where the doorknob is, where the stairs are, when he comes down the stairs. It's worth it for me to build. I think in more choreographed situations, it's a cool thing to build.

Frank Darabont, *The Green Mile*

We built every interior in the movie, save two minor exceptions—the warden's office and the prison auditorium where they're showing the movie to John Coffey. That's actually the woodmill at the Warner Hollywood lot, with those great windows. But everything else was designed and built from the ground up. Every nut and bolt, frayed electrical cord on the wall, every piece of chipped paint on the walls. I knew that I was going to spend a lot of my movie on "the mile" itself, which connects with the offices, which connects with the execution chamber, which doubles as farm equipment storage when they're not killing somebody. That whole set wanted to be very specific and very carefully designed. So Terry Marsh, my genius production designer, would go off of sketches and build his little foam-core model and we'd get to a certain point with that, and then I'd say, "Okay, let's go to an empty soundstage and tape off everything for me, please. Put the diagram right on the floor. Because I'm going to be in there for so long, and I want to go scene by scene through the movie and say, okay, here's how I kind of picture the blocking." I wound up compressing the thing, knowing that I could actually; when I wanted to make it look expansive, I could use a wider lens. Less shoe leather. So that it wouldn't take thirty paces to get from here to there, but that it would take only six perhaps. I learned on *Shawshank* that if you're going to shoot in a cell, you'd better make sure that wall flies efficiently. Because every time I had to move the wall out of, say, Tim Robbins's cell, I'd go take a nap while you guys are moving this damn thing and reseaming and repainting the corners. And on this, I said to Terry, "Terry, tell you what, let's make it like a Chinese puzzle box. Make these walls out of fiberglass; let's have it run on rails. We can—in thirty seconds we can jack the wall up. We literally slide it out of the way like a canvas. We can spin it, put it flat against the stage wall so we don't sit there trying to repaint. Let's put angle iron, just a piece of steel, as if they had constructed this brick with steel corners." It was really wonderful because no matter how many walls you needed to move for any given setup, it was done within five minutes. It was fantastic.

Rob Reiner, *A Few Good Men*

You key off of actual locations; in this case it was based on an actual true story that happened in Cuba in 1986. I went down to Guantanamo Bay, just looking around and seeing what the base looked like, the way in which the marine barracks were laid out there. Very similar to what we built. And also the topography, which we shot down at Crystal Cove down in Laguna [California]. It's virtually the same as what's down in Guantanamo Bay, Cuba. You can see the guard towers across the way that are anywhere from three hundred yards to two miles away depending on what part of the fence line you're looking at. So we tried to re-create that.

The courtroom we took a lot of dramatic license with because the actual JAG Corps in Washington are small there. And since, again, we knew we had to spend a large portion of film in the courtroom, we felt that we could take some license and make it a little better. We actually fought about the courtroom quite a bit. The story, the theme of it is big, because it's about following orders and where you draw that line of morality. But the actual scenes themselves are intimate, because it's a man on a witness stand and it's an attorney and they can't really move very much. And your jury is fixed and your gallery is fixed and the judge is fixed. So the courtroom should have some size to it, to give it a little bit of a look, but also again, it couldn't be too much, so we actually cut twenty feet off it after it had been built.

Obviously if you can shoot something in a controlled environment, it's better, as long as you get the reality.

I thought that by shooting scope [CinemaScope, a wide-screen process] it would make it a little more cinematic and not so claustrophobic. *A Few Good Men*, it's basically a courtroom drama, it's all interiors and stuff, but I thought that giving the scope might just make the picture a little bit more pleasing to the eye.

Clint Eastwood, *Unforgiven*

With the art director, walk over the spot, and I say, "We'll put this building here." We sort of kick around ideas. He'd say, "How about this," and everybody would contribute, and then somebody else might say, "Well the stable would be better here because this is the way it would be in life." I wanted the town on forty-five degrees so that I could have upwards and downward angles, and so that I could look out across the valleys. Then the art director will design the buildings on paper, and you start going through it and imagining how you would shoot it.

I wanted to shoot it like a black-and-white film. And so I even had the costumers working accordingly. There's a lot of coal-oil lighting. There's no real big illumination for a building, so you have to make the interiors look like their actual coal-oil lighting of the day, and as you know, everybody can shoot exteriors, but interiors is what separates the players in cinematography.

Clint Eastwood, *Mystic River*

The book by Dennis Lehane was so vividly written that I was very surprised when I first got in Boston and found that some of the items weren't there. For instance, the saloon at the river, so we had to build that one. Of course, Boston itself is very photogenic and these neighborhoods are all very photogenic, so everything else was pretty much there.

I like to utilize a whole set. That's why I like natural sets 'cause you can use everything, use every wall in the room.

Marc Forster, *Finding Neverland*

I really wanted to make a point to use as many real locations as possible. And then the whole fantasy sequences, we had all these limitations with the budget. So for instance, the pirate sequence, we shot at Pinewood in the studio and we built like a gimbals like a boat, part of a boat, and then the visual-effects designer said to me, "You know, you only have one shot where you can show the background. Everything else has to be in the boat. We don't have any money for anything else." I said, "Okay, but I still can shoot these other shots and then just leave them green screen for the final film." And then, and I thought if I could convince the production company that it's really worth it to put them in, then they wouldn't leave it green to release the movie. So I had this one shot budgeted but then it ended up fifteen shots. I wanted them very sort of theatri-

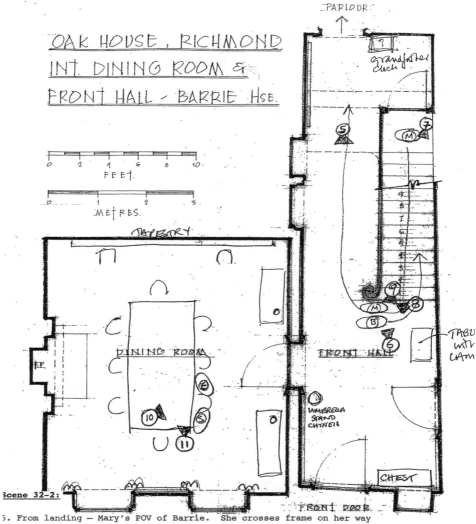

OAK HOUSE, RICHMOND
INT. DINING ROOM &
FRONT HALL - BARRIE HSE.

FEET.

METRES.

PARLOUR

grandfather clock

TAPESTRY

DINING ROOM

FRONT HALL

TABLE with LAM

UMBRELLA STAND CHINOIS

CHEST

FRONT DOOR

Scene 32-2:

5. From landing — Mary's POV of Barrie. She crosses frame on her way down.
5. OTS at Mary — carry upto close up Mary confrontation.
7. OTS at Barrie — several positions on staircase. Depends on scene timing.
8. Profile Barrie and Mary confrontation — servants in back ground.
9. OTS — close up Barrie at confrontation.
10. Servant's reaction with Barrie and Michael in back ground — start with Mary entering frame.
11. C.U. inserts on servants actions, dropping plates etc.

Camera floor plan for front hall and dining room of James Barrie's home in Finding Neverland.
(Courtesy of Marc Forster.)

Location scout photo for Finding Neverland. (Courtesy of Marc Forster.)

cal and very naive and childlike because the film deals sort of the child's point of view, and they said to me, "Oh, we don't have money to build a Western town. We only can have like one house." And I said, "One house?" And then my location manager suddenly called me up and said, "You know, I found this man like forty-five minutes outside of London who built with his friends a Western town and every weekend they'd play cowboy." So then we basically had this Western town with this entire street. And it was all green, and I don't like green somehow, because I grew up in Switzerland and everything was green and I felt like this film there's too much grass and green. So we did the digital process so we filled it up with sand. I wanted sort of these cliché, Monument Valley, John Ford kind of backdrop.

We had so many sound problems in London. Everywhere we went and all the locations I chose, I drove around, I'd say it's a great location I found and then everytime we had so many airplanes. And it was like a nightmare. And I was so excited finally being on a soundstage. It would be quiet and suddenly the stage starts to rumble. And I said, "What's going on here?" And [someone] said, "Oh, that's the Concorde taking off."

I did a lot of research of how [James] Barrie [who wrote *Peter Pan*] imagined the first performance of the play of *Peter Pan*. The Neverland we built was basically based on a lot of drawings I found from him; he had a lot of artists draw how he imagined Neverland, the fairies, the big leaves, and so on.

Scott Hicks, *Shine*

The design side of it was quite tricky. And the location side because I had made repeated pilgrimages to the Royal College of Music over the years developing the story and planning to shoot the film. It was essential to me that we shoot there just to get those little bits of connections with what was outside the window as much as anything else.

The only other thing we built was the bathroom. And it had to be that appearance of being in that tiny room and that period and overseas; it was just physically impossible. The house particularly, a family house, was an empty and somewhat derelict place that we found months ahead of time. And that enabled the designer to do wonderful things as far as I was concerned. She was able to put all of the ingredients that were part of Peter's landscape, you know, the bottles that he'd collected that we see him doing on his collecting rounds, and let the grass grow through them and dig the vegetable ground and make it appear as if things are growing. To really give the sense of a place that was lived in and had a life. And it made for those usually enormous logistical difficulties of shooting in tiny spaces, the enormity of the camera and the crew around. It's extremely restrictive but at the same time it does add. I remember when Armin Mueller-Stahl [who plays the father] walked into the set on the first day that he was involved in and he said, "I know what this is telling me; this is good." He felt the authenticity of the environment in which we were going to make this sort of extraordinary family setting. And so that was the positive element if you like.

Alexander Payne, *Sideways*

Everything is location in the film except for two shots. And basically I should say that I really only like locations. I can't stand shooting on a soundstage.

Alexander Payne location shooting on Sideways. (Sideways © 2004 courtesy of Twentieth Century Fox. All rights reserved.)

Because I want the real, I think I have a certain documentary urge with respect to fiction filmmaking. And I just like being out in the world and being in the sunshine or being in someone's house. It's also, coming from a film-school background, it's kind of how I was trained. My process has not changed from when I was making my Project 1 in Super 8 at UCLA, which is, I'm in a car and drive around and stop and knock on doors and say, "You may not believe this, but we're making a movie and can I look at your place?" And they say, "Oh, it's a mess." And I say, "It's okay. I'm sure I've seen worse." And then we walk in.

I've used the same production designer four pictures in a row, and it's during our hours in driving around together that we can start making free associations about locations and places where we're going to shoot the character and we talk a lot about class. And in a way, that's where the movie is most perfect because it exists only in her and my minds at that time. Kind of in a platonic form unsullied by realities.

The Fess Parker winery, that was a friendly location. He was into it. But of course, because we're trashing the wine, I renamed it Frass Canyon. And Frass actually is an exterminator and entomological term. It's the excrement or droppings of insects. The house I was renting up in Santa Ynez, I was finding that stuff and I called the property manager. And I said, "Yeah, there's this stuff like cornmeal." He goes, "Oh yeah, that's frass." And it was at the same time that I was looking to rename that winery.

I welcome the obstacles: you're completely in love with one location and then three days before you're supposed to shoot there, the owner gets cold feet. A lot of ego massaging in location in this type of shooting. And then you think, oh, you mourn it for about a minute and you say, "All right, goddamn it, we're going to find something better." I pick locations because they suggest cool shoots. Locations shout loudly how they want to be shot; I mean, I've never storyboarded in my life. And in one particular instance, it's an Armenian house, and the thing you always have to show in an Armenian house is the marble floor. You're not Armenian if you don't have a marble floor. So they had a stairway right there, so you could look down and get a sense of the grand entrance.

John Madden, *Shakespeare in Love*

My kind of tutelage in movies is excessively low budget and I feel comfortable trusting a real environment as the source of the feel and look of a film. And I don't mind, in fact I welcome the kind of restrictions that that brings. If it's a very small room, it forces you to shoot in a certain kind of way; if it's a very large space, you can shoot that way. And I kind of nurtured that; I would find something that would pass for Elizabethan England. That kind of Elizabethan England simply doesn't exist anymore, even in England. I was coming back from the Cannes Film Festival, and I stayed overnight in a place called Toi, which is still a medieval city, and I kind of really began to think maybe we can do it here. The streets started to feel right. I was staying in a hotel that was exactly like one of those little innyards where Ned Allen's men would have been performing and so forth. I was digging my heels in against the idea of building. Because it's not a way I've ever been able to do it before. I've built sets before but not an entire environment like that. I knew we would build the theater and that oddly enough was the other way around there because everybody was always saying, "Why can't you shoot in the Globe?" Which was the wrong theater and it's in the middle of London and it looks very disappointing for me. I mean not as a theater it isn't, but it didn't have the feel or the look or the world that I wanted. And I began to realize, right, we're going to have to build the whole thing. And the river was the main kind of nightmare. And that my location instincts won out, because the idea of shooting that on a flooded soundstage would look so preposterously phony, and it may sound odd because the whole movie is dealing with a very nonliteral realm you know. It's dealing with a realm where the imagination is free to make up its own mind what it wants to see. Shakespearean theater was based on that idea. And yet I felt that if the movie were not really grounded in a kind of grubby, smelly, muddy reality, the transcendence of poetry and of language and the kind of transport and transformation that obviously happened to audiences would not mean anything. And I felt that the whole piece could sort of topple over into artificiality unless I could find a way of grounding that. So we set about the process of building the theater, which we built on a soundstage. That was kind of an archaeological process. The remains of the actual Rose still exist.

We had to go belting into production as you always do, earlier than we thought. Like two or three weeks chopped off the preparation time and this extraordinary kind of monster was just kind of growing as the nightmare of preproduction kind of engulfed you. I used to go down at the end of every day and spend the last three hours of every day walking around on this thing as it evolved. It took, of course, the entire process of the preproduction to evolve and was only ready like the day we started shooting. But it became incredibly crucial in the whole conceptual way that the film evolved. Because it's an amazing space. It's such a cinematic space. I couldn't believe how cinematic the space became. One of the great worries of it was, of the movie for me, was, you know, that people would use the word *theatrical* about it. Which is really a no-no word in the movie business. If it's theatrical it's bad. And theater on film is not something that really has worked very often. The magic of theater doesn't transfer very easily. But as I began to see this space, first of all you have this amazing discovery about why they built them like that. It's the most brilliant performance space: The actor's never more than this row away from you wherever they are in the theater. They're wrapped right around you. You just get on the front of the stage and you feel like turning a story. It's just an extraordinary space. But particularly what was wonderful for the film was that it had three distinct realms—physical realms which, you know, fed and reflected the realms of reality within the film. A backstage world where one kind of reality existed, which is already an overlap of two, a real world of these people scratching their asses and getting their clothes on, but also a preparation for a fictional world which then became the world that you found onstage. The camera of course was free to move between, in a way that would never be true in a modern theater. And that in turn gave way to a different world outside, beyond that—the world of the audience where they are interpreting that reality. You could put the camera anywhere in there. I just couldn't find a space where the camera wasn't interesting. In particular, I suddenly realized that the division between the place onstage and the place backstage was exactly where the whole movie took place. And it became a kind of guiding principal of freedom of movement between those two things where the real goes over into the imaginative and so forth.

The town was another matter. It was completely constructed on the back lot at Shepperton. I'm a great believer in not having too much money to spend because it forces you into solutions that are much more interesting than if you had the ability to build an endless town. So what we did was build a small labyrinth with a theater at one end and a theater at the other end. Which were half theaters because the two theaters in the movie, the one theater we built, we rebuilt. They were just a series of labyrinths really. Some outrageous duplication goes on all the time in the film but you don't really notice it and you don't feel it.

Andrew Davis, *The Fugitive*

I think my instincts are always to try to make it real. But what does real mean? Sort of a heightened reality is what we wanted. I wanted it to have qualities of the old thriller with shadows and this kind of Hitchcock look of things. Very contrasty. And at the same time, we wanted to feel that we were involved in real life, and in real situations, where things were not glamorized. So the contrast between the life of Richard Kimble [the lead role played by Harrison Ford] and this beautiful, tuxedoed couple, versus him on the streets buying a janitor's outfit, was important to me. The aerials were important to me, in terms of the idea of a nest. Of being lost in a haystack. Which made the city a character in the movie.

Originally I thought they would never let me go to Chicago in the middle of winter. This would be suicide. They'd had some trouble on a film the year before. But Harrison was very smart to say, "Let's not make it a road movie. Let me come back and put myself back in the cauldron of tension here." So it was very easy to conceive the life of a surgeon, because growing up in the city and knowing doctors, and making available the University of Chicago Medical Center to use, we quickly invested ourself in creating the life of the doctor. From meeting other doctors by accident and going to their homes and looking at their art collections and designing the inside of his house to match somebody's house.

The train sequence was probably the most storyboarded because we actually had to create our own train. We had to find an empty locomotive and push it from behind. We had to have a side railing that we put in. So it was very complicated. We knew from the beginning that we were going to crash a real train. We were not going to rely on miniatures or process to make the sequence work. We would shoot as much as we could real. We actually did have models. For example, the plate of the train chasing Harrison is an Intravision shot that we created with a model. But at the same time, we did have a shot of a real train running into a camera in North Carolina. So the combination of the two of them together made it work. Intravision is a special effects optical process that allows you to look through the camera and see exactly what you're going to get. You can adjust the lighting while you're doing it, so you don't have to wait two days to see what's coming back optically. We'd do the shot list, and I'd say, "This is what we need to see," and then we'd go about talking to our special effects coordinator, and the whole team would work together and try to say, "Okay, how are we gonna do it?"

The river was an important element because it led down to running downriver and getting to the dam and the tunnels. There was a continuity, and a sort of baptism of Kimble's jumping off the dam and surviving.

We took over a grammar school on the south side of Chicago; that turned into a jail, police station, hospital, and some interrogation rooms. So that became like a mini-studio. We took over another warehouse. A huge warehouse, a former Westinghouse plant, where we built one of the tunnels of the BAM tunnels. We built the elevator shaft for the end of the movie. We built Kimble's house. So there was some major construction. At the same time, we were on location a lot. We were in neighborhoods; we were in real basements. It was a production that mixed both types of challenges. Being on location in the middle of winter, in ethnic neighborhoods downtown. I have a deep feeling for that area because that was the area right by the steel mills, where a lot of kids from my high school grew up. It's sort of an abandoned, desolate area. And when we first looked at it, everybody got real concerned. They said, "My God, it's so small and crowded and tight. It's a mess." And that's what I liked about it. That it was going to be confining. And we weren't going to take walls out and put the camera places that it shouldn't be. And we were going to be able to make it very real. The problem is, you've got all these reality television shows where video cameras are running and chasing everybody all the time, and that's the level of reality that we have to accept these days.

Michael Radford, *Il Postino*

I love working on location. I don't like working in the studio; I always feel slightly fake in the studios. On this film it was impossible really, and as Massimo [Troisi, the star] fell ill, it became even more impossible. We had to shoot as much in the studio as we possibly could. The problem about finding locations in Italy is that it's such a beautiful country that everybody goes there for their holidays and the entire coast of Italy has been built up. And to find somewhere that even resembled the 1950s, we finally ended up finding this island called Salina, in the Aeolian Islands. There's no airport or anything there, it just had the feel that I wanted. I didn't want this to look like a kind of pretty Mediterranean film. I wanted that sense of the landscape somehow as a metaphor for the interior stage of the characters, and I wanted something that was both beautiful and oppressive to this guy. He was going to have to discover that it was beautiful. So you have to feel that sense of oppression. I love those kind of big mountains and those cliffs, and we built a small fishing village. I have to tell you that I can thoroughly recommend location hunting in Italy. It consists of going from one restaurant to another restaurant and sleeping through the afternoons.

Mel Gibson, *Braveheart*

The battle scenes were the only sections of the picture that were storyboarded because of the massive amount of people and logistics and you had to have some kind of bible to fall back on when it all got to be too much. You can see the chaos that it looks like; in fact, it's not. And it was very carefully planned around a table with people's imaginations running riot about battles and tactics. There was one storyboard artist. There was myself, there was the guy doing line producing, and the camera guy and the first AD and the stunt coordinator. And we were all in there sort of cracking the whip and coming up with all kinds of ideas for what this battle could be and how it was to be done, and we had a table with egg cartons and stuff with cloths and stuff drenched over it and little plastic soldiers—and lots of cigars being smoked.

I wanted rotting carcasses and I wanted to be able to smell it; I wanted it to be really funky and down, not what people expect from the thirteenth century. People think they had castles. In fact, there was a lot more wood. They were going from wood to stone and the wood fortresses that they built really served as a kind of inside scaffolding for what would eventually become the big thick stone walls of later on. And as you went further south, there was more stone used. But it was pretty rough and primitive and we did aerial photographic scouts of what had been. We developed a little Scottish town from that, very similar to Native American dwellings, just no chimney or anything, just a hole in the roof of a rock tepee.

Cameron Crowe, *Jerry Maguire*

Well, we built a lot just because it was a complicated movie with a lot of scenes. The porch where the kissing scene took place and everything is on a stage. A lot of care was put into making it seem real. But the jewel really is, of course, the set you don't see a lot, which is where Jerry works. Every desk in that place is unique, special to the person that works there. One's a punk rocker, one is very angry about certain things in his life, and all the photos on the desk are very specific to that person.

The house was supposed to be Jerry's soul in a way. At the beginning he's sort of "shoplifting the pooty," as they say in the movie, but by the end of the movie this place that he was kind of rushing out of to move on with his life is where he has to go to begin his life. And for that you've got to have, I think, the perfect kind of place. Where you stand on the lawn and look in the window and what's inside is your future. That is how we designed the house.

Sofia Coppola, *Lost in Translation*

I had been in Tokyo a lot, throughout my twenties and then I went back before we were filming and just kind of hung around the hotel and wandered around. The hotel's kind of its own world. I was just trying to make the film like what it's like to be there for a week and a lot of jet lag.

They don't have street names in Tokyo, so trying to figure out how everyone knows where to go and then seeing Western movie stars in these ads. But there's always new trends or whatever that it's interesting to see.

Neil Jordan, *The Crying Game*

We built that glass house, because it seems an odd thing if you capture a hostage and you want to hide him and you put him in a glass house. But I had a situation where this entire thirty pages of dialogue had to happen between two guys. You were told, if somebody were hostage, you would hold them in a dungeon, wouldn't you? But if you are in a dungeon with a camera, you are finished, aren't you? I mean, what can you do? It's dark! So I said, "Okay, we have a glass house adjacent to the little farmhouse. Okay, they're in the glass house, so you've got to obscure what they see from the outside." So I say, "Okay, it's a dead glass house where all these tomato plants are hanging down so all these vines cover, obscure your view from the outside, which then creates the impression of heat, like you are in a jungle or a sweaty situation." The demands of the action plot create the design. Designers love to do things, don't they? You know, they like to create arches and curves and stuff, and you say, "No, no, it's like that." And then you have to persuade the guy that he came up with the idea. That's the most difficult thing! The main problem was to create the sense of space within confined spaces. To make things that did not look too large for the characters or for the actions. But actually gave me some space within which to compose the film. You get the set built and you bring the actors in and maybe it's not right, maybe things are not right. You sit somebody down here, and you say, "Well you can't see this guy from over here," so you get the designer to change that.

We had to create some rather little sad glittery fantasy in a bar that was in a workable shape. It was a dreadful shape, but it was the only one. The only place you could put the camera, actually, was behind the bar, so it was a nightmare. I couldn't afford to—we couldn't build anything. You're in a real location, so your choices are limited. And sometimes you come up with some interesting things—you can use mirrors, or you have to organize all the movements of the people through the only place you can put the camera.

The film that we were doing was mostly between two people, and I—the audience is with two characters for the first third of this movie. And if you use that big wide-screen format, it means you don't have to cut all the time. You can have one of their faces there and the other face there, and if it had not been wide screen, it would have been cutting from face to face to face a lot more.

The problem was, you know you are going to be in this room for at least thirty pages of script, so you better make it interesting. And her bed—I wanted to surround it with curtains. Her bed had to be about sex. The bed had to be the center of the flat, really. So I just came up with these series of curtains that surrounded her bed. It was a bit like a boudoir kind of situation, but yet it was a one-room flat, it was a loft. So I tried to build in things like that that can actually create some mystery, so you can see the character behind the curtains, or she's behind the curtains, or she's looking at something, which adds to the sensuality of it. I mean, we had so little money that we had to achieve these solutions. I prefer to be in a studio, generally, because you can control everything—the lighting, the colors.

Gary Ross, *Seabiscuit*

You're never going to do the research that a lot of your keys [heads of the various departments like sound, wardrobe, props] do. I mean, let's face it. Judianna Makovsky [the costume designer] is going to come to me and know that the gauge of buttons changed from 1933 to 1938. Now, I don't care, but she does and in a period movie especially a lot of stuff starts coming back to you and discussions begin and they're very informative discussions and you learn more. And that's what's fun about the job.

We created like a playbook that everybody had so that they could reference it.

And I disseminated it to the jockeys and the guys on the camera car and the guy operating the techno-crane 'cause he has a stick right next to somebody's head on a horse at forty-five miles an hour. So everybody knew what their part was in the play. And then in the morning we would rehearse all these with My Pretty Ponies, little toy horses, you know, and look at that, at six o'clock every morning sort of review the plays. But it was just the only way to make it safe.

And what I do is go through the script before I ever shot-list it and just write sort of a directorial bible or notes to myself for the entire movie. And it can be notes about performance. It can be notes about blocking. It can be notes about how I'm going to shoot the scene. It can be notes about design or costumes or whatever. And I'll take this little bible with me because it's a much more purely creative approach to how I want to direct than a clinical shot list would be. And I have kind of that as reference and that's a document that I use as a springboard also to begin the discussions with the actors. So it makes it easier to kind of throw the whole thing up in the air and find a happy accident 'cause I'm not clinging to something out of anxiety. I have a little bit of a blueprint and it gives me the security, then, to play with it.

Roberto Benigni, *Life Is Beautiful*

This is my first period movie. But I must say each story is a contemporary story, so we are talking about the present always. And my production designer is Danilo Donati, really one of the oldest and wonderful. He's very old and really a genius. And the [cinematographer], Tonino Delli Colli, who is very old. And they are like two little boys. They fight all the time. For example, when he chose the grand hotel, we discussed a lot with Danilo Donati about this grand hotel. So big and wide with gigantic stairs, very strange. I was really scared by this idea because a grand hotel like this in Italy doesn't exist. It was really worrying me, this big white . . . and you know the [cinematographer], they hate white! Stay away! "You can't do it white!" And then Danilo Donati decided to put in mirrors, white, mirrors! And Delli Colli left the crew. Because they are very old both, and they are two geniuses. And they are really like little kids. "Tomorrow, it will be red. Because your blood will be there." And also because Danilo Donati was thinking about the green horse. And the light, I like very much what Delli Colli did, because the light is like the sky and the reality. It's like the world, the sum of the movie. Everything, the light. And they did it with the light. In the hotel I told them to try to put a dramatic light in the first part of the movie, of course. And to try comedy light in the second part of the movie. So this was very difficult to explain. And the second part of the movie, the extermination camp, we discussed a lot because this is not a true story. But we had seen a lot about all the extermination camps. But I didn't want to put the idea of a precise extermination camp because I was not telling a true story. So I try to give the idea of the extermination camp. For example, in Italy, we have only one extermination camp in the north of Italy. It looks a little like this. But for example there is never mountains. And I choose this place because it was completely different. I didn't want to put something real. It was a question of style. And we really lost a lot of time about this, between the first and the second part of the movie, so to combine something real with something completely invented.

Martin Scorsese, *Gangs of New York*

I had the experience of drawing little pictures in a room by myself when I was a kid with nobody talking to me, and that's the kind of thing I want to get back to in a way when I'm designing the scenes. I usually lock myself away for a week or two in a room and design as much as possible the entire picture.

In *Gangs*, the opening battle scene pretty much was over a period of a number of years. I have Post-Its around in my house and I have an idea, I write it on the Post-It, like in the middle of the night or something, and I, you know, [in the] morning I collect them. I say, "That's good, yeah, maybe three cuts here." So there were certain specific moments in the battle scenes, before I'd also realize that you really need to get to your main characters. So there are certain action sequences that are designed on paper which ultimately I'd give to Joe Reidy [the assistant director] and say, "Okay, this shot, this shot, this shot, and this one cuts this, this, this is twenty-four frames, this is forty-eight, this is thirty-six, fooling around, based on montage that I really liked from a Hitchcock film or particularly Pudovkin, Eisenstein, Russian films. And then, that's how we did the entire first sequence, the first battle scene. That took three weeks just for all that.

Martin Scorsese, *The Aviator*

The first thing, I designed what I could of the flying sequences. I had a couple of pictures of the planes, black-and-white things, and I know *Hell's Angels*, the movie that Howard Hughes did, very well. Just locked myself in one of the hotels and leave TMC [The Movie Channel] on without the sound. So the older images come up. Just something that's more comforting to me. It's the movies I grew up with. And played some music and just walk around a lot and then from that process began, which then led to the next step, where Rob Legato does the visual effects and his group. He would bring me a model of what the plane may have looked like, and he'd have this little camera, fiber-optic thing and then move it around. And then he had some machine that had a little black-and-white fax and a little picture would come out and we'd draw on the picture. Then eventually the sequences came through what they call previsualization. Now this really is just the first time I've worked this way. I just normally would design the action scenes that way, by myself. But now there's previsualization and what they did was so complicated I still don't quite understand it completely. I'd say, "Look, well, you can't have that." He'd go, "No, that we can do easily. That we can do easily." "Yeah, but it's gonna cost more money." "No, it won't cost that much more because of . . ."

And so I started to get a little more bravado about it, so on the set I'd say, "Yeah, we can fix that." He says, "No, that we can't do." But these guys were amazing. I'd look at the previz and we put some music on it and it would be like a little animated cartoon. Then the other level that would be amazing was to re-create Los Angeles and that area, the Southwest, in 1927. Ah, fantastic. Yeah. Well, the town has changed, you know? And quite honestly there's a lot that we couldn't find. But Dante Ferretti [the production designer] and myself and his group, his wife, Francesca, we've worked together for fourteen years now. And basically we had to build pretty much. And I love working on real locations too because it's lived in, it has a life. The walls are alive when you go on a real location. It has ambience already as soon as you walk in. But on this one the thrill was to re-create the Cocoanut Grove. In those days it was going to the nightclub with the actress, getting a picture taken. So we built the Cocoanut Grove to scale. So in the design, we had to use sets; we had to build. We actually made Hughes's house just a little bigger. His den where he worked a little bigger. And I built the screening room a little bigger to move around in. Also in the scenes where he's cracking up, the walls kind of stretch and that sort of thing. We built the interior [of the plane, the Hercules], and that was an extremely difficult sequence to shoot. There were over two hundred shots we had designed and we couldn't always get back to them.

The other element of design was the use of color. And color to me is very important. I love color and I love black and white. But when I was a kid, I'd see a movie in three-strip Technicolor. There was nothing like it. It was palpable. You could taste the colors. But there were also films made in two color, the cheaper version of color, Cinecolor. Sometimes you'd see like the sky was green, you know? Roy Rogers would be riding and I was about seven or eight years old and there's this green sky and his shirt looks pink, okay, and the grass looks a little blue, but it doesn't matter. Boy, this is magic, you know? This is really what it must be like to be out there. I come from the tenements; I mean, I want to go out in the West. And what I felt was that if we're gonna do the old Hollywood of '27 to 1947, I would create it with the color of that period 'cause in my mind it's almost like a Proustian thing or it's a sense memory of seeing those films on a screen, the magic of that world, what it must have been like and what it is like still. There's still an aspect of magic to it.

More than half the picture was designed for two-color Technicolor blue and red. Katharine Hepburn in the Cocoanut Grove, when he takes her flying, that dress is the perfect color I wanted, but that dress was actually . . . it's a kind of a beige. The reality on set was mustard green. If you actually walked on the set, it looked like craziness, I mean, wah. And, " You're sure this is [Okay?]" "Yeah, don't worry. The color's gonna come out blue." And then eventually Rob Legato worked out a system digitally where you pull the color right out. I knew that some of those films in two color had a richer quality to them. The face, skin tones are always off, but I like that. I like that blue, the gleam of the silver plane. The golf course is blue. I saw a movie called *Blue Grass of Kentucky* and the grass was blue. It was 1951. It was Cinecolor. And so it was almost like thinking back and looking at old photographs that are hand tinted in a way. And eventually the film slips into a three-color process by the end of the picture when he's in the Senate. It's fairly much normal color at that point.

Sam Mendes, *American Beauty*

One of the things I loved about Conrad's works [Conrad Hall, his cinematographer] is that his blacks are black and his whites are white, and he yearns for the days of black-and-white photography because it's all about values. It's all about light. This is a testament to Conrad really. You get a sequence like Annette Bening coming into Jane's room when she ends up slapping her. She comes in, in a house in Brentwood. Jane turns to the window on the Warner Ranch, she turns to the mirror on the Warner Ranch, and then she runs to the window on another set, which is built elsewhere. And it's three successive shots in three different places. And I challenge anyone to spot that.

I mean, obviously, that's part of the art of the cinematographer, is to bind all those things together.

My reference points all tended to be photography. What would I have on my wall when we were making the movie was Edward Hopper and Norman Rockwell and that very white cryogenic, pure but deadly light that comes in Norman Rockwell paintings, and those very solitary composed poetic Edward Hopper images, often with people trapped behind glass, people trapped within frames and that sense of loneliness and desolation, and yet great contained emotion. All those things were what I wanted to be in the film, and what I was searching for was something that hovered a foot above reality almost the whole time. So the journey between the real and the fantastic—literally fantastic, his fantasy scenes—was a very short journey. We deliberately, particularly in the first half an hour of the film, used tableaux and almost deliberately two-dimensional images, to then give depth to them later on in the movie and to give the lie to what you thought was a deliberately almost presented cliché in the first twenty minutes. And as far as the production designer was concerned, I found myself taking stuff out of the frame all the time. Taking cars off the streets, wetting down the streets to give it darkness.

Spike Jonze, *Being John Malkovich*

I wanted it to look very flat and very milky blacks and low contrast, and just sort of banal, because I thought it would be a fun place to take off into discovering a portal into John Malkovich, and so we did film tests and kept underexposing it more and more, and they'd come back and we'd go more. And finally got it to where we liked it and Lance Acord, the cinematographer, looked over at me, and he's like, "Well okay, but you're going to have to stick up for me on this one." And the wardrobe is a friend of mine named Casey Storm, who I've worked with since some of my first videos, and Casey and I would drive around in the city, L.A. or New York or wherever, and just take photos of people from the car with the long lens and get a lot of ideas from that.

We talked a lot about what the "portal" would look like. At one point in the script it was written as a membranous tunnel. I just wanted to sort of make sure—it was a big thing—when this door opens and to keep in the sort of reality that we've created and stay with it, so as we started visualizing opening up the door from this office and seeing a membranous tunnel, whatever that means, fleshy—and it did didn't feel right, so we talked about a lot of different things to make it more sort of gradually shifting from this office reality into something else. And it took a long time but we finally came up with the obvious solution, dirt, which seemed to work good.

Mike Leigh, *Secrets & Lies*

Now, finding locations for my sorts of films, even though they are, ultimately, quote-unquote, "ordinary places," is a difficult one. Because what happens is that this day looms on the horizon when we will go out to a location that has been dressed and prepared, which is one of the series of locations, and we will start to shoot a coherent picture. We not only talk about where it might be, but we choose the whole world, the whole spirit of the film as it's growing. Now when there is no script and story and

I don't know the locations. The speed with which that date races towards you is terrifyingly quick! What happens is, we tend to arrange one or two main locations. Usually one location is booked for the entire shoot, so you can start there and go back there, and it's a sort of fail-safe. And there are other locations that are found spontaneously, because I'm still making it up as we shoot, and we go and do things as we go.

When we came to *Naked*, it began to appear to me what kind of film that I felt I wanted to make. We talked about color and tone. We shot tests. We decided to shoot AGFA [a film stock] and used the bleach process and all of those things. And that, still without having started to make the film or know what the film really was. In *Secrets & Lies*, we took as a point of reference the quality of high-speed photography and chose Fujicolor for that reason.

Steven Spielberg, *Amistad*

When I read the script, I pretty much knew that I wanted the film to have a certain look, and I wanted the look to be Goya, especially in his late dark period. And when we looked at those pictures and we saw some of those paintings—we knew what the mood of the film was going to be. The production designer [Rick Carter] did a lot of conceptual paintings with some illustrators he brought in, and I'd be up there on a stepladder with a Panaflex inside the mouth of a T. rex and he'd be trying to feed me these big pictures up a second stepladder! But a necessity of the schedule created a kind of spontaneity that actually benefited the movie. I didn't storyboard *Amistad*. I didn't storyboard *Schindler's List*. But I did storyboard all of *Lost World* and all of *Jurassic Park*. The size and the logistics of the film kind of dictates what we need to share with every member of the crew.

We principally shot the movie in Newport, Rhode Island, and we used all the old seventeenth-century houses and squares and courthouses. That was all very authentic, so most of the light, even though it's augmented by units coming through the windows, or by hitting gryfs [gryflon is plastic reflective material] and bouncing into the windows, I'd say the movie was about 90 percent about location.

Steven Spielberg, *Saving Private Ryan*

I didn't do any storyboards for this movie because those soldiers and those cameramen didn't have any storyboards to key off of in 1944 and we took a kind of method-actor approach to directing and to performing in the picture. We just used each day to kind of inform us where we should be and who we should be.

The design once again came from history. I hired Tom Sanders, who was an assistant art director on *Hook* in 1991. I liked him a lot. Then he went on to become a production designer; he did *Braveheart* and some other wonderful pictures. We just basically got all the British and the American flyovers of Omaha Beach. Because they did a lot of flyovers before the invasion. And when they were building the Belgian gates and they were building all the tank traps and all the barbed wire, all that was in construction, we were photographing it up and down the beach, months before the invasion. So we got hold of those key kind of aerial reconnaissance photographs. And basically, Tom

Sanders simply duplicated what was once a part of reality. The same thing with the town of Vermeil and with the central town in the story. Those were actual pictures of Charaton and pictures of San Mara Gliess and a lot of the French towns that had been devastated and had been kind of denuded of trees. That was just part of history and those still photographs helped Tom to make his determinations of how he was going to lay out the sets.

We did a lot of camera experiments. I had seen the Robert Capa [photos], all; there's eight of them left. Robert Capa was the photojournalist who took three hundred or four hundred shots of first-wave D-day Omaha Beach and the lab in Britain had melted all the shots. The developer was so excited to see the shots and made key mistakes and ruined all but eight stills. Those eight stills have survived and they've been printed again and again in magazines, in history books, and those eight stills totally told me the look of the movie. I showed those eight stills to Janusz [Kaminski, the cinematographer] and I said, How do we get this look? What do we do because it's all blurry, it's got stuff on the lens, and it's right down low? And we began to do tests on the back lot at Universal. I'll never forget our first test. We took a camera and put some extras in army uniforms and we lined them up and we photographed them and I took one of those huge drills, those big industrial Black and Decker drills, took the bit off and instead just used the drill as a large vibrator. And basically had the on/off switch and I would hold the drill up to the camera, and when I pressed on, the camera would vibrate, and when we'd turn it off, it would stop. And when we saw the dailies the next day, it gave the most neurotic affect to the movie. The vibration was subtle enough to create a subconscious neurotic feeling to it. And we substituted the Black and Decker for an actual device called Lenshaker that you actually put onto the lens and it does shake the elements of the lens. And there was another technique: I saw hundreds of hours of documentaries and I always wondered, how come in those WWII black-and-white documentaries when there's an explosion, you can count each piece of dirt that goes into the air. Whereas in a modern action movie when there's an explosion it's a beautiful flower eruption, it's a beautiful orange, yellow, black, and white flower erupting, and it's just kind of like, glamorous. And Janusz was saying, "Well I think it's because the old Bell and Howell cameras had an open forty-five degree shutter." So there was no blurring possible. So we took poor Panavision [a company that makes cameras], we took their camera and deconstructed a Panaflex. Totally deconstructed it, stripped the lenses of coating, 'cause lenses are coated you know to make me look good. I mean if I was in front of the camera. And we took all that off and basically opened the shutter up to either 45 degrees or 90 degrees as opposed to 180 degrees and when you do that, there's no blurring. It almost looks like every frame is a machine gun, like every frame is a bullet coming from a machine gun. And that combined with intermittent vibrations to the lens and just the way the camera was handheld and where it was placed. Several times I actually put a blood pack with a squib on it and I would put the blood just under the lens and I would trigger the squib so simply the lens would be splattered with blood. Because I wanted to deconstruct the look of the picture. I didn't want the picture to look like a slick, glamorous John Wayne war movie.

Ang Lee, *Crouching Tiger, Hidden Dragon*

You can start with the color pallet, the concept, with how you envision, you know, red means passion to me. Let's find some red desert. So I take them to location scouting and we start to dreaming of the movie from there on. Green is the repressive one and gray is at night, and during daytime—need a lot of embroidery. Some clothes would take them like two months, four people so you really have to work with them way ahead of time. We're mimicking Chinese painting. We're shooting low contrast. A lot of negative space typical for Ching [dynasty].

I describe how I see it. Then they show me drawing, rough drawings, and then once we choose one, they keep refining it. Like that cave at the end, is conception I want it be like a woman's womb.

Taylor Hackford, *Ray*

Usually with flashbacks you desaturate it; you show that it's in the past. I didn't want to do that in this film because, you know, Ray Charles could see when he was young and I wanted the flashbacks to be like the color, almost supersaturated, like a young boy seeing a spring day for the first time. All those colors. And then we stepped on the linear part of our movie. Ray Charles once he got on the road, he never stopped, and you must give the audience that sense. We didn't have the money to shoot major productions. So we used stock footage. For early on, we had done our research and I found stock footage from all these places. This footage itself was bad. We have 8mm from 1946, 16mm Kodachrome from '47. We have some 35mm. But every single piece of stock footage gives us the large scope of wherever you are in the world. We shot the whole film in Louisiana so we couldn't go anyplace. That was all predetermined, and the idea of desaturating, doing a bleach bypass on our main part of the story, helped us integrate that footage into the film because that, in and of itself, was deteriorating our footage so that it could work.

We've done a lot of work in this guild [the Directors Guild of America] to try to get incentives, both statewise and now we have a federal incentive to bring production back to this country. With me and this film, I just refused from a different point of view [to shoot out of the country]. I mean we want to get our film made. So if that's the place you have to go, you have to go. The difference is, it's not just architecture. Sometimes it's human architecture. This is a film that deals with the African American milieu, and I needed this film to be made in the South. I needed my extras to be real Americans, not Canadians who mostly are from Jamaica. In a way the film should have been in Georgia, you know; Ray Charles had a history in Georgia: "Georgia on My Mind." Steve Altman [the production designer] and I went to Atlanta and we were looking for a city and then a surrounding area of rural area for all these different historical places, because we were looking for New York, Chicago, Seattle, Atlanta, Houston, L.A. all in one place. And the problem we found immediately with Atlanta is, Atlanta has torn down all its historic buildings. The guild had helped Louisiana write their tax incentive legislation so we went to Louisiana. My second home is New Orleans. They love their tradition and there's a lot of old period buildings there. There's a stink about a location that works. And when you get in there, you can feel it.

You know, Ray Charles was constantly on the road. That means he's constantly in hotels. What you don't want to do is go and move here, spend a half day here or a third of a day here, take the time to move here to hotel rooms, because hotel rooms are ubiquitous. And so what Steve did is that we went into a warehouse and we built a modular four-hotel-rooms situation. So that we saved time and while we were moving to another place he'd re-dress another room with wallpaper and so forth. And we moved into a lot of clubs. Ray Charles in his career went from a working musician in the "chitlins circuit," in these little clubs where, before our *American Bandstand*, every single town had its own dance style. But as Ray Charles got successful, as he crossed over into the white audience, he grew into bigger venues. We had money for about two hundred extras on certain days, but we never had money for more.

But Ray, one of the things he described to me 'cause he grew up in Georgia and was raised in northern Florida right at the border, he remembered colors. He knew the blue of the sky, he knew the green, and he remembered the red earth of Georgia. He always talked about that red earth that he used to run barefoot on. He didn't even wear shoes until he was seven years old. And we get some dump trucks and this red earth of Georgia and we spread it out. And one of the great arts is the breaking down of costumes. Where the costumes fit the character instead of making it look like the costume's wearing the character. These are working people. They didn't have a lot of clothes. I had a very specific vision for this film. But when I showed up on the weekend to look at the set that he'd [Steve Altman] dressed, we designed this little house and I looked across the street and there's this dead tree with these bottles hanging from it. And I went, "What the hell is that? And what's it based on?" Because it's such a very specific image. And he said, "That I saw when I was scouting for my father [the film director Robert Altman] on a film in Mississippi. I saw a bottle tree. It's what the slaves had when they came." And it came from West Africa. And there was a specific tradition of taking those bottles to capture evil spirits. The thing hit me immediately that it was so great for my film when the boy could see; this is something he saw every day. It's raining, it's sunny, and it gets more and more dim. It gets further and further away as he goes blind. So it's the last image that he remembered in his life.

Afterwards with the wind blowing you can hear it. You know it's still there, of course, but you can't see it. This image I used all the way through the film. I asked Ray if he'd ever seen one when he was a kid, and he said yes. But the fact is that that image is something that is indelible to my movie and my designers threw it in there and my first response was it's phony, and he said, "No." And he gave me research that went all the way back to Africa. And there it is. So it's these relationships. We don't work alone. It's a collaborative medium.

Taylor Hackford on the set of Ray. (Ray courtesy of Universal Studios Licensing LLLP.)

Gus Van Sant, *Good Will Hunting*

We talked about the design but we [he and Missy Stewart, his production designer] kind of had enough of a camaraderie that she sort of went off and did it, and I would often be surprised—just sort of showing up and seeing what she had done. One of the issues was trying to match the Toronto interiors with the Boston exteriors. Usually when I go into a film, there are a lot of styles that are in your head, and you're looking at films with the cinematographer. We were watching these sort of example of films that we were kind of trying to get ideas from. One of the things I'd always try to do in my past films was to try and get a sort of natural light going so that the natural light from window is lighting the scene, and you don't have to do much interior shifting of lights, which usually takes up a lot of time. You know, like the changing of an angle can sometimes eat up thirty to forty minutes of time for the cinematographer. I've always tried to get this going with cinematographers, where you just sort of light the set and then you can move the camera around within the set. And it usually never works out that way when you're there doing it. I told Jean Yves [Escoffier, the cinematographer] this, and he did it. He knew what to do and what we wanted to do. He accomplished that, so that our turnaround time for cameras was like five minutes, which was pretty amazing, and it made it so that the actors worked harder because they couldn't really take breaks. It made it so that I was shooting twice as much film as any other film that I did.

The first film I did was completely storyboarded with like five hundred pages of drawings, and I used that in a Hitchcockian sense. And that was a very low-budget film. We could handle all those different drawings; we could get the shots. Then when I did *Drugstore Cowboy*, I was faced with an eighty-person crew. I realized that just changing your shot became a huge ordeal, and I couldn't keep with the storyboard I had drawn, so I got used to shooting a scene after rehearsing it and getting the action down, choosing the first angle and then deciding what the second angle is.

Quentin Tarantino, *Pulp Fiction*

I don't storyboard because I can't draw and I don't like anyone else's drawings. They always get the framing wrong as far as I'm concerned. But I can light, so I describe everything in great detail.

We didn't have enough money to build what Marsellus would call his house. I had a budget of $8 million on *Pulp*, and I knew—"Wow, this is the first time I've had some real money to make a movie." And I was like, "Okay, I have a lot of money, but I don't have that much money. So I'm going to give myself one big Hollywood thing." And that was Jack Rabbit's Slims. Everything else was like a little independent movie, if you look at it, but that was my big thing. So I created this restaurant.

James L. Brooks, *As Good As It Gets*

I always like storyboards because if you hand them to somebody, everybody will go away and look at that, and then you can figure out what you are doing.

Curtis Hanson, *L.A. Confidential*

I do not storyboard, unless it's a situation for a stunt in order that everybody can see exactly what the shot is and anticipate what to build for safety reasons. In terms of communicating with the cameraman, I prefer not to storyboard. Unless, for example, the shootout at the Victory Motel, I actually did a list, a shot list; it wasn't storyboarded until again, for safety's sake, we storyboarded certain aspects of it so that the effects people could see exactly what the expectation was.

I grew up in L.A. and in a sense feel as though I've been researching this picture all my life. And I've always wanted to deal with the city of my childhood memory and it was very ambitious logistically in that we had forty-five locations to find, and my dream was to do it all on location. I wanted to actually find real locations and shoot in what would appear in a casual way, as though we were not interested in the set dressing. There's always a tendency I feel, as a moviegoer, when one looks at movies that are period pictures, where the movie somehow becomes about the period instead of about the story and the characters. I screened a number of pictures that were shot in the '50s. Pictures by directors who had a very lean, no-nonsense style, like Robert Aldrich and Don Siegel and Sam Fuller and so forth, to show that when they shot the scenes on the streets, there was almost a semidocumentary feel to it. It was as though they'd put the camera down and shot because they didn't care about the cars or any of that because it was all ordinary.

Mirrors and reflections are a thing that runs through *L.A. Confidential*, with this theme of illusion and reality, image and reality, in the city of illusion, in Los Angeles. It was constructed in such a way that several of the characters have moments of truth. For instance Kevin Spacey in the bar looking in the mirror at his own reflection and seeing it's like looking at the portrait of Dorian Gray. His eyes become filled with self-loathing and he sees what he has become. The character that Guy Pearce plays in the beginning of the movie—he's behind the mirror watching as Kevin Spacey is being interrogated, and in the middle of the movie, Guy's on the other side of the mirror doing the interrogating, and at the very end of the movie, when he's finally telling the truth, so to speak, all the cops are outside looking at him, and he then looks in the mirror.

Peter Jackson, *The Lord of the Rings: The Return of the King*

I storyboarded a lot of the first movie and kind of ran out of time and so we didn't have a huge amount of storyboards for the second and third one. But I've never really stuck to storyboards. I've always just done storyboards as a really cheap convenient way of having a practice of the film beforehand.

What I like to do is to start with drawings of a set, if it's a big set or even a small one, and then I like to make models of them so that you can actually get a little camera and you can actually have a look around. Back in about 1998 we built a model of Helms Deep and we got these little plastic soldiers and we kind of worked out the strategy of the battle.

We pretended that Tolkien was writing about history and because he was a professor and put so much detail, extraneous detail to some degree for a filmmaker, into his books and he invented these languages, Elvish and Dwarf, and he spent fourteen years writing *The Lord of the Rings,* and his interest was from a scholarly point of view as much as from an entertainment point of view, that we had a lot of material that we were able to use to give it the semblance of history, 'cause that's obviously all that you can do is to make it seem authentic.

I love paintings and illustrations and when we are beginning a movie, and it doesn't really matter what the subject matter of the film is, I love starting with paintings. And we have a great team in New Zealand of artists who were just able to paint and draw the most beautiful pictures. And in the case of *Lord of the Rings*, we also brought in a couple of artists who we had admired [and] who had illustrated the Tolkien books for years. Minas Tirith, the big multitiered city, fulfills the function in the story of being a very sort of ancient, faded imperial place. So a lot of it's based on the gravitas of that sort of Roman architecture and the faded grandeur of a bygone era. And even with the Elvish architecture, and the Elves are a culture that, obviously, we were creating that never existed, but we looked to art nouveau for that because we just felt that in Tolkien's mind Elves were populating this world, our world, seven thousand years ago, which is when all this was supposed to take place, and we just thought that maybe art nouveau is the last remnant that they left us. We based the design, we tried to base everything, on some form of reality that we could understand.

But you know, when you're faking authenticity—which to some degree is what movies are going to do—it's great to have all this detail and Tolkien was so serious in his academia and his love of ancient language.

James Cameron, *Titanic*

The biggest challenge in making this picture was to get past the technical challenges, which were so enormous and daunting for everyone concerned because they were an order of magnitude beyond what we had done previously. We started doing a lot of testing. We did a lot of previsualization. We got a model of the ship and went around it with a little lipstick camera, making hard copies of that, drew on them and that sort of thing. We did a tremendous amount of figuring out light placement, and how much of it would have to be practical and built in. We'd do a lot of camera tests especially with Kate and Leo, to really find out what focal length lenses worked with them. Eventually we just decided: we are trying to take the audience into a time period and let them inhabit that and live in it. We want it to be rich and not desaturated. We want it to look like Kodachrome. We eventually wound up opting for very little filtration and going for strong colors as much as possible. Then of course that impacted the costume design and the production design as well.

We never really used storyboards that much. We built a twenty-five-foot-long study model of the ship. We built models of the interior spaces based on old reference, used a small chip video camera, so we had several weeks of previsualization. We had the luxury on this film, because we were dealing with a known and defined space. If we were doing a science fiction film, we would have had to do rough production design drawings, some kinds of storyboards, and then convert that into models or maquettes. We took the twenty-five-foot study model, drove down to an empty field in Rosarito Beach, stuck it out on a bluff, and watched what the sun did to it during the day. We kept turning it and moving it and finally said, "Okay, this is exactly where the thing should go. Now build it here—except, seven hundred and eighty feet long." We actually worked from the plans of the ship. And he [Peter Lamont, the production designer] had an interesting challenge because I would not let him diverge from what it was. I said, "I want the *Titanic*, and I want it exact." *The Guinness Book of World Records* called us up and apparently it's the biggest set ever. But we only built one side and the whole top. And for the first time, I think in the fourteen or fifteen *Titanic* projects that have been put on film over many years, for the first time Harland and Wolff actually opened their plans drawers and we got the blueprints to the ship! Because it had always been kind of a black mark for them, which frankly it shouldn't have been because there was nothing wrong with the ship; they just drove it into an iceberg! You drive a Volvo into a bridge abutment; you are gonna get the same effect!

We went in with a very, very clear idea of the game plan. At the time that the film was green lit, all the sets were blueprinted, all the tank and riser systems were all blueprinted. To achieve the time scale which we had set out to do, which was to do the entire thing including building the set, then shooting the movie, posting [editing and mixing music and sound], and delivering it, was supposed to be thirteen months. In that previsualization phase, we sort of merged together, figuring out the effects. If the *Titanic* really existed, this would be a cool shot. Okay, now, how much set do we need, how's it going to be done with a model, how much of it is CG [computer graphics], CG water? And you eventually realize, if you try to do all the effects, it's going to cost you even more because the effects are not cheap. At a certain point as a storyteller, you go, "My God, I've got to have something to work with. Something that I can see, because I've got to react to something too because the actors need it and I need it as well." You can't preconceptualize everything.

Peter Weir, *The Truman Show*

Dennis Gassner [the production designer] got involved very early on. I needed a top person and I was familiar with his work. We met and got on and he was hired truly months before the start of preproduction in fact. To do research and so on. The key was the town. We had to find the town. First, I thought of doing it here and joining up the key back lots of Universal and Warner and a little bit of Paramount. I was going to sort of construct a town out of the existing standing sets and streets, but it would have tipped the film into a more theatrical comic direction, with a Western street or the Paris café corner. But it was tempting and so I photographed it all and we were looking at that. It wasn't right, and then it was suggested to me, there's this little town in the Florida seaside. And it was quite a remarkable experiment really. Architectural experiment where the people had built in the style you might say of the Southern vernacular of the United States. These little clapboard houses. So of course I sent a camera crew; it looked interesting. I then began the difficult negotiation. These people were very sensitive about what we were going to do obviously physically, but also in terms of how the town was portrayed. Because part of the architectural community of course condemns what they're doing as sort of retro and Disneyish. In fact Disney came down and had a long look at it. The kids play in the streets and they live the life that we all lived from my generation. Where kids could go out and play in the streets in safety and live in this very pretty seaside town. The great thing was in the end they decided against

Production location for The Truman Show. *(Courtesy of Paramount Pictures and Peter Weir.)*

cash and they said, "We haven't got a school, build us a school." It was great to go back recently and walk through the school.

As with many things in this film, it had to be done with an apparent effortless quality. This film is in danger of being something that would be too much of a brain tease for the audience if they couldn't just relax and go with it. I had to in a sense, subvert the form of the movie. I wanted to turn the audience into viewers of the *Truman Show* just like the characters we see from time to time within the film. And I wanted them to assume that they knew all about it. They knew they were in a dome so I would just have to give you a little glimpse here, a word there, a phrase there rather than the awful feeling that I as the filmmaker am telling you information.

It was really an aesthetic choice. The wide angle and the minuteness of cameras was done to occasionally give the audience a reminder that they were being watched. I liked very much from the silent era where they would have all kinds of frame shapes around the lens and were free to experiment. Sometimes triangles and all kinds of things to focus your attention on what you're interested in. And so we would shoot a lot of them and then I decided it was too risky. We made up a number of gobos [devices covering part of the lens] that we would be able to put around the lens or have the lens shoot through. Then I decided it was much better to do it optically. I had a lot of fancy stuff in the film that I took out, finally. Again to make the audience have a cinema experience and then reveal all that was to be revealed, but not to in a way to distract them.

I don't use storyboards very much, although I did for the critical sequence, the storm. I like to draw them myself, though. I find I draw almost everything. I keep saying I've got to go to a drawing class. These stick figures are becoming embarrassing. But I love to draw little frames. And sometimes I'll give those to a professional to have them drawn up more fully.

Production construction of ship for Master and Commander:
The Far Side of the World. *(© 2003 Twentieth Century Fox and Peter Weir.)*

Peter Weir, *Master and Commander: The Far Side of the World*

Often in these movies from the past they would raise headroom below decks for ease of moving cameras and so on, but we stuck to the actual head heights and it was uncomfortable, but I think the reality was important as part of the experience.

Steven Soderbergh, *Erin Brockovich*

That's my weakest area, production design and costumes, I have to say. I rely very, very heavily on those members of the crew 'cause I have no background in it. I just sort of become that irritating "I don't know what I want, but that's not it" person. Driving around in a van looking for locations, in those vans with like ten people, eight of them on cell phones, including the driver, and then you pile out, uh, and you look at it, and you go, "Uh, eh, well, yeah, I guess. How far is it from the hotel?" Scouting is my least favorite part of the process.

The funny thing about the wardrobe is, if I showed Julia that wardrobe when I first met her, she wouldn't have done the film. There is just no way. 'Cause it was the first thing she talked about—what is she going to wear? And I assured her that it would all be done with the utmost taste: "Uh, it's gonna be great. It's gonna be," you know, "no worries." And um, what was hilarious was by the time we finished, one day she walked onto the set and said, "This skirt is too long." Then I knew we'd totally, you know, we've turned her. The trump card was that stuff was tame compared to what the real Erin wears.

Anthony Minghella, *The English Patient*

The first time I drove anywhere near a location and I saw how many trucks there were, my stomach just churned and churned. Because it was massive. I think we had over forty trucks that went from here to the desert. We had to build roads! We had to build a road into the Sahara because, funnily enough, there aren't any roads there. I went to the desert a year before we started shooting, and it was so gorgeous to be there, and it was so cleansing and so extraordinary. Then when we went back there a year later, I loathed every single second of it because it was so inhospitable and cold, bone-chillingly cold. It was also totally against the spirit of making films, which is repetition. If you ask Ralph Fiennes to walk up a sand dune and he does it too quickly, you're stopped, as we say in England, because when he comes back, there are the footpaths of the first go-round—and so you know, the insanity ensues very quickly. The day we were there we were rained out, so that the place we went for was completely gone. When you're trying to roll a truck down the side of a hill and they discover they can't do it and you've moved all the equipment there and you can't do it on that hill, then you try and use what you have. You try and live in the moment that you have.

I drew every shot in the film repeatedly. Partly because I was terrified of the scope of this film—and so I thought, the more I know, the more I'll feel like I'm not a jerk when I turn up every day. And I'd rather have that than the screenplay.

We built tons of stuff—the church which Hana is flown round in and most of the monastery. We built the exterior and the interior of the cave in the location. Stuart Craig [the production designer] said, "What do you want to see at all times? My job is to give you that back." So I'd go and I'd say, "I want to see that, but that's not right." And he'd say, "So then, we'll make that bit, and if you want that ravine to lead into a cave, then we'd better find some way of doing that." You're the sum of your own decisions.

•7•

Rehearsal

James L. Brooks, *As Good As It Gets*

$\mathscr{I}$ love rehearsal. I've had great rehearsals where I don't even touch the script. I think that what kind of rehearsal depends on who the actors are. When you have something called a rehearsal, basically all you are saying is the system goes away and lets you talk to the actors for a certain length of time. And that's so hard to come by and it means everything. It means how you communicate; it means what you know about them, what they know about you, how quickly you can talk to each other when you're filming. I just think it's everything.

Rob Reiner, *A Few Good Men*

I do a lot of rehearsal. I mean some of the pieces I've done are like theater pieces. Particularly *A Few Good Men*. It's a courtroom drama. It's like theater. And I go through the whole thing in a two-week period, and I rope out, tape out, all the sets on a soundstage.

I find that the fear is always that you are gonna lose spontaneity. And the fact is you do. You lose it in a big way. But then you regain it. You have the spontaneity right away, at that first read through, and you hear how it sounds and everybody sounds good. Then you put it on its feet and it gets worse and worse and worse and it's really starting to stink. Then it turns the corner. If you stay with it long enough, you get—something a little bit better than you ever had before, with a little greater understanding and a little bit more depth.

[On *All in the Family*] we'd read the script around the table Monday morning. We'd be hysterical laughing, it was great, we'd put it on its feet, and the first couple times it was funny. By Wednesday or Thursday these jokes are lying there; I mean, they're just dead. We've all said them, and we've all heard them a lot, but we kept saying, "Have faith; stay with it. The audience is going to hear it for the first time." They haven't been through this process. And if you can find a new way to make it fresh, not only will you have preserved a well-crafted joke, but also the audience is hearing it for the first time.

[In *Misery*] Jimmy Caan didn't like to rehearse so much. And Kathy Bates is from theater and she loves to rehearse. So that was difficult. I had to wind up rehearsing a little less than Kathy would have liked, and a lot more than Jimmy would have liked. Jimmy was frightened he would lose the spontaneity, and he had to use a wheelchair in that film. And he would say, "I want to see what it's like when I first get on the set and just feel what it's gonna be like and experience it." And I said, "Jim, you've never been in wheelchair before. If you have to get in a wheelchair, it's gonna take you hours; you're not gonna be able to do it." I said, "What you gotta do," and he knew it. I said, "You get in that wheelchair and spend a lot of time in it so that you can get that wheelchair to do anything you want, spin this way, turn that way, move back." I said, "Then you can make it as awkward or as easy as you want it to, rather than always be struggling with trying to make it work."

[In *A Few Good Men* in the rehearsal] I had the luck of having Jack Nicholson there. He knows what he's doing, and he comes to play, every time out, full-out performance! And what it says to a lot of the other actors is, "Oooooh, I better get on my game here because this guy's coming to play! So I can't hold back; I've got to come up to him." He sets the tone.

What you are trying to do is get to the point where you are realizing the script as best as it is and maybe adding just a little bit more spin to it, just with their performances.

Anthony Minghella, *The English Patient*

I rehearse. I come from the theater and I think the actors need to rehearse and they get better through rehearsing and I get better and know more about what can be done and what can be eliminated.

Sam Mendes, *American Beauty*

In rehearsals, I encouraged the actors to improvise. Annette going off. That dialogue she has with herself? That was an improvisation that we scripted. It was much longer, believe me, when Annette improvised. She went on for about five minutes. But we then pulled out the things that we thought were best and put them into the script. I think we changed a fair amount, but the spirit and the story of the script, they are unchanged.

Barry Levinson, *Bugsy*

The first screenplay I made was *And Justice for All*. And Al Pacino wanted a reading of it. I wasn't the director. I was just there. They had a bunch of really terrific actors. And what happened was Al Pacino maybe not wanting to give a performance and every other actor not wanting to upstage him, they are doing a little less. And everybody's doing a little less. And the point is I had no idea what anyone was saying. I didn't know what the movie was about.

The idea of putting like twelve actors around the table is the most petrifying thought to me. So I kind of hear a movie in my head to a degree and I'd rather just put it on the floor and work it out.

So in a sense it's like a constant rehearsal on film that you keep shooting. And a lot of times you're looking for the imperfection of it. Because sometimes what happens is you get a nice piece of professional work, but the professional work doesn't give you that surprise. And sometimes there's a struggle to say the lines, maybe a struggle of not remembering what to say; that is the same as not knowing what to say in life. That may be good. And those are the moments that you kind of treasure.

Steven Spielberg, *Amistad*

I don't like rehearsal. I can generalize one thing on most of my movies—I don't rehearse unless the actor truly needs the rehearsal because that's what the actor requires. I'll read through a piece, but I don't do it often. I've done a number of readings to determine for myself whether I should direct the movie. I've never committed to a movie based on one of the read throughs. I don't know what that means. On *The Color Purple* we did a read through with all the actors, and there were fantastic moments that evolved and existed and dissipated in my conference room and never occurred again anywhere on film. And it was a brutal lesson to learn, that sometimes you cannot capture lightning in a bottle. Sometimes you really have to trust that when the "mojos" are working, there's gonna be some kind of magic happening on the set that day, and it's all gonna happen when the cameras are moving.

I think an actor really needs you to believe in him and her. If you simply believe in him and the actress, it's amazing what they can do for you.

Steven Spielberg, *Saving Private Ryan*

In this case there was really nothing to rehearse. There was another kind of rehearsal. All the actors went to basic training and became soldiers for a week. Captain Dale Dye, who was our technical consultant, took Tom Hanks and the other eight actors and brought them to a small bivouacked area near where we shot the film, which is near British Aerospace, outside of London. And he put them through six days of grueling, treacherous, torturous training. And it was a bad week. It rained every day and every night. And the actors all wanted to go home. And they wanted to quit the movie about the second day in. And Tom called me one day in the editing room and I was cutting *Amistad* at the time, and Tom said, "We're losing our entire cast. They're walking out. They're calling their agents. They're saying it's humiliation, and they're being humiliated every day, and people are yelling at them. They haven't been yelled at since they were children at home. What do we do here?" And I just said, "Well, Tom, I'm here and you're there. And you're a director. You just did *That Thing You Do!*, so do that thing you do and save this cast." And he did. He rallied the troops, and from that kind of near disaster came a real bonding of the entire cast, to the point that when I showed up, I was the outsider. Because I hadn't been yelling at anybody, and I hadn't been in their lives, and I only met about two or three of the actors anyway for the first time. And they weren't listening to me. They were listening to Dale Dye and Tom Hanks, and I showed up—I had my name on the back of the chair and everything—they didn't care about that. And I had to win my way into their hearts and minds because they weren't accepting me right away. When I'd say something, they'd all look at Tom Hanks or Dale Dye. And so I had to kind of prove myself, and it took awhile. But it was a great experience to know that they went through that experience. Because what they really brought out of it, even though it was only five days and not the ninety days that most soldiers spend in basic training, in much worse conditions, they brought with them a respect of the combat veteran. And they came out of it really understanding that we weren't just making an entertaining, escapist kind of summer action movie, but we were making a movie that was really meant to memorialize the WWII veteran. And I don't think any of them realized that's what we were determined to do until they had gone through that process.

Ang Lee, *Crouching Tiger, Hidden Dragon*

Rehearsing start with me on casting process; when you read the person, it's hard for me to carry conversation in English. Working is easier so I shoot straight to the reading. So I have them do, prepared and do the scene. Like rehearsal, and I "demolish" them, one way, two way, and stretch them do different things and see, you know. There's two purposes. One is just to establish that I'm in control. The second thing is that see how they respond to your direction: "Do it like you resent him; try to push him away." Then just see how they respond.

Sometimes like the previous movie [*Ride with the Devil*] and this one, I will set up a month of boot camp 'cause that was Civil War, very specific historical skills and look and habits. All the kids, they come into Kansas City a month before shooting and I set them to like thirteen-hour program every day. It's like concentration camp, training camp. And this one for martial arts. For Jen [played by Ziyi Zhang], for example, she has to go to martial arts early in the morning and then, 'cause she's such a modern, sassy person and is no grace to her, and I had her every day do one hour, just to sit still doing Chinese calligraphy lessons, then horseback and rehearsing and dialogue and learning to wear that big thing on top of her head and the Manchurian shoes. For about a month and a half. And swordsmanship I keep them busy. And I will participate as much as I can. That's when I observe them. It's like coaching basketball team. You don't want to spend the most of their energy in rehearsing, in training, but for the game. Just watch them talking to each other and see how the chemistry will work, we discover things that you might be able to use in, from real life. Like if you sense friendship, you use that. If you sense jealousy, that's easy to catch and use that for real.

Oliver Stone, *JFK*

I rehearse a lot. It allows us freedom. Once you have developed in a rehearsal an attitude, then we can go against it. And I find that very valuable. But the movie is a debate. The debate starts with the rehearsal.

We budget usually three weeks in advance. We do one week in wherever most of the actors are. And the second week we move to location and we rehearse on location as much as we can. Not all the sets are ready, obviously, but we do the best we can. Then I stop and I do some rewrites.

Whenever we start a new scene, we rehearse it again only with the actors; I ask the crew to leave. And I take the set with the actors and we work it out. We agree to agree, synchronize our watches, so to speak. We block it out. And often it's quite different than what we did several weeks before. But we've now done it three times. This is the third time. The crew comes back. We show them the rehearsal, often indifferently, because we want to save it. And then we go and we shoot. We had the liberty of going through it three different times and trying three different things, or maybe three similar things. But it becomes a payoff. We've made an event; we've built up to a moment.

I believe in rehearsal. But I believe in going against the rehearsal too. As I believe in preparing the script, but also going against the script too.

Stephen Daldry, *The Hours*

I like to rehearse and dealing with a lot scenes with a lot of "yap" in it so that it's a very important process of investigation into the text. It's hard because the film world on the whole doesn't really, in my experience, doesn't quite understand what you need to rehearse.

And the railway station scene—it's a very long scene—it's a very difficult scene between those two characters. But three weeks beforehand we took three days and I went up with the actors and we shot the train station and then rehearsed from there for three days. Which was tricky, you know, but it was absolutely vital. Also because, you know, I was thinking, well, I didn't know how much movement. So much about rehearsals is about staging.

Barbra Streisand, *The Prince of Tides*

I knew I had to have a reading because I needed to hear this piece, I needed to see it. And I was devastated by what I saw. I thought, this doesn't work. But I learned a lot from it, and I started writing. It changed a lot from hearing that reading.

In terms of rehearsal, I only like to rehearse certain things, things that have to do with technical stuff. Otherwise, I like to capture the actor's spontaneity, his first instincts, on film—then go from there.

Roman Polanski, *The Pianist*

I like rehearsing when you have reason for it. I like theater. I started in the theater so instinctively, I always think that more tears in the maneuvers, less blood in the battle. But there are certain films when it's absolutely superfluous, like this one.

Mike Newell, *Four Weddings and a Funeral*

We rehearsed for a couple of weeks and I like rehearsal because I enjoy the whole business of acting. We tried all sorts of things and a kind of chemistry emerged. There is rarely such a thing as natural chemistry. There is mostly people who must make a chemistry together, and because they are actors they get on and do. There's that phrase that people use to you, "You've got to get good performance," which I rather mistrust. I don't think you GET performances; I think actors GIVE performances and what you have to do is sweep the ground in front of them so there's nothing for them to trip on. I mean, of course, you have to set guidelines and you have to be clear with them about what's necessary, but if you've got the casting process right, it should work, so long as they don't stumble.

Mel Gibson, *Braveheart*

Ofttimes we rehearse the last thing of an evening or a day when you'd know you'd have to come in tomorrow morning and you'd have an idea of how you wanted it to go during the rehearsal. Sometimes you end up ripping pages out and say, "Hey, we don't need that."

In between takes you'll stand around and yak about it, who the person is, what's his particular dilemma and why. Just a lot of questions, and sometimes I pose the questions, and sometimes they pose the questions, and you're just talking in kind of abstract terms. And you can reach for all kinds of situations from stage plays you've seen, to old movies. Nothing's out of bounds.

James Cameron, *Titanic*

I don't like to overrehearse. You want to give the actors a sense that they are gonna be able to explore on the day. So what I did with Kate [Winslet] and Leo [DiCaprio], was I spent a week a couple of hours a day, two, three hours a day and it was mostly improv [improvisation] work; it was mostly just figuring kind of who their characters were to each other and working on that chemistry. Leo was still struggling a lot with his guy and how to play him, just because he always sort of looks for a dark side and that's really not what the character was all about. Finally I said, "Look, it's a lot easier to do the stuff you've been doing than to be Jimmy Stewart. Because to have so little of what I think of as flashy stuff in the part and to be mesmerizing to an audience 100 percent of the time that you are on the camera is a great acting challenge." Once he realized it was hard, then he was down for it! It's only when he thought it was too easy that he didn't want to do it!

Mike Leigh, *Secrets & Lies*

What I tend to do is to have a sort of pyramid where we start rehearsals with two or three people and it builds up. People are contracted to join in as it develops. And their contracts are constructed so that they are contracted to drop out during the shoot, but with an extension, which has to be taken up before the beginning of principal photography. It's a curious combination of being creative and mathematical.

Curtis Hanson, *L.A. Confidential*

Rehearsal to me is invaluable. I use it. I don't think of it as rehearsing for performance as much as I do rehearsing for content. To me it's the opportunity to be with the actors, read through the script without them actually acting it, but just kind of reading it and maybe they go up to let us say, second gear, just to kind of feel what it feels like. It's the time where, in a relaxed mode without the crew, without the pressure of time, you can talk about the scenes and talk about the intent of each line, if need be, and with some actors it's necessary to talk about the intent of each line because they want to challenge it and feel it's right.

The rehearsal period on this picture was unique in that I had these two Australians, and they both have Australian accents. So I brought them over actually seven weeks before we started shooting. I wanted them to become comfortable with the language so that they wouldn't have to be thinking about it when they were performing, but also comfortable with me, and I felt the picture rested on their ability to pull off these parts. So I went through every day with them for however much time it was necessary, given scenes, and then gradually I would feather in the other actors.

John Madden, *Shakespeare in Love*

We rehearsed for about three weeks. Which is much longer than I would ever normally do. Gwyneth for example had never actually performed Shakespeare, so dealing with the language and understanding how the language works and so forth was part of that. It was also building a life for the actors. And so much of the time, I knew I was going to have to rely on the core group of players in the movie, to have a life that was going on at the edge of the frame. Because it needed to feel real all the time in order for something to come out of it, for something to transcend from it. And we had dances and we had fights and so forth. And the movie is extraordinarily patterned. It's not something you necessarily spot the first time around, but the balcony scene happens three times in the movie, and the people are changing places all the time, and changing sexes all the time. There are all kinds of patterns going on. So it's a matter of working those out so that the actors understood. The physical stuff between Joe and Gwyneth was something that we, I wouldn't say rehearsed, but we certainly talked a great deal about what that would be. I don't like to rehearse too much for movies. I operate on a sort of touch-and-go policy, in aeronautical terms. Where you just kind of land on the material for a moment, just to prime it, so the actors are aware of what might be in the scene, and then you take off again quickly. So that when you're there, in the white heat of the moment, trying to decide exactly how you're going to shoot it, and how it's going to be played, there's still something left to discover.

Michael Mann, *The Insider*

I don't want anything I would want to shoot to occur in rehearsals. So there were a couple of scenes in which the subtext was so obvious that I actually wrote phantom dialogue that I had the actors learn and we did, and it was the dialogue of the subtext.

It wasn't the dialogue of the text. I usually design some kind of curriculum about how an actor's going to acquire that character. What experiences he has to feel, he has to do, he has to actually be able to perform. I mean it may be Russell [Crowe] stumbling through some chemistry experiment in some high school in the Palisades, but it's enough to have done it and smelled it and been there. An actor doesn't need that much because their learning curve is spectacularly high, because of their ability to imitate.

I had Russell do Olympic pistol shooting, which has no relationship to this character. The real Jeffrey Wigand knew Japanese. And his appreciation for Japanese culture is because this is a man who is avidly, very aggressively, ordering the present, because he perceives schizophrenia right over there on the horizon kind of coming this way, and so it's a desperate kind of maintenance. So things being very symmetrical and very ordered. Which also means if I want to elicit a certain reaction from Jeffrey, all I have to have Al do is reach over and start messing up where the plates are, and Jeffrey will get very—Russ will get very disturbed.

One thing about Al's performance, he really became a skilled journalist. I had arranged for him to interview people at the FBI in Washington and just do everything. I don't believe you can drop into a character that deeply, where it's seamless, unless you've experienced the ability to do it.

Baz Luhrmann, *Moulin Rouge*

We had four months of full-time rehearsals. And that is starting with dance workshop in the morning and then we'd have scene work in the afternoon, the odd absinthe party at night to keep everybody sort of going, and then it would all start all over again. When the actors came into the workshops, they would truly and absolutely affect text development. It was their film, their story; they could tell it as well as anybody else in the team.

One of those emotional scenes between Ewan [McGregor] and Nicole [Kidman] which went for weeks and weeks and weeks, because not only does Nicole have to die, but because it's a heightened theatrical language, she has to die with the perfect tear and the hair and you know the moment and then it's "Cut, cut, cut," and three hours to get it all rigged up again, you know? So the ability to go over and work with those actors in a very private tiny room, and I mean that metaphorically, to go over and have shorthand of language came from an extremely elaborate and an extremely involved preproduction rehearsal period.

And there's no question if we hadn't been backed in the extra expenditure that's involved in a four-month actor development period, I wouldn't be here today.

Rob Marshall, *Chicago*

I went into a three-month workshop with my team of dancers and my dance arranger. One of the last things that we did was the whole "Razzle Dazzle" sequence because I really couldn't crack that. And I originally thought, well, you know what, we'll just shoot it as a separate number and it was just going to be a sort of circus number. And then I realized it's just going to sit there and I knew I needed to wrap story around the number. Because at a certain point musicals just don't work when you're just waiting for the next number and just sitting there. It needs to be all interlocked into the story. And so we worked that out literally in rehearsals.

Richard cannot tap dance. "You're gonna have to teach me that." I said, "Okay. Great. I can do that." 'Cause I knew, see, tap is all about rhythm and because he's a musician it was easier. He worked for three months, killed himself every day, you know. We used to hear him screaming and swearing at himself down the hall. Because it was, it's hard.

We had six weeks of rehearsal and just about every moment of that was rehearsing the numbers. I had to kind of get these people up to this sort of place. And so in a way when we started shooting I felt underrehearsed in terms of the scene work. So we did some on weekends as well and did it on the day. We had a reading of the whole piece, which we rehearsed for two days, which I think shocked the actors. We're going to rehearse? I remember [Queen] Latifah saying, "We're going to rehearse a reading? What the hell's that?" Musicals you kind of have to rehearse because it's all, it's all about rhythm. And so we rehearsed it for two days and then did the reading as a performance, which helped enormously because we got a real sense of how everything played and what felt too short or, you know, two back-to-back songs, not enough breath. We did it on a soundstage. And we had an audience. And it, ultimately, it was a really good thing because everybody stepped up to the plate in a whole different way. It was like "showtime" and I remember Renée [Zellweger] was like, is she singing or is she not singing. I said, "You have to understand something. This is all about process. You can't stop that process. You gotta jump in sometime. It's all people that love you and want you to do great." And it was a totally different tone from that day on. I knew that this was going to be this wonderful time where everybody got a sense of the whole, those six weeks of rehearsal . . . we created a company, and that's rare.

When I began conceptualizing, you know, the three months that I had alone with my team was so valuable because that's when there's no principals there. It's just us and it's really just spitballing in a room. Now, a lot of people think when you're choreographing or creating a sequence, a dance sequence, that you're up dancing. I don't. I spend very little time on my feet doing that. That's like the last thing that happens. You sit around and you discuss ideas. And you know I had this huge ghost of Bob Fosse [the director who created the Broadway show] and I had to sort of wrestle with that, and because clearly he's a genius and a mentor of mine, but I wanted to do my own version of *Chicago*. So what I did was I went about reconceptualizing every number from what it had been originally. And with "Reach for the Gun," I was looking for a new attack on the number. And clearly the metaphor that Billy Flynn is the master puppeteer is what led me to the idea that he would be the master puppeteer of all these reporters, as marionettes. First, when I come up with an idea that's like that I, for a long time I think it's terrible, you know? You think, "Oh, that's an interesting idea," when you first come up with it. And then you're brushing your teeth in the morning and you're, "That's like the worst idea in the world. It's going to be so horrible." But then you come around with it again and you start realizing that it could work, it does make sense.

M. Night Shyamalan, *The Sixth Sense*

We do a read through, and I see where the worry points are going to be. And oftentimes, because I really like minimal type of acting when I hear the read through, I do hear moments where I'm like, oh, man, that was perfect. And especially with Haley [Joel Osment], who's just going fucking hundred miles an hour at the read through, and everybody has to jack up their performances because this little kid came to the table and he's pouring it out, and so everybody starts like—I'm like, hey, everybody, chill out—and they're full-out performing it, and by the end of the movie on our read through, the whole room's crying and everyone's like, oh my God, this is going to be great. And I'm like, oh man, I didn't have the cameras on any of that.

Andrew Davis, *The Fugitive*

There was rehearsal time in the sense that I did go around with Harrison [Ford], for example, and with Tommy [Lee Jones], and showed them where they were going to be living and working. I wanted their feedback on dressings and character things that they would want to have. What kind of personal items, things that would make you feel better about this. Actors like this are very resourceful. They'll come up with wonderful ideas for you.

You rehearse to find out what you have to change. And I haven't done a dramatic piece where you're sitting in a room for six minutes talking to each other. There's hardly a scene in these movies that are longer than two minutes.

Certain actors do not want to rehearse. Certain directors don't want to give scripts to people. And there are advantages to not letting people know too much. They can get stale, they can preconceive things, and then they get upset when it doesn't work. At the same time, it would be wonderful to have somebody rehearse and really know what they're doing. I think that both techniques are viable, and valuable, and should be used within one movie.

Michael Radford, *Il Postino*

Philippe Noiret is a great, great movie actor. He knows precisely what to do. You don't have to have any great discussion with him. When I first met him I said, "I think Pablo Neruda this, Pablo Neruda that," and I went through a whole kind of "schpiel" of about what I thought he was and he looked at me and he said, "Hmm, I find that very interesting what you said. You know what I think about Pablo Neruda?" And I said, "What?" He said, "I think he's a man, when he sits down, who sits down like this. He doesn't sit down like this." And he had it. He had it absolutely down, because he [Neruda] was an extrovert, he was generous man; so he never crossed his legs throughout the entire picture and that was the only real discussion we had. In terms of dealing with his performance, he has in the film a very small space to move, a very small arc of character. The balance to achieve with Philippe was how cold he would be towards the guy, so he could just warm up enough to feel that this guy had touched him. What I did basically with Philippe was to shoot practically every piece of dialogue that he had in two different ways. We'd do a colder version and a warmer version because I knew in the editing rooms I would be able to judge it, but I couldn't quite judge it on the set, particularly as he was doing it to a blank space [Massimo Troisi, his costar, often wasn't there to act with Noiret because Massimo was seriously ill].

Ron Howard, *A Beautiful Mind*

I had a couple of weeks of rehearsal, although a lot of it was eaten up with makeup test time 'cause that was so crucial with the aging process. I also like to try to get to as many of the practical locations as possible to actually rehearse there. Not to ever get any scene up to speed, but what I try to use the rehearsal period for is a kind of an extended prep. But it's a chance for the actors to get to know each other, and in this case, also to do research, ongoing research. I like to try to get the significant questions out on the table ahead of time as much as possible. Doesn't necessarily mean we're gonna have all the answers. But it's nice to not get surprised day after day after day with something really significant and important. And so I try to focus enough energy, apply enough discipline, put enough pressure on those couple of weeks so that all the scenes get a good looking at and I get a sense of how the actors work, because that's always very interesting. You know, some people are great in the first couple of takes; other people need a few to warm up. Some are sort of reluctant and procrastinators. Others, you know, hit the ground with a million ideas. Others—brilliant improvisationally—you know, some not. Important to know all that.

I learned that Russell [Crowe] was going to go through periods where he was really terrified dealing with his character—really terrified. And largely because there was so little research that he could tap into for the younger John Nash—no film, no tape. And to understand the disease, there are fifty different very significant symptoms that you could choose from. I said, "Let's choose a handful, you pick 'em, we'll pick 'em together." And we looked at documentary footage. I had done interviews with some people with schizophrenia myself, and of course we had lots of documentation and research. I said, "Let's go down the list and let's choose because later on in the movie, we're gonna reveal the fact that you were ill all along." The screenplay makes it seem like he's sort of absolutely a-okay, and then we find out. I didn't think that was playing fair. At the same time, you want to preserve the surprise. Russell agreed with me, but his instinct was to go a little too far too fast. So we began discussing it and modulating it, and we basically came up with five or six little behaviors that—my idea was he could play them as eccentricities during the first part of the movie, and you'd think, "Well, here's, here's the genius." You know, "Why does he do that?" And later, that gesture would be, you know, played with more intensity, and you'd begin to realize, "No, that's an effect of the disease." And so slowly but surely I had to keep working with Russell and sort of just being very patient about it with him as he explored. And if I got too judgmental too quickly, I could see him close up. And by the time we were shooting, we had a good program working.

Peter Weir, *The Truman Show*

Rehearsal? No, I don't at all. It doesn't all happen until everyone's in costume and props. The invented world, the magic world, it comes alive. I come alive. I can't draw chalk on the floor, that kind of thing. It seems sort of comical to me. I must say it's my own approach. I have trouble sometimes with actors. Jeff Bridges for example said to me, "Boy, I'm really nervous about that." For his sake, I did set up a rehearsal. But I said, rather than do the lines from the film, let's improvise the rehearsal. And we ended up really I think just laughing.

In terms of the friend, Noah Emmerich, I cast him firstly because he is such a warm personality. And then I said, "This is breaking your heart. You hate what you're doing. You grew up with Truman, as a kid." And we worked out back stories, always working out back stories, which I often did by the way with a more conventional film. I loved to talk about who they were and where they came from. We worked out that he'd been told at twelve the truth of his situation. He moved to the town when he was seven; he was told to make friends with that little boy over there. "Truman, he's your kind of boy; go and make friends with him." So at twelve, his parents said, "We want to have a talk with you, and sit down." He thought it was going to be about sex. He said, "I already know all about that, Dad." And he said, "No. This is, you know television?" "Sure." "Do you like television?" "Yes, I do." "Well, you're on it." And he said, "That day, I lost my innocence." With the parents telling him. So he had all that kind of back story. So there was emotion for him there.

Peter Weir, *Master and Commander: The Far Side of the World*

Mainly I make them improv. I could never have a hall and mark the floor out and that kind of thing. The sets, costumes, and so on are terribly important to me. But what I do like to do is to spend time with them before we shoot, dinner and sort of hanging out a bit. And I find a lot of things come up through that kind of not talking about the actual character and so on. And sometimes the conversation will lead back to the character. But I'll find myself therefore on set sometimes eventually saying, "Remember that when we had dinner you mentioned about your uncle or something? Didn't you say so-and-so?" Relevant to the scene. And then on the day, yeah, I just block it out in a very conventional way. I usually ask the crew to step out and leave us with the set. Generally talking about anything but the performance, just about the props or the layout of the room or how do you feel about sitting there and so on.

I think when the camera rolls for me, that's when it begins. And I don't like too much talk about it, about the sort of motivations and things. I like to work all the way around the thing, and then when it happens, I like to actually think it's sort of real.

With the boys, to create a sense of fun so it wouldn't seem sort of so inhibiting, it would be lots of ad-libs in London in a hall and we'd say this will be the cabin, these cushions here represent the hammock. And so I'd just make things up and say, "Let's do an improvisation where you're doing this, that, and the other," and get them laughing and get an enjoyment into it and they say, "Let's try that such and such a scene." And "Okay, the line sounds . . . you're kind of annunciating the line too clearly. What would you say in modern life? All right. Now let's just fiddle that a little bit and just say that, sounds more natural." So it was important for the feeling of fun and I wasn't going to be kind of a remote figure and that we would change anything that sounded false.

Peter Jackson, *The Lord of the Rings: The Fellowship of the Ring*

We rehearsed, but the rehearsal, I find is like, you know two or three weeks before we started shooting and I'd be having to have meeting here, meeting here, meeting with the DP [cinematographer], meeting with the costume designer, and, you know, I'd be rehearsing from like one till three, rehearsal. And that isn't much time to do anything, really. What we did rehearse in the time that we had was we essentially rehearsed our first week of shooting. Because I was very much aware that if we fell behind schedule in the first week, if we sort of got off the rails, the studio would probably go crazy because we were looking at a fifty- to sixty-week shoot. And didn't want anything to go wrong schedule-wise, you know, in the first week that would create some knee-jerk reaction from the studios. We went on locations where we were gonna shoot, and we just blocked through the scene, chose the camera angles, and we actually blocked through our first five days of shooting.

Peter Jackson, *The Lord of the Rings: The Return of the King*

We had our actors, the ones that needed were taught Elvish. There's a guy over here actually who's an Elvish scholar that we used. There are such things. And it was important for those seven people in the world that understand Elvish we wanted to get it right.

What we usually did at the very beginning of a movie is to have the cast, when they arrive, which is some weeks before we start shooting, to have them come around to our house. And we sort of have a read through of the script where there's not performance. It's not about the acting and the subtleties of the lines. It's simply just sitting there and reading. And I usually read all the descriptive passages and then the actors do their dialogue lines. And that's actually, to be quite honest, more of a benefit for the script than anything because we are realizing what's starting to work and what's not and we are just involving everybody in those discussions. That also is useful because it gives everybody an overview of what we're trying to achieve in certain scenes.

Clint Eastwood, *Mystic River*

The rhythm and speech, you can't help but take it on when you're in that neighborhood the way they use "Os" and "Bawston" and all that. The actors all went back on their own and visited with Dennis Lehane [the author of the book] and visited state troopers and visited various neighborhoods. They were all so enthusiastic about the material and the words to be said that they all did a tremendous amount of research.

Neil Jordan, *The Crying Game*

I find the most important moment is when you bring the actors onto the set. Because you know they've imagined the scene in their minds and you've constructed the set, where the door is or where all the pivotal, important objects are. That's when I rehearse.

Spike Jonze, *Being John Malkovich*

And when I say rehearse, I would never get the actors up on their feet because I think that you just want to fill up their petrol tank so that they can explode in front of the cameras. There is this terrible sense that, oh, don't do it now because you may not be able to—or you may get it as you want it, or as I want it—and then be trying to remember what you did, which is the worst possible thing you can do as an actor. It needs to be in the moment. I quite like them holding scripts. I quite like them not being in character yet. I just need to get the smell in my nostrils and then I'll leave them alone. I encourage them to invent their histories, invent their relationships, invent everything about them. Malkovich read the script and thought it was funny but I don't know if he ever thought it was ever going to get made or anything like that. When I met with him, he actually encouraged us to be meaner. Which was really liberating. On the set Malkovich was so relaxed about it that he freed everybody up to not like oh my God, like worrying about making fun of John Malkovich. He was so loose about it that he made everybody else on the set really comfortable with it.

Christopher Nolan, *Memento*

And as far as rehearsing with the actors and all the rest, I was amazed at how little preparation you get to do with actors on real movies. But the film I'd made before, I rehearsed with my actors for six months before I shot anything. We'd get together a couple of evenings a week and work through scenes. So I had actors who would know the film like a stage play and who had been through everything so many times, so that we could just find a location at the last minute.

Guy [Pearce] came up from Australia and we rehearsed for two weeks, which I've now discovered is actually quite a long period of time. For me it just seemed like nothing.

It seemed crazy. But what I also found is that the different actors required different approaches to rehearsal. And Guy is a very meticulous actor and wanted to really go through everything with me. And we went to one of the motels where we were gonna shoot scenes of him there and actually did that on location. And rehearsed and worked stuff through and tweaked the script and so forth. Carrie-Anne [Moss] was much happier to sort of save it for the day and just jump in and do it then.

Gus Van Sant, *Good Will Hunting*

I'm used to about two weeks of rehearsal time. It'll be say two hours in the morning and two hours in the afternoon, pretty short periods, where we're reading through it and acting out scenes and we're probably trying to get to know each other. Sometimes there's some going off the page and just doing the character without going from the script, just inventing things. Also during that time there's costuming and gearing up and getting ready. I'm totally in favor of keeping out of the way of the performance because you can definitely jump in there and screw things up. I always let the actors sort of come up with a bunch of things and maybe there's an editing process or advising process, but there's not a whole lot of monitoring the performance or the actor, unless they really want it. Sometimes an actor will really want you to sort of explain exactly what to do, and you can do that.

Sofia Coppola, *Lost in Translation*

We didn't have time to rehearse. I like to rehearse, but the actors just came a few days before shooting so we were kind of figuring it out as we went. But we shot the movie as much in order as we could so it's pretty in continuity. So the actors were getting to know each other and the characters and then when they were supposed to be closer, we had already spent time together. So I think that was helpful.

Martin Scorsese, *Gangs of New York*

A lot of the films I've made are urban and people are in kitchens or bars or in church or in cars and that sort of thing, and we were able to write certain dialogue sometimes improvising with the actors, myself, and with the writers. Recording it on audiotape about six times, then taking it home, getting it transcribed, and then looking at all the transcripts and then building the escalation of the scene 'cause it's about escalation. And then writing up a new scene and having the actors work on that. I don't have any experience in theater. So ultimately, once you read the scenes in a hotel room, then it would be always best to take it to location and work it out in location and I'll usually tell actors at a certain point, "Here I'm going to want to do this. Do you think you could come here?" But invariably I really try to be surprised by the actors. I want to be the audience, and sometimes I've forgot that I've put screen directions in there and I see them do something, say, "That's interesting." And they say, "It was in the script." I say, "No. How did that happen? Who's been reading the script?" It's an old joke. But the idea of trying anything—because there's no mistakes in a rehearsal, in a sense. Try it, try it, try it. What was interesting for me with *Gangs* that we kept rewriting scenes and so the rehearsal really became about costuming and it became about body language. It's about proximity, how close a person is to you, because immediately that's hostile. The sets themselves became a little town in a way. And it became more like a painting, a kind of living painting, where Daniel [Day-Lewis] would move a certain way, Leo [DiCaprio] had his certain moves, Cameron [Diaz], all of them and they sort of inhabited these old engravings in a way. And a lot of the scenes were in bars or were in theaters and that sort of thing, so I could actually rehearse or read the lines upstairs in a dressing room, but it really was a matter of sitting on the set, smelling the wood, the way the costumes felt, as if they stepped out of time.

Martin Scorsese, *The Aviator*

For the cast, I screened *His Girl Friday* in 35mm so they get a sense of the nature of the rapid-fire dialogue of the period. I mean, journalists of the period, they didn't have video cameras. They had to write down what you said. They had to ask the questions fast. They had to get in there fast. And getting a picture then, they had to get a bulb in there. The bulb had to be pushed out. Somebody broke it. It really was a process. So they had to talk quickly. And also the sense of body language. So watching *His Girl Friday* was a key. *His Girl Friday* and a number of other films, *Mystery of the Wax Museum*. The wisecracking reporters that I guess at the time was more like Walter Winchell. For Cate Blanchett I screened every one of Katharine Hepburn's films in 35mm from *A Bill of Divorcement*, her first film, up through *Philadelphia Story* because that's where you sort of leave her in a way. That means, in order, wherever she was, including the ones that weren't that successful, *Spitfire* or *Sylvia Scarlett*, which is a remarkable film, sort of invoking the work of George Cukor to a certain extent with the actors and also later on some interviews that Dick Cavett did of Katharine Hepburn to get a sense of the strength and yet the vulnerability behind it. We hardly talked very much about it. I just showed her these films.

Gary Ross, *Seabiscuit*

The rehearsal process before I shoot is as much for me as it is for the actors. It's about finding certain intentions that I can remember on the day. So I'll play with it. Especially as the writer, you can get locked into kind of the metronome of the rhythm in your head and you have to yank yourself out of that. And so you have to investigate different alternatives and different motivations and different meanings for the scene or nuances there. And for me the rehearsal process is discovering all those shades and I'll make notes in my script so that on the day, when I'm less clearheaded and I have so many more things to worry about, I have at least a document where I can go back to what the original performance intentions were.

CUT TO
NASH'S POV
PARCHER
WIDE ANGLE

"ROSEN? THAT QUACK."

137-7

CUT TO
NASH

"RAND HAS NO RECORD
OF YOU"

137-8

HIGH ANGLE
PAST LIGHT BULB
NOTE: FLICKERING LIGHT

"I'M SORRY YOU HAD TO
GO THROUGH THIS"

137-9

PAN WITH
PARCHER

"YOUR WIFE"

137-10

Storyboard for A Beautiful Mind *(Courtesy of Universal Studios Licensing LLLP and Ron Howard.)*

CHICAGO SC. 29   STORYBOARD—R.HOBBS
DIR—R.MARSHALL

CHICAGO SC. 29   STORYBOARD—R.HOBBS
DIR—R.MARSHALL

IC) PUSH INTO CAM   BACK OF PADDY WAGON

3) FLASH GOES OFF

2) OTS ON REPORTER CAR PULLING UP — 'A' TRAIN B/G

3A) ROXIE STRIKES A POSE

2A) THEY GET OUT & RUN FWD   ②

3B) D.A. PUSHES HER INTO WAGON   ③

Storyboards for Chicago. *(Courtesy of Miramax Films and Rob Marshall.)*

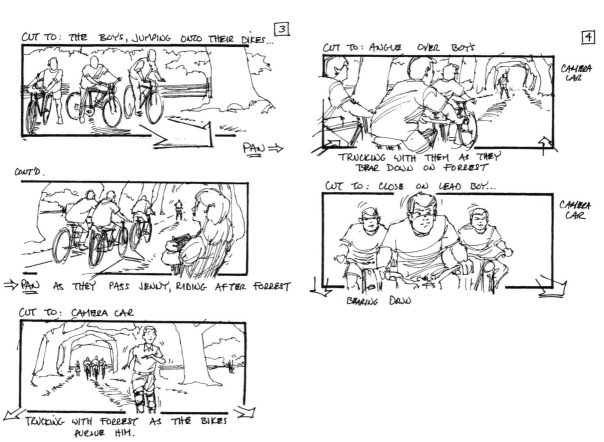

Forrest Gump *storyboard sequence of young Gump running away (Courtesy of Paramount Pictures and Robert Zemeckis.)*

CUT TO:

ANGLE ON FORREST'S LEGS, BRACES PUMPING FURIOUSLY...

→ TRUCK W/ FORREST

cont'd

... SO FAST THAT THEY EXPLODE OFF OF HIS LEGS.

cont'd

SHOT WIDENS... AS FORREST SPEEDS UP... FREE OF HIS BRACES

cont'd

AND CAMERA STOPS AND PANS AS FORREST RUNS AWAY...

cont'd

AS THE BOY'S RACE INTO FRAME

Forrest Gump *storyboard (continued)*

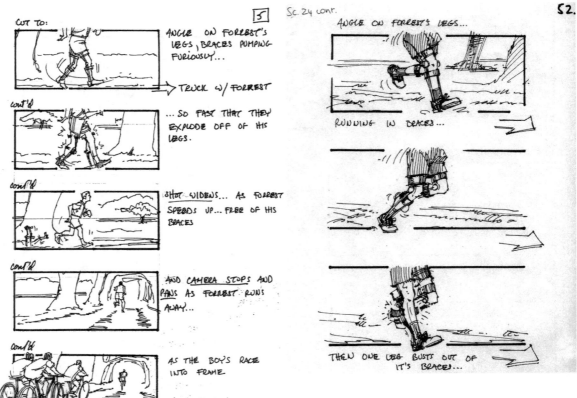

ANGLE ON FORREST'S LEGS...

RUNNING IN BRACES...

THEN ONE LEG BUSTS OUT OF IT'S BRACES...

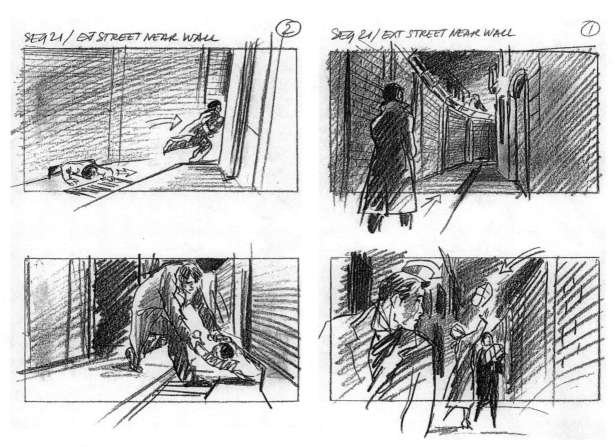

Storyboard designs from The Pianist *(Courtesy of Universal Studios Licensing LLLP and Roman Polanski.)*

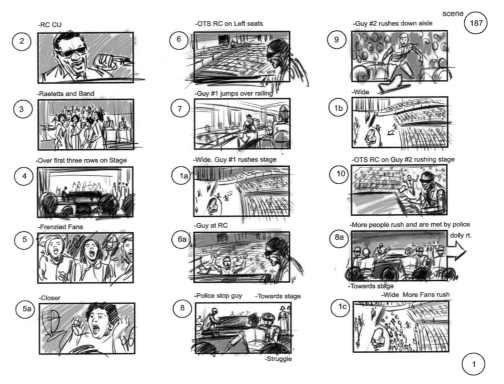

Storyboard for "Unchain My Heart" sequence from Ray (Courtesy of Universal Studios Licensing LLLP, Taylor Hackford, and Ray Prado.)

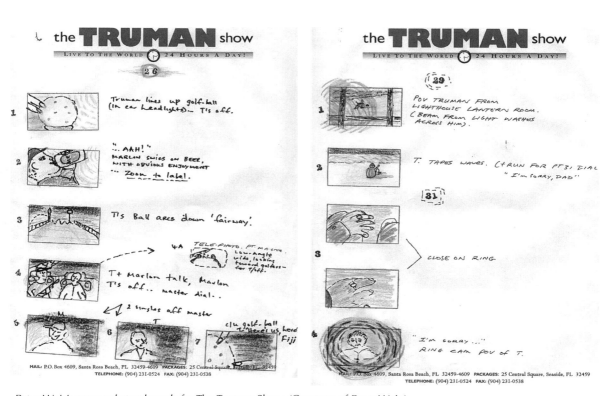

Peter Weir's personal storyboards for The Truman Show *(Courtesy of Peter Weir.)*

92 FIRE!   4

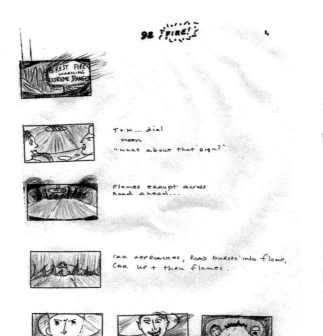

T+M ... dial
MERYL
"what about that sign?"

Flames errupt across
road ahead...

CAR APPROACHES, ROAD bursts into flame,
CAR up + thru flames.

MASTER c.us thru fire   2 shot drive thru fire.

Peter Weir's personal storyboards (continued)

180

A.
CAM
①
B.

2 waves of searchers converge —
Rear wave followed by searchlight
mounted on vehicle..
(Looking East toward Modica)

Searchers from 1st wave,
backlit by mounted Searchlight.
(plus other cuts – clu's etc on
subsequent takes).

②

Wide-angle, tracking (vehicle)
Close on Pluto, snarling + growling
into camera.
(Pluto + Spencer come from Barrymore Place
group...).

③

Left-wing of Barrymore Place group
appear – pan them to centre to
join group from Rear + Right

Imperceptable zoom back
as group marches toward camera.

• 8 •

Production: The Shoot

Gus Van Sant, *Good Will Hunting*

*Y*ou are channeling everybody's energy, the cinematographer's, the actors', everyone else involved in the production coming together and kind of trying to channel something to make the scene come alive.

I'd often find out that you'd put the cameras say, in point A, and since you couldn't stand in point A, you'd have to stand over here. But during the shooting, you'd realize that point B was a better angle! Then, you'd move the camera over to point B. It was really frustrating. Then you'd realize that, okay, you have this side and that side and you're sort of starting to create like a philosophy of that particular scene, which you're drawing from sort of a history of all kinds of things: storyboards that you've done in the past, films you've seen. There's sort of a dictionary you've built up in your head by the time you've done three or four films that you start to be able to think on the set pretty fast. And you can do pretty tricky things, even though you are just thinking them up on the set.

I think for me, it's mainly keeping everybody comfortable, very comfortable, where they can make a mistake and it's okay to try something new, or don't be afraid to goof because you can always roll again. And once everybody's really comfortable, the different styles and the different experiences kind of equal out and then people can have fun together. I like to do just a couple takes if it's appropriate, depending on the actor.

There's the curious thing of the mojo being right the day that's kind of a hard one because from the first say week or two weeks of shooting a film, hopefully you've gotten it, you've gotten the mojo right each day and you sort of brought something in focus in each scene. And by the third or fourth week, you have to match yourself because you've done this day in and day out. And a Monday or Tuesday or Wednesday or Friday, there will be a scene, it could be a small scene, and there's a sort of helpless feeling that the director has because they know they have to once again bring all the forces that they had on all the other scenes together and you just try and do it.

The least experienced actor on *Good Will Hunting* was Tom [John Mighton], who was the assistant to Lambeau, and probably one of the most experienced actors was Stellan Skarsgård, he was playing Lambeau, so they were really interesting, and they were very comfortable playing across from each other. Tom, I think, had never been in a play or a movie or anything. He was a real mathematician, though, so he sort of had this whole presence that he brought to the screen. He could ad-lib, he could do all these great things, and Stellan would just be amazed.

163

Sam Mendes, *American Beauty*

It's so difficult talking about working with actors because I think one of the things you learn very quickly in the theater is you've got to treat everybody completely differently, depending on what they want and how they want to work on a role. Kevin [Spacey] wants to joke and be on his mobile phone; he doesn't want it to be serious. And you call action and he's like turning on a laser beam. But somebody like Chris Cooper, he wants to be in total silence. Or Annette [Bening] will be listening to her Walkman for fifteen minutes quietly in a corner. And your job is to bring them to the same point at the same time. And there are as many ways of directing actors as there are actors. In a way, you're very, very secretly trying to get people to bring themselves to the table, parts of themselves that they wouldn't have exposed before. But really a lot of it is just creating an atmosphere in an environment where people are free to make fools of themselves and be human and allow themselves to be vulnerable. You have to keep going until you get what you want out of that particular actor, and you have to have the skill to know when to say what you need to say. And I think that that's something that comes with experience and instinct. I really do, I think it's an instinctive thing. One little sentence can be the key. Sometimes there's a way inwards through something that's very external. So you feel an actor's gesticulating too much. Their energy's wrong. It's not coming from their face. You don't say, "Your energy's not coming from your face; you're gesticulating too much." You might just say, "Can you just hold the knife and fork in the shot, please," and it comes out of their face. I don't want them to think with their outside eye at all. I want them to be simply thinking with their inner eye.

A lot of my job with Kevin was to take away Kevin's outside eye. Because his sense of self-censorship and his awareness of what he's doing is so extreme. I mean, if it's the raising of a right eyebrow. He's aware of everything his face and his body is doing. A lot of what you see on film is quite late takes when he was messing around.

Spike Jonze, *Being John Malkovich*

I'd ask all the actors how they liked to be directed. I asked other directors. Cameron Crowe told me something, I talked to him, and he told me, when you're on the set, right after you say, "Cut," just make a connection with your actors and make sure they get the information, they know you're there with them, and that that is the most important relationship on the set.

M. Night Shyamalan, *The Sixth Sense*

I try to be very good cop, better cop. And the good thing is there's a real desire to please me. For example, we had that car scene that we did, and everyone was aware that was our big emotional moment in the movie, the car scene with the mom and the kid. So we get to the shoot day and this is about three-quarters into the shooting of the movie, and they shoot the scene and they're way too jacked up, like really emotional from the first line, and I say, "We've got to go somewhere; let's not start at the finish line here." So Haley [Joel Osment] was up first, which we generally did—have him blow it out first—and he did it. And he was just way too hot from the beginning, emotional from the beginning. I had to take him out and say, "Relax, let's just go. Don't worry about the ending and don't worry about crying and all that stuff." And he did it again, too hot, too hot. And so for the only time in the movie, I had to piece it together line by line, where I'd go to my script and I'd go, got these three, got these three, got these three, we've done the scene. And so I turned it around and Toni [Collette] has blown it out now, four times, just exquisitely and we get around [to shoot her angle] and she's burnt. And I had to remind her again where the character was, the subtext. And I walked away and I go, "All right, great, check the gate [a term used to ensure that there are no problems inside the camera]. Let's go." And so I'm walking away and I get about fifty feet and the first AD [assistant director] comes running over and grabs me and he goes, "Gotta come back to the car quick." And so I come back to the car. They're both crying their eyes out because they think they failed me in the big moment. And I said, "Oh my God." I opened the door, and I said, "I promise you, I'm not disappointed. I promise you we did not leave this scene without it being perfect. It's going to be the best scene in the movie. Trust me. Do you trust me?" With Bruce [Willis], in particular, his acting style he likes to actually take the piss out of you a little bit. In a kind of way. So he'll be like joking with this girl over here and making fun of this person. And meanwhile I see his eyes glazing over. He's getting emotional. And a lot of times he'd direct it at me, and it took me like the first four days to get that this is his thing, you know? Where he would kind of bust me in front of the set. In a kind of way so the attention was on me and he's getting ready, and he's getting his thing up. And what I did was—I just did what I normally do in situations like that—I gave it back to him. So he'd give me piss and be like, yeah, this is going to be a good scene; you're going to be directing commercials after this. And like everybody on the set would get quiet and I'd go, "[cough] *Hudson Hawk* [a failed movie that Bruce Willis played in]." And there would be equality, you know?

Andrew Davis, *The Fugitive*

The real challenge for me was to keep the balance between what Tommy [Lee Jones] had to work with and what Harrison [Ford] had to work with, which is really the much more difficult part. Harrison had nobody to talk to. He was left alone. He had to play everything on his face, which is really difficult acting. Trying to create the balance between these two characters.

Tommy Lee Jones was very concerned about shooting a gun in a public place as a U.S. marshal probably would not do. And rightfully so, he was concerned about it being irresponsible. And yet dramatically for the film and the kind of entertainment that that gave us, we went ahead and did it anyway.

If it involved stunts or anything dangerous, it was all very storyboarded and very exacting. But in terms of things that just felt like we needed to do something, for example, the end of the sequence in City Hall where Harrison runs into the parade, we met Mayor Daly before we started shooting, and I realized the parade was coming; and so this opportunity became available to shoot the actual parade, and we basically winged it. We had some hidden cameras, and we had a great Steadicam operator [a camera rig that allows the operator to move freely], and we prepared it, but it needed that kind of spontaneous, "anything could happen" quality to make it be believable.

There were no parts for Joe Pantoliano. But Tommy needed somebody to play with, a really solid actor to improvise with, and to be the straight man to. So I said to Joey, "Listen, you're gonna have to make up all your own stuff." He created that part and gave great life to that group of marshals, and they hung out together.

We started shooting with Harrison's beard, for continuity. And we started in jail; then we went into his apartment. And we had enough for a forty-minute movie on the night of the fund-raiser, and the murder, knowing that we were never going to use it in continuity, knowing that it would be long and flaccid. But the reason for doing that was to be able to keep the memory of his wife alive through the whole movie. To keep that kind of emotional pulse alive.

We built a set piece on top of a two-hundred-foot dam that was about twelve feet long, and we created the actual scene where Harrison turns around, looks down, and we were two hundred feet up, wired on our ankles. It was freezing, it was blowing, very dangerous. And we took a couple articulated dummies and threw them over the camera. We dropped a couple out of some helicopters, and somehow magically it worked.

Usually the first day of shooting is easy because you've done so much planning. The fifth day, forget it: you don't know what you're doing. But the first day, everybody's been so wired, and the shot lists, and going to bed early.

Tom Mack was the assistant director, and he is a great guy. This guy knows how to take two hundred extras and set them into a scene and give them life and work with his assistants to make it work depending on what the details are, of propping people and dressing people and lighting the set. It takes a lot of energy to get what you need in front of the camera.

We were actually writing the script, staging it, rehearsing it, and shooting it all at once. I was very concerned we would have a ten-minute trial sequence in the movie and it would be very boring in the first reel. One of the two actors with Harrison is a sergeant in the Chicago department; the other is an actor who's had an interesting background with the police himself, and so both of them have a certain reality to what's going on. Harrison was wise enough to say to me, "Andy, don't tell me the questions. Just let them interrogate me. I don't want to know what they're going to ask me." And so it was totally improvised. We had a Steadicam and another camera working, or maybe two cameras, and we would do the scene a couple times, and then we would revise the questions a little bit. And it was the end of a very long day, and I said, "Harrison, great, we're done." And I was just going to stick around and shoot a couple cuts of the cops talking. And Harrison was on his way to his car to leave, and he said, "What the hell are they doing up there?" And the next thing he was back, sitting next to the camera, playing off-screen for these guys. And that's the kind of actor he is. And I think somebody said to me, "What are you shooting those extras for? Why are you doing coverage on those guys?" And it was only after they saw the film that they understood that you needed these two cops to indict this guy, and it was their mistaken judgment that caused him to be sent down the river.

I shoot two cameras all the time. I make it very, very difficult for the sound man. Who, in spite of all of his complaining, has been nominated [for an Academy Award] twice now for the last two films. But basically, because of the improvising we do, it's very important to me to be able to have two sizes of the same performance so I can get in and out, to have cutaways of other people reacting to things. The Steadicam operator is a real artist. I don't think I could live without this type of talent and the equipment. It's given the ability to be fluid and to not have to do so much coverage and cutting. So we always had three cameras available to us to shoot at any time.

It's better to try to find a camera position or move that takes you in one piece, one fell swoop, right past and you're into it. And it was important for me to keep the camera moving, whether it be cutting or panning or actually moving, in order to keep this search. There's a lot of point-of-view shots in this movie. It's Harrison looking, people looking for Harrison. And to make you feel like you're in the middle of the movie, rather than standing back and observing it.

I just think that you can get more out of yourself and the people who are there contributing if you open it up and say, "What if?" Come with an idea. There are some days on this movie that I was lucky to know in my head what the one-liner was on the strip board [the schedule of what is to be shot day by day]. "Harrison rents an apartment," that was what I had to do. And the details of how people spoke to each other, it was all worked out in the basement, as the room was being lit. Or as this woman, who had never been in a movie, got past being with Harrison Ford and started talking. She came in; she was chewing gum. And I didn't tell her to take the gum out of her mouth. And that was something I never would have thought of. And so those kind of things make it real.

Did I know exactly how I was going to shoot a sequence? No, I didn't. We, for example, had to experiment to see what kind of rig we could use that would allow us to dolly fast enough for Tommy and Harrison to run full speed, and still keep in front of them and turn corners. So between the grip [crew member who moves equipment]

Andrew Davis on the set of The Fugitive. *(The Fugitive © Warner Bros.,
a division of Time Warner Entertainment Company L.P. All rights reserved.)*

and the Steadicam operator, we actually put the Steadicam on a dolly and used it that way. At the end of the movie, when everybody left, we had some short ends [unused negative] left, and I took some shots of the city off my balcony while everybody was going home. And those are some of the cutaways of Jeroen Krabbé looking down as Harrison's pushing him over.

Steven Soderbergh, *Erin Brockovich* and *Traffic*

When you're an actor, you have to feign that innocence about your destiny all day long and you have to do it out of sequence. And it's really hard. And so the people that do it well I have enormous respect for. So I'm totally performance driven.

It never gets any easier is the problem, at least in my experience. It's just you have to believe that the parachute will open. And it only opens after you've reconciled to hitting the ground.

I think it's very important to hang out with the crew at the bar—I'm only being partially facetious—just to sort of get a temperature of what's happening. I try and read the script a lot. And you'd be surprised how often you don't and you find yourself drifting off compass a degree or two a day. And two weeks later you're somewhere else. At times I'll just go back and read again just make sure that I haven't lost sight of what enthused me at the beginning when I first got attached to the idea.

What's interesting in working with someone like Benicio [Del Toro], for instance, is—which I encourage—is you never know quite what's going to happen. I mean, the script had him saying, "I don't want to go there." But it didn't go as far as he went. It didn't get as tense, and Benicio just said, "Well, if I thought it wasn't safe, I'd get out," you know, "and they've got to stop me. If those guys don't convince me to not get out of the car, I'm just going to get out." I mean, I said, "Great." And it added something, you know?

Benicio had come up with the idea of the cut to the pool. Benicio said, "Well, I don't know. I mean, if I didn't want to be recorded, I think I'd go to a swimming pool." And I thought, "Oh, what a great cut."

I've reshot on every film I've made, including *sex, lies, and videotape*. The good news is I've never gone over budget, so the good news is, I've always had money left over. And I always go back and say, "That's gotta be better; it's just not working." Especially when you're talking about the end of the movie, which is really the only thing people walk out of the theater with. I'm very concerned that things are landing correctly. As soon as you say the word *reshoot*, the actors, you know, the blood drains from their face. But I think most people like the opportunity to go back and try it again.

Well, the reason I decided to shoot [Soderbergh is credited as the cinematographer] *Traffic* myself was I just wanted to try some things and push certain ideas a little and didn't really have the time to get into discussions about a lot of them. And that's not a knock; it's just that even [James] Planette, my gaffer, would often come over and say, "Ah, you realize the windows are twelve stops overexposed." I'd go, "Yeah, I know. Let's go." And you know I don't have to worry about being hired.

Here's the good thing about having all of the dinners with actors and stuff is you can go up and go, "Uh, faster." And they go . . . okay. That's the benefit of building up this bond beforehand, is you get in, you can go up and say, um, "FFB," which

Steven Soderbergh on the set of Traffic. *(*Traffic *courtesy of Universal Studios Licensing LLLP.)*

means faster, funnier, better. And then, they go, "No problem." And that's that. I don't have time for stuff that has nothing to do with the work. I just don't. You know? And life's too short and work's too hard and the days are long, and if somebody's not going to just be with the program, then I, you know, I really don't have time for them.

I did a lot with multiple cameras on *Traffic* and a lot on *Erin*, almost constantly, and *The Limey*. And *Out of Sight*. On *Traffic* I'd shoot a wide shot with, you know, a 35mm [lens] and a close-up with a hundred at the same time, and that was just the aesthetic of that thing. I'd be on A camera and this fantastic operator on the other camera, Gary Jay, who I'd worked with before. Extraordinary. And I'd put him on the long lens because he's really gifted.

We shot *Traffic* in fifty-two days. It was like 1,650 setups [different camera positions]; on a movie like that, we had a couple of fifty set-up days. But that's rare.

Ron Howard, *A Beautiful Mind*

It was the most difficult movie I've ever made. There's a very important scene in the . . . the bedroom between John and Alicia Nash, where she is making this sort of dangerous decision to not to hospitalize him, but instead support him and protect him. And there was a version of it written and the scene had been my idea to begin with because I wanted to represent an even larger idea of that sort that had occurred in the real story between John and Alicia Nash. I wanted to work on this scene. It just wasn't quite right. And we began talking about the true story. We began talking about what we had learned. And at that moment Jennifer Connelly and Russell Crowe were interacting very well, very creatively, and we were trying out a lot of different ideas, and I was throwing out ideas, and one moment, Russell literally dropped to his knee and put his hand on my chest, and suddenly, he was becoming Jennifer. And I had this line about "I need to believe," but it was always awkward, and Russell sort of did it. And it turned the whole scene around. Now it got completely rewritten, completely changed. I remember ending that meeting and thinking to myself, "This is what I love to do." I was at the center of sort of a creative swirl. And when we shot it, in fact, it was the easiest scene we shot in the whole picture.

At one point Russell said, "I'm gonna just keep—instead of trying to hit the point—it's gonna be easier for me if we run a little series of takes. I don't need a lot of 'em, and let me play." And having directed a lot of really strong improvisational actors in comedies, this idea didn't scare me at all. It was freaking other people out a little bit, because they'd see Russell, and he'd be too big in a take. And I'd be saying, "Oh, great, great. Okay, let's try another." And Russell basically said, "Let me play, and you find the truth in it." And we did shoot in sequence. And so we could keep developing these things more or less in order, which was a huge advantage in this particular case, because it was really about building nuance upon nuance then undoing it, and then building it up again.

James Cameron, *Titanic*

I was dealing with a large number of actors, a lot of ensemble scenes where everybody was gonna be watching each other work. I made a decision early on to just say to everybody going in, "We're gonna shoot a lot of takes. So you got lots of room to figure out . . . if we've got it we'll move on." But we gave everybody permission to explore, to screw up, to find different ways of doing the scene on film in case there is that lucky accident early on that is something that you could not have predicted. Fortunately for me and my working process, Kate [Winslet] and Leo [DiCaprio] especially were very much the way I like to work, where they just get into the scene and just work and start playing off of it. Really take six was always better than take five, and take seven was always better than take six. In fact, we were doing Leo's, Jack's death scene, and I had done a lot on him and we both felt really happy with it. And I turned around on Kate, and Leo was giving Kate what she needed and doing better than when he'd been on camera! I said, "Leo, you son of a bitch, you're better off camera than you were on camera!" He says, "I know, I'm always better off camera!" And Kate laughs, and then Leo says, "And so are you!!" When Kate finished that scene, she went off and cried for an hour in the arms of the makeup artist who was kind of her confidant on the set. Just to come down from the emotion of having done the scene and keeping it at that peak for so long. It's not a question of the director pulling the plug. It's getting the actors to stop once they've got the bit in their teeth. Because they feel that they are closing in on something. They don't want to stop. And I like working with actors like that. I feel like we don't want to leave that space. We've spent all these months, and in my case maybe two years, to get to that moment, hours to light it, all this preparation, months to build the set and all the costumes and everything, to get to that moment, and to walk away from it without it being the best that everybody there can do is foolish.

The way I approached all the scenes on the film, I worked with a thing that my brother invented, which is a video viewfinder system. It sends a video picture to the monitor station, so I can actually kind of line up the shots by holding the actual lens that we're going to use for the scene or for the shot. But I don't go right to that. What I like to do is get the actors into the space and get some lights on. The lighting especially on the interiors of the ship was primarily done, or was meant to look, all "sourcey" [realistic] from the practical fixtures and so then I ask the crew to step out of the way and the actors are like in sweats and stuff, and on a particular scene [at the table scene] we might spend an hour and a half just figuring out who was sitting where and what are the currents. The dynamic of the scene changed the seating around a lot. We had to play it; we had to see what it meant to everybody. And then once we had that sort of roughed in, we started figuring out the angles. I decided to move the camera in virtually every shot of the film and to impose a kind of sort of semimodern style on 1912. I wanted to give it a vitality and a life and an energy. When you start moving the camera, it starts to get in the way from an editing standpoint, so I had to figure out when in the moving master [a shot that photographs the whole scene] exact camera cutting, what lines I wanted when I was likely to be wide, when I was likely to be in close, and make a lot of those decisions before the fact. And sometimes I would even say, "Okay, I wanna do a couple of different versions of this. One where the moves start a few lines earlier, just in case, because I'm thinking editorially I might come off him, but I might wait till she answers." I'm thinking editing-wise as I'm shooting. So you let them run with the line for a while, and if you don't see anything that you like better, and this is a subjective area, I mean, sometimes your own preconception is so in place, but I try to be very open like that, and if the actors can come up with a better way to say the words, then give them the space.

Leo and I were talking about a scene the night before. It was one of those rare occasions where we actually did think we got a big thing coming up tomorrow, let's sit and talk about it. I'd done a little rewriting on that scene, and Leo said, "I'd like to try something to make contact with Cal, you know, throw him something or something like that." I said, "Let's have him smoking a cigarette," and he said, "Yeah, I could throw him some matches, because I was smoking in an earlier scene and it came out of that." And then the question is, Okay, now where are we going to do it? And then finding the right line to put that exclamation point at the end of. And I think it landed in the right spot, but that was a collaborative effort. Leo is the kind of guy that has a lot of ideas and I like that. You know, some actors have a few ideas and they really hold onto them. It's like "If you don't use it, then you don't love me." But I think the actors that I feel most comfortable with are the ones that have a lot of ideas and just spew them out there, and they are gifts, and if you want to use them, use them, and if you don't, don't.

James L. Brooks, *As Good As It Gets*

I tend to have insomnia when I'm shooting.

On a lot of days, you say, we are all here to serve the actors, and that's your message to the crew. I think the most exciting day is when you change your mind and something totally different happens. *As Good As It Gets* there were two examples: one was the hospital scene, where Greg Kinnear was beaten up and scarred. There were a few jokes in that scene I thought to relieve the tension with the idea to play it almost farcically and we were able to take the scene in a new direction and have pure fun. I

James Cameron on the set of Titanic. *(Still from* Titanic *© 1997 courtesy of Twentieth Century Fox and Paramount Pictures Corporation. All rights reserved.)*

do, do a lot of takes. The other one: there was a letter in the script that Helen Hunt's character wrote to Jack Nicholson's character. Helen said, "I'd like to know what was in the letter." And then I wrote the letter. And I wrote a lot of pages about what she wrote; it was sort of fun. And then she handwrote everything I typed. So now he had this great prop. He had twenty pages of this prop and it was never intended for her to read the letter. And it was a very problematic scene from the story point of view for me. And then, it's just one of the great days where—"What if you read the letter to him?"—and that became the solution to the scene. I was always worried about these three people going to Baltimore. How do we justify it. How do we get there? How do we believe it? And somehow that letter got me over a huge hump.

What you are asking the actors to do is to lose self-consciousness. It's a very difficult thing to do. Sometimes you're asking them to risk being bad, which is the hardest thing for anybody to do. Stretching, testing your limits, it's a very scary place to be.

But I think the big responsibility you have is—let's move on. "Let's move on" should be your pledge to the actors that you really have it. That's what that should mean.

The last scene in this picture we had to do within the first days of shooting, and it was ludicrous that we're out there doing the last scenes in the picture, especially for somebody like me, because I tend to be linear in my thinking. We did it and there was a moment there, because he wasn't supposed to kiss the girl, and I said in the middle of the take, "Kiss her." It was a good kiss and we went home, and I don't know how many months later, the scene wasn't right, because it was glib with that kiss. And it wasn't played correctly. There was too much emotion in it. It was a cranky kind of scene and it was based on stuff that I believed in when I was writing it. And that didn't turn out to be true. And we went back and the performance became simpler, and we solved some choreography. And that was an example of not getting it right and going back.

The worst moment was one day when it just wasn't happening and it was serious, it's embarrassing and it's frustrating to the actors out there and the director's saying, "Do it again," and that's some indication that he didn't do it right. I think the great thing about Jack is his willingness to humble himself. I had to send the crew home and I was a little behind schedule. I'd never done it before, and I hope I never have to do it again, but suddenly it was just the two of us. And we talked for four hours. And Jack can remember what we said and I can't, because I felt it was just that we gave ourselves the time. And we just sent everybody away and it was just a matter of respect, respect for the process, that we're not machines.

Rob Reiner, *A Few Good Men*

Jack Nicholson has one of the biggest laughs in the picture, when he says "Hi, Danny, how is your old man?" and he [Tom Cruise] says, "He passed away seven years ago." And then you cut to Jack and he says, "Don't I feel like the fuckin' asshole," and he didn't get it right at all. I'm one of these guys that gives line readings. Most guys don't do [that], they hate it, actors hate it. I find that, if you don't give them a bad line reading, most actors will take it and then make it their own anyway. That's the easiest way to communicate. I would say to him, "Jack, what you gotta do is hold the smile. Hold the smile in your face. Let the line break the attitude." He would always break the attitude, when he heard that the guy passed away. I said, "Your attitude is what's delivering the line. You have to let the line deliver the attitude, rather then having your attitude drop, because then you've already delivered the line; the line then is anticlimactic." And he finally got it. He did it, and it's right.

I do have a cinematographer come into the rehearsal period after I've worked a little bit with the actors, so at least he gets a sense of where people are going to be moving. At that point, I'll make a shot list up for the day. I'll sit with the script supervisor and I'll tell her I want all these shots and she writes every one of them down, and then as you go along, as you're working the scene, sometimes another shot will make itself known to you.

I don't like a lot of takes because that's what the rehearsal period was for—to know what we're doing. And then we're out there, and let's just go for it. I mean obviously if it doesn't work, then you got to do it over, but I rarely see double digits on the slate [the clapboard used to mark the number of each take to synchronize picture and sound].

I'll help actors out, I mean, some actors, like Kathy Bates. She said, "Tell me how you want me to do it," and I'd act it out for her. Or Tom would say the same thing, "What do you want me to do and I'll do it." And I would just act it out for them. I'll show them. It's not a great way to do it, if you can't act, but I can act so it's a tool that I can use to communicate when I want and then I say, "You've got to obviously make it yours and do it the way you would do it."

I don't stage for the camera—I let the actors do what they do, and then I photograph that rather than determine that this is the way I want the camera to move and I want to place the actors in it. You go in there and you rehearse the scene. Once the cameraman and all the key department heads look at that, send the actors off to get made up and all, and then you do your work and go about the lighting and try to avoid the craft service table [where food is served] as best you can! Because it's very dangerous if you start in early in the morning; I could be a hundred pounds heavier by the end of the picture and I have a problem with that!

Anybody who's been with a director during the making of a film and had a relationship or marriage, they get a lot of gold stars, because it's all consuming. You're working twelve- to fourteen-hour days, every day, and you basically don't have time for anything except to have dinner, go to sleep, and then get up the next day. And I always tell the people the toughest thing about directing is the physical part of it. Get as much rest as you can and sit down as much as you can during the course of the day.

Michael Mann, *The Insider*

Wigand was an obsessive-compulsive, very dystonic, very arrhythmic, and I wanted to bring you into his perception. So there's a lot of use of negative space and sometimes, if you just move it right, then I am the person. And you don't know it until the camera is on your shoulder and you're looking through the viewfinder and you make that slightest shift and you just, you match your footsteps to his, and somehow I'm with him, I'm him. I can't explain it any other way than that, except it's an emotional state that as a director you just fall into it. Of course, I'm falling into it, I'm shooting it, then the audience is going to be there as well.

I have my own real detailed analysis of what the scene is supposed to do, And that's what I'm reminding myself of, and some options I want. So I do a lot of prep. And I prefer doing it the night before rather than getting up in the morning.

It's visual, it's language, it's this character. If Al [Pacino] is going to be aggressive in a Japanese restaurant because he explodes, there's different ways he can explode. What are the different ways I want him to explode? We'll get in there and do a little blocking, block a few moves, and maybe run the lines once or something like that. But the way I'm shooting, shooting in this direction, I don't shoot traditional coverage. I don't shoot masters and automatically go into close-ups. I'll probably double up cameras and have a wide shot from here and also in a tighter lens, because I usually work with two, sometimes three, cameras simultaneously. I like to maintain the actors' concentration, so I don't like a noisy set. The best days go something like this: The blocking happened the night before. We determined the first setup. I walk through it with everybody; then we wrap the unit. We come back the next morning and we walk right on. I bring them in from their motor homes and we just go right to work, start shooting.

There's a scene in the hotel room where Jeffrey and Lowell meet for the very first

Michael Mann on the set of The Insider. *(*The Insider *courtesy of Touchstone Pictures. All rights reserved.)*

time, and I wanted to use very bright shafts of light as if they had the power of feeling like an interrogation. They had to feel absolutely natural; all the camera work it had to feel like a fortuitous accident. And so there's kind of a conspiracy worked out between myself, the production designer, the set decorator, and Dante [Spinotti, the cameraman] that the chair is very awkwardly placed in the room, too awkwardly removed from the table, and Pacino is back on the sofa, just immobile like a stone and he's one and a half stops underexposed, and at a key point Jeffrey revealed a bunch of stuff and he says, "That's as far as I go," and Al leans forward and says, "As far as you go where?" And he leans forward into being a stop and a half overexposed and his black eyes, which are like lasers, just are riveting.

We shot the whole Japanese restaurant scene with traditional eye lines. With Jeffrey on the left and Al on the right. And when we had finished the scene and we were about to wrap, I looked at it and it suddenly occurred to me that if I could cut into these—switch screen direction totally—it would be kind of brutally precise, perpendicular to the two actors and just go back and forth between these two, that it would give a punctuation that would signal the conflict. Because two men walked into a situation expecting to almost celebrate their newfound bonding, and instead wound up getting into a fight and both characters' expectations wind up being blown out by the end of the scene. So the idea of getting the violence of that was just spontaneous.

Michael Radford, *Il Postino*

We had this terrible problem of Massimo being mortally ill through the shoot. Any preconceptions, any idea I had about how I would shoot this picture, went straight out the window. Under normal circumstances, I don't rehearse. What I tend to go for is what I call "the tingle." It's like when you're on the set you feel the chemistry of the scene, and suddenly it happens. It's very hard to put your finger on what it is, but you know when it's not there. Now very often that actually only happens when the camera is running. I also feel the same thing when I set up a shot—I find the tingle to feel, yes, this shot is the right one. So the night before I'm usually having some food, relaxing and not really thinking about the next day. I tend not to be very good at night because I tend to drink a lot. It helps you sleep and I wake up very, very drunk. It helps you unwind and stuff and this particular film was particularly difficult—if I'd wanted to rehearse, I couldn't. So I'd wake up the next morning—I'd wake up very early in the morning, then concentrate the mind, and I sort of think through the scene, and I think approximately the parameters of it. I don't storyboard things. Maybe if it's a big crowd scene or a big scene, I'll have a storyboard to make everybody else feel confident, but I very rarely stick to it. But it gives you somewhere to go.

[Each] morning I'd have to see how Massimo was. He would come onto the set about five o'clock in the afternoon. He couldn't go to any of the locations which I had chosen, so I had to redo everything, rethink everything. Every day it was another day where I had to rethink everything. He could only walk three steps and he'd have to sit down. So we had to find places where we could shoot him sitting down. I don't shoot master shots quite often; I don't work that way. For me, there is a shot which is at the center of a scene. That shot I would shoot at the end of the day when Massimo came on board.

I discovered that actors spend an awful lot of time on the set sitting about or feeding lines to other actors or waiting for the lighting or doing shots in which they're not recognizable, and if you cut all that out, you've got that hour or hour and a half with an actor when you're going to do his close-ups.

Now, Massimo was a brilliant, brilliant comedian. And comedians have exquisite timing, and what it meant was that usually on the first or second take, he was at his best, he was cooking. And if you started to repeat too often, it went away and then you'd have to do fifteen or twenty takes and he wasn't physically capable of doing that. So what I would do is, I would make sure that by the time he came on the set, this main shot we were going to do would be technically perfect.

Massimo was a comic, not a dramatic actor. And all I knew was that I wanted to pull him back. This is often really basically what you spend your time doing with actors. This is what I could bring to the film, as slight resonance in the way that he behaved. He was used to making comic movies, where he would take the script, he would sit down, and he would just improvise. He'd never learned lines in his life before! He started to learn his lines, he said, "God, you know, you're making me learn these lines," and then he would come up to me and he'd say, "You know, I just got this urge to do a little something in this scene. Would you mind?" And I'd say, "A little something, as long as it doesn't last too long." Then he would come up with a brilliant piece of improvisation, absolutely brilliant.

After about three weeks into a picture, the picture is your life. You wake up and you see the characters in front of you; you don't see the actors.

The whole film is handheld [the camera is held by the operator rather than being locked down to a tripod or dolly]. We had a Movie Cam which is not designed to be held on the shoulder. I said to Stefano [Coletta], the camera operator, "I want this to be handheld for a number of reasons. One, I feel it gives the sense of immediacy to the picture. The second is, I know that you're going to be able to adjust instantaneously and improvise if Massimo does something, so we won't have to reshoot it." And he said, "Okay." And it was unbelievable; he was so strong. All the tracking shots that we did, I would sit him on a dolly with a camera on his shoulder.

I used to say far too much in the old days. I try to avoid that now. It confuses an actor. An actor is reaching out for something and if you're as clear as possible, even if you don't quite get it right that time around, you've got another take. You let the actor do it and then you adjust it again. If you say too much, it's confusing. I always avoid acting it out in front of them. I think that to me, if you can't find the words to express it, then you don't know what you want. But then again, these are not hard and fast rules; these are just things that make me feel good. So I try to find an adjective which basically characterizes that particular moment.

You don't get any atmosphere on a video [assist, used to see what the camera sees] and I tend to work a lot with atmosphere. I tend often to just listen with the cans [earphones]; I shut my eyes. I often listen rather than look. Particularly towards the middle of a picture when I know pretty much what the actors are looking like. You stand where the script supervisor is standing. She or he always finds the best spot, so I stand back, I watch, and then I walk up to her and say, "Get out of the way!"

It's about creating the circumstances in which something untoward can happen, because that's when it comes to life. You have a screenplay, but actually what you're hoping for is for something else to happen. In the movie there's a scene, a long scene, which is my personal favorite when he discovers the poetry within himself and he starts to record the sounds of the island. Now, I'd written that as the central moment in the film, but the interesting thing is, I couldn't shoot it with Massimo. So at any spare moment, I would start to improvise scenes: the sea would be rough and I would get the double [a "look-alike" for the actor used usually to stand in while lights are being positioned] and the telegraph operator and we'd shoot. We had about eight little scenes. You just see a hand coming up from behind a bush or something like that. But it lacked the presence of Massimo, it lacked his presence, and I knew I wasn't going to get away with it. And on the last day of shooting, when I thought he was going to go for his heart transplant operation, I just went up to him and I said, "Massimo, these are the shots; just read the shot list that we've done." And he sat on the bed and he read this shot list. And when we got into the cutting room, it was the most powerful thing I'd ever seen. I actually had tears in my eyes when I was watching it. And it was better than I could have ever imagined.

Scott Hicks, *Shine*

I wanted to create around the camera an environment that I thought was going to be really conducive to getting this character of David [Helfgott]. Particularly with Geoffrey Rush being nude in the filmmaking process the last thing I wanted was this cut and thrust that can go on around the camera. Geoffrey Simpson [the cinematographer] has a very centered, calm personality. He works with a crew that again invites a good mix of genders.

[Another issue was that] John Gielgud doesn't travel these days and so it was important that we had somewhere in London. He comes up from the country. He works for four hours a day, which by the time you take your lunch break out and make-up and wardrobe, it really boils down to about two hours in the day that you're working with him. So you have to use that energy that's available very carefully.

We decided to start shooting because I was in mortal terror of us running out of money. If we started shooting in Australia, I thought there won't be enough to afford going to London at the end. I mean the whole film was shot in forty-two days and in London we were there for a total of seven or eight days shooting in which we had to get quite enormous elements of styles as far as the film is concerned. It's a small film but the big concert scene we saw is a central piece of it. And in the end, it was put together in one of those wonderful sort of movie things where we shot the concert, as it were, in the Royal College of Music with their orchestra and all the rest of it. But to me it was like some donut because there was a gigantic hole in the middle which was all of Noah Taylor's work at the piano. And that was all shot on the stage in Adelaide. It had to be shot on the first day of shooting because we then had to cut Noah's hair for the second half of the shooting. And the concert pianist whose hands were doubling for Noah was in London. So he flew to Adelaide for a day. He got off the plane and was led to the set. We did all his stuff and wheeled him back to the airport and put him on a plane. We didn't even know if he survived. And that was just symptomatic of trying to put something together on two continents on a very slender budget.

Christopher Nolan, *Memento*

When you come to shoot, you spend all day working on the star. And then this poor person, who's, you know, been waiting all day to sort of do their thing, they get twenty minutes before the light's going. And it's like "Okay, you're on. Do it." And that's the take you have to use. And that's just sort of the reality of how you're telling the story and which character you're closer to.

The scene I shot with Guy Pearce and Carrie-Anne Moss, probably in the first week of shooting, and I'm a bit of a pragmatist, thinking in terms of time and all the rest and we shot Guy's close-up, and it's a scene where he reveals, quite early on in the film, how frustrating and upsetting this fact that he can't remember things is. And I felt, you know, you needed to see that early in the film to sort of carry that with you. And I shot this close-up, and after I got something I was very happy with, I said, "Well, okay, you know, it's getting late. Are you okay with this? It's time to move on." And he said, "No, I'm not. You know, I haven't done it yet." And at that moment, I'm either gonna, you know, say, "Look, it's good enough, and, you know, you have to trust me," or see what else he can do. He did one more take, and it was one of these moments where the actor is so in the moment it was just completely transcendent. And you're there; I mean, I don't use the monitor, so I'm sort of, you know, looking at it with my eyes about four feet away, and it's just completely real. It's not acting. And suddenly you realize that, with the right actor in the right role at the right time and all the rest, you're gonna be able to have a lot of fun.

There's a scene in the beginning of the film where I had a sequence we filmed in reverse. And I wanted to shoot everything on the original negative and not use any special effects. And it was very confusing to a lot of people on the crew. And you know, we had a lot of discussion with the effects of how we were gonna do this. There was one thing we just couldn't get, and that was [when] the shell casing pops out the gun. And in the end, I found myself, you know, on my hands and knees, just out of frame, and I just blew at it as we shot and we just ran it forwards. And you know, at that moment, I suddenly realized that even those millions of dollars and trucks and all this stuff I'm not used to, it's exactly the same as being in your back garden sort of messing around.

Sofia Coppola, *Lost in Translation*

It's always a surprise when you shoot even if it's exactly the dialogue from the script. Actors always bring something that you hadn't thought of. You try to be open to the things that happen and adapt to that. When we shot the Suntori photo shoot with Bill Murray, I was just making things up that the photographer would say and then Bill Murray just came back with things, and that was pretty entertaining for me when we were shooting.

In Tokyo we would see something and then incorporate it into the movie, just scenes of them running through this big intersections. There definitely were things that just came from being there and seeing something interesting and seeing a pachinko parlor and let's shoot in there. When we shot in the hospital, Bill Murray sitting by that little old man, we just had him sitting next to him and eventually they started talking.

One of the women was the daughter of the little old man and she had brought him and we asked her to sit and be in the scene, and then of course she started laughing when her dad was talking to Bill Murray and I figured that's what would [be] in real life if you saw that. You'd probably laugh at seeing Bill Murray and this little old man. And I remember one of the ADs [assistant directors] saying, "Oh, should we stop? Should we cut?" And it was like, no, that's what would happen. I just sort of left it going as long as we could and then eventually, I think we ran out of film.

Some of it was scripted and then we just let the cameras roll and I would just make up questions and she responded and she [Anna Faris] was really funny about improvising the other stuff about liking Mexican food. I just remember doing interviews in Japan and you find yourself saying kind of just dumb things.

Shooting in the hotel was more of these kind of intimate dialogue scenes, and when we were running around the city, we were just kind of being documentary-style about it. It's hard, I think, to shot-list before the actors have gotten there 'cause you don't know what ideas they're going to come up with and it's going to change.

There are certain shots that when I was working on the script I pictured a certain way, and so when you're approaching it, you plan for that. But then you come up with other things. I agree about just keeping it as informal with just keeping the cameras rolling.

We did some rehearsing [in the "rip my stockings" scene], which was interesting because the actress didn't speak English and we don't speak Japanese and it was a lot of physical wrestling going on. But we kept asking her to really try to take him down and make it look as real as possible.

We were looking at the script and I would change a lot of dialogue as we were shooting, but I never felt like the dialogue in that scene really had the emotion that I wanted—to kind of have that moment of acknowledgment between them [the last

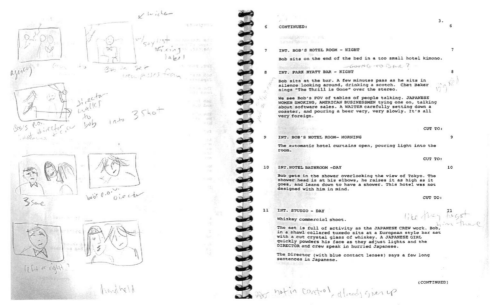

Sofia Coppola's script notes for Lost in Translation. *(Courtesy of Universal Studios Licensing LLLP and Sofia Coppola.)*

encounter with Bill Murray and Scarlett Johansson where he whispers something to her]. So I was talking to my brother about I think it was Godard [the French film-maker], that they would just say numbers and then figure out the dialogue later—so that was where that came from. I talked about, well, kind of just whisper about, tell her about this. And then when we were shooting it was, we realized it was nicer just to have it between them. So that was something that came about on the shoot. And I also in one take asked him to really kiss her, which wasn't in the script. And I like that because it was a real reaction as she wasn't expecting him to kiss her.

Well, we did 'em [shooting two cameras simultaneously] so we didn't have to do coverage. We'd have one on Bill and one on Scarlett and that way we could improvise things. Or just because of time because our schedule was so short. Or sometimes my brother would take a camera and go shoot second unit somewhere else.

I remember a scene that I liked on paper of Bill and Scarlett having breakfast together and they were just, it was six in the morning, we had been shooting all night, and they were in bad moods and we were getting kicked out of the location. And it just didn't work. We ended up cutting it out because we didn't need it. So there's always moments where things don't come together. And the scene where they're talking all night in bed, we started that and that was kind of off to a bad start. We were all just tired 'cause we'd hadn't taken a break in a long time. And my producer, Ross [Katz], said, "Why don't we just all go home and try this again tomorrow?" and I was worried that we were falling behind and could we really do that. But I'm so glad that we came back fresh and started again.

There's always moments where you kind of get stuck and you have to try something else. And I kind of picked up a habit from my dad [Francis Ford Coppola] of talking during the scene when you're shooting and just saying things to the actor while you're filming, while the camera is running, just to kind of change gears, or you'll say something to the actor that they're not expecting at all. If I wanted a reaction from Bill Murray, I would whisper to Scarlett to say something that wasn't in the script and to see if you can get a real reaction. I think it helps always talking during the scene because then they have to think about what you're saying and also just leaving the camera rolling after the scene is done because always the actor for a moment comes up with something. Inevitably something else happens if you just leave the camera rolling. Sometimes that's an interesting little moment that you can use somewhere else. I just always thought that was normal 'cause I always saw my dad do that, so I'm just in the habit of talking—the sound doesn't like it.

Mike Newell, *Four Weddings and a Funeral*

We all know spontaneity is the pearl without price, and how do you produce spontaneity? There are times at least when the spontaneity is out of kilter with what is needed. And then you're dealing with nuance and trying to produce a whole different atmosphere. And sometimes you don't talk sense to them at all. Hugh Grant tells a story that I once said to him, "Hugh, it needs to be a little quicker—thus, I feel perhaps a fraction slower." Now, that made absolute sense to me. What I was trying to do was produce nuance in him. That's my torment is to try and get spontaneity with nuance.

There's a scene in the film after the funeral where the leading character makes up his mind he'd better marry somebody. The whole scene floats on the brink of sentimentality. And so what I tried to do was to find a way of him not being sentimental. So I got him to be harder and harder and what happened in fact was, he simply came out lunatically neurotic and angry, and people looked at the scene and said, "What on earth is it, he's angry about?" I can't remember how I cured it. I suppose we looped it. But it was raining and rain is something that drives rationality from your head. Water and celluloid they don't mix. Part of the reason why I got it wrong was that it was raining and I lost my reason. And people just want to be somewhere else. That's when the mistakes happen and that's when you start to chase ideas that you should never have chased.

I suppose the thing that's most frightening about acting is that you constantly think to yourself, tomorrow I might not have an idea. It might not happen tomorrow. Because whether it looks self-evident or not, acting does need, actually, a lot of ideas. I always try to read what I'm going to do the next day before. I have a kind of superstition about that, that it'll never go right if you try to do it in the car on the way out. I try to get there an hour or an hour and a half before everybody else starts to do their work.

Ang Lee, *Crouching Tiger, Hidden Dragon*

I think fear is just about the strongest emotion we have. I think it's definitely stronger than hate or love or guilt; I think it's strongest. That's why it pump up the most adrenaline and juice, creative juice. So maybe that's useful. And sometimes you have to be seen, the sheer existence of just staying, sit there, maybe empty headed but still look contemplative, be watched. I just want to go back and make a Chinese language film. The budget is small here, but it's titanic over there. So it's like wild, wild West. I pretty much create every detail, every way of things doing on my own. It's a big responsibility but I see as a great adventure.

After a few takes they begin to get an idea. Then you ask them not to anticipate a certain fight, look genuine. So to me action is the extension of characterization and relationship. How they fight each other is how they respond and relate to each other, which is really pain in the neck for the choreographer. He'll drag me and say, "I know what you want. You're not going to get it." From take 12 on, it's just getting worse, not better. And I will go on to take 36 and I really immobilize them. So it's harder than acting actually. Acting on top with martial art is kind of cruel.

Shooting martial [arts is] often something very different from everything else. It's guerilla filmmaking but highly sophisticated. The choreographer, they just do it right there for one camera angle and they shoot that really quickly. The way they use the mobile head, they call a hot pod, was just amazing. I never see it so agile with this Hong Kong crew. I try not to use handheld because if we can do gracefully, why do that?

I always think that "What you want to do storyboard?" you know? Why do you want to make a motion picture to feel a still picture? We have a saying in China, "You don't want to cut your foot to feel your shoes." But I think bigger production you will have to, as a tool for communication especially, special effects. But I don't like storyboarding. I try to plan as much as I can but just not the way that choreographer [of the bamboo fighting sequence] works. He won't gear up until he is on the set. I try to drag him to do rehearsing but on the set he'll change everything. Very low tech, just hanging them up and do the thing and remove the wire, you know, digitally. That's all we do. I really dream about doing the flying shot from top, only with big wire and digital remove can reach that. And we cannot afford the Hollywood big cables. So they swing a lot and the actors get banged to the wall quite a bit.

In that bamboo sequence actually, the first three days are practically unusable. None of the shots make into [the movie]. It just look like they being hanged. Then they learn, yeah, you do that and if you touch the bamboo like, if you let go a little bit, so swing, so they gradually figure out pretty much on the set. We got a couple of lucky days when it's drizzle so we can cut the bamboo, put it on a platform to do the close shots.

You know, we're lucky we spend months making a movie. You can allow yourself to screw it up many times but still you find a way to come back. Change a scene so to amend this problem you made here. So it's not that serious unless you have a big shot, like one shot something crash and unless something like that you don't have to be that nervous. The night before I might just think about what I do next day or just try to get relaxed. In this case, I be lucky if I can manage some sleep. I don't social with the crews. I think it's . . . they have a lot of burden just to look at me all day long for like twenty hours. All they try to do is try to please me, give what I want. So I don't really want to be seen when we're not working. I found at the end of the day is probably not a good idea to think about the movie. I think going to the set when I'm fresh, I think that's the best time to think about what I do for that day.

I try to grab thoughts, and is like meditation. The more you try to grab it, the more escape, scattered, and you're thinking about something that led you to think of something else which is irrelevant and you start to get a little panic and then you have to tell yourself if today screw up, we still have chance to amend it in the future. Not until I see it really happening when I rehearse actors, see the real set, see the real thing, or talk about how we do certain shots, then something might click.

Well, for the experienced actor is about breaking down their confidence, you know. They try things and you analyze it and make them realize that's not right. Just keep doing that. Keep defeating their confidence so they become real, genuine. And for the younger actors, you pump up. I think for the young ones you need the freshness from shooting. You need to direct them to where you want them to be and try to capture the effort. That's genuine. For the more experienced one, I think it's about tell them what not to do. Just keep, keep at it, you know, try different things, distract them, whatever you can do. Some of the really great actors you can just tell them, you know, be more genuine, be more this and that, and they give you that. I feel a lot of sympathy for the actors.

Michelle [Yeoh] is the most expensive star in Asia. But she was always seen as action movies but she never get a chance to do dramatic acting. So she was like virginal to this field. So she is a combination of star, experienced veteran action star. On the other hand, she's like a little girl, totally pulling my hand. Very insecure. So she'll look at me like a kid actor looking at me.

Movies are made of many shots. Not every shot is, or should be, brilliant. You know, if you got 50 percent, you're in very good shape because the impression put together will be okay. If the actor is really unworkable, you shoot from many angle and hopefully something can cut together. When that happens, is very unfair to the other actors 'cause they know they're being undercovered and they're in the background so every time you do a take, they have be all the time very good. And that will spend most of the day; when you turn around to them, you don't have enough time and then they are spent already. So they will hate that particular actor.

Mel Gibson, *Braveheart*

I try to know what each scene means and why I want it there, and how to tell that story the best way. It's not always with action and dialogue either. Sometimes it's just "Where do you throw the camera?"

I'm not too good at articulating what I want, sometimes. People on the crew would sometimes be "What is he doing?" And sometimes, I couldn't explain it. It's kind of like you're doing a million things at the same time, and you think they can read your mind. But I think the key is to be open to things that other people see. Like the cinematographer [John Toll], because he made some tremendous contributions, as did the first AD [David Tomblin]. I thought, "That is a great idea; I'm gonna take it."

I'd have to do a lot of technical things like they had to sew this damn thing into my head every day, not a brain, but the wig. And I actually had to have some kind of closed-circuit television set up on two screens to see the kinds of things they were doing.

I rarely lost my temper or anything. It was one of those things that I thought, "I can't lose my temper; I've seen guys do that and it just destroys everything."

The battle sequences were six weeks. It's a twenty-two minute sequence and I had eight cameras going some days. As an actor, I don't like the multiple-camera thing at all. I don't know what to work for because I think, perhaps vainly, that you're using a

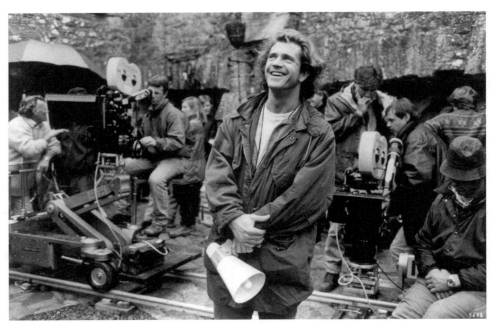

Mel Gibson on the set of Braveheart. *(*Braveheart *© 1995 Paramount Pictures. All rights reserved. Courtesy of Paramount Pictures. Photography by Andrew Cooper.)*

specific viewpoint, and that you show what you want and you can't do that for two viewpoints.

I remember, a few times in particular, I just couldn't get what I wanted. I think it was the largest amount of takes I did, partly because I wasn't quite sure what I wanted. It was a little bit of hit and miss for a while, and then, I started getting in there with the actor and talking in between takes. Then he started to get freaked out, because we never did this many takes. And I said, it was my fault because I don't know what I want yet. I did want something different from him, but I didn't want to go up there and dictate things to him, and we talked about the oddest things. We eventually got to this discussion about something else we both had seen, and that sort of got a meeting of the minds going and this guy who was wonderfully talented came in and just knocked it off in one take. And it was just perfect and it was worth it.

One of the things I learned early on from Peter Weir, and it's just a general thing, is that you take a scene and if it seems lifeless or it's not working, you do it twice as fast as you think you need to. And oftentimes, that's when it comes to life.

Some actors I've worked with have very different methods. There's no right way to do anything.

There was three thousand [extras]; that was the largest amount of people I had to deal with. There was a huge system set up with loudspeakers. I felt like I was some kind of fascist in Spain. There was a delay on everything you said, but then you could hear it echoing back off the hill and stuff. They were getting it loud and clear. There was a whole lot of time spent in amping everybody, because I think that there must be something very distressing and I've experienced myself, you know, when you're in a scene where they stick you out on a hilltop someplace and they got like long lenses and everybody looks like an ant and you think, "What the fuck are they doing?" It's kind of, you're not connected to it somehow. And it's very important to give someone something that they can hook onto emotionally so that they do their best, and that they have a sense they're a part of it. One time, I remember, it was the last shot of the film, when they're all coming down the hill in slow motion and stuff, and I had three cameras. They all ran down. It took a long time to set up. They ran down and did the whole thing and then I watched the video monitors back and some of the guys coming down are horsing around and laughing and all this kind of stuff. This is one of the times when it backfired on me, when it was toward the end of the shoot and I was pretty cranky, and this is one of the occasions I lost my temper. And I just like, I said, "We saw that on the video monitor. Some of you are horsing around and laughing." And it went from, "I'll find out who you are, from the picture." By this time I was totally insane. We were eighty-five days in and I was pretty ratty. And it ended with insulting all their mothers, collectively. It stirred them up and I'll never do anything like that again, because I had to pay the price for that two weeks later. And I didn't even think about what had gone on before because you're so busy. And it rolls off me, like water off a duck's back, because I'm just single minded and insane. But these people really got offended by that and they think, "Ah, we'll catch up with him one day." And they did. I had another scene where it was in the London town square where there was always not enough extras. We got these army guys to fill up all the spaces and they remembered what I said on the hill that day, and we armed them all with turnips, potatoes, and every conceivable fruit. So there I am like Bozo at the fair, big goofy target, being wheeled through, and these guys decided to practice their cricket on me. A nineteen-, twenty-year-old arm going for all it's worth with a turnip, this is not funny; this is an instrument of death.

Some of the pressures of the financial and time pressures will force you into decisions, frantic decisions, and you'll just do the most incredible things, like you'll have to shoot in the rain and it gives the film a wonderful look. I learned that from George Miller [who directed Gibson in *Mad Max* and *Road Warrior*], just shoot no matter what.

Anthony Minghella, *The English Patient*

Saul [Zaentz, the producer] tells a story about me which is entirely true which is that he left the filming for one day, and I fell over and broke my ankle. So his diagnosis of the whole film is that the minute he turned his back, I couldn't even stand up by myself.

Walter [Murch, the editor] gave me this totem every day. For the 127 days of shooting, he gave me 127 mottoes. They were extremely deep and aphoristic: "Remember what you've forgotten and forget what you've remembered."

One thing that I try to do is never take the screenplay with me when I'm shooting, because I don't want to be the writer on set. And so I try to leave that behind and learn and be surprised by the day.

It was a road movie of epic proportions. You take everything with you and throw as much of it away as you can and focus on the real thing—which is the human being. However beautiful the locations we had, however ravishing Tuscany is or Africa is, I'd rather watch a human being against a wall. In the end, you're there for the actors, who are wonderful and give you a commitment.

What you're looking for is to eliminate forgery because audiences can smell it from a thousand miles away. They want to feel as if they're somehow invisible participants.

When you make a scene about sexual behavior in films, it's the most difficult thing. Not because we're embarrassed by sex, as we are, and I'm a particularly prudish personality, but because it's like a required scene and so you don't want to do scenes of people who pretend to make love to each other, because it's the moment where you most see the artifice. You want to get as far away from dealing with the mechanics as possible. And particularly in this case where I wanted the electric charge of the film to really be something. I wanted you to feel that these people were resisting emotion, unwilling participants in this event, rather than running into each other's arms. So everything to me was how to set up a dynamic when they finally came together.

The job, as I understand it, of directing is to create a space in which actors feel empowered and the more space you take up as a director, the less room they've got. If you push them and pull them and tug them, they are just rocked around by you. At the same time if you do nothing, they can't see the space they're working in.

Peter Jackson, *The Lord of the Rings: The Fellowship of the Ring*

It was an interesting combination of incredibly careful planning combined with totally seat-of-your-pants kind of make-it-up-as-you-go-along kind of experience.

About two or three months of shooting, back in 1999, end of '99, we went down on our first location shoot, which was in Queenstown, this beautiful place in the south of New Zealand, and we didn't take any weather sets with us, any cover, any weather cover, because our plan with the weather cover was, we'll shoot in the rain, you see. We thought, oh, Tolkien, rain, it'll look gray, and if it rains, we'll just keep on shooting. And that was what we thought. It was very clever. But what we didn't count on is, a storm had hit just as we were arriving in Queenstown, and the location that we were gonna shoot at was along this sort of road along the lake. And the road had been washed away. So we . . . it wasn't a case of shooting in the rain anymore; we couldn't actually drive to our location. So we were suddenly in a situation where we had to think of what to do, and Queenstown doesn't have any sets or studios or even any big warehouses, so we looked around, and we found the squash court of the local hotel was a reasonable size. So we asked the hotel if we could build a set on their squash court very quickly, a cover set that we had to build like in twenty-four hours. And the only set we could fit in there, 'cause it was very small, and the only set we felt we could build fast enough, was a set that we needed for the third movie. And it was a very intense scene between Frodo and Sam. And so I had to go to Sean Astin and Elijah Wood and I had to say, "Look, guys, we're gonna start shooting tomorrow. We're building a set overnight, and we're gonna shoot the scene from the middle of the third film." And none of us, including the actors, have got their heads into the third movie. And Elijah was freaking out. Because especially for his character—Frodo—is really intense by the time he gets to the third movie. And it was a whole head space that Elijah hadn't gone to yet. So Sean said, "Why don't you start by shooting my angles first? And then that'll give Elijah time to get up to speed?" And we thought, "Great, okay, that's, that's a good idea." So we spent a couple of days in this squash court shooting this complicated scene, but shooting all the coverage looking past Elijah at Sean, 'cause it was like a two-hander [a scene with only two actors]. Or three, with the little animated creatures. So by the time we were at the end of our second day, Elijah was good. He was right into the scene, and he said, "This is great; this is great." And then we found out that the road had been repaired, so we could get to our location. So we said, "Okay, well look, we're just gonna pull out of this scene now 'cause we gotta go shoot our location stuff." And anyway, we returned to Queenstown a couple more times during the course of the next year, 'cause we had twelve more months of shooting to go, so we asked the hotel if we could just leave the set standing for a few weeks, because obviously, we were gonna come back again. And they said, "Sure, okay." And every time we went back to Queenstown, the weather was good. And so we'd always shoot our exteriors there, and then we'd move on. And this set stood on this squash court for a year.

The most valuable thing for me, which I love, is the blocking process at the beginning of each day. And this is more for the drama-based scenes obviously. What I do is, the first hour of the day we'd usually devote to blocking, which is essentially a rehearsal, really. And the actors would come on set, we would look at the storyboards, and we'd say, "Okay, if we shot the storyboards, this is what we'd be shooting." And the actors would play the scene out. And then we'd say, "Okay, how could we improve it? What can we do to make this better?" And at that point, you're sort of throwing your storyboards out the door.

And, and I love looking through the lens and so we'd put the lens on a viewfinder and I'd just have the actors playing. We'd do the scene without the lens a couple of times, just from a purely performance point of view, to talk about the blocking and where people should be, and then I'd just have actors run the scene five or six times for me, just a low-energy performance, 'cause it wasn't a performance rehearsal at that point, and I'd walk around with my eye just fixed totally to the camera—to the lens, so it was excluding all else. And I'd try to just . . . because I like moving the camera when the camera is sort of a participant in the scene, and I'd just get them to run it over and over and I'd just be walking around trying to find those little sweet moments with a little bit of a camera move here or there that would help the scene come together.

The First World War, I remember, was used in a scene in the middle of the movie where Frodo had to volunteer to take the ring to Mordor. He has to stand up in this meeting and say, "I will do it." And what, to me, was important was not just that show of Frodo, but the show of Gandalf reacting to that. And we shot a couple of takes with Ian [McKellen] where I didn't think he was really giving me what we needed, and I, and I said to him, "Just imagine that you're a father and it's 1915. And you're in the drawing room, in some Edwardian drawing room, and you've just, and you're talking to some friend of yours, and you just hear your son behind you, saying, "Dad, I've just joined up. I'm going to France tomorrow." And I said, "Just give me that moment, Ian." So, and he did, and it was great.

Peter Jackson, *The Lord of the Rings: The Two Towers*

When we were shooting scenes with Gandalf and we didn't quite know why but we figured it was something to do with the gels on the lights, if there was a particular kind of a blue-green gel on the light, we'd film him and he looked great and everything and when we saw the dailies his nose would be black, like the rubber part of it would just have gone black. It was like he had frostbite or something. It was terrible. And Ian would ask me how the stuff looked the next day, and I'd say, "Oh, it was great, it was great." And then we'd have to put it through a computer. We had to repaint his nose back to being flesh colored again.

We shot all the scenes with Gollum with Andy Serkis and then basically, we either had the animators copying his performance, or in some cases the animators couldn't if he was walking down a vertical rock face or something. Then the animators would animate that the traditional way. He was in like a skintight kind of leotard and it was like flesh colored because the lighting reference was quite helpful. The thing that the animators did which was amazing is, they actually managed to re-create the nuances in his face because we built a computer version of Gollum after very carefully studying all the muscles in Andy's.

I just think the first hour of the day is where I get the most valuable rehearsal. You know, especially when the actors know who they're playing. You're not really talking to them so much about the fact they're doing things wrong because I kind of believe ultimately they know more about the characters than me. You know, it's like they start to own the character. And I like to just run through, at the beginning of the day; I like to have everybody there run through the scene three or four times, and you actually get actors on this film that didn't learn their lines until the first run-through. They would just arrive on set, they'd maybe had a cursory look at the script beforehand, or maybe they'd had it under their hotel door the night before. But we would run through the scene three, four, five, six times just low energy, not giving it full, just low energy.

They'd be programming it, the scene, into their minds and I'd be walking around with a viewfinder just exploring how we could shoot the scene. And so by the end of an hour, a very valuable hour, we sort of knew the shots we were going to shoot that day; the actors had had a good run-through of the scene. We hadn't talked about any specifics because I don't believe, it's not much point, in talking to an actor in detail about something they're doing wrong until you actually have the camera and the film rolling. I had a good relationship with all the actors and if they got "stroppy" or had a different opinion, then I'd just simply say, "Well, listen, I'm happy to shoot your version but s'long as, as you're happy to shoot mine." And it wasn't necessarily that my vision always got used.

I'm sort of always stunned by actors because they give so much and they have to trust you. And I certainly feel a great deal of responsibility for them, for their careers, for their work, you know, and so it was important for me to serve them.

We usually use between one and two hundred extras and then we use computer people to sort of put beyond that. But I find the best way to work with the extras is to explain to them exactly what's happening. Don't sort of keep anything away from them. Explain the situation, explain what their role in it is, what they're supposed to be reacting to. And then really from my experience the process is to just pull them back, because extras generally like to give it everything they've got, and stopping extras from overacting becomes the mission really. Of course while we were shooting I was concentrating on what the lead actors were doing and when I thought that I had the take that I wanted, before we broke the set up I'd always want to go back and actually study the replays to look and see if there were any extras that were stuffing it up. Because you can just have an extra doing a really silly thing and suddenly, there's a horrible time in the cutting room. Normally for drama we'd use two cameras, one or two cameras. And then for sort of extra scenes probably three, maybe four. Never more than four.

When we came to principal photography we, based on the little planning that we'd done, we knew what bits of set we needed to make. So we then built the set and we did the stunt shooting and obviously the stuff with the actors—the dialogue, the drama—and then a couple of years later, this last year 2002, we then did all the computer work where we were able to shoot the miniature again for real and put all the little CG [computer-generated] soldiers into it. It was interesting shooting the battle. I found out—and it was sort of obvious when you think about it—that the battle scene became uninteresting if we cut away from our principals for too long.

I'm talking to second unit [the group of filmmakers shooting additional material while the main unit is working with the actors] about what sort of shots are that I'm imagining and what the action is. We had a little bit of the battle storyboarded but not a huge amount. And I'm just describing what I wanted to do 'cause I tried to create a little story in the battle. I didn't want the battle to be just a cacophony of action. I wanted people to be able to follow what was actually happening in the battle so that you sort of were aware of the different strategies. The second units were just shooting endless nights in the rain with drenched extras. It was amazing. It was a superhuman effort.

Peter Jackson, *The Lord of the Rings: The Return of the King*

There was a scene we did in *The Two Towers* where Viggo [Mortensen] had to kick an Orc helmet and he kicked the helmet and broke his toes and sort of dropped on his

Peter Jackson on the set of The Lord of the Rings. *(The Lord of the Rings: The Return of the King ©*
MMIII, New Line Productions, Inc.™ The Saul Zaentz Company d/b/c Tolkien Enterprises under
license to New Line Productions, Inc. All rights reserved. Photo by Pierre Vinet.
Photo appears courtesy of New Line Productions.)

knees kind of screaming, staying in character. It was supposed to be a moment of grief
and I thought, wow, this is really powerful. And then we noticed him limping around
afterwards and we said, "You okay? " And we, sort of the medic, forced him to take
his boot off and his toes were all kind of blackened and red and swollen and he'd broken
two toes.

I tried to be as flexible and organic as I possibly could at all times. I mean, which
may not be the sort of thing you'd think I could do with a film like this.

Whether you're writing or whether you're editing or shooting, every day there's
something you can make a little bit better and improve. And so I try to make the most
of those opportunities. And I love doing pick-up shooting as well. And the way that
we structured our shoot is, we shot our fifteen months of production where we did all
three movies and then we had one year of postproduction for each film, and each of
the three movies we did the same thing where we'd start the year looking at the edit
and you'd start to realize all the flaws in the movie and you'd start to see where it wasn't
working and where it could be better and things that you didn't think of two years ago.
And then we brought the actors back to New Zealand and we shot for another four or
five weeks during the middle of each of the years and we would then have that wonderful, wonderful opportunity just to sort of, just to finesse and craft and shape the movie.

You know, actors in prosthetics [makeup devices that cover the face transforming
it], it's interesting because a lot of people can just get swallowed up in prosthetics and
they disappear and they just get overwhelmed with it. But you have to have actors, I
guess, who are prepared to just push their facial muscles and use their eyes a lot. I mean,
there's so much about the eyes. Obviously, our key character who we had in prosthetics
was John Rhys-Davies, who plays Gimli the Dwarf, and he has prosthetics over his

entire face. And I said to him, "Listen, I really think Dwarves should have quite pronounced foreheads and a hook nose and I just have this image of what a Dwarf should be like." Obviously, the size thing, we were going to shrink him down, but there was just this face. And I just remember John putting up a resistance against that and I understood because he'd just arrived in New Zealand having committed to fifteen months of shooting with us, and we'd discussed prosthetics on the phone, but I think he just felt he was going to be able to talk me out of it. And I felt for him because once you commit a person like that to prosthetics, it means for the next fifteen months they are arriving for makeup at three o'clock in the morning and needed on set at seven thirty in the morning. It's a huge thing, and I bullied him into doing it, you know, and we did a test. We shot him as Gimli without prosthetics, so we put a beard on him and a wig but just with his face and then we put him in the chair and did prosthetics and then we shot another test so we had the two of them side by side. And the prosthetic version just looked much more like a dwarf. And John Rhys-Davies started to have an allergic reaction to the glues and the solvents, and every time he put the prosthetics on and take them off at the end of the day he was all puffy around the eyes and sort of red skin and raw and it was very difficult for him. And we ended up with a situation where he came back to do a pick-up [an added shot] and his face went crazy and so we looked around to find a double for John because ultimately it was prosthetics, and John was okay with this and the only guy we could find was, literally, a guy walking along the road. And he turned out to be Russian and couldn't speak any English. And then we shot a dialogue scene where Gimli was walking along talking. And so we had the Russian guy learn the dialogue sort of phonetically, and we did it in a really low-budget way and we had John Rhys-Davies without the makeup walking six feet behind reading the lines. And the boom operator had the boom on John and the cameraman had the camera on the Russian guy who was mouthing and John was doing perfect lip synch live as we were shooting. And that shot's in the movie.

And Ian Holm would come to me when he first arrived in New Zealand and he'd say, "Now listen, Peter, you might find me a bit odd." I said, "Okay." And he said, "I just like doing things and playing 'round and giving you choices." And I said, "Oh well, choices are great and that's good." He said, "So let me do a few things and then you can tell me if you're not getting what you want and it's fine."

Ian McKellen, on the other hand, is somebody who just likes to get his head into what the scene is and what his character should be and tries to nail this same thing take after take. And so Ian Holm is just doing different things every time, like putting emphasis on different words. And after about the fourth take, Ian McKellen pulls me aside and says, "Do you like what Ian Holm's doing?" And it's "Yeah." And he said, "I've never thought about doing that, but it's sort of interesting, isn't it?" And I said, "Yeah, yeah, it's interesting." And then if you're not getting what you want, you kind of, you obviously, you eventually, you steer. But I don't do more than five or six takes normally and I love if you're shooting and you're running through the scene, whatever the shot is—whether a close-up or a wider shot—I love not calling for the camera to cut but just saying, "Okay, let's just try that one more time," and keep rolling and get at the top and do it again. And sometimes we would roll through three, four, five runs of the entire scene and often the film would just run out. It just keeps this fluid thing because every time you get this formal structure of "Okay, we're going to shoot," makeup and checks [phrase used for other crew members like wardrobe and hair and props to "check" continuity] come in, everyone kind of tenses up. And you do it and then you cut and then it's like another ten or twelve minutes and everybody's makeup again. I just like breaking through all that and the best way of doing that is just to keep the cameras rolling. If we're doing quite complicated dolly or crane shots, I'd just crank the dolly back to the beginning, everyone would go back to their opening marks, and let's just go again and just get that kind of, make it less formal, less structured.

The challenge for me some of the time was towards the end just trying to combat the exhaustion that I was feeling. Sometimes you would turn up on set at the beginning of the day and your brain is just dead and you realize you've got no good ideas for what to do today if an actor's not giving you quite what you want. What I sometimes do, which I always find works quite well, if we've just gone through six or seven takes and I can't quite think of the words anymore to say, I just sort of beckon them over and I'd actually just run the last take or last two or three takes back on the screen for them to look at. And I never found an actor that didn't like doing that. And I'd sit down and I'd actually talk through a whole take, which might cover several lines of dialogue, and I'd be quite open and honest. I'd say, "Listen, I love this moment that you're doing here and I think that's great. I really believe that." And then I would get to the problem area. I'd just say, "And I'm not believing this. This is what my problem is. Look at your face. I'm not believing that moment." And they'd look and they'd get it. Almost every time I found that the actor would say, "Right. Okay. Good." And they'd just storm back on set.

I think sometimes there's occasions where the directors have to be as good an actor as their actors. You can't let people see that you're floundering at times.

One of the things I do too sometimes when something's not quite right or when you suspect that you could get better but you've sort of hit a brick wall is sometimes I just say, "Okay, let's just try one last take. We've got to move on so we'll just do it one more time." And once you've put that gauntlet down, this is the last chance they're going to get, often, you get a great take. But you had to tell them that. You're not doing any more.

Curtis Hanson, *L.A. Confidential*

I try with every scene to have formed a visual key that I don't want to lose sight of in terms of the visual telling of the story. For instance, in the liquor store where Russell Crowe sees Kim Basinger for the first time, to me, the visual key of that is this moving point of view that reveals her, because that's an image that he's going to carry with him for a long time. So I have that in my head, going to the set.

In *L.A. Confidential*, there were so many sets it was usually a matter of going to a new set each day, so I would get there first and I would meet with the cameraman and the first assistant director and talk about the general thing that we hoped to accomplish. Then when the actors would show up, get everybody else out. Then it would be just the two actors and me and I let them just kind of do it and see what's comfortable for them, and then I would try to sort of nudge them into a situation. Working with the actors is, to me, the fun part actually of directing. Because I think that's where the magic happens. I find each actor is different, and I think that my job is to create the environment in which that specific actor can shine. Some actors really want very specific guidance—as much as saying, for instance, "When you say this line, in the next take, I want you to look into his eyes." And others don't want or need that. Some actors obviously need a lot of takes, and some don't. I do as many takes as it takes. I've found myself caught in the middle, certainly as I think we all have, with actors who sometimes give it all that first time. Then you get diminishing returns as they need more. As you get to know the actors, and again this is something I try to achieve in rehearsal period, I start then having a plan that when these actors are working together, which actor do I shoot first. Let the actor who likes a lot of takes—let him be off camera, for instance, so that he's kind of warming up through the early part of the shootings. I try to do as little coverage as possible.

It's interesting. we're dealing with a time period, that of course, was before Russell Crowe and Guy Pearce were born. Number one, they're from another country so there's the cultural thing to deal with and the language and also as it happens, neither of them is a fan of old movies. That they didn't even know much about. So it was a laborious process and different with the two of them. Russell was somebody who had a dialect coach and broke down his lines phonetically each single line. Whereas Guy Pearce has a remarkable ear and what he did was imitate me.

Frank Darabont, *The Shawshank Redemption*

In anybody's working life [there] is going to be a wave pattern. We, all of us, had what we would count as bad luck as well as good. There's another kind of luck, which is very important. Which has to do with intuition. You could have a lucky day of shooting, and I think that you're best not to ask questions about that. I think you are best to let that be, and let it happen to you, because it will happen to you. But it isn't going to happen to you if you look at it, and if you worry about it, and if you try to produce it. I find a lot of working is actually about not thinking about it, hammering at it, not trying to dissect it.

Oh, the actors, boy, sometimes they make you feel like Lillian Gish on the ice flow. I find myself being Zelig [a Woody Allen character who is a living chameleon] a lot. I'm the human barometer. Every actor is a different person and every different person needs a different thing from you, so I always find that I'm trying to be all directors to all actors. I'm always trying to assess an actor. I think you need to know when to get out of their way as much as when to be in their face. I always talk individually and always in whispers. I'm the antithesis of Dick Donner [director of the *Lethal Weapon* movies], you know, Mr. Bullhorn Voice. I love watching him work. He's such a thrill to watch. He's like a force of nature. He will talk to the actors in the back of the auditorium; he will tell them what to do from there. And it makes it seem initiated. I can't do that.

Frank Darabont, *The Green Mile*

My preparation the night before is to try to drive home as safely as possible, and at least try and hit the bed when I fall over. That's my preparation. When I start off in the morning, it's really a matter of, okay, I've got this scene to do, and I need a little bit of quiet space to reread the scene, purely as a viewer, purely as a reader, and remember what the intention of that scene was. Part of the job of directing is being a barometer of what any given actor needs. Because I learned fairly early on that when it comes to working with an actor like Morgan Freeman, Morgan doesn't really need much. He wants to know what direction he should turn. And when do we roll? He comes from a very intuitive place; there's not much conceptual discussion that needs to go on with him. And if you have conceptual discussions because you feel like you need to do your job, their eyes will glaze over, if they're that kind of an actor. I'd rather just leave them alone, let them do what they do. Morgan's a fantastic actor and why mess with him? Why mess with his process? Tim Robbins, on the other hand, is a very conceptual person. He doesn't come instantly from here [the heart]; he has to process it all through here [the head], so there's a lot more dialogue that goes on between director and actor in that situation. And there are all these various measures in between. So you're always kind of trying to figure out who needs what and give it to them. You don't want to give them too much or too little. You don't want to shortchange anybody. And in terms of having problems, if I had a problem with a take, we roll another take. Until the actor finds his comfort level or finds his moment that is true, and then, once I know I've got it, then we move on. And if he needs some kind of assurance or comfort level from me, I'm there to give it to him.

Ridley Scott, *Black Hawk Down*

Mayhem has to be, like every scene, has to be like a dialogue scene 'cause if I do that piecemeal, in the conventional manner, like there, there, there, there, there, I'll be there for twenty-five weeks, and I didn't have that time, I had this pending SAG [Screen Actors Guild] strike. So that was a reality check. So we shot for just about fifteen weeks. And it was very unconventional in the sense that the actors wanting their motivation. I'd say "What motivation you want?" And "You get slaughtered by a four-hundred-pound commando." And "I'm gonna chuck everything at you. You know where the marks are. You know who you're shouting at. Ready, action. Let's do it."

I've spent years operating camera, and I know lenses inside out. You got two thousand commercials operating, you know lenses upside down. And so the first few movies I loved the process of operating. It's one of the best jobs on the floor. And you know, you see the bells go off right there—half of it's visceral. So how I work: It's "Gather around, Okay, that's yours. That's yours. You're gonna cover this. You're gonna get Charlie, Pete, and Fred, who are gonna be shooting in this direction. But there's gonna come in behind them a heavy recoilless rifle that's gonna be shooting at them. They're gonna turn. That'll go onto Fred over here. And now you've got a different camera." And Slavomir [Idziak, the cinematographer] is going "Oh, ew," you know, because fortunately the sun is here. I said, "Slav, after ten o'clock it's top light and there's a lot of dust flying, so that always helps."

First AD [assistant director] is essential. People never mention first ADs. First ADs are money in the bank if you get the right guy, okay? It's Terry Needham, right? So reliable, that the pyramid beneath them will be formidable, right? So you got two thousand for lunch, breakfast, and dinner and turning up at the tents to get the costume and handed the weapon. And you don't get paid at the end of the day unless you come back and give me the weaponry and the clothes, right? First time probably in, maybe, years they've got an ordered structure to deal with on a daily basis. A total shoot of sixteen weeks.

In the morning? Right, "Gather round the Humvee. This is what we're gonna do." And I love that, you know?

Sam [Shepard] is a sweetheart, really great guy, actually. And he's a good play-wright—great playwright, actually. And so I fully expected him to come and write everything. And he didn't. And he just said, "You just want me to say all this stuff? God almighty." But really super laid back. And Sam's one of those fortunate actors that whatever he puts on his head, the hat, he somehow becomes an iconographic—is that the word—image of what it will be. Whether he's a cowboy or a general. So that's real easy for me. He kinda walks in and he's kind of just right, you know? He's always just right.

Cameron Crowe, *Jerry Maguire*

I was able to direct rather quickly and enjoy the process more than I ever had before because of the time I'd spent directing in my head.

Renée [Zellweger] does have an utterly real quality. And you find that you torture an actor like that sometimes because, say you have them do a breakup scene twenty, thirty, forty times from different angles, and they're in shreds, because it's real, they're breaking up every time.

Rob Marshall, *Chicago*

The first day of school is frightening always. I can't imagine any actor is completely confident about their work. To me it is all about positive reinforcement. And I think that if you don't have that atmosphere, I don't know how people can feel safe enough to try things. And I knew all these actors were doing these unbelievably brave things. Richard Gere is throwing his arms in the air and walking down steps. That was scary for him! But freeing at the same time too. And having the dancers from Broadway who were so supportive, I mean, that's a real community, and to have them there just saying, "Go. Great." And I remember seeing them in the corner working with Renée [Zell-weger] showing her something or showing Richard something. All that camaraderie helps. You can't buy that really.

I remember speaking to Catherine [Zeta-Jones] and Renée when we were shoot-ing the final number, and I said you have to imagine that this club act you're doing is like Monica Lewinsky and Linda Tripp. I had all these reporters up in the air and they all had to land, boomp. I thought I had one in the can, but I didn't. There was always one guy just a little late. So he was erased right out with CGI [computer graphic imaging] effects.

I had four cameras rolling a lot of the time on the big numbers. One would be moving back and forth across the audience. One would be from the side. One would be on maybe just a puppet or two, you know. And the thing is, when you're moving fast, you kind of say, "Fish and hunt and find something else," you know. I think I have that. And they'd scream to you, "Rob, I think I got that," you know. And the tricky thing is, of course, you have four monitors and it's, it's really daunting to try and make sure, you know, did you get it? And you sort of, at the end of it, you're like kind of frozen, like, I don't know. There was like a good moment in that one. Over three days I guess we probably did a number seventy-five times. I tried to be careful not to overdo so many times that they couldn't do it. Catherine doing "I Can't Do It Alone," sliding down a pole or sliding on her front or landing on a chair and, you know, I had no idea until she showed me the next day the bruises on her legs.

Baz Luhrmann, *Moulin Rouge*

I was shooting the cancan sequence and the girls could only do it, you'd be lucky, do it three times. We'd shoot it 'cause we didn't wanna cool 'em down. So I went over and went, "You think we can go one more?" And it's like "We'll have to ask around of the girls." And they were, like, after, you know, four months of rehearsals and waiting, they were like, "Yeah, we're in." So off we go, "Action," and as they went around, right, I spontaneously had this notion that, in the real Moulin Rouge, the girls would dance around the men and they would sort of seduce them onto the floor. It became sort of like, you know, sort of like techno lap dancing was the idea, right? And so I started to call, I had this call for the extras, which was unbridled lust, you know, so to jade them up. And I said to the girls, "Now dance out to the men." And they sort of started dancing out to the men and dragging them onto the floor, and it kept going on and on and on and on, they've had the music on loop. So then people started like writhing on the floor, and there was like, you know, this kind of bacchanalian outbreak, that went on and on and on. The music stopped, and the cameras kept rolling and rolling and rolling, and so for a moment there, there was a sort of true, sort of orgy-esque bacchanal that may have happened in the Moulin Rouge, and I forgot all the pain for just ten minutes, and then we went back to work. Anyway, that was a peak [moment].

During the process of making the film, and I think that it's fundamental in musical process, which is draft and redraft. I mean, during the making of *Wizard of Oz,* you know, I mean*,* "[Somewhere over the] Rainbow" almost didn't make it in [the movie]. You know, they'd do a number with Judy Garland, say that's not working, and so—draft and redraft. "Marmalade," for example, came in after I shot the pitch with Jim Broadbent going, you know, "If life's an awful bore . . ." And we thought, "Gee, you need to understand that these girls are for sale." And so I thought, well, "*Voulez vous coucher avec moi, ce soir*" [the song]. So we go in, we reshot it, girls sang the chorus, drop that back in.

We were going to do that thing, put them in the blue room, shrink them right down [to make the actor appear smaller]. It was totally prohibitive to the power of the actor for Toulouse. And it was such an ensemble piece. So many times I needed these very high-powered actors working incredible cues at an amazing velocity. So ultimately 90 percent it's John [Leguizamo] on his knees, all right? Because what I quickly realized too is that if we're all standing around normal height, he's just basically a head bobbing into the frame, you know. His two legs would stick out like this at the back. And if you saw that in profile, he had blue socks on—we'd just rub it out. So the back of the legs would be rubbed out. The illusion of his height is less important than he act the role and that he's engaged with the other actors.

Now, on the set, Nicole [Kidman] is doing that kind of Katharine Hepburn physical comedy sequence, and what that would be about is I would be like fanning the flames. So she'd be like, "Oh, no, no, no." You know, she's doing the orgasm and I'm going, "Further, further, further," and Ewan [McGregor] is going, "Do you think this is too much?" and I'm going, "Are you kidding?" And sort of like driving them to go further and further. And then, once we'd got to extreme, driving it right back and grounding it. Do both ends, from extremely heightened, high comic style and then it grades down—you know, song, dance, and finally you're moving into high tragedy. And it has to strip away and get simpler and simpler and simpler until finally it's just the two kids backstage against black. With all that stuff, in the end it's just a two-hander.

John Madden, *Shakespeare in Love*

The camera is an accomplice to the language. You have an instinct about when you want your camera to move and when you don't. When you feel that movement is going to generate some visceral sense when that moment is right, and when it's right for the camera to be still and just observe. Usually that's when you hear music, or when you know you're going to be using music. And I have this bizarre habit of sort of humming whenever I'm doing a moving shot, or sort of thinking about a moving shot, which is a strange sight to behold. I find that what I do is, I try and prepare as much as I possibly can, think about everything, every possibility, so that I can throw everything out when I get there and then do something else. Which is where the anxiety comes in for me. In certain sequences, you do exactly what you intended to do.

It seems to me that you don't want to have a method of working. A director's responsibility is to be able to pull completely different sensibilities into the service of the story you're trying to tell. And that involves I think being sensitive to and recognizing a particular route that people have to take to get there. Gwyneth [Paltrow] and Joe [Fiennes], for example, totally different actors. Have totally different ways of working. Joe's very, very, very exploratory and has a tendency, almost as soon as he's found one thing, to distrust what he's found and want to go find something else. That's partly his own nature, partly just where he is in his profession, I suppose. Still searching. Gwyneth by contrast is extraordinarily accurate and very instinctive about where she's going to go. She doesn't want to land at all until the camera turns over. I think she's frightened the genie will get out of the bottle. She perhaps doesn't trust herself as much as she could. What I think I have to do in that circumstance is to create a kind of bridge so that I can negotiate the problems one actor is having with the way the other actor might be receiving it. And I always do that with the text or the scene or whatever, to create an imaginative world that they can all believe in. And somehow then you've got a way of negotiating what's going on rather than saying, "Gee, are you having trouble? Do you want to take an aspirin?" You can't do it that way. You go back into the world that you've created, the imaginative world you've created, and that you're all engaged in, trying to create for other people. But it's difficult. Sometimes an actor will get trapped. And of course you go through the process of a large number of takes. Which seems to make matters worse. Often I just walk away at that point. Often I'll even shoot something else. Come around and shoot the reverse again. That's another thing I did a great deal in this movie. I'd say, "Let's go on," and then we'd shoot something else, and then I'd go back and shoot the reverse again. Because with this material it was so strange how elusive it could be. Every actor would come up and go, "I don't know, was that all right? Did that work? I didn't quite feel that was right. Was it funny?" And we all knew what he meant. It was just very, very hard material to target. I have to restrain my instinct not to want to go again, because I am so committed to this idea that there might be something I haven't yet discovered, which is a pain in the ass for producers who work with me. I'm not saying I want to do thousands and thousands of takes. I gave every actor a rule that they could call upon, which was that if they ever wanted one more take, when I had called it a day, they could have that. The interesting thing about a movie is that, of course, you learn about what it is as you go along, and it has things to teach you about what you're doing and the way you're approaching it and the way you're telling the story as you go along.

Roman Polanski, *The Pianist*

I believe that the actors instinctively take right places in a situation that is given to them. If you have the proper geography, a room, for example, or an apartment, the best thing is to let them do it. They, of course, desperately ask for the instruction and I try to cheat them out of it, you know, and just coax them so they do it by themselves. And then I see what looks right, what looks phony, and then I intervene and try to shape it up into a scene. I don't like to decide how the actors are going to evolve around a scene beforehand. I think it's like having a terrific suit made by a great tailor and then trying to look for the guy that will fit it. I prefer to do it the other way around.

I knew that the toughest stuff comes at the end so we decided to shoot it first. In other words, we started with the end of the picture and we gradually went to the beginning through this five months of work. Also for another reason, that I wanted him [Adrien Brody] to lose a lot of weight and it was impossible to ask an actor to lose weight throughout the shoot. And he lost thirty pounds before we started picture. He was weak. And you know, people who are weak are easier to maneuver.

On the script we had the exact date on every scene. We knew how much time evolved between one scene and the other and what period of the year it was because we wanted to be truthful with this as well. So that when there is winter, it had to be a winter.

Sometimes suddenly we had a reshoot of a little scene and we had to use prosthetics and wigs and things like that to put Adrien back in the continuity. He would come on the set and where he would ask me, "Where should I sit? Here or there?" My answer was usually evasive, you see, because I wanted to use his instinct, you know. I try to avoid the situation when an actor is asking himself a question what he should do. Just do it. Just do it. And then you see things which are not right and you see the things which don't function for the camera purposes so sometimes you have to modify this action. And then I would say, "How do you feel about moving over here?" And he would say, "No, it doesn't feel right." So we would have to change the camera position, you know. I really try to accommodate the actor first and to film it afterwards. In a certain sense it's sort of documentary approach on your own set, you see; you let the actors do their thing and you just film it.

I try to use psychology to get what I want. It doesn't always work. I think that if an actor doesn't trust a director, it's better not to work with him. It's not worth the struggle. And if it happens early in the rehearsals or readings, it's better to quit.

I love giving lines to the actors, you see, which some bitterly resent, but never mind.

I find myself—very important to close my eyes sometimes and trying to recall what I have seen and what I had had in my mind before I even came to the set, before I started this whole adventure and trying to be as faithful to it as possible. So when I am on a set sometimes I know I have arguments because I ask for a little detail to be on the left and not on the right and people don't understand why I want it this way. To them it seems all the same. But to me it's very important that it's the way I have thought of it.

Those big extra scenes, the big crowd scenes were made in Poland and those people were fantastic. They were really selected by my assistants, took months to get them because they needed to be emaciated, thin. Most of them had to have some kind of Semitic physique. I think sixteen hundred was the maximum we had. And as I would find myself sometimes in the middle of a scene when it all looked so real that I had to pinch myself to say it's only a movie. It was very hard work, you know, to dress them; to, to make them up takes four hours as usually they would get up at four o'clock and sometimes stay there until the sun set and there was never a single complaint.

We had to cheat a lot because when you look out of the window, you don't see enough, you know. It had to give the impression that it's really being seen by the character but in fact the camera would have to be much further out.

We dug holes in the road and some people were real, some stuntmen, with the body not real. So the head and the arms could react when the car was running over the body, which was not real.

Quentin Tarantino, *Pulp Fiction*

I very much, as far as shooting is concerned, believe in the "robbing Peter to pay Paul" principle. This scene needs four days to do, but I'll make it up because I'll do this scene in half a day, because I'm gonna nail it in rehearsal and I'll be able to take care of it that way. That 10 percent that I'm wrong is always the worst day on the set. All the stuff that we had at the pawn shop, that was one of the practical locations, and I was just really abusing the crew that day because we only had one day set aside for that, when we absolutely, positively needed two. It was Monday and we're going really late. I tried never to abuse the crew until Friday and that's cool because that's no problem; they're going to have two days off and it's going to be cool. But you don't want to have them go until four o'clock in the morning on a Monday. And then you have this scene coming up and my first AD [assistant director] actually describes it, I've never heard this term before, "fear of shooting." This thing coming up that you were so dreading about doing, it's going to be so sensitive and everything that you do everything so you don't have to shoot.

Apparently actors hate it when you say, "Just have fun with it." What's that mean? The thing is, just trying to give them little minute adjustments.

[In working with one particular actor] we show up, and I just want to do a run-through, without the crew, just the actors sitting down, me, and the first AD. And I'm like, "Is he going to be able to remember his lines?" And he couldn't do it. In fact, not only could he not do it, he started to almost have a nervous breakdown. That was due to age and fear, and then one by one the other actors couldn't deal with it anymore and one by one they started leaving and all the crew sees is outside the different actors walking through the door. I'm like, "Oh my God! I've got to rewrite this whole scene. What am I going to do?" And it was the only time I had like complete despair and actually my first AD [assistant director] saved me. She said to me, "You know what, Quentin, I think you just need to start shooting with him and it'll work out. Give him a chance." I don't very often use two cameras but this time, I want a camera here on him and I want a camera here on him. And I said, "What we're going to do is basically we're just gonna go through the speech until he forgets his lines." And he ended up doing great. It was start, stop, start, stop, start, stop.

On *Pulp*, whether it be the adrenaline-shot scene, the whole thing where they're trying to bring her back, or any of the cinematic stuff that's got to work, that's always kinda scary that day before because if it doesn't work, it didn't work because I didn't do it right. Maybe another director would've.

Stephen Daldry, *The Hours*

The great problem we had, in terms of shooting, is that the women, the actresses, who are used to being in control of articulating the emotional arc of a movie or of a play, they were not in control. So they didn't understand a lot of decisions that were being made. When we would get to the set, we're persnickety, which I think was unusual, you know, saying to actresses you really shouldn't add the "um" there. If we wanted the "um" we would have written the "um." I always wonder whether they teach it at Julliard [famed New York school of performing arts]. There's a couple of things that I wonder about—one is the look away before they speak. It's particularly [with] young actors. They're given a line, look away, and then come back before the next line. I wonder whether they teach this at Julliard to pause before the active verb 'cause, you know, you can't cut. The actor will know they can't cut in the pause before the active verb; you can't cut away 'cause you're waiting for the verb in the sentence. It's a very good trick, so you just say, "Don't pause before the active verb for fuck's sake."

I'll spend the morning rehearsing actually on set. I know there's a hundred people hanging around outside and they're all going, "What the fuck?" And some actors don't like rehearsing and say, "Well, you know, where d'you want me?" I say, "I've got absolutely no idea. You know, where'd you want to go? If you redo the scene, then we'll work out where the camera is." "Well, show me the frame." I said, "I wouldn't know where the frame could possibly be unless I know what you're going to do." And sometimes, you know, actors don't want to do it. So I didn't say, "Meryl, you're going to have to do the breakdown 'cause I've got to know what you're going to do, darling." You know, "I've got to know whether this is going to be any good." But I'm slightly different because on the whole I do know more about the characters than you do. You do get into points of conflict. They're quite rare, but then it's a process of cajoling and bullying and flattering. Never ever underestimate how valuable flattery really is.

The child in the birthday party scene is listening to John C. Reilly declare quite a complicated view of the family. What the child mostly is listening to is me telling him "Jack and the Beanstalk" and you use those reactions from the child. Or when Julianne Moore says to the little boy, you know, "I love you," and the little boy smiles, I think what I actually said to him was "We're gonna finish soon."

With Meryl, you know, you just carry on shooting really until either we'd get fed up or we had to move on. Later Meryl said that she was a little surprised I go to, like, twenty-two takes. And I'd be doing it for the fun. I'd be doing it to keep working, you know, just to keep exploring and see what else can happen. Sometimes "let's do it again" was good enough. It can be very personal 'cause it's very dependent on your relationship with the actor and any relationship with an actor is like, you know, it's like a love affair. It's like you're falling in love with someone and it becomes very intimate and very personal and incredibly private. It's very much about the particular things that you hope are going to release the actor in one particular moment. Sometimes you just want to be utterly surprised. And sometimes you've got an idea and sometimes you know that they're again nowhere near the full potential of what they could actually be doing at that particular moment. So you got to keep pushing them to go there. And sometimes you gotta do terrible things like make them angry and get them wound up.

I was blessed with an extraordinary cast who'd also spent a lot of time in the theater, so the great advantage for me is that you have a shared methodology and a shared approach so you can actually say to Meryl Streep, "You know, if we start lifting inflections at the end of sentences, we'll have much more energy in this," you know. And she'll know exactly what you're talking about.

I still have to recover from the fact that the [cinematographer] is looking through the camera and not me! The video assist is useless. So you tend to just look at the actors live.

Neil Jordan, *The Crying Game*

First of all, you've got to put the camera somewhere, you know, and I'd say, somewhere around there and it was not specific enough. They used to call me "There-ish" because they'd say, "Where would you like me to put the camera?" And I'd say, "There-ish."

People think if they are doing loads of things, that they're actually acting. Very often it's just to get everything simple so the only gestures are the necessary ones.

With Forest [Whitaker], the main thing was to get his accent right, because he's from Texas. So I found this taxi driver in London, and I heard his accent. I was in the back of the taxi, and this guy had slightly a bit of Caribbean and the north London accent. And I thought for Forest, the way was the Caribbean accent. So I got this guy to read the whole script into a tape and he became Forest's driver. And this guy then came to drive me insane because he'd be sitting at the back of the set, and we'd be doing the little scenes and Forest would look and say, "Was that okay?" When people get a hint of power, they really take it!

The first day is a disaster generally! Everybody is nervous with each other and the actors are nervous and generally I end up redoing it.

The night before, I write out everything I want to get in the next day. Like I'm my own mother, saying to me, "You have to get this tomorrow or when you come home, you're not going to get any dinner!" And I just write out the shots I want to achieve. And it's a strange thing if you want a certain bit of emotion at a certain moment. I try to make a list of what I actually want. I even write out what I want the weather to be like. And then you get to the next day, and everything changes. I go out and talk through the scene with the actors. It's a bit deceitful really, to say, I want them to move from here to there for the purposes that I want, but I want to get them to do what I want them to do on their own accord. But sometimes I'm wrong. Sometimes they would move places naturally and it is perfect for the scene.

I try to operate the camera, you know, on the rehearsal. And sometimes I try to give the operators shots that he can't do! Because you do see things differently when you are looking through the lens. I don't believe anybody in the world can draw what happens through a specific lens through a moving camera with a moving object.

When you do long takes that are like twenty-two minutes long, when you are putting a lot of film through the camera, and you have to do that twelve times, that is exhausting for everyone concerned.

I think acting is a mysterious thing. Sometimes when you get nonactors, Jaye Davidson was a nonactor, and they're doing this stuff and it's terribly leaden and you're saying, "Well, okay, if I get it a bit faster I could use it or maybe I cover [shooting the same scene from different angles] it in these different ways." And then suddenly one day the guy begins to act and you say, "Why is he acting now, not before?!"

You hope the spirit of the roles is going into the actors. You hope the actors are being as generous to the characters as you were when you were writing them. And you hope they kind of get involved in the emotional traumas of their characters.

I think the danger with me is that sometimes I like excessive performances. There's something in me, and I have to watch it, that likes bigness; and I've come to realize that that's a dangerous tendency of mine in part.

I try to work at the rhythms of the whole, of what the finished film will be. And in the scene let's say of dialogue, where there's progressive intensity between two characters, I try and design it so that the broadest thing you see is first, and the tightest thing you see is at the end of the scene, you know, the closest thing you see is at the end.

You try and work out how you want it to be seen. [In *The Crying Game*] we've had all this tranquil but terribly tense kind of moments between two men. I want this gunfire to come from nowhere—it's like demonic, it's like vengeance of God or something. So I don't want you to see the source of the gunfire. Or perhaps just want to see the helicopter up there. So I just draw out the different shots that I want and give them to the special effects people to work out what to see—the glass house, to see every pane just explode. And you say, "Can you do this? Will this be the most effective thing?" Maybe there's something else to come up with more punch. And are those stunt scenes you work out what you want to see? But you're in the hands of what actually can be physically done at times.

A main problem was, Could you look at a man with a hood over his face and could he engross you? Now Forest took care of that problem just because of his emotional power and the way he uses his voice and his language, or the way he struggled with this, or the way he went into exhaustion. I wanted to see his mouth; the little bit of humanity that Stephen Rea exhibits towards the character is, he rolls up the hood and holds it up to there. Now you can write that down—"He rolls up the hood and you see his mouth"—but try doing it. The thing keeps slipping literally, and when he struggles to get it up to show his face, he'd do it once or twice and the whole thing would come off! So the take would be ruined.

Robert Zemeckis, *Forrest Gump*

My preparation is actually I don't write anything down until I'm in the car; that's when I start doing my shot list. But I think about it the night before. I dream, I have nightmares about it the night before. It's kind of broken down into the days when I can go directly to the set and the days when I have to go to the hair and makeup trailer first, which is the place I always hate to go, because I know they're always gossiping. But on the day that I have to go in there, then that's the day I'm not quite sure about something and I don't want to ever, in front of a crew, act like I'm not quite sure what we're going to do that day. My feeling is that you always have to act like you know what you're doing, no matter if you have no idea what you're doing! The scene in Jenny's dorm, I never knew how it was going to work and I was very worried. And Tom [Hanks] and I sorted that out on the day. The problem was, after he had this premature ejaculation, it was written that he got very disturbed and distraught about it. And Tom realized Jenny should have the punch line in this scene. Jenny should break the ice. And then we wrote that right there and that's what made the scene work. The days that are terrifying are the ones when you've cast this day player [an actor who works only one day on the picture] and a great actor, but you cast him four months before the day he works and here you've got this whole film company who's been making this movie for four months. Everybody's got a shorthand, and he walks onto the set and he's in a completely different movie. And those are the days that I know when we make our salary, because then you've got to step out away from the monitor, go up there in front of the camera, and say, "Okay, that was really good. Can you try this for me? Just try this for me." My job is to sit there and say, "You're feeling really angry here, well, not that angry, little less angry." It's a level thing. I don't try to talk in any kind of mysterious psychoanalytical way to the actors at all. Kurt Russell, when we were doing *Used Cars* by the end of the movie, said, "I got to the point where I could hear how you'd say the word *cut*, and I would know whether we'd be doing it again or not."

The actor that played Bubba [Mykelti Williamson] said, "I want to have my lip look like this." I didn't think of that. He thought of that and I immediately said, "That's great. Go ahead!" Because usually actors are always saying the opposite, "You mean you want me to look like my lip's sticking [out]?" They always want to look beautiful. But Mykelti is a very handsome guy; he really wanted to find that in the character.

Steven Spielberg, *Amistad*

In a sense, everybody has to kind of keep up with me, because I'm running all around the set finding shots and everybody's sort of running behind me and I don't often communicate when I'm in a kind of frenzy. The only person I really collaborate with when I get inspired is Janusz [Kaminski], the DP. And Janusz has to hear what my thoughts are not just for this shot. I'm trying to set up for the next five or six shots, because Janusz has to know and make an informed decision artistically about how the whole sequence is going to look. And we'll have many discussions, and because we're close personal friends, we often discuss this off the set. So by the time they come on the set, even though I don't know my shots until I walk on the set that morning, we know how that scene is going to appear, how it's going to look. But in terms of shooting, I shoot very quickly. I shoot with one camera. I don't like multiple cameras. You never can get a true eye line [where the actor is looking] with a second camera—the eye line is false. So that the A camera is beautiful, the actor is talking personally to the actor off right. But the B camera—the actor is talking even three or four inches off the personal emotional connection with the other person he is speaking to. It's not personal. So I tend to use just one camera.

On *Amistad*, I tried something I had never done before, because I had never shot nineteenth century, I had never shot anything out of the twentieth century, in terms of subject matter. I'm notorious for moving my camera around. I move it all the time. I've moved it all my career, and I thought, what if I didn't move my camera except four times in *Amistad*? And the four camera moves were only going to be at moments where I wanted a kind of epiphany. Because I really respect the old directors that don't even use close-ups until they require an epiphany to happen. I think that Howard Hawks was one of the greatest directors in terms of saving the close-up, and John Ford as well. I found the shots ahead of time and I actually wrote them in the script. One where Cinque stood up and said, "Give us free."

The first thing I do is to try to find the theme of the scene. I try to determine for myself, "What am I trying to tell the audience?" Not about every single line the people are speaking, but "Where am I trying to go with this scene? What is the idea that I'm trying to arrive at?" And the idea might be a plot point, but I feel if a scene doesn't engine a story forward, then that scene has no reason to be in the movie. If there is an indulgent moment where the photography is beautiful or there's a happy accident that happened with one of the children, and you kind of hate to lose it, but it really isn't going to help the next scene, then it really shouldn't be in the picture at all. I kind of make those determinations the night before or the week before.

When I get to the scene, I allow the actors to block themselves to begin with. I've found that left of their own devices, actors would prefer to stand in one place and do seven pages of dialogue and not go anywhere. There are actors who will say, "You know, it would be great if I came in here and got up on this line and moved on that breath." But for the most part it tends to be a static rehearsal, and that's when I've got to figure out where I want them to move and why. So there's a lot of blocking time. I take about an hour and a half to light, maybe two hours to block and light a master. But then once the master is lit, then pretty much the camera goes very quickly from setup to setup. I do a lot of reverses [shots in opposite direction], and I like to do a lot of reverse masters. I have four masters per scene. On *Amistad* there were at least four, sometimes five masters per scene. I camera cut my films. I play just what I know I'm gonna use in that master. Because, when I first began directing, I did nine pages of dialogue from twenty-five angles and got to the editing room, and after about nine years of experience, I realized, "Look at all the waste I never put in my movies." And I've kind of learned as I've gotten more experienced to pretty much know where I want to use the values at the moment. And then I can do what they call "camera cut."

A lot of times, to get performance, it's sometimes important not to talk too much to the actor. Because I find that if you talk too much to the actor, the actor is simply a reflex of your own, and the actor isn't bringing any value or any ideas to the part. Each actor has a different way of communicating what he or she wants to say on film. And I often find that if an actor is having a great deal of difficulty with an emotion, like crying or like bringing themselves to anger—and I've recently worked with an actress who couldn't cry and an actor who couldn't get angry—what I've done is, I've walked away. And I've allowed the actor to get so mad at themselves for my walking away and saying, "Well, we can try something else." The actor gets so furious with themself that once I see them working themselves up, I say, "Now we'll shoot! Come on back!" And they can usually deliver. But it's not really playing tricks on the actors; it's being able to recognize when the actor is not comfortable with a scene. And often what really helps an actor to get to a place where you're happy, the director is happy, is simply going off somewhere and talking about the whole movie, just a couple of sentences, what the movie means to me, and why this scene is important. And then you let the actor work it out, and I promise you, almost every time they work it out for themselves.

Djimon [Hounsou, who plays Cinque, the leader of the slave revolt] is such a gifted individual that I wish I could take credit for his performance. I didn't have to do anything with him. He was in character. His mood was right. He understood every breath he took and why he had to take that breath, and he made my job really easy.

When Anthony Hopkins began to do the scene and the camera was rolling, I forgot I was on a movie set—and when the take was over, I forgot I was the director, I forgot there was a camera in the room, and I thought that somebody had invited me to a theater to watch a play. Anthony Hopkins really didn't like to go beyond three or four takes and I knew he had gotten it and he knew he had gotten it, and oftentimes it's frustrating for actors who pretty much know they've got it but the director is still sort of amorphously looking for something else that could be even better. And I think that the biggest challenge to be a director is when to walk away from something, when you are pretty certain you have it.

When I first met Peter [Firth, who plays the English captain] for this, the one thing we talked about was—in order to get the audience to believe him, that there really was slavery and he really was looking for slave ships and his job was to destroy slave colonies—that we had talked about stillness—that if he didn't move at all and everything was just the words, he didn't blink, he didn't move his head, he didn't gesture, that there would be such economy and such power and such focus from him that it would all come from his eyes and from his voice. So he didn't move.

Steven Spielberg, *Saving Private Ryan*

I put myself in the role of a combat cameraman, which in a sense would be a lot better than putting myself in the role of an overseer, which most directors are. In most of my films, I'm an overseer; I try to give to all of you the most comprehensive angle that will tell you the most about what I'm trying to tell you. Whereas I was concerned about deconstructing this movie and I was more concerned of putting you through the eyes of someone who couldn't see very well. Which is why my assistant director kept coming over to me and saying, "Why do you have a thousand actors on the beach if the camera's so low it only sees twenty-five people? I don't understand why you have all these poor Irish soldiers coming out every day and getting wet and getting hypothermia and standing in the water; you only see twenty-five people in the foreground." And I kept saying, "Well if I stand up with the camera I'll get shot; I can't stand up." Let's really assume the point of view of John Huston when he made *The Battle for San Pietro*, that great documentary.

I shot the film in continuity. Which I hadn't done since *E.T.* And I only did it in *E.T.* because I wanted the children to understand where they were yesterday so they could figure out where they were today. And I started in the Higgins boats and I shot the movie in complete continuity, and I think more than anything else, the script evolved on location. Because the moments we were putting on film were telling us what the next moments needed to be. And in that sense it wasn't the formal process of a director and a writer in a room trying to find out who the dominant forces were and who the subordinate forces were.

Tom Hanks was actually saying, "Don't make my character better." He had so many lines in the original screenplay and Tom just insisted, he said, "You know, I don't want to talk in this movie. There's too much to experience; I don't want to speak." So we wound up cutting out I'd say three-quarters of Tom's dialogue. And it was a choice that Tom made. Tom came to me and said, "Please cut out these lines. I wouldn't be lecturing my troops, I'd be leading them, not lecturing them."

When we were first starting the movie, we used the Irish army. I had between 750 and 1,000 actual soldiers from the Irish army, not including our own stunt people and our own actors. And we did not use the Irish navy. Because of that the Irish army was throwing up in the boats all day, and they were really sick, and that was the day that the general of the Irish army chose to come down and pay our location a visit. And because the seas were rough that day, and I wanted to get rough seas, because in fact when they made the crossing the seas were horrendous. It was the most inclement conditions you can imagine that all those soldiers had to cross the channel. And so what happened was we had bad seas, we sent the boats out, and there were big waves breaking over the Higgins boats, the flat bottom. And the general took one look at his boys out there, and he called us all in. And he sent the entire army back to their homes. And we were without the army. Then I was taken to task. I was sent in to the Irish colonel's tent the next morning and I had to do what they call formal dressing down. They read a proclamation that condemned my inhumanity to their troops, and my reaction to that dressing down was going to determine whether the Irish army came back and finished the movie or not. So I just took it. I just sat there and took it. And when it was all over, I had a piece of paper in my pocket, and I pulled it out, and I had a proclamation which I had written the night before which was basically a proclamation that marveled and raved at the courage of the Irish army. So they condemned us, and we celebrated them, and we hugged and we kissed and we began to shoot the movie again. The whole movie took fifty-nine days to shoot, but disproportionate in that figure, it took twenty-four days to shoot just the landings on Omaha Beach.

I used a very unfortunate word which is often misunderstood. In an earlier response where I said I was like a "method director." And people say, "Ooh, the 'method!'" What a horrible Stanislavsky term that is. That simply means that you let the environment, you let the circumstances around you, you let the immediate moment inspire you. You look for the inspiration. You look for all the mojos. And in starting the movie in continuity, at least everyone knew we had to open the boats and the rangers had to come out of the boats, and they had to take some defilade behind those Belgian gates, those big steel crosses. So at least everyone was prepared the first day. They knew where we were shooting. And I had it laid out in blocks of two or three days. We would try to take the beach the same way the rangers took the beach. The first day we would try to just get from the Higgins boats to the Belgian gates. The third day of shooting we would simply try to get from the Belgian gates to the seawall. That turned into five days of shooting just to get to the seawall. But it was kind of like taking a beach on a relatively safe method. And that's all we had to do. My support crew, the special effects people especially, the stunt people, had to know what blocks we were shooting from day to day because there were so many charges. You have to understand that they created a grid of squibs and explosions, and the actors were trained where not to be. And we beat it into them where they could not be and where they had to be. And so there were so many safety meetings on this film. Most of the time was taken with repeated safety meetings. So accidentally one of my actors wouldn't wander into an area where we had taken the stakes out with the red tape that marked the danger zones. We didn't want anybody wandering into those areas. Those are only for the stuntmen. And we had a tremendous contingent of stuntmen on this picture. I was more concerned with people getting hurt than I was about getting the shot. So most of the time was spent, "Okay, are you sure you know where you must not go? And if you get any sand in your eyes, will you please stop and not continue the shot? Don't anybody be a hero. Drop your gun or just go like this, and say, 'I'm out of the shot,' and we'll stop everything, we'll start over again." So much of it was like a football game. Huddling before each shot. And every shot I held my breath. There wasn't one shot in this movie where we didn't have some effect going off because this wasn't a CGI [computer graphic imaging] movie. This wasn't a special effect film. This was a physical effect picture. There wasn't one moment where we weren't all just saying, "Oh, please God, don't let anything go wrong here."

I found that it worked really well, especially when I was shooting over the German machine gun emplacements, to simply let the cameramen find their shots and not tell them anything. And I pretty much left it up to them to get the shots. So in a sense, there were many little moments of individual directing efforts on the part of the camera operators. This was one moment where you could actually go to a camera operator and say, "For those two shots, you directed this picture, not me." And because I gave Mitch [Dubin], our main operator, a chance really to respond to being shot at. Because he was running behind the rangers, right up to the beach. And there was one shot that I'll never forget that he did. I don't know what brought him to do it, but I had put a number of soldiers on the ground who were really in agony, and as Mitch was running through the fields following Tom Hanks with explosions going off and the casement firing down at them, for some reason, he caught some guy out of the side of his eye, and he brought the camera down and just showed the face of a soldier who was screaming in pain, and then came back off of him again and came back up again. I didn't tell him to do that. The environment was so intense, with such firepower seemingly coming down at Mitch that he just became intuitive with the camera and made intuitive choices, as many of the operators made, as all the signal corps cameramen in the '40s made when they were actually out there in the Pacific, in Europe, trying to document WWII.

There were very few Steadicam shots. Probably no Steadicam shots at all anywhere on Omaha Beach. It was all handheld. And it was handheld with the shaker lens, and I would run behind with a monitor, with a small handheld monitor, so I at least had some idea what we were getting.

The scene where Giovanni Ribisi tells the story of his mother, pretending he's asleep—I had first of all shot his death and his death was probably one of the most emotional things I'd ever been around as a director. And we shot it all day. It was torture for everybody. But it came off so well when I first cut the film together that I realized that Giovanni didn't have a story that prepared you to know him or care about him enough to care about his death. So I asked the writer to come back, and I asked him to write a scene, and I said let's go into a church, and let's do a scene with Giovanni talking about his mother. So that scene was written after the film was in first cut.

Everybody had ideas. Every actor came that morning with an idea of how they wanted to react to what they knew was going to be coming at them. I remember one day I went over to Tom Hanks, and we were shooting the capturing of what we called Steamboat Willie—the Wehrmacht soldier. And I had been feeling and empathizing with Tom the whole time, wondering when he was going to break, because I wanted him to break at some point. I didn't know when or how, and Tom was looking for a moment to break, but he didn't know when and how either. And one day I walked over to him. I said, "You want to just try something? What if you just kind of walked over to the crater, and you sit down, you take out your map, you look at it, and you just start to lose it. And you just lose it." And Tom, he's an amazing person to work with. Instead of sitting with me and analyzing why he would lose it at that moment, and whether it was the right time, and whether he was really prepared for a crying scene, he went, "Okay." So we set up two cameras. One on a slow dolly, and one with 85mm lens just on Tom's face, and Tom went, and he did that moment. And he broke down, and he cried. And he cried as long as he needed to cry. And at the end of that, he was a wreck. He got up and he had to leave the set. He had to go behind some rubble. And he came back to me and he said, "Do you want to do it again?" I said, "No. Do you?" He said, "No." And that was it. That was the first take. It was in the movie.

We've all shot in rain before, we all had rain experiences, and rain's a very debilitating form of environment that you bring down on yourself and your company. But in this movie it really helped everybody feel miserable, because they were. And there was one little moment I remember in that scene with the French girl, where he was handing her off to a stranger. And the idea was that she would come back to her dad. And I thought that a natural thing would be, just personally, because I've got a lot of kids, that if I handed one of my kids off to a stranger, I would expect my kid to slap me across the face. So I told her, I said, "When you come back to your dad, I want you to beat him. I want you to slap him as hard as you can across the face." And she just couldn't do it. She just couldn't hit anybody across the face. And this wonderful actor took her aside behind the scenes and said, "It won't hurt; I promise you it won't hurt." And she just tapped him like this, and he said, "No, hit me harder, harder." And he prepared her. When we went to do the scene, she really hauled off and slapped him. She really hit him a number of times. And then she came over to me after that and she said, "Can I do it again?"

Martin Scorsese, *Gangs of New York*

It became like a live organism in a way, particularly in the scene, the theater scene, where they're doing *Uncle Tom's Cabin*. The four hundred guys in there, with the top hats, and for four or five days you'd see one person move, they'd all move with him. You see it in the film when the gun goes off. You see everybody move back, instinctively.

I love that stuff, where the actor is sort of looking almost as if he's looking in the lens; it makes such a strong connection emotionally with the other person. But in reality to do that the lens has gotta be where the head of the other actor is. So you have the other actor's head tucked in and the actors are wonderful. They do it. Looking right to a little mark right on the edge of the lens. I've seen a lot of this in [Stanley] Kubrick's films. And I had Daniel [Day-Lewis] sitting there and John [C. Reilly] and we started improvising the scene. The scene was only three-quarters of a page. And at one point Daniel said, "I have a crazy idea." I said, "What?" "I think . . . ." I said, "No, no, no, just do it. I'm shooting it." And it was the moment where he says, "I'm really interested in getting this; I want the kid who hurt this poor little rabbit," but he breaks down crying. And John hadn't expected it and then he said, "Well, I can go further," and he took the rabbit pelt and put it on his head as if he was pronouncing sentence, and then we did long improvisations on John's angle. And that's a sort of thing, to have that kind of life occur was really something.

Ultimately it was like paintings: the more I felt that the people were inhabiting those sets or inhabiting those images, it was like I'd want it to go wider and wider rather than closer. Michael Ballhaus [the cinematographer] and myself played around with positioning people. No movement at all. It may have been too posed. The women in the bed, it was one of those things. I said, "No, no, we need the whole set." We were rushing; I said, "Okay, we could just do an overhead."

There's three hundred men fighting each other and the kid is running between them. I mean, it's, we're trying to make it as realistic, as real as possible, make the kids understand it as much as possible that this is real. And when you get chased, we're gonna catch you, so you better run, you know. And the kids were really great that way.

Vic Armstrong is a second-unit director who has been in the business a long, long time. And he came on the picture and then he did for another six weeks bits and pieces for me. And I showed him a scene in *Potemkin* [the film masterpiece of 1925 by Sergei Eisenstein], where the sailor is washing a dish that says, "Give us this day our daily bread," and they had just, they had no food, you know? So he's looking at the dish and looking at the dish and whock! He breaks the dish. And it's about fifteen shots. And I'm looking at this. I've seen it many times. I'd say, "That's interesting." What's interesting to me is that when he pulled back his arm, they kept cutting to his shoulder, but the action already had been completed. But the power and the anger was here. I said. "Let's just start shooting bits and pieces," I said, "You figure out the action to intercut, but you track from left to right and do it, start at forty-eight frames, go to thirty-six, go to twenty-four, go back. And the next, do another take just the opposite." And then the last battle scene with a mass of Union troops coming in, into Five Points, that was done with seven cameras pretty much in one day. And then I designed some scenes and Vic continued for another few weeks shooting bits and pieces, and by that point according to designs and drawings and things we were pulling out with money and what we could afford, what we couldn't afford—I had three units going. And I would just go from unit to unit. With a golf cart.

Martin Scorsese, *The Aviator*

I was shooting a lot of green screen [a process where the actors are photographed against a green- or blue-colored screen and then the environment is added into the image in postproduction], which is a whole other thing I never really used. We had [Leonardo] DiCaprio in this cockpit being knocked around on one soundstage and then—we were going behind schedule and wanted to finish, and we did finish on schedule—it was a fairly well-planned film—and so they said, "Marty, we want you to come over to soundstage B because we're gonna show you something." And I'd run over there and I look around. There's all these people in the crew I never saw before. So who are these? So I sit down and I see the set is the shot where I want the wheel going through the roof, and the guys were gonna get it for me and the special effects people there too, working on it. And they explained to me, my assistant director looked at me, Joe Reedy, and said "Marty, I want you to understand that if you want another take, it will take seven hours. That's where the wheel's gonna hit. It's gonna come this way." "Right." "And there's where the camera."—"I know."—"We got this covered."—"That's slow motion, this one is that. The woman in the foreground is gonna be put in later because we shot that earlier with you."—"Yeah, that's right. We shot that yesterday." "Okay." So I said, "And are you ready now?" He said, "No," he said, "we'll get you, we'll get you back." So I went back, shot some more green screen. And then hours later they took me onstage. And I sat down again. Again, I say, "Who are these people?" They said, "They're here for the day to do this shot." I said, "Oh." and I realized that again when he said, "You understand of course that if something, you

Martin Scorsese. (The Aviator © 2004 under license from Miramax Film Corp. All rights reserved.)

don't like something, uh, it would take seven hours to do a second take." I said, "Yeah, I get it now," because I figured whatever happens, I'm gonna have to like this. I'm gonna have to really love it. And I had some friends with me. We're sitting and all of a sudden that thing hit. Boy, it was great. It was terrific. And we played back on video and it was fantastic.

The part of Howard Hughes that Leo played, the twenty years, it was literally shot way out of continuity. Because of actors' schedules and different location problems here and there, I mean, two days of the week he'd be twenty-six years old and three other days forty-six. I mean it was very hard for him.

There was one [shot] we had a serious problem with. It was a shot of Leo flying the Hercules at the end, which starts with the whole plane that goes all the way in, all the way in to his eyes. That one, that one took a little doing.

Once they're around a table, it's okay to use the two cameras. It's just sometimes you certainly sacrifice composition and lighting as a problem. That's a serious problem.

Clint Eastwood, *Unforgiven*

Some people perform at their very best early in the game, and maybe they'll disintegrate and you can bring it back up. I like to set the atmosphere and just kind of go through it, and as we're going through and setting cameras, I'll just have the actors just talk through it: "Don't try to put too much into it." And in *Unforgiven*, I had Gene Hackman, and I had Morgan Freeman, two of the fastest startup actors I had ever worked with. Gene is one of those guys who—I think he is one of America's best actors, he just is ready to go immediately. You start the rehearsal and you're going, "My God, why aren't we rolling?" And so what I would do is start rolling early. I'd say, "Let's just rehearse this on film."

I like improvisation, I must say, I like that feeling of that first time. And I guess a lot of the directors I've worked with out of television and everything didn't have the benefit of rehearsals so you want to expedite things fast. Jessica Walter, in the very first film I ever directed [*Play Misty for Me*], she was one of those kinds who loved to rehearse on film, loved it, that first time out of the box. Now it isn't always ideal and sometimes it won't be as good. Sometimes you may do three or four takes. There may be something in that first take, though, that's great. There may be a section of it that is just fabulous, and you may never recapture it again. I think that's the advantage of film—you can try things and see what happens and you don't have to use it.

I think a director's most important function is probably a comfort zone that he can set up for the actors, because every actor has a certain insecurity level when they first come on. It's a very frightening experience—you are up in front of a lot of people you don't know, and all of the sudden you are going to start spouting dialogue you've thought about, but you've never heard it come out of your mouth. Then, you set a comfort zone, try to make everybody feel very, very much at ease, and sometimes you can do that by saying, "Well, here are all the props and stuff, and you walk around and you do this, and the cameraman will be here, we'll be lining up some things," and you give the actors a chance to be free and wander about and get it, and all of the sudden—boom!—they're ready to go.

The main thing I always tell other directors is "Get more sleep than anyone else," and so I go to bed relatively early and try to get a decent night's sleep and go in with

Clint Eastwood on the set of Unforgiven. *(*Unforgiven *© Warner Bros., a division of Time Warner Entertainment Company L.P. All rights reserved.)*

absolute will. You are gonna will these shots. They're going to be made. Never look back and never think negatively that "Oh gee, what happens?" I hate the expression—a lot of times people use—"Oh, I'm afraid of this, I'm afraid that won't work." If you are afraid, then you shouldn't be there.

With the actors, I kind of start out kind of gradually. Sometimes a European technique, where the director shows the actors what to do, is effective only if the actor asks for it. I remember Vittorio De Sica [Italian director of such masterpieces as *The Bicycle Thief* and *Two Women*] insists on acting out every part for every actor. I don't do that unless the actor gets "salty" with you. I had one actor once who insisted on going into a corner, and we were trying to stage a scene in his room. It was an interesting room—it had a lot of nice set decorations put up there—and he says, "Well, I feel better over here in this corner." Well, there's nothing more dull than shooting into a wall that's flat. I kept saying, "Well, you know it's such a bad place to be," and he says, "Well, this is where I feel it." And I said, "Well, I tell you what—why don't you try it where I feel it out here?" And he's going, "Well, how would you do it?" And so I thought, I've got to appeal to this guy's ego, so I walk over to this window and say, "You feel this light coming, see this light coming through the window, see how it hits? Now it's really dramatic; it makes your face look sensational." So all of the sudden, this guy's going "Yeah, yeah, that's okay, that sounds good!" So pretty soon I got him out into the room. Sometimes you have to be a little bit of an amateur psychologist or psychiatrist.

My first three or four films, I shot exactly what I wanted. Then later on as time goes by sometimes you give yourself a luxury of shooting a little extra footage or extra angles that you think might be effective, but you have some sort of doubt about.

The first two films that I did I used video [connected to the camera that shows what the camera sees and can be replayed with a VCR]. I found it helpful in some ways, but I found it also something that could be very abused. A lot of times I'd see the shot and we had to put the video player in a trailer. So I'd go back to the trailer and I'd hear this rumble behind me, and I'd look and here's all the actors and half the crew, everybody's come and they're all going to see the shot. And after a while the actors are saying, "Well, I could do one more and could I have my hair fixed and makeup?" So I finally would only use it on my own close-up, something I was in doubt about, a crane shot or something like that. And then in recent years, I've just discontinued using it altogether.

I know there's a lot of precedent for actors, dating back since the beginning of filmmaking, actors who have directed themselves, but I don't recommend it as a usual way. Sometimes you'll say, "Well, wait a second—I'm in this scene, but I'm only about 40 percent in here because I'm really thinking technically and I'm worried about the other actors, the light on them." I remember years ago, I was doing a film with an actor, an older actor, and he was having trouble with his dialogue. So I started kind of rooting for him, and we'd have the camera over here, and I'd be kind of mouthing it along with him. When the camera came around here, I was mouthing along with him again! And the camera operator said, "You know, you were mouthing his lines with him." And the shot was on me!

Nowadays television has trained the eye to look at cinematography differently than when we grew up, because we grew up looking at [John] Ford pictures and [Orson] Welles and various people that would do some very bold work. And nowadays sometimes people are afraid, a little more cautious. I'll look through the lens at times; I'll have a stand-in go through it if I have to be in a shot or if it's a sequence. Naturally films that you're not in are much easier, but I'll look through the lens maybe on a rehearsal of some kind or maybe it's a simple shot and I know what the lens is and I know what it's seeing.

Clint Eastwood, *Mystic River*

I'm always looking for accidents, mistakes, and I love things when the actors are forced to think outside the box a little bit. I guess the biggest accident that I can think of was Tim Robbins: He comes out and he lights a cigarette on the porch. And the matchbook explodes in his face. It just blows up. But he goes like this, and he's looking down and he stayed in character and he walked out. And so I printed it. I said, "Print. Thanks, and we'll go on and we'll move over here." And he's looking like "You can't be serious." But it was great. It was just a natural thing. He stayed in character, he looked down to where the matches might have gone two stories down, and then he came over and he stayed in character with the film. And those are little things that sometimes little human aspects that you can't buy in a film. If you tell somebody to do that, then they become sort of studied or forced, but if you allow the actor to have that kind of freedom, then you can enjoy it more.

I did a film some years ago with Meryl Streep. When I showed her the rough cut of the film, she said, "God, you printed all my mistakes." And I said, "Yeah, I did, but your mistakes are wonderful." You are trying to give the illusion that these lines are said for the very first time. And sometimes with me, they are. But if they don't work, you go back and you mold it or you have story points that you have to accentuate. But by and large, I like actors to have freedom. I think it's very important.

Sometimes I'll go on the set by myself and just block it out in my mind. And then other times I'll have the cinematographer watching and then I'll say, "Here's what you do," and "We're gonna do this." And sometimes the actors will do something that's just brilliant. Just by their own instincts they do something that's great and you say, "Let's just follow this around. Don't change a thing." And it just all depends. There's no real rule to it.

We were doing a shot on Kevin Bacon and Laurence Fishburne and I just wanted to do it in one shot. I didn't want to do any coverage or anything. So we tried a take and we had to go down a hallway and we only had so much hallway, and it came to an end. The guys came to an end. We couldn't get the scene in. So I kept saying, I said, "I'm going to give you a Frank Capra direction. 'Just talk faster.'" And so we tried that, and that didn't work. And finally we're going down and we were just barely, just missing getting this in the one shot. And so finally I said, "Okay. You're Rosalind Russell and you're Cary Grant, and this is *His Girl Friday*. So you know how they used to talk in those things? You're listening but at the same token you're anticipating and going right over it like people do a lot of times in conversation." And boom, one take. Print. And we were through.

If I feel a scene's very, very difficult for an actor, very, very emotional, I'll set the scene up so that I know the actor can do it the first time, if it works for 'em. And in this picture it was kind of a dream cast. So they were all ready to go. They were all ready on the very first time. So I could just say, "Okay, we're going to come out here and we're going to follow you down here, and then you're going to come around and we're going to end up on you and then you'll come around again and we'll end up on him." And the actors would fall right into it. If you don't have people like that, then you have to kind of maybe get a little bit more diagram. But this idea of putting a mark down on the floor and saying that that's, you're wedded to that, is pretty inhibiting. And if you start explaining when to look up and all that, it gets very mechanical. You can just watch an actor's eyes get tense. And to me, the tension should be what the character has to give, not in the tension on the set. And so if it's a highly intense scene, I want the adrenaline of that scene to be in the acting, not in the fact that there's a lot of uncomfortable crap going around. So I'll try to keep everything down. I keep the sets extremely quiet so I can just go like that and they roll. I don't have to say, "Action," I don't have to say, "Roll 'em." I can just ease 'em right into it. So all their adrenaline is in the emotion that they have to put forward to that scene, not in somebody coming out and hitting a monstrous clapper in front of their face and saying, "Go." So these are just tricks. I direct the way I like to be directed. We printed every first take. A couple times maybe something technically, or something wasn't right. But by and large, those actors, actors like that are ready to go. Sometimes we'd be walking through an alley and I just would want to keep the take in one piece so I'd say, "At a certain point in the scene, why don't you come around here so I can feature you in the over shoulder; then we'll move forward and then you come around the other person," and just vice versa like that so they just go around. And that kind of thing you have to sort of block it slightly. But the actors know and it's not like the old days when you'd do sort of a master shot and everybody'd upstage each other. In a movie, you upstage yourself, you're out of focus. You can't do that so everybody, everybody is very generous, and the generosity of actors to actors is one of the things that makes it all click.

The way you could do it with these people. You just start right in and fire away. And we did a scene and then the coverage they did a couple takes, various takes on Sean [Penn] because sometimes it would get jumbled up or what have you. But by and large, he can play with such intensity that you don't want to burn him out and get anything less than that 100 percent thing you've gotten. So sometimes I'll change cutting around to adapt, matching-wise, to what the actor has done rather than try to say, "Hey, Mac, try to match up to the last shot." I'll maybe come back and revamp another shot so that the matching fits.

With the young kids I'd say, "Go play ball for a while. Go play." And pretty soon they get talking and they get hanging out together and you can almost sneak up behind them with a Steadicam and shoot dialogue if you wanted that kind of an atmosphere. When they were in the yard explaining that one of the kids had been abducted, I just said, "Just tell 'em the story. Don't pay any attention to any dialogue. You just tell these men down here what happened." And so they were all overlapping each other and doing all kinds of natural things.

Sean has a very pointed scene where he's talking about his daughter being murdered and he couldn't cry for her, and he improvised a line. He says, "I just want to hug her one more time." You can't buy that. An actor says that—that's why that's the first take. But I set that scene up so it would only be one take and just a slight creep in. But because I knew that he's going to burn, you just can't do a scene like that too many times.

I used to find if I got a director who wouldn't print anything until take 8 or 9 or something, I'd find I'd coast seven takes. I'd just kind of wander around and finally they'd print one and you'd go, "Jesus, I don't want that." but if they know you're trying for it—and I learned this from Don Siegel [director of *Dirty Harry*] and a lot of those old-timers, the John Ford school. They used to all do that because they were, these guys were serious, get-things-done-type people. And I worked with William Wellman [director of *The Public Enemy, A Star Is Born, The Ox-Bow Incident*] one time and he was like that. They're ready to go, so you've got to be ready to go. So pretty soon you all stay in the mood, and if you keep the atmosphere proper on the set, then everybody is ready to fire when ready.

I've worked with people who did that [shooting multiple cameras]. But then there's the other theory. Two theories. One that you'd solve all the matching problems. But the other is that you get two mediocres instead of one excellent. You have to compromise one angle somewhere.

I don't use an instant replay. I just don't. I used to use them. The first picture I did thirty-four years ago. But I found that most good actors really don't want to see themselves. They don't want to see anything. They just want to feel it from the inside. And maybe they want to see it later or something, but I don't think they want to see it during the process. However, like we were talking earlier, there's no rules. But the way it is now, I just never use the instant replay. I just depend on my own thing. I use a little tiny plasma screen that's flat with a handle on it, and I'll carry that around and I can look at the setup so I don't have to always be eyeballing the camera. I can look at the setup or the framing and stuff like that, so I'll be watching the scene and sometimes I'll just glance at that. It's radio controlled into the camera. But I don't like instant replay. It forms a committee right away, and I don't want to form a committee.

To help an actor I might say, "There's a couple points you're missing here," and explain, "I think that if you tried it, maybe, with this thought or maybe try it with a little different mental attitude and see where it comes out." But most of the time, your actors are pretty smart and they're ready to contribute greatly. If you don't suppress them in any way, they will bring you all kinds of contributions that you can utilize. One good thing about not being a writer, though it's a big disadvantage and I certainly admire people who can do it, is that I'm not wedded to any of the dialogue. If something else can be said in a different way and it's more comfortable for the performer, then I would prefer to go that way. Sometimes a little bit messy or a little bit raggedy kind of works well for you because it seems more human, more lifelike.

Clint Eastwood, *Million Dollar Baby*

I shoot a lot leaner than I used to. Once in a while you get with directors that shoot a ton of footage and then others, I've worked with the leanest shooter I've ever known in my life was Vittorio De Sica. He'd shoot and he'd give you a rough cut the next day. And it was because he only shot exactly what he wanted. And Don Siegel was a little bit like that. Like Sam Fuller [director of *Steel Helmet, Shock Corridor, The Big Red One*], like Budd Boetticher [*Bullfighter and the Lady*]. They didn't have the budgets to do a lot so they had to know exactly where they were going. And so from Don I learned that I may not always get it right away, but I'm always trying for it right away. And that way I find that crews kind of are with you 'cause they feel like you're going somewhere. And so that's been philosophically mine.

I still like occasionally to do scenes all in one piece, but if you do, you gotta make sure your rhythm's right.

By and large I kind of know what I'm going to shoot when I go in, in the morning and—and I kind of have the architecture but I don't necessarily plan shots or anything. I just go in and we just start in. They're in there in the subconscious and I just bring 'em out to the conscious mind. I used to do shot lists when I started. I'd put everything on the back of the opposite page and exactly how I was going to do it but I find myself not doing it that way when I get in there. So I figured what the hell, might as well just swing along with it.

Children are the greatest actors in the world if you just don't rehearse 'em and beat 'em up. If you wear 'em down, they'll become the stiffest, the worst. In *Perfect World* I had to cast the boy. He wasn't the best technical actor. He was the worst technical actor, but he was the best of moments. He listened the best. The kid would lean out of the shot and he'd come back in, and he was doing all these things. And I said, "God, this guy is amazing." But you had to get him right away. And so I would shoot the kid first usually because I could get the camera rolling without him even knowing it, and sometimes I'd do a lot of that.

I had had another scene where another child was supposed to be in the shot and she was supposed to break down, and she was a good actress but there's always that wall when they get to reality. And they said, "Oh, she can't be in the scene. She can't work for a while. She bumped her head on the side of a truck when she was outside the stage." And I said, "No kidding,"—I sound like one of these cruel guys out of the '20s that used to beat the kids and tell them their dog was dead—I said, "Could I see her just for a moment. Let me see if I can calm her down." Well I came in and she was crying and the scene was this other actress had to go in and comfort her. And we had the camera on a Steadicam, so I just said to the guy, "Go in," and we start shooting. And if you keep your set organized and if the set is not loud and you don't have a lot of people talking—and we don't, we used closed radios and everything so there's not a lot of noise going on—you can go right away. And I just go and the crew didn't even know we were shooting. My eight-year-old came on the set and her hair was all scroungy and she looked like she had been rolling in the dirt. And I looked at her and I said, "Yeah, that could be Hilary [Swank] when she was a little girl." I said, "Bring Morgan back next week. I've got a little thing I just want to. Don't tell her she's going to be in anything." And so they just brought her in and put her in there and I started talking to her and had Hilary start talking, chatting with her. Then pretty soon I just started rolling the camera, didn't tell her, and, you know, always end-sticks [this is when you slate or mark the beginning or the end of the shot with what is called a clapper, which makes noise to synchronize and identify sound and picture for editing], kinda like on a Western. And I say, "Now, don't do anything. Now just sit there and just talk about that dog and feel how it is. That dog is the only thing you got in the world. And now you look over and you see this lady here and that's it." And you can do that with kids.

I never recommend directing and performing in a film. It's . . . I started out of necessity. That's the only way I could get the directing job. I swore after the last picture, *Mystic River*, that I would never act again. I was going to stay on the back side of the camera. I loved it there, loved watching the younger people. Then all of a sudden the role comes along, and you never say never because a role comes along that intrigues you. I carry a little plasma screen with a handle on it. I may look at it and say, "Well, yeah, hmm. He looks good today." And put it down and just kind of step back and forget about it. But it's difficult to kind of keep throwing that switch in your mind and get into the performing thing and forget about it; you just have to have faith in yourself. You know when you're clicking on all eight cylinders and you know when you're on seven. And it's just a question of making sure you get to where you want to be in that particular thing. It's all done by feel. It's not done by any great intellect. It's not an intellectual art form and you have to emotionally put yourself into it and go for it. I did certain scenes in the picture that included myself which I didn't even rehearse. I just set the camera and I'd say to the other actor, "How do you feel about this?" And he'd say, "I'm ready," and so we'd shoot it. It doesn't always work. But in this case it did because the material was very strong and everybody was on top of their game.

I'm usually shooting before they know what happens, so everybody stays very relaxed. I also, I never use the word *Action* because I don't want that moment when the clapper hits too hard. The clapper guy has to be really quiet. Everything is really quiet, and I just say, "Okay, any time you're ready," And then at the end I just stop or whatever and "Enough of this crap," sometimes I say that. "Enough of this crap over here."

Roberto Benigni, *Life Is Beautiful*

Working with this little boy [Giorgio Cantarini] during shooting—it's like working with a giraffe, with an oak tree—what can I say? I put the camera there with a sea, what can I say to the sea, go home? No! The little boy was a very poor boy, very wonderful, pure really, but because it was first time for him, he couldn't learn by heart his lines and the concentration was one minute and a half. He thought to shoot a movie it takes two hours, like to watch.

In order to protect him, he's not an actor, I couldn't shoot with him together a master. Because he was imitating me, like a little monkey. He's full of energy and he was just imitating me. But when I was acting with him, it was impossible because he didn't know his lines. I was just telling him. So I adapted to the boy. It's a kid direction.

For me, I don't sleep the night before. And my dreams, they are directing, maybe my unconscious. I am dreaming somebody is telling to me, "What are you doing? What are you doing?" Very directly. And I can't sleep during the shooting because I feel that I don't know where I am going. Like Columbus, maybe I think to discover India, and I find America. I am sure that I am going toward something, and then I discover another direction, and I won't discover India. When I read the diary of Christopher Columbus, the crew wanted to come back, and I feel sometimes that I am never sure. A lot of the time, I'm not certain what to do. And the crew, they feel everything, and this is good. The director makes the feeling, and that's very good. And when I am only actor in movies, I like to have this feeling very much. I can feel very much the director. And so I'm thinking, when I'm directing, maybe I am doing this. And that's good. And I feel when the ship is going in another direction, or it's a moment when I'm not sure about what I'm doing, everybody, actors especially, they feel it. So I'm inventing. Because art is something you feel, but you cannot explain. And actors, they have to feel. I think this. So when I start to explain, "You are bourgeoisie." I feel like a real idiot. Because the script is there. I so offensive to explain.

Peter Weir, *The Truman Show*

What I do is use music. I'll go home and I'll have a quick bite. I find Japanese food's the best to eat in a shoot. Easily digested. And I'll play music for an hour or so and do all my thinking for the next day on some level. Not sort of literally. But I find that music stops me thinking. Because we all know jobs are mostly practical. And necessarily so. And the danger is that you won't have the door open to the inspiration. How do you keep it open? So for me music is probably one of the key ways. A good walk and so forth is good, but it stops the intellect. And you switch on to some other thing as the music goes through your head. And then I'll go, "Oh God," and write something down. It sort of almost works as simply as that for me. I have certain pieces to get me into certain moods that relate to the film. And then next morning, going to work sometimes, which is a very difficult time, that first approach to work, just getting everybody going. And so I'll play the music often very loud to myself. Because when you think about it, imagine you can cram your trailer with Gauguins and Van Goghs and all the great art of the history of the world, and Michelangelo's sculptures, and walk through your trailer and feel all this stuff, and go out and direct, but you can't. You can with music, the treasure of the world.

Peter Weir, *Master and Commander: The Far Side of the World*

There was one specific week of shooting on the Galapagos Islands where you could not deviate from the path. We had very, very strict supervision from the Ecuadorian National Parks because there were tortoise eggs off to the side or rare plants. And you couldn't touch the animals. So it was sort of like Mack Sennett [director of slapstick comedies] time in the sense that I'd keep the actors and camera very close behind ready to go for it and improvise a scene with a sea lion, if it was lying there or a bird that was kind of wandering about. But what a wonderful way to shoot, you know? They knew their characters well. And they had their equipment that naturalists would have and so forth. So they'd be brought forward, the cameras would roll, and we picked up some wonderful spontaneous stuff.

I always think, when I finished a scene, is there anything I can get for free, you know, within the lighting setup. And I'll grab stuff sometimes and improvise. There was one scene that did not work in which the dialogue was flat, so I said, "Look, I've got a problem. It's not working. You can feel it yourselves." There was about six of them in the scene. I said, "Everybody back off. Let's talk. What do you think? What could you say? What would you say?" And so we cooked up a new scene, wrote it on the spot. It was in the middle of the doldrums and they were beginning to think that their ship was under some sort of curse and they had a Jonah. They'd all had experience, I think, at improvisation, and so in a fairly short time we got the scene, and we rewrote it together.

After the first day's dailies of seeing this young boy [Max Pirkis, who plays Midshipman Blakeney], it was as if he had an actor, an old actor's soul in his body. And I tried to talk to him about it at one point, as others did, and he didn't want to talk about it. How do you do it? How are you doing this? Only thing I noticed he'd yawn before every take. But not a normal yawn, a kind of an odd yawn. I think he went into some sort of hypnotic trance. His part was not enlarged but definitely I gave him more challenges to do, and you could ask him to repeat things. That's essentially the difference between an amateur and a professional. The amateur can get it once or twice. Once you get into the hard grind of multiple takes, forget it. 'Cause they say, "I don't feel it." And you say, "Well, that's what acting is, you're faking it." But with Max Pirkis I could, as with an experienced sort of virtuoso performer say, "Could you just look down before you say that last line and then look up 'cause I'm catching your eyes in this close-up in a very particular way," and he could do that.

I do a lot of storyboards, particularly for this picture. I work with the storyboard artist Dan Sweetman. I also do my own little drawings. I'll go into the set on my own at night or in the morning sometimes and sort of be each character to some extent. But then, you don't want to overwhelm the actors with your ideas. It's always a very interesting moment. You could bombard an actor with "I think you're here, you pick up the water, right? And then you look up and you're surprised. And then you go back, and that'll be a wonderful moment," and the actor looks at you. And the actor says, "Why don't you play the part?" So you have to pretend that you don't sometimes have an idea. And sometimes you don't. Of course, there are days where really the muse disappears and you're in a really bad way and you're leaning more heavily on your actors and your cameraman. But generally speaking, I think you're always looking for the truth of the scene; you're looking for the truth of the shot. And somehow, if the scene is rightly in the movie, it will come. You will know where to put the camera. The actor will say, "I think I should be already in the room. Coming through the door it just doesn't feel right, it's awkward." And so on. And so in a strange way it's as if you're like iron filings drawn to a magnet. In a picture like this, in a lot of movies today, two-camera pictures, we work with Steadicam with Harry Garvin on that and Don Reddy on handheld camera, on a gimbal—everything was moving all the time, rarely used sticks [a tripod]. But ideally, I'd prefer to work with one camera and there's one place to put it, and that's good discipline for you with one camera. It's sort of, well, where should it be? With two cameras, you can defer it, so you have "a bob each way," as we say in Australia. One of them will work or we'll use both.

I think if you have a problem with a scene, it often needs rewriting or it shouldn't

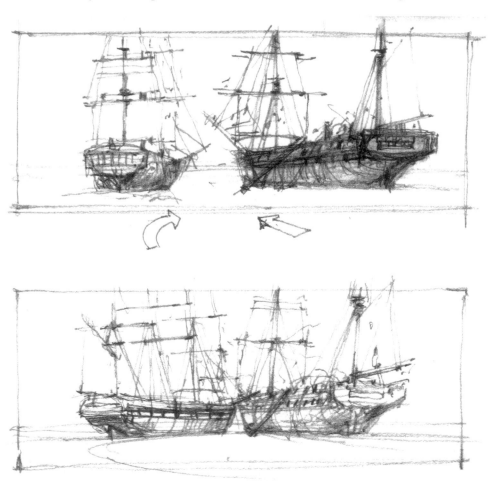

Production design for battle scene for Master and Commander:
The Far Side of the World. *(Courtesy of Peter Weir.)*

be in the movie. It often amuses me when I say, I'll see a scene drop out in the cutting room and I'll say, "You know? We always had trouble with that scene. We had trouble with it in the writing; we had trouble with it in the directing." It was just not truthful.

I'm kind of like six, seven takes. I like the energy to be pretty high right from the start. I think it's all about energy, a lot of this thing we do. And you can have bad days. The energy is awkward and down. But if you're fortunate, most days the energy is up. And in they come and you're rapidly shooting. But I do like a kind of reckless energy. That is to say, you might just drop everything. You might just sort of say, "Let's just do a wide shot on this, you know? Let's drop all that fancy tracking shot. What's that for? It's wasting everybody's time and there's so many marks it's getting complicated for the actors. Let's just do a wide shot." Double or nothing, gamble on it, you know? And so I like to think the script's a blueprint; anything can happen on the day. And you can only do that when you've got a good, strong structure where your script has got a good spinal column, as it were. Then you can wander off, try things, and come back.

That terrible moment where your scene is really not working and you sense it's a problem with the actor—and if you speak up, particularly in a confined space—the crew picks it up. So what I'll tend to do is change the angle, I think. And so you say, "Great. We've got that one. Let's go over here. Let's do another master of it." So you really then just a wink and a nudge with Alan [Disler, the cameraperson] who'll know. And then there's the time taken to change the thing around: You'll go and have a cup of coffee, maybe, with the actor and just say, "Did you feel this works? Were you happy with that?" And I'll say, "Well, we're going to do it; it'll get covered from the top again." But I think sometimes that forward momentum everybody loves to feel, all right, we've got that angle—otherwise it can get bogged down.

Barry Levinson, *Bugsy*

You may spend twelve hours a day, and out of that maybe walk away with two minutes of usable film. So the concentration of the director on the set has to be very, very focused. You can't miss a moment because you never know when those two minutes will happen.

Sometimes the blocking [the actors' movement] is not clear and then I'll just let the actors keep playing around with it as we keep evolving into some kind of blocking that begins to make sense and feels comfortable. When you approach a new scene, there's always a certain amount of trepidation. So just really being very comfortable with it and trying the blocking that makes sense, like you might say, "It'd be nice if we went over towards the window." But rather than saying to the actor, "Why don't you go to the window?" Because then they say, "Why do I have to go to the window?" It's better that they went to the window and got there by themselves. It's a little bit like trying to get what you want and at the same time not wanting to be so demanding that we're restricting the process. I like to give an actor as much room as possible to explore anything that might come up. And the performance may change radically as we begin to play with it.

It's not always the words themselves. It is the struggle to say the words and what they may represent other than the actual words. And that's kind of what I'm trying to evolve to in the easiest way of sneaking up on the performance. You have to work in different ways with different actors. I did *Good Morning, Vietnam*, and I had a classroom of all of these Vietnamese, none of them could act or knew anything about it. And what we did was just try to keep the camera and hide it. You don't say, "Action"; you don't say anything. You just sort of launch them. And somehow they don't even know that they're being filmed anymore. They don't really know. There's a cause and effect that's taking place, and yet the script is being serviced to some degree. Because a lot of times they will say different things that may be better than what we have. And they're not aware of it. You have to find a way to get their behavior on film without intimidating them.

Sometimes it takes longer for some actors to warm up than others. Some of them are there in that earlier take, and others are fourteen takes in, that's when they're starting to cook. That's a dilemma. You have to find some way that it's going to start to work.

Certain blocking suggests certain things. And then from that, between the blocking and what some ideas you have in terms of visualization, you will find the day's work and how it should take place.

In *Bugsy* I wanted to end up with Bugsy and Virginia behind the movie screen, because they were sort of like these people who wanted to be movie stars but never were. I knew I wanted to get to that. I didn't know how to get there. When the actors were kind of playing it, all of a sudden I said to Allen Daviau [the cinematographer], "We'll pick them up from the time they come through the door." They go around the room, we go behind the screen, one's behind the screen, one is in the clear—and it suddenly evolved into the entire scene as one take.

I like to use two cameras a lot. I'll put them anywhere, maybe at very odd angles to one another. A lot of times I find that the B camera, which is supposedly in the wrong place, is actually better than the one that's in the right place. We don't want to compromise a shot and the look of the film. But at the same time I think that you can find certain parameters that you can work within. And sometimes that second camera, which is slightly off, may be more interesting in a way, because it can't give you all of the information. And I found that a lot of times not having the total information engages the audience slightly more than having all the information. Most scenes in the film are two cameras, unless you've designed a specific shot for one camera.

Oliver Stone, *JFK*

People will tell you that my set's pretty wild, it's chaotic. Which is good, because each day is the day of birth. No matter how much you rehearsed it and how good it was in rehearsal three months before, it doesn't mean shit when you're out there. That's when it starts.

We had five cameras on certain days: we were running around between cameras. So many angles suggested themselves naturally at Dealy Plaza that a storyboard would've minimized the scene. Why limit yourself?

On the day of the final rehearsal, I might change the position radically and say, the point of view is totally wrong. It really should be inside this person or inside that person, or outside this. Or the entire movement of this should not be six shots. It should be one shot. And that will happen right then and there, and he'll [the cameraperson] go crazy because the lighting scheme has to change. But better that than shoot it and not be happy with it.

I can't sit there and wait for two hours while the cameraman lights. I just don't have that kind of patience. Certain directors do.

I usually get out in less than six takes. Could be the script, could be an actor, the camera, the lighting. I occasionally go seventeen, twenty-seven but very rarely.

How do you deal with the actors that start late? And I've had that problem many times. John Huston [director of *The Treasure of Sierra Madre, Prizzi's Honor*] had a great solution. He just announced that he was doing one or two takes. And the actors realized that it was for real. He did both and he walked away. There is some truth to that because it does force them to concentrate. I don't admire people that assume that film is free. It isn't. It's a privilege. I don't like people that just sit there for seven takes and warm up. It's a waste of everybody's time and energy. The crew is trying from take 1. I want it to work on take 1.

I encourage my actors to overlap all the time. I love the Wellesian technique. But there are certain actors who really—a line of dialogue is sacred to them. There are some actors that don't like to be changed at the last second.

I torture the sound man. Because I often like to do extreme close-up with an extreme wide [angle] at the same time. And they hate that.

BARRY LEVINSON: "I basically just mike everybody, whether they're on camera or not. They're going to have a wireless [microphone]."

BARBRA STREISAND: "They're the worst. I can tell you that from the actor's point of view. They're horrible."

OLIVER STONE: "My people don't like wireless either."

BARRY LEVINSON: "But it works extremely well. I did it in Thailand with all the people over there and you're able to use it. I like to mike everyone, whether they're on camera or off camera because sometimes things happen, because when we talk we overlap one another, all the time. It has to do with rhythms."

When I was doing *Diner*, we got into the diner scenes—I had not directed a movie before—and we started to shoot, we're looking this direction, and the actors are talking, and then the sound technician says after the take, "You've got a problem because we've got these overlaps." I said, "Yeah." He said, "But they're off camera." I said, "I know." He said, "But they're off mike." So I said, "Why can't they be miked? Why don't we mike them?" He said, "Because you can make the overlaps later in editing." In real life when we talk we overlap one another, all the time. So I prefer to struggle with the overlapping in the editing room rather than try to invent it.

Barbra Streisand, *Prince of Tides*

I like to know what I'm going to do, then to throw it away. Because I get bored easily. I don't like to do that many number of takes. A lot of the time I stage things in just one shot. I mean I just don't want to cover it because it's too boring. I kind of like that living on the edge of danger, the risk factor.

I have a video 8 camera and I go around and I do the shots that I see in my head.

I have also models near the sets. I like to know what I'm going to do. Does a wall have to move? What has to happen to get this shot?

I always imagine how I want it to be in my head. But I don't want to impose that on actors, at first. I impose it, if they don't come up with something better. I like to use reality and use what is—use the day, use the snow, use a prop I didn't see before. And so be open to the moment, be present in the moment.

I do find it fascinating that most actors would like to be told what to do. But I do like when the actor brings very definite opinions. Because again it forces this debate, the energy, and the aliveness.

Storyboarding that rape sequence I had done way before I had a set. So one reality exists on paper. Then when I'm on the set, then I don't look at them anymore. I love being able to be flexible and bending to what is, the reality that exists.

On *Yentl* David Watkins [the cinematographer] lit the set. So you could go any-where. So that I could do ten-minute masters and have two cameras that had to be choreographed to avoid each other.

Gary Ross, *Seabiscuit*

The actor who played the young Tobey Maguire would not let go of his father in the scene and just hung onto him. And I kept rolling. And he literally would not let him go and they just fell into an improv spontaneously while we were shooting. And it's the best part of the scene. Once they got past my dialogue, they got into the good stuff. It was spontaneous and kind of magical and wonderful. And it came from this young actor, a fifteen-year-old sort of having the guts to just go with it and not let go and hang on, which just amazed me from a kid of his age. I was just incredibly thankful.

Right before that scene I said, "What would have been the worst horse to be taken down from?" And he, Gary Stevens [who plays the jockey George Woolf] went, "Silver Charm." He has such amazing ability to get right there for somebody who hadn't acted much, and tears came to his eyes and we just rolled quickly. You know, like really quickly.

I previsualize a lot of the movie so when the actors show up, the blocking's pretty clear in my head, what I'm shooting's pretty clear in my head. But that doesn't mean that there isn't room for spontaneity, both in terms of the way I shoot it or in terms of the way we blocked it or what we're going to do. And the actors are absolutely an integral part of that conversation. But it does mean the conversation starts with—we're going to be here, you're going to be here, and we're going to do this. You know, the only day I didn't like is when I had to go inside and shoot a dinner table. Everything else was fine. I like being outside in the wind and the dirt and all that stuff and being in this world. No one likes to shoot a dinner table. I'd much rather shoot horses going forty-five miles an hour.

The first thing an actor has to do is not be watching themselves act, to remove the self-consciousness. So I've had with some actors video assist [where you can play back the shot scene on a monitor] just be lethal, where I won't let an actor look at it. I've hid the monitor, in fact. When the actor just says, "Okay, what am I doing wrong?" And then they start watching themselves act, you're done. You're not climbing out of that hole.

I think it's different for every actor. Chris Cooper is a very, very private man. The conversations between us are, he wants to know, as a reflection back, what I'm seeing. Jeff Bridges is the opposite. He'll want to get in and sort of gnash into the detail and try different options and try different things and sort of shuffle the cards a little bit differently. If it's not working, we'll find another way to shape the scene instead of just beating the horse to death. And then everybody gets tense and they feel it and the takes are climbing and it becomes a very counterproductive situation and you need to kind of mix that up and change it up. If what you're just dealing with is performance and you're pretty convinced that it's performance, get them to relax and try something new and maybe investigate a different interpretation so that the judgment leaves, so that it doesn't become about the "right" answer. It's okay, that's an answer, this is another answer, let's mix this up.

Alexander Payne, *Sideways*

We shot a 140-page script in forty-nine days, rarely working a twelve-hour day.

The scene when they're having dinner, that was improvised. Thomas Haden Church is really a funny guy and would sometimes in a read through add some funny lines and I'd put those in the script. But generally I work off pretty tight scripts and like it.

Where they're all having dinner together that dissolve-y montage feel, that was indicated in the screenplay, that it would be bits and pieces of their having dinner. And I had my little laundry list of shots to get. And basically I had the four actors and told them, "Have dinner." And then the cameraman and I had two cameras up—one for more two-shots and the other on a tighter lens searching. And then you find exactly how it works only in the moment of shooting.

Thomas Church's breakdown—that particular one—the first thing of that whole scene we shot was the close-up, his close-up 'cause he was understandably a little bit nervous about doing it and I knew he wouldn't go many takes. So we went two or three, and two cameras on him. Because I needed naturalism and because the script was long, I had told the actors to speak as quickly as possible, for a shot, reverse shot I would put up two cameras, and also so they can overlap and talk over and it wouldn't be a problem in editing. So a lot of it is when those two guys are together in restaurants and in the bar scene where Jack says, "I think I'm falling in love with another woman and wanna back out of my marriage," that was all with two cameras. Sometimes when you have two cameras up or three, it makes the actors more natural I think because then they don't know which way to look. They don't know which camera is on.

Marc Forster, *Finding Neverland*

I love the British stage actors. I'm just a huge fan of them, and the British comedians. So I brought them sort of all together and a lot of the comic sequences in the film were all improvised. They weren't in the script, Toby [Jones], who plays Smee, came up with this whole improvisation, "Oh, you look better on four legs than on two," and "You're a better dog," "You're a wonderful dog," before he goes on stage.

Actually we shot the bench scene between Freddie [Highmore] and Johnny [Depp], and I wanted them to disappear from the bench and just have the umbrella left there and this hat on the bench as they disappear. So we had this motion-control rig and we get there and Johnny says, "Oh, these rigs always break. I dealt with them with Tim Burton. They always break." I said "No." That was my first motion-control experience. So "No, no, no, this is top quality, doesn't break." So anyway, we like start shooting the motion control and it starts to rain slightly. Next thing I know that the rig starts breaking down so the rig doesn't work anymore.

So then I said, "Okay, let's just keep covering the scene." The rain gets heavier. The one camera suddenly breaks. And then the next camera has an issue with the lens. And so the whole thing was a disaster. And the performances were amazing. So the AD says to me we can't continue to shoot. I went to Johnny and told him, "Look, we have to come back in a few weeks to reshoot the scene." And then I went to Freddie, who plays Peter, and I was mortified because I said, "Can you get the performance again?" The performance was so right and he only had like three or four takes in him because he was so emotional and he's such a different kid than he is actually on-screen. He's like playful and funny. So then I went up to his trailer and knocked on the door and tried to explain it to him. And his father was sitting in the corner, and he said to me, "Oh, I'm so glad, Marc, because I wasn't on today." So then in three weeks later we came back and that close-up where the teardrops was take 3. I basically asked him to look into the camera and sort of break the fourth wall and have this connection with the audience. But that tear dropping was him. The tears just were welling up and then just this tear dropped and it was like incredible. It was magic.

When we were in the theater, the idea was once Wendy and Peter are on the rock and Peter says to Wendy she should take off, the idea was that the camera becomes the kite and the camera sort of flies into the theater and it was a very expensive shot and my producer suddenly saw the previs [previsualization, which is done with small cameras or digital effects to show what a shot might look like] and got all excited so we had this motion-control rig. I said to the line producer, "Please don't try to save any money on this because we only have this theater for a certain amount of time." If that motion-control rig breaks down, that's it. We didn't have enough extras so we broke it down in sort of four pieces. You have, with a crane, a piece up to the chandelier, then a piece swinging over the audience, and every piece picks up the next piece and then we only had two hundred extras, which we moved around in the theater. And then ultimately the shot ends up on Peter, and because the camera comes with incredible speed into him, there were all these security issues that the camera wouldn't fly off and into his face. So we had these two stunt people next to him. I said, "We can't put these two people in there. They don't look like period faces; they look like stunt people." But you know, security issues were more important.

I thought it would be much more psychologically interesting to jump back and forth and so I shot the same scene obviously twice, once in a fantasy and once in reality, and used the same lenses and everything to match it. *Neverland* was very tight because of the hours of the children, and so we had this really limited times to shoot. So I never had the luxury and I always had to think everything through—really what I want to shoot.

Taylor Hackford, *Ray*

We were working on a schedule. You just don't have time. I had a brilliant, brilliant actor playing the role [Jamie Foxx] and also a great ensemble cast—but we probably never went past three takes. We just couldn't. You had to move and also fight Louisiana weather and I also knew that I had all this montaging material I needed to get. And I sent my second-unit director [responsible for additional shots in a movie that don't have the main actors in the shots], Ray [Prado], out in rural Louisiana and said these are the things that you've gotta get. And he got great imagery. We were trying to, basically to take the point of view, when Ray Charles could see until he was five years old. And those are the only images in his head, so as he's going through cold turkey, his heroin withdrawals, really deal with those images.

We went into the Sanger Theater, which has got four or five thousand seats, and I had two hundred extras. And so when I'm shooting past Ray down into the close shots and you've got real people moving, but everything else in that whole theater is dead. Nobody is there. And I have to say to Jamie, "You're playing to the house. You're playing to the people way up in the balcony and you've got to feel that energy." But it's imagined energy. And then we leave and then Raymond Prado came in with those two hundred extras. And he literally would move them around the theater, change their costumes over the whole day, matching the lighting effects, get the music playing, having them move and clap exactly the same. And then, 'cause I'd shot here with locked-down cameras with Ray in the foreground, we tiled them [an old film process where you create a crowd from moving around a small group of people called the tile and doing a series of shots and combining them all into one shot to fill the space].

I'm a fan of tail slates [where the clapper marks the film at the end of a "take" rather than the beginning]; it's a much better way to get into a scene and it does not start the whole sequence with a rock.

I use multiple cameras. With children I think it's vital. If you've got children, their attention span is very short. You better make sure it's covered so you're not going in and saying, "Okay, we did the wide, now we're doing the tight, now we're doing this," because you're not going to get the continuity, not to mention just the spontaneity of the moment. I didn't have a lot of takes. I couldn't go for a long time. So the idea that I would do two cameras gave me more coverage [various shots of the same scene] and allowed me to get through it much, much quicker.

•9•

Postproduction: Editing

Barry Levinson, *Bugsy*

I've worked with the same editor [Stu Linder] for all the films I've done, so I only know from working with one person. And he only has one assistant. I always feel like we're sort of making a home movie. What's nice is when you've made movies and you've built up a group of people, there's a shorthand, so you don't have to explain your sensibility. And he cuts very quickly. What I don't do is see an assemblage of the whole film, because it may be like a nightmare. Unless the segments are sort of cut and rhythmically feel the way they were intended to be, there's no need to see the whole film. I feel all the scenes have to make sense on their own and be as tight as possible. Then you watch the whole film and then you begin to cut back on it. So there's a long period until I actually see it for the first time.

Oliver Stone, *JFK*

Because we had four months, I had four editor teams and four different rooms. I've always promoted from within. All my editors have come up from being assistants to the previous editors who all left me at one point or another. They've had enough of me. I've burned them out. We had community meetings every day where we'd look at various stages of various cuts. They worked around the clock. I gave each one as much independence as I wanted them to feel as free as actors, to try anything. As long as they ultimately conform to a zeitgeist of the whole. And I tried to run this as a democracy. Generally it was five votes, four editors and me, and sometimes it would be one against four!

In month two if editor B was not working well with what he had and wasn't flowing, then it would be given to editor C, who wanted to work on it. There were conflicting styles at points. And that was part of the director's job, to make sure that it blended. The four editors would choose things they felt closest to. Like with actors, there's a natural flow to editing as there's a natural flow to writing. We were playing with time—present, past, and future—so it was totally disassociative editing. We were not bound by any strictures at all of conventional editing. I felt totally free. It's a free association. We wanted to go with MTV. I love MTV. I said, "Let's go for consciousness; this is what it's about—put a splinter in the brain." In the first draft [of the screenplay] there were so many flashbacks on each page that it was an unreadable script. I took all the flashbacks out, of course, intending to put them back in—in the editing room. And we did it. If anything, we added more flashbacks. The scene with Ferrie confessing in the motel room with Kevin [Costner] we must have cut fourteen times, with three different editor teams. It was the scene that was totally disassociative. It's all jump cut [where the editing, rather than appearing seamless and unnoticeable, instead "bounces" around].

John Madden, *Shakespeare in Love*

I've certainly worked on movies where I've turned the film upside down in postproduction. I'm not necessarily disrespectful of the script, but you can make extraordinary discoveries. On this one, that was not the case. Because I had to commit so completely to the way it was going to be at the shooting stage that it was just a matter of hoping that it would go together right.

I worked on a movie with an editor who was cutting the movie and we were cutting a scene, and I said, "Geez, look at that. That's the wrong chair in that scene." And he said, "What do you mean?" And I said, "That's not the chair that was in the scene the last time we were in this room." And he said, "What, we've been in this room before?" He'd been working the whole movie and he never realized that it was the same location. And it's absolutely true.

Ridley Scott, *Black Hawk Down*

It is kind of a director's medium, and also is the editor's medium. There's a guy sitting in a darkroom somewhere, and in some respect you can say we're having all the fun, right? But it's not so, 'cause editor's love the process of being in the editing room, where the story is finally adjusted or told.

Neil Jordan, *The Crying Game*

Sometimes the editor can put two shots together that can change everything that you've designed. And it was interesting on this film. There was an editor from Hong Kong, and I come into the editing room and he's done a really solid cut of the film. But half the way through, I realize that his understanding of English is not what I thought it was. He's not fully hearing what the different actors are saying. And it was very interesting because he was responding to the most basic things, which was the emotion in the actors' faces. And there was a lot of dialogue in this film. And sometimes I would have to clear up the dialogue issue. But he was responding to the most basic thing, which is the picture in front of him.

Spike Jonze, *Being John Malkovich*

I was trying to hold on desperately to the movie that I had worked on the script, prepped, shot, and this was like—it's almost like when you get in an editing room, you have to kind of let go of all that and now watch the footage you have. And like the editor, he would suggest a scene, and we'd say, "No, we need that," and I'd get defensive and think we'd need it and a month or two later we'd end up dropping that scene and figuring out how to get the information we need from that scene into a different place, or maybe we don't need the information at all.

Andrew Davis, *The Fugitive*

Actually dailies [the raw footage that is shot on day and then developed in a laboratory to be projected or seen on tape the next day] are probably one of the most enjoyable parts for me. Because you work so hard, you're nervous, and you're trying to put everything together, and you go to see dailies and you say, "My God, we really got something. There's a story here."

I like to tell the story with picture and with collage. And then when you stop, and you listen to dialogue, it should be the real fine flavorings and seasonings of the characters. So there are a lot of sequences put together with music. I hear pieces of music and it's all there. It's dramatic, it's got everything in place, all you have to do is put pictures to it. I think you're constantly building with pictures and with sound effects and dialogue and music to create this whole kind of environment. We brought in some younger editors to help support what was going on. And we would literally change off sequences. Somebody would take a sequence, and then work on it, and then they'd say, "Well, you try a shot at it."

There have been situations where people say, "Well, why do we need this? What is this all about?" And then they go to the screening, and people laugh or respond to it, and they go, "I think we need it." So that's nice. We dropped a lot of sequences, just for pace, and feelings that Harrison shouldn't have. There was a scene where Harrison stopped in a café and met a woman and saw his face on television, and nervously got up and walked away. And we decided we didn't want to have him be warm and in the café. We wanted to keep the pressure on the story.

I'm not one of these directors who believe a lot in testing and responding to the audience's needs. It's not that I'm arrogant; I'd just rather not have to deal with it. But luckily we got these incredible scores [at the test screening]. It was like 97 percent "excellent" and "very good." It was like the highest scores Warner Bros. had ever gotten on any test screening. And we went to the screening the next day to show at the studio, and we had all these cards [with the scores from the test audience]. So it went very easy. They basically said, "Don't touch it. Leave it alone." We made a thousand changes after that screening. But it was very supportive. And actually I remember Harrison saying he had never been to a meeting after a first screening that had been so smooth. So we were very, very lucky.

Martin Scorsese, *Gangs of New York*

That something becomes something else—I still have that fascination with moving pictures that you cut one shot of movement to another shot of movement and there's a third movement. There's something else going on. The cut makes it. You may not even see the cut, but when each person in the audience, when they all get it, it's amazing, you know. It's this extraordinary magic that occurs putting images together.

Martin Scorsese, *The Aviator*

I do move around and wait for a cut. When we were cutting on a KEM or Movieola [two mechanical editing machines that cut film, rather than electronic editing machines that cut digitally], I'd be able to say, "Okay, make this change, make that change." And I'd get up, walk around fifteen, twenty minutes. But with the new computer editing, I say, "Okay, make this, do that," then I get up. As I'm halfway out of the chair, the cut's made. It's not fair. Gotta give me some time to think about the thing, you know. Now what do I know? "It looks exactly, no, wait a minute. What d'ja do?" It becomes an extremely anxiety-ridden process.

It's always very mathematical. And ultimately at a certain point, in the case of *Aviator* we put a red light on outside the door—"don't interrupt." 'Cause it's usually, you know, there's a frantic phone call or something and you've worked for something like for an hour and a half, two hours, or a day, and now you're gonna look at it for like twenty minutes of the film. And sure enough, there's always someone who comes in. So we started a red-light system, which she [Thelma Schoonmaker, his editor who has worked with him on nineteen films] forgets to put on sometimes and I get mad, then I put it on. It's like two old, married people arguing. "It's too cold in here; it's too warm." That sort of thing. In *Aviator* there was a scene that I designed in the editing. I wanted an effect where this Howard Hughes character is beginning to crack up and he sees an older gentleman sweeping up, and he looks at him and he gets kind of unnerved and he tells his associate, "Who is that?" So I had this idea that it'd be interesting if we're tracking in on the face of Howard. But don't get too close. Do three tracks, and each time you start a little later and end up a little closer. Now intercut with those on the guy sweeping up, but moving up on the broom, and each time you cut it gets a little closer and higher and higher and by the time you're full on Leo's [DiCaprio] face you're on the man's face, who looks up at him. He's kind of seeing what he might become in the future. And I said, "I know that it'll work if you're moving in, two moving-in shots. But one moving in and one tilting up, I don't know, it's like scratching your head and rubbing your stomach at the same time." And we tried everything. I mean, I shot that man with the broom for ages and I said, "It's not going to work." But I mean she found a way while we were mixing the film, she found a way to make it work with me, based on a concept I had that wasn't quite that well-enough defined. She wouldn't give up until she found something. And ultimately she actually intercut three cuts later in the future of him in his nervous breakdown scene so it made it more mysterious and I took a look at it and said, "Leave it in. It's good."

We're all dealing with narrative film and all this kind of seamless cutting. You know, it's William Wyler [director of *The Best Years of Our Lives* and *Ben-Hur*] and John Ford [director of *My Darling Clementine* and *The Grapes of Wrath*] made for a different time. The screen was one-three-three, it was gigantic you could actually do a scene and see the full character from midrange, right below the knee, and you could feel the body language of the actors. Now, it's really a new language and has a lot to do with the small screen, and I find I enjoy it and sometimes I say, "Let's just push it." It isn't seamless for me anyway. I think sometimes just pushing the story forward. I found when I was doing *Mean Streets* I had twenty-four days shooting and I just didn't get some scenes. We just didn't have the time. And I didn't get connective tissue and suddenly a guy's in a bar and they're standing up and talking and suddenly they have to sit down. And I had no coverage of them getting to the table. So I just jumped them sitting at the table. But on the jump cut a sound of a chair scraping, as if they're pulling a chair out. And the audience never noticed it.

In these new DVDs I don't like to show scenes that we didn't want to put in. If we didn't wanna put 'em in, why are you showing them to the people? It's kind of like it's a selling device for the DVD, more people see it. I understand. But people have to understand as part of an editing process you do lose a lot of things that you like, you know. And so I'm always against that so many documentaries explain exactly [how] the film is made, how the special effects are done, and it kind of breaks away the magic I think.

Gary Ross, *Seabiscuit*

These postproductions are so tight now you're multitasking so many things at once. We literally were on the mixing stage while we were on the recording stage while we were finalizing our visual effects while we were still making picture changes. This stuff sort of crunches down in a way that did not used to be.

Steven Spielberg, *Amistad*

I've worked with my editor Michael Kahn for twenty-two years now, and Johnny Williams [the composer] for twenty-four years, so we've been a team for almost as long as I've been making feature films. My process editorially is, I like to cut on the set. I spend my lunch hours in the editing room and my evenings in the editing room with Michael. I do that for several reasons: number one, I do a lot of reshooting, and I like to know that the set is still standing before we strike it [take it down]. I can see the entire scene assembled if I need another couple of shots. My process is—I don't know the movie before I make the movie. I only come to discover the movie as I'm making it. And editing, more than shooting, helps me discover the film and the story I'm trying to tell. And I don't believe in the Avid or Lightworks [electronic editing]. I only work on the movie on the KEM [a flatbed film editing machine]. I'm old fashioned. Even though the Avid is truly a more facile piece of technology, it doesn't give me more thinking time. It's very valuable when the assistants are pulling trims [individual strips of film that have been cut and categorized] to change a cut, or make a new cut, that I have ten minutes or twelve minutes to walk around and think about my movie. I think really fast on the set, but I don't think fast in the editing room.

Steven Spielberg, *Saving Private Ryan*

The postproduction on this particular film happened during the production of this particular film. There was no postproduction! We were editing every single day we were shooting it. Mike Kahn, the editor, he was a day behind the dailies, a day behind the production. So I was able to see whole sequences assembled before we left the set. And that was very important because I didn't quite know what kind of a movie I was going to make. And I had most of Omaha Beach cut together just before we left for England for the rest of our picture. And that really helped me. It really helped me to go back and fix things and correct mistakes I had made when the sets were still standing. The biggest thing in postproduction was sound, on my film. Because we pretty much locked [the images in final cut] *Saving Private Ryan,* I'd say a month, after we came back from England. And most of the time took, with Gary Rydstrom and Gary Summers, the sound designers, putting together the sound design, which I just think is the most brilliant thing I've ever heard these guys do before.

Mike Newell, *Four Weddings and a Funeral*

The editor shows me stuff as we go. But then usually what happens is that he asks me to stay away. The great thing about most editors, I find, is that they show you not necessarily what's on the page, but what actually was in the head. And it's in the cutting room that the shit really happens, studio stuff, money stuff, disappointment, rage, "Why didn't we do this? It doesn't work does it?" And he must make up his mind where he's going to stand, and usually a good one will stand with you. They are your right arm. They're people with great strength and great character. They are very accomplished and they're usually very clever people, very perceptive.

Sam Mendes, *American Beauty*

And I think, particularly with electronic editing, it's so easy to make cuts at speed and so easy to make a cut, and so you don't think hard enough sometimes about what you're doing. But the biggest change that took place on the movie happened all in the editing room, no question. In the version that I shot, the kids, Ricky and Jane, were accused and found guilty of Lester's murder, even though they hadn't done it. And the movie ended in a series of scenes, which I shot as one long succession of left to right tracking shots. Very, very slow. And Lester's voiceover at the end was much longer. He had many more memories, which I showed in black and white, and took us through courtrooms and police stations and bedrooms. It was a very long kind of montage. And the movie had such a power when Lester was killed, I realized that it reduced it with every scene, with every bit of knowledge as to what happened to the characters thereafter. And so I reconfigured what had been a very carefully storyboarded planned sequence and made it something completely different. It was a whole different ending to the film.

Marc Forster, *Finding Neverland*

Usually with my editor, at the beginning, I'm really a control freak. When I was in film school I just cut all my shorts myself. So when I shoot, usually I edit in my head sort of what I want because I usually have very limited time and limited funds.

Neverland didn't start editing until I finished the picture. There was one moment when Johnny Depp is in the park and opens the paper and then discovers the family, Kate Winslet in the background. And he [the editor Matt Chesse] said to me, "Look, I think maybe because there was this whole pedophilia issue, if he sits in the park and looks through his paper, it might be like 'peeping Tom' and people will not get your joke, but if the maid cuts out the review of the paper that his latest play was in . . ." So we actually on the last day shot that scene. I was really thankful that he called me up. And he was editing in L.A. and I was shooting in London.

The tricky scene to edit was when she walks into Neverland because Neverland, the concept was just having all these fairies and Indians and all these pirates. And we shot that in a day with three cameras, one on a crane, one on a Steadicam, and just some static positions. And I felt like just to cut it together was a sort of montage, and I always have problems with montages because they just make me nervous and just like I get a little horrified by them. And then I said to my editor, "Look, I don't know how to cut this together. I don't know how to do it. That's the only thing in the film I don't have a concept for. Just make it work." And then he did, he cut it, and I loved it.

Curtis Hanson, *L.A. Confidential*

I let the editor do exactly what he wants while I'm shooting. That's their time to be creative. I watch dailies every day with the editor and then give any thoughts I have about specific takes that are in my mind, the key take. But beyond that I let them do their cut. I will go in on the weekend, sometimes at night, into the editing room and look at a few scenes as they have them, just to give them my two cents to be helpful, but also to kind of recharge my own batteries. In the editing room, I'll give many notes, go away, and let them execute them. And then as we keep refining, I'll end up being there more and more. And ultimately, I'm there all the time.

Stephen Daldry, *The Hours*

I'm a fan of the pick-up. You can watch the previews, and you fret about speeches and think what else can you do. One of my favorite speeches that Meryl Streep has in the film is—she's on bed and she's talking to Claire Danes—and eight months later we just thought we could just make it a little bit better. Hard to get them together, you know, and it was by chance that they could come back. But what I love is that a year later there's a series of shots which are a year apart within the speech. And I don't think you'd know.

Peter Jackson, *The Lord of the Rings: The Fellowship of the Ring*

We have a strong philosophy in believing in pick-up shooting, and in each of the *Lord of the Rings* movies during the postproduction period we've had two or three weeks of shooting pick-ups. And these aren't pick-ups because we have previewed the film and the scores are bad and everyone's got this knee-jerk reaction, "Oh my God, we have to fix it," because we've never actually previewed the films. These have never been seen by an audience. We preview them for ourselves. I mean, we're just like, we cut the movie together, we look at it, and basically the filmmakers sit there as their own preview audience and just feel what we like about the film, feel what we don't like, what's working, what can be improved. We then write some more script to fix the things that we want to fix, to improve the things. The actors come back down to New Zealand and we shoot for two or three more weeks. And for every film that I make in the future I'm always going to build in that period of additional shooting because it's such a valuable tool to filmmaking. And you just organically develop the thing right away through to the very end.

Peter Jackson, *The Lord of the Rings: The Two Towers*

There's a shot where there's these hundred Elves in formation have to march up this causeway. And we did three or four takes. And for various reasons, you know, there was only one that was really any good, which was the one in the film. But when I got to the cutting room, I didn't see it on the set, but they're all marching with their bows sort of perfectly up in the air, and right the way in the middle of the shot, one of the extras had kicked the bottom of the bow and this bow goes "boing!" and completely spoiled it. So fortunately, we're living in an age where we're able to go into computer and paint the bow out doing its little thing and just leave it sticking up.

So we sort of in the editing, we kind of had a thing where it wasn't really a hard-and-fast rule but I think it worked out that if you have two or three shots without one of your leads, then go back to your lead. And also, the thing with the battle that I found too is, it wasn't just about the fighting. It was about the lead-up to the battle. I think any good battle scene in a movie is as much about the kind of the agonizing, slow build-up to the battle.

Robert Zemeckis, *Forrest Gump*

The editorial process—it's my favorite part of filmmaking, because all the madness and insanity and pressure of shooting is over. When you wrap [end of shoot], it just instantly funnels to just you, your editor, and your film—and you don't have to worry whether it's rainy out or if the sun is coming up. I call my editor "my second brain." He's the guy who you really have to rely on. I never seem to get enough time to edit because it's always rushing into these release dates [when the picture is scheduled to be in the theaters]. But I'll look at what he's cutting when I'm shooting and we'll talk about it later. But I can't focus on it, so I put the distance there. He's roughing it in and making his cut and I don't really start working with him until we get into the cutting room.

Roberto Benigni, *Life Is Beautiful*

Editing is really the moment where the movie takes the energy. It's there, it's the body. It's wonderful because you can watch the little sign of the face, first time. Everything is in tumult, of course, but it's stinging every organ of your body. You cannot judge exactly, but this moment for me is the most wonderful.

M. Night Shyamalan, *The Sixth Sense*

The thing I find about editing is, I'm trying to create a new rhythm and magic in the editing room. It's a big deal when you make a cut. It's a change of thought; it's a change of rhythm to understand when you would need to get off a character and when you would need to come back. I was really upset about that, when I nailed some scenes and it wasn't fitting together right. And I'm like, "I'm telling you, this was perfect when we shot it." And now it's not. I don't have the rhythm at all. And so for me, now the editing process has become more and more a confirmation of what I did right or did wrong.

My favorite scene in the movie is not in the movie, which is the last scene in the movie. And I think maybe Bruce's [Willis] best performance. And that was a decision in the editing room because of a directorial tonal choice that I made.

Peter Weir, *The Truman Show*

The nightmare is, your structure isn't there. The nightmare is, you don't know where you're going. That's the way I've had it. Anyone with a long career has had it. But you know what you aim for, and hopefully have most of the time, is a solid skeleton for the film before you start. And you've got to go with it. You've got to learn off your dailies. But in this case, it was incredibly much in detail. As it happened with the umpteen drafts of the script, so in the cuts—I've never had so many cuts. I think I got as high as seventeen full cuts.

If the tone wasn't right, the balance shifts. You were thrown out of the movie. I had to give you a movie experience. And it had to be about movies, rather than about television. So in fine-tuning, I put this in pretty standard sort of changes. But you couldn't know until you tested them on the screen.

The new editing systems are sensational in the possibilities they give us. Like you are cutting your picture as you go along. It's amazing, the speed with which you can assemble a cut. But on the other hand you still have to get into the theater. You can get into terrible dangers looking at the monitor, in terms of cutting too fast sometimes or missing details, going too close.

Frank Darabont, *The Shawshank Redemption*

You always want to get the thing as tight as you can. A journalist once asked Abraham Lincoln how long a man's legs should be—long enough to reach the ground.

Frank Darabont, *The Green Mile*

I love being in the editing room because I feel like I'm finally getting to make the movie. The real job occurs, which is right there with your editor. And you're really discovering your film. You're really putting it together. You're writing the final draft of the film right there.

Mike Leigh, *Secrets & Lies*

The film is made in the cutting room, and you really do have to have someone you click with. I've been blessed with Jon Gregory. And the thing about an editor like him, particularly with my kind of material, which grows as the film is being shot, he's just got an ability to take that material and put it together in a way that really makes sense.

Rob Reiner, *A Few Good Men*

A film editor has to understand the film because he's helping you shape the film and tell a story. So if he doesn't get what story you're telling, it's gonna be painstaking because you're gonna have to deal with every single cut.

I don't conceptualize for the editing room, because most of the things I do, they're very character driven. If the performance is right or better in one take than another, I may decide, "Well, I'm gonna stay with him a little longer," and that I can't determine until I actually put the stuff on film. I won't make a predetermination of how I'm gonna cut it beforehand.

I change performance tremendously in the editing room. I love doing this stuff. I will take the dialogue of one take, the dialogue of another take, marry that line and put it in the mouth of that third take, because I like the way the person looks on the certain take, but I don't like the way the dialogue's coming out. You can all of the sudden create another performance.

The digital stuff, I think there's obviously value to doing it. It's a lot shorter. I think you gain something, but you also give something up. You gain obviously speed, but there is a gestation period that you need, I think, to see a film come together and think about what you want with a film, and how you're shaping it. And I think you lose that. The instantaneousness of video editing I think takes that.

James Cameron, *Titanic*

When I did *Strange Days* with Kathryn Bigelow [the director], she asked me to get involved in the editing and I wound up cutting a number of action sequence scenes and sort of mastered the Avid [an electronic digital editing machine] on that so then I decided on *Titanic* that I'd cut the picture myself. Eventually I decided to bring in Richard Harris, who I'd worked with on two previous films, because I really believe that in the editing room you've got to have somebody to talk to and to put another perspective. I knew I was going to be living at the editing room so I just cut to the chase and put the editing room at my house. The way I preferred to work on *Titanic* was, I would divide up the show: "You guys work on these scenes, you work on those, and I'm gonna work on these because I sort of know what to do and I can do it faster than explaining it." And we'd all be working at the same time and I'd look at their cuts and

I'd ask them to come in and look at my cuts and comment. And then I'd say, "Okay, why don't you go take this thing that I've been working on and go see if you can work with this idea, that idea, which aren't quite right and give me that thing that you've been working on." So we just all would sort of play musical chairs and I think that was a strengthening process, because it went through a number of sets of eyes and hands. I asked the studio for more time, which by the way, I think is the great triumph of the film, is that we actually said, "You know what? We're gonna fuck this up if we go for this release date and I think we need another month in the editing room." And the studio said, "Yes," and that doesn't happen very often. They said, "You know what? We don't want to screw this up. First of all, we've got a lot of money in it; secondly I think you've got a chance of doing something really pretty cool here." So they gave us the extra time. So I wound up going back over nibbling out a few frames here and a few frames there, and it was kind of a marinating process, literally just sitting in that room by myself for about a month just running the sequences over and over. And suddenly something will pop. You've seen the thing five hundred times; something will pop out that you've never thought of before. Or you'll remember a shot that was from another scene and you put it in and it just changes everything. And the very last thing I do when we're really confident with the cut that we're almost there is, I sit in the screening room and run the conformed picture with the image flopped in the gate. Because I find that as I've watched the scene over and over and over, my eye has learned where to go next in the next shot before that shot has come on the screen. So I wanted to short circuit that pretrained response. It's a way of seeing the film for the first time; you only get to do it once but you can learn a lot from it.

Quentin Tarantino, *Pulp Fiction*

If I wanted to make *Pulp Fiction* move like a bullet—the movie is two hours and twenty minutes—I guess I could've taken twenty minutes outta there. I didn't want to. I mean if I do a movie that's supposed to work like that, that's exactly how I'll do it, but that's not how I want to do it. And that's not how I want to do this one. Like when you get to a scene like Jack Rabbit Slim's, part of the whole idea is the whole thrust of that story was the date, the date, the date. When we got there, I didn't want to do like it normally is in a movie—ha, ha, ha—dance. Like everything's been condensed. I wanted us to be on a date; I wanted—the whole thing's been building up to that. I don't want to shorten it. I wanted them to be uncomfortable with each other. I didn't want all of the sudden they just start sparkling dialogue. They don't know what to say to each other. I wanted it to be uncomfortable. I shot it so it was that way. But what you have going on is just the constant talks. If you were to lose this, this would move a lot quicker and we achieve the same thing, but much less painfully. But I think the pain is part of it. So it's the constant process of whittling it down and then saying, "Nope, I know we could lose this and no one would know it was lost," but I would know, and it's not just because I'm holding onto my baby—it's supposed to work that way.

Michael Radford, *Il Postino*

The editing process for me is the process I'm least good at actually; I tend to try and put everything in the can [metal containers that hold the film]. I did shoot a lot of cover.

And it became instantly apparent that these long scenes between the two of them just held. So we made that the linchpin of the movie. And we cut this in a very old-fashioned way. Tom Priestley, who cut all my other pictures, was very much an old-fashioned Hollywood editor, who liked to hunch himself over the Movieola [an editing machine] and not let you see what was going on. And to that extent you can keep a distance, you can come back and have a fresh eye. With Roberto [Perpignani, the editor], it was a total collaboration. He doesn't like to work on his own; he likes to really just sit there and talk it through and put it together while you're there and you have a look at it. And I loved that. It was like going back to film school. And like in shooting you have to be alert. You shoot a scene and then you throw away all the preconceptions as to why you shot that scene when you get into the cutting room. I mean it's an absurd situation: you've shot a scene for a particular reason and you use it for an entirely different reason.

We were two months in postproduction, from the day we finished shooting to the day we had to deliver the print. I did actually recut it afterwards. I have to tell about the mix [where the sounds are mixed together dialogue, music, and sound effects] on this picture because it was like nothing else. First, you have a lot of Italians. They dub pictures a lot [dubbing is replacing dialogue recorded while shooting with dialogue recorded in a studio, often with voices different than the original actors'], so they have a dubbing director who comes in and he starts to dub all the actors. You've got these performances out of people and he brings other people in and redoes the performances for you!

Ang Lee, *Crouching Tiger, Hidden Dragon*

I work with same editor all my career, all seven films. I got him from interviewing him. He just came in and talk like very clearly and I found a person that has just the opposite taste of me. I think is important you get along with them because you talk to them more than I talk to my wife. I choose Tim Squyres and stick with him. He has just from the way I look at film, performance, music, all the way down to the food we order, is totally opposite. And I think it's a good chemistry. I don't think I want somebody who thinks just like me. To me, editing is the most enjoyable part of filmmaking, though. You don't have to deal with the actor. Sometimes smoothly is better for me; sometimes jumpy is because make a jump, break people's habit of watching something. It provokes thoughts and emotion and it appear to be stronger. You know, when I'm shooting, I'm living the fantasy. I don't want to see editor's version of reality. It really deflate my courage and everything. I spend a big part of the beginning of editing process just relearn my footage. I thought it's going to be like this, and that's why I get mad at the editor. I didn't mean that but then a lot of time he was right.

Scott Hicks, *Shine*

The editor [Pip Karmel] and I were in need of some therapy I think by the end.

For me the very central decisions that you make are the cinematographer, the designer, and the editor. When all the pyrotechnics of shooting have stopped and you're confronted with the material out of which you're going to fashion the film, it's essential that first of all you share the same sense of humor. That's going to get you through that very long and difficult process of fashioning the film.

Running through the rain is actually a really good example of the process of working with the editor. I had in my mind an image of a continuous thirty-second shot of David running through the rain where he's really at his lowest depth. But of course this is extremely difficult to do when you're shooting high speed with an actor who's running parallel with the camera in the rain at night. We really had slender resources in which to try and execute. So when we saw the rushes [the developed film projected on screen], it was a disappointment. There was no one take that was executed to the perfection that I wanted. And the editor said, "Frankly, this is rubbish. You're going to have to forget about this scene completely and think of something else." So in the end, I said, "But look, that bit's good and look there's a good bit. Take them and jump-cut them and use this piece of Rachmaninoff, and I'll come back on Thursday and show me what you've done."

Taylor Hackford, *Ray*

I met an editor and we talked. We didn't know each other. And I went to Louisiana to start shooting, and we had a very intense schedule. So I was shooting, you know, a lot of material. We didn't have money for dailies so we were going to look digitally on a monitor. And about two weeks into the shoot this man's father died. And he had to leave the picture. So for about a month and, you know, I didn't have anybody. An editor was suggested to me. I looked at his credits. He cut *Star Wars* and *Ferris Bueller's Day Off*, and he was obviously a good cutter but I didn't know the man. He flew down. Paul Hirsch. We went out and we spent the day together. And this is one of those things where you just have to look in the eyes of the person and get his sensibility. And I talked about what my concept was for the film and what I was going for. A couple of things hit me very nicely. His mother was a dancer and he'd been a musician. And I liked that 'cause I thought of this film as a musical. I wanted the action and the narrative to flow forward. And montaging, since I'm covering thirty years in a life, was going to be very important. And I looked him in the eye. I said, "Listen, I'm going with you," and that was it. He went back to Los Angeles. He wasn't on the set. And he started gathering the footage. And I got these calls saying, "I'm looking at the footage. It's speaking to me, and I think I see what you want. Tell me one thing—are you the kind of director that tries to get it in the first one or do you work towards a performance and the last take?" And I said, "That's what I do. I work towards getting a performance, each step, making nuances, and then I go for that." He said, "Thank you. That's it."

I never look at footage by this point in my career: I know what I'm shooting, I cover myself, I'm not going to get myself in a hole. And so I look at what the editor has put together and then I get in and I never leave the editing room after that. In this instance, after he had cut the film and I went in, you know, my heart was pounding, you know, because who knows what it is going to be. And literally, we started looking at his assemblage. About a minute in, I could just feel myself, you know, settle down into the chair because he did a brilliant job. And then once I looked at his cut, he and I started working together and we worked every day and he got nominated. Paul developed a really wonderful sense of wipes. You know, it's a period film. We were creating a kind of suite that I think was helping us get throughout this piece and get forward and move forward over this thirty, really thirty-five years.

This film was moving on three levels. We had the linear story moving forward with Ray Charles. And we also had flashbacks, which was kind of a ghost story of what had happened to him and his loss of his brother at the beginning the flashbacks all took place at the beginning of the film. We take the journey; about a third into his career the flashbacks had finished. And in the editing room we realized that was wrong. And we stretched the flashbacks out throughout the whole film. And when we got to a certain place where we had inserted them, which they hadn't been inserted in the script, the film worked. And that process of discovery and invention is the great joy. It's just a fantastic process of being in the editing room. The last rewrite is in the editing room. Always.

Anthony Minghella, *The English Patient*

The editor becomes the filmmaker with you, in what was for me, ten months of the process.

Mel Gibson, *Braveheart*

It was a real "the two of us" kind of process. I'd give him [Steven Rosenblum] what he needed and he was putting it together the way I wanted it and even better than I wanted it. And I was like, "Wow, this is even better than someone's fine cut, this rough cut" [rough cut is the earliest version of the edited film]. And every day we'd go in and occasionally we'd start choking each other. You know how that is. You'd come to a difference of an opinion. But we'd got around that problem because I got, you know those punching puppets; I got a nun and he got the fighting rabbi, so we'd be sitting there and we'd be punching the shit out of each other with these puppets until we start laughing and then we'd throw the puppets away and then get back to it. It would avoid direct confrontation.

What's on the floor was stuff that I'd labored too much to make a point, and I thought, "You get it already." And also, I'm not a big fan of testing it with audiences, but it's important because that's who it's for. If you're sitting in a theater somewhere and fifteen or twenty-five women get up and go, "Oh my God!" and get up and run from the theater screaming, you know you've got to lighten up somewhere.

Alexander Payne, *Sideways*

I've worked with the same editor [Kevin Tent] for all four of my features, I'm also with him all the time—it's very much like having a cowriter. I mean, I cowrite my scripts and then in a way coedit. He will cut together sample scenes so that I have a basic idea if it's working or not or if I need to pick up a shot I dropped and that sort of thing. But I don't pay too much attention to it. I even have fallen out of the habit of watching dailies. I'll sort of spot-check them and now you can get 'em on DVD and kind of zip through 'em. It's just my fourth feature so I'm still very much learning. But I find myself increasingly seeing directing as [Akira] Kurosawa [director of *Rashômon*, *The Seven Samurai*, *Ran*] said, the only reason to write and direct is you get things to edit, and although I'm not editing while directing, I'm always thinking about editing while directing and harvesting shots to put together and even having the actors do it a couple different ways 'cause I'm not sure exactly how it might play in the finished film. And rhythm, rhythm, anticipating what the rhythm of the film might be.

But one thing that came in editing was the flashes forward to Miles's calling—'cause as scripted and shot, he makes an excuse and he gets up and he goes to the bathroom and actually tries the men's room and it's locked, and it's only there waiting for the men's room then he sees the pay phone and fights himself, "No, I won't call—no I won't call—ah, to hell with it, I'm gonna call." And I had all these cool shots. You know, dollying into the phone and as he runs to the phone dollying in on him and that sort of thing. But in editing, the picture was running too long. I mean, I think it's even slightly too long as it is in its finished form. So you're always thinking, how can we speed X-Y-Z section of the picture? And I somehow came in one morning and thought what if we try that kind of flashes forward or flashes back thinking about calling and then suddenly he's just there. And we just fooled around with it one day and found that it was kind of cool. One of the beautiful and mysterious things about film is that you never know how a film will later function and you kind of can't foresee what you're going to have to lose. You don't know that in the script form. Otherwise, you would have cut it out of the script, especially when working with low budgets when they're kind of forcing you to have as few days as possible. You don't know how a film functions until it exists. And it tells you how it wants to be. And then you start screening it for people and that part of this film is too long, so what can we pull out of there either by tightening what exists or can you make big power cuts. And I actually welcome cutting scenes. The tighter you get a film, the more the audience starts to make connections. And this whole thing about "Oh, I lost that scene" or romanticizing it, idealizing it—I don't really feel that at all. You know, you trim a steak, you gotta cut into the meat. But one consolation these days is the ability to include those scenes on DVD.

Clint Eastwood, *Unforgiven*

I enjoy the shooting process, but I also enjoy being finished! I love being done! And the idea of going to a cutting room with two people or one person or an assistant or two editors is just heaven. You go in there and you stand there and you think, it's done, for better or for worse. So now the question [is] to glue it all together and see how it comes out.

I feel editing. I see the editing as I do it. I preedit in my mind. Once the film is all assembled, I'll go through it and I'll do a "cruel cut." What I call a "cruel cut" is I dump everything I think is unnecessary. And then I kind of think, well, this moment's missing, so I get it back to what I think plays and then I try to stay away from it for at least two weeks. Because the more you look at it, the duller it plays because you get brain dead.

Vittorio De Sica [the Italian director of *The Bicycle Thief* and *Two Women*] had a rough cut the next day, after he finished shooting. But he only shot what he wanted to use. He just "camera cut" the film [shooting only those shots that will be used in the final edit of the movie]. But other people will take a lot of time. Three weeks to four weeks is about as long I can stay in there with any kind of sanity.

Once you've been on the set, you remember every frame of that film that's shot. There's no way it can ever escape you.

Clint Eastwood, *Million Dollar Baby*

I've worked with the same editor [Joel Cox] for twenty-five years and he knows exactly what I'm doing 'cause I just give him the film that I've shot. There's nothing to jumble around particularly.

Once in a while if you do a defensive maneuver where something doesn't work, then you go back to the drawing board. I can talk to him on the phone and tell him how I see it and go in the next day and it's exactly that way. And then you look at it and you go, "Nah, I was wrong. Change it up a little bit."

I edit near my home up in Carmel but I don't stay in the editing room with the editor because if I do, I go brain dead. I try to find every excuse in the world to leave. So we'll get something started and he'll say, "Okay, well, I'll frame that in." Now he says, frame that in and then in the meantime I'll play nine holes of golf or something. And editorially, Joel reads my mind. In the particular case of *Million Dollar Baby* I was also knocking at the music to go with the scenes. And so eventually the film just kind of went together much as I had anticipated it would. But there are scenes you trash. You just get into the rhythm of the picture and you find this scene is redundant of something else that we've already seen and it may be an emotional scene and it's very difficult to do because you've spent time on it and you think they're nice shots but you trash 'em. I never put 'em in a DVD because once they're trash, that's it. I never want to see 'em again. And so you have to sort of make up your mind that's going to be your vision. The cutting is actually the way you finalize your vision of the picture. And editing is an exciting process because you don't have a hundred people or whatever size crew you have. You don't have 'em standing around looking at you. You don't have an assistant saying, "What's the next setup?" And when you don't know, you have to make up something. You have the computer. You're sitting there with an Avid. The cuts go so quick so you have to make the decisions quicker. In the old days of the Movieola [the first mechanical film editing machine], my prior editor, he'd stand on the film and it would rip right out of the Movieola and he'd just tear the film and I'd say, "Well, that's a perfect place to cut, I guess."

I did the montage of her training. I shot all the pieces but I hadn't really drawn it out so we just kinda started assembling it. You just sort of mold it there on the computer. It became the choice in the editing room as to whether to just go from straight cuts to a soft dissolve or a soft cut where you either do a four-foot dissolve or a six-foot dissolve, or go to black. And we started out the film with that format, going from black right into the sequences, and we just decided to keep that all the way.

Steven Soderbergh, *Erin Brockovich* and *Traffic*

I like that sort of jagged, messy quality. When I started making films, I was a real perfectionist, or at least I was a formalist, and it was really leading me down a dead end and I sort of went in the other direction. I've become more sloppy and it's more fun. With this handheld-multiple-camera aesthetic. It really lends itself to abbreviating and truncating action and movement. As Godard said, "Cut out the boring bits." I cut my first three films myself, but since then I've had some terrific editors. A great editor can really find the film that you've almost got but that didn't quite, you know, sometimes you're your own worst enemy. You just don't see stuff.

I would look at stuff but not give any notes. I'd just figure, I'll get to it when we get there 'cause there is a very different mind-set. Being—when you're on the set, it's all instinct; it's not reflective at all, not contemplative. You're in it and present. And when you're in the editing room, it's just very different. Very two dimensional. You have time when you can look at things. And what's interesting, I think, for the editors is that—you know what it took to get the shot—and they don't know that. They're just looking at the shot. So yeah, you're waiting for these kudos to come over the phone and they just see the stuff and they go, "Yeah, I saw it." They don't know what went into it. They're just looking at, which is good because they are the audience, they're the first audience.

I think emotional transitions within scenes and literal transitions from sequence to sequence are some of the most important elements in any film.

James L. Brooks, *As Good As It Gets*

My editor, Richie Marks, who I've done every picture with, and composer Hans Zimmer, are like family members to me. Editing is everything to me; it's where the performance is at. It's amazing how much you change the performance. It's extraordinary. And it's in the editing room also where filmmaking gets religious. I think just the focus and attitude towards the film in the editing room is pure.

•10•

Postproduction: Music and Sound

Rob Reiner, *A Few Good Men*

$\mathcal{W}$ell, it's obvious music is critical. I mean, you can look at certain films without music and then with music and all of a sudden they become alive and they're lifted. I mean, they talk about *Chariots of Fire* as being one of those films that when it was screened without music they'd say, "What is this?" and then with music, lifted that film.

I work very closely with the composer. I will sit with him, go through it, put a temp [temporary] score together which gives you a jumping-off point. With the composer and with the music editor, the three of us will get together and we'll get some selections, put it up against the picture, you know, from other pictures, and then I'll actually sit with the composer, after he's done his initial pass and he'll play me on his synclavier [an electronic keyboard that can simulate sounds of a variety of other instruments] the things that he's got, and then you'll say, "Oooooh, I want to add some horns in there, or on that cue I want to go down." I know a little bit about music so I can communicate a little bit with him as to what I want. That there's been a lot of music but you don't know that there's music, that's what I tried to get so that you don't hear the music but it's there.

Sofia Coppola, *Lost in Translation*

I worked with Brian Reitzell [the music producer] when I was writing the script, and we would just listen to records and he would make me a compilation CD that I would listen to when I was writing. And I would talk to him about what I wanted it to feel like and that I wanted it to have this kind of dreamy feeling 'cause when you're there, you're so jet lagged that the neon and everything takes on another quality. And then— just like the karaoke songs—some of that just came about when we were shooting.

The score—most of it was done by Kevin Shields. I listened to his music when I was writing, and then I sent him tapes of dailies and he wrote some songs, but in the edit, I think, was when we tried new songs in different places. And so it wasn't, I think, a traditional scoring. It was more like having different songs and placing them.

Well, one of my favorite parts is working with Richard Beggs, our sound designer, who's just a real artist and he just comes up with things that I wouldn't think of. And on this, he went back to Japan and just filmed the hallways and the elevator, the wind, and really notices that stuff. So working with him added a whole other atmosphere. We made the sounds of the city kind of overwhelming, what it's like to be there when you're hearing music from every corner and then the hotel is so quiet and just the wind in the tunnels.

But one of my favorite things that he did was in the scene in the club where Bill Murray is carrying Scarlett down the hallway; the song from the scene before, it's just a buzz so it sounds like your ears ringing from what you heard that night and just kind of the residue of the song in the hallway.

Peter Jackson, *The Lord of the Rings: The Return of the King*

I love sound. I just think it's a wonderfully creative part of the process. We have a great sound effects team. And they're incredibly inventive. The footsteps of the big, big elephant creatures—we wanted this tremendous weight to hit the ground and so they used to get these concrete blocks like about six foot square and they used to crane them up in the air over a piece of glass and put about five or six microphones all around and then press a button and release these huge concrete blocks and smash 'em to the ground. One of the difficult things with sound effects recording is in urban areas, obviously, is just getting exterior sounds quiet enough. So they often used to go to a cemetery which was about ten miles away and record things at a cemetery. But the way that you can create mood and atmosphere and ambience with sound is just phenomenal.

We've been utterly spoiled really on these movies because Howard Shore, our composer, with the exception of a couple of smaller films he did, he's basically worked on our movies nonstop for four years. Music's been a technically or logistically difficult part of the process for us in the sense that our films are long, and there's so many visual-effects shots that need to be put in all the way through the film, which only happens the year that we're doing the postproduction. And Howard needs a lot of time to write the music because he's writing over three hours of score. And it's always just been real difficult to give Howard things that he can write that are things that you're confident are not going to change. And often they do change, and Howard's a composer that hates to edit music. You know, you've delivered a shot that's forty-eight frames long and you just want to take three frames off either end just to kind of tighten it up. And of course, if the music's been recorded, it really causes trouble.

Quentin Tarantino, *Pulp Fiction*

Part of the way I find the music is, I figure out how the opening credit sequence is going to be. And I try to figure out what song I'm going to use for the opening credit sequence because basically I feel if I'm playing a song, a piece of music over the opening credit sequence, this is the rhythm that movie is supposed to play at.

Peter Weir, *Master and Commander: The Far Side of the World*

The ship being so alive, wooden ship, everything's moving, everything's making a sound, that when I spoke to Richard King [sound designer] about the sound design, I said to him that I was not going to look at a big score for this movie because I did want the sounds of the ship to come through and for the audience to experience that. So I held back on music, tried to use it only where it was very important. Richard went out and recorded a lot of it and then created a kind of wonderful wind machine and he drove around with that getting creeks and groans and flapping in this remarkable sort of land yacht. And I love sound. He knows that. And Richard would send stuff over as we were going through the year's editing.

Music was a very big thing for the ship's crew and for the officers. And anybody could tell a story or who was something of a poet and was much appreciated by these men. And given the choice of instruments, the doctor with the cello and Jack, the violin, that was their sound. So I thought at one point that that's how the kind of score might go. That we would play one instrument or the other. And I think I was playing that piece, that Bach piece, during the scripting period and so one morning in the cutting room it was a case of saying, let's try that out of the Galapagos.

John Madden, *Shakespeare in Love*

As far as music is concerned, every Peter Weir film I've ever seen, the music has kind of lived with me for years afterwards. And I work very, very much the same way as he does. There's a sort of atmosphere a film has for me. And Peter has always had an incredibly identifiable atmosphere. And the music is very, very crucial to me. I listen to music all the time in making a film. A certain kind of music which feels kind of right for me. And Stephen Warbeck, the composer, whom I obviously worked very closely with, is unbelievably low tech. He's more low tech than you could possibly imagine. He has one piano, which has bits of old sandwiches clogging the keys up. But it's wonderful because he's totally free. The way we usually work is, he throws out a few themes, or a few ideas, which then start to build into something else. Or they join up. Or we try them in different places, and we move them around. And we constantly draft and redraft and redraft the music. I end up living in his house, contributing to the sandwiches on the keyboard. And that, on this movie, was incredibly important. Because the patterns in the film are also musical patterns. In this case, we'd obviously committed to the music beforehand. Because of the dance music, it's part of the whole vocabulary of the film. So more than any other one I've done, I think the music was kind of essential.

Clint Eastwood, *Unforgiven*

I've had it happen in my early days: somebody comes back with a sweeping score that's just kind of overwhelming and you're going, "Uh, where's this go?" So you end up having to dump half of it. I usually have a fairly good concept of what I hear for the film. I've written a lot of music and I've written music for three of the films that I've worked on, and I wrote the theme for *Unforgiven*. I just didn't want music to come in and overwhelm everything. I wanted it to be very supportive to the film, but not dominant.

Clint Eastwood, *Mystic River*

Years ago working with Sergio Leone [director of *For a Few Dollars More* and *The Good, the Bad and the Ugly*], working with Italian-made movies, we didn't shoot any sound, just kind of scratch tracks and everything. You start appreciating the sound. But they put it in—in a style, very stylistically, so it wasn't real. But then later on I started appreciating sound more and sound becomes a big part of a movie to me. The Foley [where sound effects are made on a stage to match the action—like footsteps] is probably one of the most unexciting stages you can go to. But at the same time, it's very important. All those little things like the squeak of the shoes it is very important. We had a wonderful composer on the picture [Mr. Eastwood wrote the score!]. I have written themes for *Unforgiven* and *The Bridges of Madison County* and pictures along the way over the years. But in this one, I sort of mocked up a very, very simplistic theme actually that represented the three guys. I did it on a piano and the triad was supposed to represent the three fellas and then I built it out from there and wrote several bridges to it and then we came in and did the pieces and put artificial oboes and cellos and what have you on the computer. And it sounded pretty good; actually you could have gone with it that way. We mocked up the score and then we put it in as we were editing. So I scored the movie as we were editing the picture together. Lenny Niehaus then orchestrated all the parts and set it in and did it with the Boston Symphony. Sound in general, I think it's at least 40 percent of the movie sometimes.

Martin Scorsese, *Gangs of New York*

I usually listen to music a lot and I find that shooting music to the bars of music—in *The Last Waltz* or in *New York, New York*—I was able to take like four bars of music and it was one camera or one position for the camera, not four cameras. It edited very easily. You see five or six shots; you've got the whole piece. But it's developing those shots and getting the camera move and the performers to move a certain way.

Gary Ross, *Seabiscuit*

When I write a script now, I'm very cognizant of how I'm going to use sound in a scene. When I'm shooting a scene, I'm very cognizant of how I'm going to use sound later. For example, the scene with Jeff Bridges holding his son—I'd always intended for you to barely hear the scream, to whack the track out. And I actually stole the trick from *Breaker Morant* [directed by Bruce Beresford] 'cause they used wind so beautifully. I mean, nothing evokes silence like wind does. And so as I pulled the track out into that kind of almost MOS [literally *"mit out sprechen/sound"*—meaning just that—without sound] scream on Jeff's part. So a lot of that stuff was actually sort of predesigned. And we had wonderful, wonderful sound mixers. Andy Nelson may be the greatest sound mixer in the world, and his deft touch was something so artistic.

I had worked with Randy Newman [the composer] on *Pleasantville* and worked with him again here. I wanted bluegrass 'cause there's something crazy about it that screaming bluegrass fiddle. This is a boy thrust from innocence into a world that's gone mad on him. Out of economic desperation, these guys are throwing each other off horses and beating the crap out of each other. So I wanted to have that almost super-accelerated crazy bluegrass fiddle going on as he's trying to get his bearings going on. And I just thought bluegrass was appropriate and Randy thought the same thing.

Ang Lee, *Crouching Tiger, Hidden Dragon*

I think basically music is the tool, major tool to save the movie. You see what you're lacking or where you would like to suggest the audience to view this way or that way. I think that's a great tool. You know, composers are busy. You have to hire them in pretty much preproduction [of the] film; otherwise, they lock up something else [that is, take another job].

Barry Levinson, *Bugsy*

If I'm using source music, I'll lay the source music [as distinguished from underscoring written by the composer] over a scene early on. There's a dynamic that music is very influential on images and does change things radically.

[Ennio] Morricone, the composer, doesn't speak any English so you have a translator. So when you watch the movie, she's speaking Italian, explaining the dialogue. It's quite an experience but what he's really talking about is in tones and textures and feelings and emotions. He wants to know what is the feeling, what does the character feel.

Morricone was explaining to me how he worked with Sergio Leone [Italian director of "spaghetti Westerns" like *A Fistful of Dollars* and *Once Upon a Time in America*]. And Leone would explain the movie to him before he made it. He would just tell him the story and Morricone would write the music. And then he would go off and shoot the film to the music.

Mel Gibson, *Braveheart*

I actually approached the making of the film from a very musical point of view. I found things that to me sounded primitive and Celtic and with lots of percussion and I grew to love the sound of the pipes. And at rushes I had this whole collection of discs and I'd slip these things on for certain sequences at the dailies and it really used to make it come to life. We finally sat there with the LSO [London Symphony Orchestra], a group of guys with strange little things, instruments, sort of like bamboo with bits of gaffer's tape rolled around it and just blowing into hunks of bamboo and hitting themselves on the heads with things.

[In the battle sequence] I knew I didn't want any music once they clashed. The music was gone then. I just wanted it to be like a pretty raw experience for the audiences as much as it was for me. And just have it be as real and as ugly and crowded and crammed as possible.

Steven Soderbergh, *Erin Brockovich* and *Traffic*

The scores that for my films tend to be more tonal and atmospheric than they do kind of traditional scores. I guess that's just my taste. And so I'm for the composers probably frustratingly inarticulate 'cause I'm not a musician. I'm again sitting there half the time sort of eating ice cream and [saying], "It's not sad enough."

   We had music as soon as I had a first assembly [the editor's first version of the film]—I started laying in stuff.

Sam Mendes, *American Beauty*

Well, I'm also lucky to work with Tom Newman, who's a genius. That piece of music at the beginning of the movie he couldn't get right, and I kept saying, "No," to. And I think he nearly killed me. There were a couple of occasions when I thought he was actually going to deck me. Because I just said, "No, no, no"—because what I was trying to do is be both mischievous and serious, to have epic and domestic in the same piece of music. And I also wanted to start, to create a sort of formative piece of music, which increased in tempo and intensity—it's basically creating an interesting sequence out of a boring day. There was temp music everywhere, and all different styles, and Tom really bound it into one coherent voice.

Andrew Davis, *The Fugitive*

Aaron Copland is one of my favorite composers, and James Newton Howard [the composer] gives you that kind of human, warm Americana quality. And he also is very rhythmic and hip. So he can give you the best of both worlds.

   He was the first person who I showed a long, linear, forty-minute version of the opening, which was really sort of flaccid. And he looked at it, and his mouth fell open. He said, "You've got a hit movie here." I said, "What are you talking about? There's so much work to be done."

   He was working on the score while we were still shooting. And actually was getting clips of sequences just thematically to think about: a chase theme or a haunting theme. And actually we used James's music for the temp screening we had. We had some discussions about tone, and whether it was too funereal, or it needed to be more heroic. Just conceptual conversations. But it was very collaborative, and he was very open to all these discussions.

M. Night Shyamalan, *The Sixth Sense*

I'm not a big fan of temps; I think it's a big problem, actually. You spend so much of your time in post going, "Let me see what this looks like?" And you look at your forty-five CDs that are sitting next to you and you decide what the rhythm of the music of your movie—no matter what you do it has an effect on you for the rest. And it's also a crutch in editing. I'd seen the movie played two hours and five minutes with no music.

And it was pretty wild. It was a very quiet, arty movie. And so I knew the movie could exist with not a piece of music in it. And so one of my things that I didn't have the balls to do was to not put music in until the first ghost appears. You know, when she walks by the doorway? Imagine that, you've been watching for an hour, no music. And then she walks by—dah dah. You know? Everybody would have wet their pants at that point. But I didn't have the balls to go the first hour without music.

Michael Radford, *Il Postino*

I have very great difficulty with music always. It's a difficulty because it's the one area in which you can't meddle yourself. It's a great leap in the dark and it's often a very expensive leap in the dark. You try to express in ordinary language something which is inexpressible. Because musicians think in different ways. The world is divided into musicians and people who can't do music. I started off this movie with Ennio Morricone. He would kind of sit around a grand piano in his apartment and thump out a theme. And he's one of the great composers, no doubt about it. I said to him one day, "I'd like the music to be discreet in this picture." And he looked at me and said, "I don't do discreet music." So he rang me up and said, "I'm off this picture." So I moved onto this guy [Luis Bacalov] who'd done the music for [Federico] Fellini's *City of Women*, who is the best collaborator for an ignoramus like me. He is an extraordinary musician, both as a player and as a composer. I'd said, "I want something that's popular, that'll catch people's attention, but is discreet." And he came up with the perfect thing and he improvised all that piano in the studio. It was just fantastic.

I think there's lots of different types of film music: there's film music that tells the interior state of the mind of the characters; there's music which "G's" up the action. I wanted a music that gave a flavor of an atmosphere to the entire film. But of course, composers like to think logically and they want "Mario's theme." And I'd say, "Yeah, okay, if you want. We'll call it that." And here's a guy who really knows movies, so he knows very well that the moment you've got the stuff there, that somehow or another, you're going to change it all around. It was written for one thing and it's much better for something else.

Into the final mix we've got sixteen tracks up and I'd go to the dubbing mixer [the sound technician who mixes the various sounds and music together] and we're sitting in the big studio right in the middle of Cinecittà [the Italian studio in Rome]. And I say, "Look, can I have a look at the dubbing charts, just to see where we are?" And he looks up at me and says, "Que? [Italian for "What?"] What are dubbing charts?" He said, "No, here we put it up and let's see what happens." "Where did you learn that from?" He said, "The maestro, you know, Fellini." I said, "Fellini used to have six months; we've got eight days to dub this thing." We spent seven days dubbing two reels. He would forget, he would literally forget what was coming up, "Huh? Oh . . ." and this went on for seven days and wonderfully Italian, and we had one day to dub the rest of the picture. The composer came in the middle of the dub and he said, "What's going on here?" And the composer said, "I'm going to do the music." And the guy said, "Yeah, I could do with a spare pair of hands; this is getting difficult." And then we had a party.

Robert Zemeckis, *Forrest Gump*

When you can have a relationship with your composer—that is like gold—because you don't have any objectivity anymore. You say, "I don't know if this thing works. We're going to have to shore it up with music," and Al Silvestri, who I've collaborated with on the last six movies, says, "No." He says, "I wouldn't know what to write—I just don't hear any music there."

The hard part for *Forrest* was we had all these records that we put in the movie [the music supervisor was Joel Sill]. And just wading through thirty years of music and trying to figure out how to work that into the film, that was what I think took most of our time in the editing room.

Oliver Stone, *JFK*

I called John Williams, who I'd worked with on *Born on the Fourth of July*. I thought it was a very emotional score and I was in accord with his aesthetic. I asked John, "Do you have any time? Can you give us thirty days?" I said, "Come to Dallas. Come to Dealy Plaza and experience it with us." He was there the first two weeks of shooting. He had a special feeling for John Kennedy. So in a sense he's written a requiem in his head already. And that was the main theme of the movie. And then in addition to that he wrote our temp [temporary] score for us, before we edited. He gave us a conspirator theme for the Cubans—for Oswald he gave us a modification of that. He gave us a family theme for Jim [Garrison, the part played by Kevin Costner] and his wife and children. So there were three pieces and several miscellaneous pieces written by the time we were halfway through shooting. Essentially he'd written the score before the film was finished.

Steven Spielberg, *Amistad*

John Williams [the composer] always surprises me. There's never a score that he has written that I haven't been thoroughly moved and thoroughly surprised that he was capable of bringing a whole genre to something that he'd never knew how to do before.

James Cameron, *Titanic*

I'd worked with James Horner [the composer] on *Aliens*. I thought he'd done some spectacularly emotional scores in the last few years. He worked on the film for, I think, eight months. He said, "I'm gonna just do this movie. I'm not taking any other gig." Our very first meeting, he had seen a lot of the footage. He sat and looked at over a period of several days I think thirty hours of daily selects, just to steep himself in the images. Nothing had been cut yet. He gave me some ideas he was thinking of. He was talking about Celtic instrumentations and kind of a traditional Irish sound, which I like, and the use of voice, which I thought was great. My only requests of him were "Don't do a conventional period score. I don't want to hear a big violin section." And he said, "No violins?" And I said, "Find another way to be emotional." I said, "Just work on melody for the first two months." Just sit at your piano and when you've got one or two great themes, and you can play it on the piano, you're 90 percent of the way there. And the first time he played the three main melodies of the score for me, I literally cried at the first one and more so on the second one. And I knew I was there, and he hadn't really written a bit of the score proper yet.

James L. Brooks, *As Good As It Gets*

At the very end of the road, we had a picture that was getting laughs and was short of it's emotional life. And I was almost at the point of giving up and deploring this and he wouldn't let me. And part of what he [Hans Zimmer, the composer] kept on saying to me and part of what he was able to do with the music meant that the ambitions I'd always had for the picture at the beginning were the ambitions I still had at the end. I finished with the same ambitions, and I almost didn't. That was working closely with somebody.

Barbra Streisand, *The Prince of Tides*

When I was doing *Nuts*—I didn't feel the film required much music—that's why I could compose the thirteen-minute score. I believe this is such an alive process—I mean, just last week I was redoing the sound for videotape. I thought I made the music too loud in spots in the film, so now I've changed the music balance for video. So I don't think it's done till it's done. Usually my first instincts about levels are the best—then you start to overthink it. Of course, film to me is like a symphony with slow adagio movements and fast staccato sections.

I had much less music at the beginning of previews. But then, I had a very "slow pace" score on my audience response cards. So every time I got a slow pace, I would add more music. And every time I added more music, the pace box went up. The music would keep it going.

I've also had a musician who plays all synthesized sounds come to the dubbing stage and play experimentally to the film—like in silent pictures.

Curtis Hanson, *L.A. Confidential*

There are many songs in the movie, and I, in fact, picked quite a few of them when we were writing the script. The advantage of having picked them in front, I found, was that I was actually able to play them on the set, when we were shooting, which was helpful. For instance, Kevin Spacey looking in the mirror—he was able to actually hear Dean Martin on the jukebox, which helped him feel what the thing would feel like in the movie. But it also helps me feel what the scene ultimately would feel like.

Jerry Goldsmith was my choice of composer, and he had a sort of odd job because all of these songs were already in the movie when I first showed it to him. He didn't have to worry about setting the period or even defining the characters because you have the song already doing that. He had to weave it all together so that the songs and the score didn't feel like they were in different movies. And then use his score to underline the emotions. The idea that I'd had in terms of the songs was that there would be this continuing motif of a trumpet. And then Jerry took that trumpet and put it into the score, which is actually a contemporary score, but it feels like it's wed to the songs.

Neil Jordan, *The Crying Game*

In *The Crying Game,* I tried to use a series of songs in an ironic way. In general I don't like the use of popular songs in movies because I suppose I'm not a great fan of rock and roll. Someday I'd love to make a film without music, actually just with natural sounds.

Frank Darabont, *The Shawshank Redemption*

You want the music to elicit some kind of emotional connection, and yet do it in such a way that is not obvious—it doesn't draw attention to itself in a way that I've seen other composers do, who will hit you over the head with four hundred violins at the key moment. Then comes the funny point where you've temp scored [put in a temporary score] your movie with cues from *A River Runs through It* and *Scent of a Woman* and *Dances with Wolves* and you've mixed the movie and you've test screened it and you pretty much love your score and then comes the day, you have the new one. "Oh wait a minute—that doesn't sound right—why doesn't that sound right?" Well, well, idiot, because it's not *Dances with Wolves*!

Michael Mann, *The Insider*

The mix is probably the fourth total writing of the movie. As you get closer to the end, you truly have the totality of the movie that you haven't had since the first time it all came together in your head. Everything you're doing is only to have what you need to make that film, to forge your film in the editing room. One of the last things I did was blow out all of the masters that we shot of the final mix because I wanted to raise the center channel, I think, two db [decibels] all the way across the board. And so of course everybody in postproduction at Disney thought I was completely nuts. We were now three db hotter than the optimum. It made the difference between the performances existing on-screen and coming out into the theater. And it's a tiny change, but it had a radical effect. And those are the things you just don't get until the film is totally complete.

The Best and the Worst

Barry Levinson, *Bugsy*

𝒯he shooting of it is what I love the most. Because there are so many things that are happening so quickly, and so many things that you have to fix, and so many surprises that take place, and so many interesting people that you work with, that that explosion that's going on all the time creates an adrenaline rush in a way. It's almost euphoric at times.

Even part of the pain is the pleasure, because you're trying to get something on a scene and it's not working. It's just sort of laying there; it has no life. That's painful, but at the same time it's exciting to make it work. The area that I like the least is the aftermath, in terms of talking, in terms of the press, because somehow it begins to minimize it in some way. In the final analysis, when you look back, you're not sure how you got it all done. You don't know how it all came together. And it's all of those people and all of those moments that make up a film. And it's magic. And you can't explain it.

Stephen Daldry, *The Hours*

I've only ever wanted to be a director, all my life. And I feel I'm incredibly lucky. If I could find something else that was as good, if I got as big a rush, then I'm sure I'd be a drug addict. I'd love to be an alcoholic, you know. And I'm sure these things would be amazingly available to me. Being an obsessive personality. So directing keeps me alive literally. And the worst thing about it is when I'm not good; that's when I find it the most crippling.

Neil Jordan, *The Crying Game*

The trouble with making a film is, it's the most pleasurable thing in the world. Because your whole day is filled. You wake up in the morning, you tumble out of bed, there's a car there, it takes you to the set, and it's great. What more stimulating thing can you do than, the first thing, talk to two actors or begin to worry about the paint on a bit of scenery. I find it actually, at it's best, it's the most pleasurable form of spending a day you can imagine. You're busy, and then you go out to dinner at night. If you are off on an artistic bent, everything you possibly could want to do in some states you get to do, if you direct a film.

The worst part for me is the plane flights because I live in Ireland. And for better or for worse this strange place [Los Angeles] is the center of the world, film industry, so I keep having to make the ten-hour flight back and forwards and back and forwards, and I'm terrified of flying, so that for me is the worst!

Andrew Davis, *The Fugitive*

The pleasure is collaborating. It's sort of being a part of the circus. Being able to walk in and do anything you want to do. Being taken seriously when they shouldn't take you seriously. That's the greatest fun for me. It's also tremendous to have people enjoy your movie.

The hardest part I guess is being second-guessed. When you have a kind of vision of things, and you want to pursue it, and you want to try to experiment. And there may be people around saying, "What is that about? Why do you want to try that?" I know that it can be very lonely out there, even though you're the director, and you're supposed to be the captain of the ship and there's a lot of responsibility and a lot of burden on your shoulders. And it's a question of finding a support mechanism and a team of people to share that with.

Barbra Streisand, *The Prince of Tides*

I get very obsessed till I get the script right. I can't sleep, I can't think straight. Then it's worrisome during preproduction. I mean, getting all the casting right. You go through the angst of that.

But there are really so many pleasures on a day-to-day basis. I love the discipline of we have this amount of time, we have this amount of money, we have this amount of energy. There is such an aliveness, such a spontaneity to every day, every moment, every problem, trying to capture the truth of the moment, trying to create an atmosphere where the actor is free to bare his soul—to reveal his truth.

Cameron Crowe, *Jerry Maguire*

The worst part is dealing with the casting process.
The best part is when something simple becomes the real soul of your movie.

Rob Marshall, *Chicago*

I guess the best part of it for me are the relationships that you create, that camaraderie.

Roberto Benigni, *Life Is Beautiful*

The best—it's wonderful to tell a story. And to draw it like it is. This is a kind of a gift. Wonderful! For me this is so fascinating, I am completely captured by this idea. And the worst is when I cannot tell a story, because it's very, very painful. The sorrow, making a movie, is very, very deep. I have pleasure, but there is a side that is so painful making a movie. But this is life.

Clint Eastwood, *Unforgiven*

The best is having the opportunity to interpret an artful piece of writing that you admire and the ability to interpret that and to watch it evolve is great fun. It has some great satisfying moments and it has some terrifying moments along the way. And there's that final terrifying moment when you let go of it and put it out for the public and say, "Is anybody going to see this?" I think there's a point in every film that's about three-quarters of the way through, you are going, "Does anybody really want to see this?"

Clint Eastwood, *Mystic River*

Directing's great fun if you allow yourself to enjoy it. I think the older I get, the more I enjoy it because you're more relaxed and you don't seem to put as many obstacles on yourself. I think editing is the most fun, the least pressure anyway because there's no longer a whole crew, you no longer feel responsible, you're no longer obliged to the weather, you're no longer anything. All you're doing is several people sitting in a room looking at things and putting together what you envisioned.

And the worst part, I think, is production meetings at the beginning, where you have to go in and sit in production meetings and everybody sits around and has a little thing and says, "Well, what about on the props, now? Do you want a little tiny flag to kind of go on the deal?" And you're going, I don't really give a crap, but I have to act like I do. Though I like wardrobe. I think it's a very important part. The actual going in and fittings and all that kind of stuff. Especially for the actor.

The best thing about not acting is not having anybody come up and pull at you all the time. Your hair, and they're spraying you. And then how the hell can an actor [do] any kind of a scene when everybody's pulled at you for ten minutes before the scene goes? But that's the genius of good actors is they can do that. They can shut off their mind and then go ahead and do that. But to me, those are the two worst.

Gary Ross, *Seabiscuit*

The worst part is fighting about money. Fighting about budgets. What if the set was smaller? What if it didn't have a floor? What if it didn't have a roof? Do you really need a thousand extras? Could you get by with seven hundred? Well, what about six hundred? And you're being pecked to death, so that's a drag.

The best moments of this entire process, from start to finish, are just when you get a good day and you let the van go and you walk home alone, back to the base camp, and you just have the satisfaction of seeing this thing coalesce. And there's absolutely no better feeling in the world.

Taylor Hackford, *Ray*

I spent thirteen years trying to raise the money for this film and that was the most difficult part of the film—the most arduous, the most painful. By the time, you know, we finally thought we were going, Jamie [Foxx] was on, the money fell out. Always the nightmare.

Once we started going, it was a dream, it was fantastic.

Sofia Coppola, *Lost in Translation*

Shot lists are the worst, my least favorite part.

Just to be able to think up anything and then to have all these people there helping you make that is, I can't imagine anything better or more fun to do.

When I was in the middle of shooting, I was thinking, "This is so hard. I don't ever want to do this again. I don't know why I do this." And then at the end, of course, I'm like, "I want to do that again." So it's a weird thing where you forget about the hard part and think about the part you enjoy.

Gus Van Sant, *Good Will Hunting*

The worst is probably shooting. It's the toughest period. It's just something that's a necessary evil! But also it's probably the best too, because it's the part that you always talk about; when you're talking about filmmaking, it's the most exciting. I remember Dennis Hopper, I heard say once: "The only thing worse than making a film is not making a film." Or waiting to make one.

Michael Mann, *The Insider*

I think probably the best is a couple of moments when something's really being realized. There's a very tense dialogue scene between Russell [Crowe] actually and his wife; he does all the talking, kind of a soliloquy. And those were the kinds of performances that I would always operate [the camera on] and I'd just really be right in there. And just to see around his eyes, the connectedness that he had with the moment, and we all feel connected. So that, and mixing [the sounds] with Andy Nelson would be a similar experience. We'd happen to hit something right where everything's conspiring to hit a certain harmonic in terms of the film dramatically and emotionally, and you hit it.

The worst—probably things that get in the way of concentration. We had a hurricane watch in the Bahamas, so suddenly one-day shooting became a half-day shooting.

Scott Hicks, *Shine*

The worst part is turning up on any given day when suddenly you don't have an idea in your head and you hope when those forty faces turn to you, and you try not to show the panic and you work your way through it.

The best part are those days when everything lays out in front of you and you see things so clearly. You find exactly where to put the camera. You're in tune with what you're doing.

Peter Weir, *The Truman Show*

I would say that it becomes an addiction. It's hard to imagine giving it up. I remember meeting Fred Zinnemann [director of *High Noon*, *A Man for All Seasons*, and *Julia*] in the latter years of his life in London, and he was like a small bird with a cane, having a cup of tea in his office, and he said, "You know I don't think I will ever make another film." And I thought he was joking. The man was in his eighties. And I luckily didn't laugh. I said, "Well, who knows." But I realized that of course he was a young man. Creatively of course you don't age in the same way. And I found it very touching.

Peter Weir, *Master and Commander: The Far Side of the World*

The weather. It's just tremendous tension in a day. I don't mind any tension that's part of the job, but the weather you just can't do anything. You've shot half a day and it's been bright and sunny, and over lunchtime it comes not just overcast. It's a storm coming, you know? And you say, "It's interesting light." And they say, "Yeah, if we moved fast and you drop a couple of angles, reshoot the morning's material." That's my worst nightmare. Do you do that? Do you go with it? What do you do? Weather. Drives me nuts sometimes. I remember seeing Alfred Hitchcock when I was a film student, in his last film he made, *Frenzy*, in London. Sitting in his chair outside on the location and he said to his AD, "What are we waiting for?" And the AD said, crouching down, "The sun, Mr. Hitchcock." And he looked up and I thought, "God, even Alfred Hitchcock."

Another worst—the first cut. You're convinced you've made the worst film of all time

Steven Soderbergh, *Erin Brockovich* and *Traffic*

The only thing that gets me down is when I feel like I fell short, I missed it, I just didn't get it. I didn't work hard enough; I didn't know enough. And that's the worst feeling in the world. And you basically just have to keep getting on the horse, you know, and keep moving.

I like everything about it. God, I would do any job on a film. I have done most of them. And I like 'em all. I just think it's fascinating. It's the best job in the world. The best to me is when I'm surprised by an actor, when I see something that just is startling in the right way, that is so true and, you know, lifelike. I live for that. I mean, when that happens you just want to celebrate.

Peter Jackson, *The Lord of the Rings: The Fellowship of the Ring*

The best of being a director is imagining a movie in your mind. A movie that you'd like to see that nobody else is making, so you can't go and rent it. And then going and trying to put the jigsaw puzzle together to somehow end up close to what was in your mind. So you're actually making a film for yourself; you're making a film that you want to see. That, that's what I love about directing.

The worst is simply, I mean, it's, it's the pressure, it's the stress. The worst, actually, to me, always revolves around the weather, actually. Weather is what I hate, standing in a field and getting snowed on.

Peter Jackson, *The Lord of the Rings: The Two Towers*

The best part is you just feel like you're a child. It's not really a profession that grown-ups should be doing.

The worst part is when people say it's costing too much and you've got to cut your budget.

All you really have at the end of it is, you've had this wonderful experience. And whether it does well or doesn't do well, you've had this experience with them and so that's something you treasure.

The worst part for me in a funny way was that you're the only one that takes the full journey. In other words, you begin and then you meet a few people along the way that you're working with and then you go into rehearsal and you go into shooting it, and those are a new family. But then you lose little families along the way. They go away and you're still there and you're working sort of, with sort of a new family, your postproduction family.

Peter Jackson, *The Lord of the Rings: The Return of the King*

It's the honor of being in one of the most unusual professions in the world in which you can sit and imagine something in your head, just like everybody in the world does, you know? Imagine something. Except with our profession, you then have this huge team of incredibly talented people who kill themselves to try to get what's in your head out on-screen so the rest of the world can enjoy it. I can't think of anything quite like it. I guest the most fun part for me is writing when there's no constraints and the imagination's going crazy.

The worst part is the toll on your family.

James L. Brooks, *As Good As It Gets*

Exhaustion. And I guess maybe worst and best is maybe the loss of yourself.

Baz Luhrmann, *Moulin Rouge*

I think the worst part of it is the responsibility. It's one thing for me to go and do something with my life but it's another thing to bring other people with you. So the weight of that responsibility and what you feel you owe them.

The best part is the fulfillment, having done it. That you feel useful and worth-while.

John Madden, *Shakespeare in Love*

For me having the ability to say, "No, I want it to be this way," is absolutely wonderful. And there are times when you want somebody else to be asked all the questions. I go through the best and the worst every single day. You go to bed at night, thinking this is an absolutely fantastic job. And you get up in the morning wanting to go anywhere but where you're going.

Ron Howard, *A Beautiful Mind*

It's that adrenaline that I can feel when, sort of, you know, creative ideas are coalescing. Mine, others, somehow, you know, problems are getting solved in a way that I find exciting.

Rob Reiner, *A Few Good Men*

The best part is having directed. It's expressing yourself, your thoughts and your feelings.
   The worst part is the hours. They're just brutal, and you gain too much weight!!

Steven Spielberg, *Amistad*

The worst part of directing a movie for me is getting up early in the morning. I hate that! I just hate getting up before the birds and driving to work in the dark and then watching the sun rise as you pull into the main gate of the studio, that's tough. And the other worst thing about making a movie is having a thousand people ask you a thousand questions every day, every hour. And having to answer everyone's questions and having to be so attentive and so responsible and there to be everyone's friend and psychoanalyst. And that's draining.
   One of the greatest things about directing is you gain yourself. You sort of are reborn every time you make a new movie. And you see yourself differently, every time you make a movie. I think our films tend to inform us. We grew up with them, and we also sadly watch our films, watch our children, grow up, graduate, and within the space of a year, they belong to somebody else and they go away.

Steven Spielberg, *Saving Private Ryan*

I think the best thing about directing is when you've had a thought that somehow is better than the thought you had. And that's a nice feeling.

The worst thing about directing I think is something that we all have to go through, and that's that moment where you are judged. I think the judgment is the worst part about being a director. Starting with whoever you show the picture to first, whether it's your wife, or your partner, your best friend, the studio, and then eventually the critics, and then eventually the public. That for me is where I go into hiding if I can.

Frank Darabont, *The Shawshank Redemption*

Wasn't it Milos Forman [director of *One Flew over the Cuckoo's Nest* and *Amadeus*] who said shooting a movie was a necessary evil to get into the editing room? That's really my favorite place to be. That's where you can actually concentrate your focus on making the film.

I think my least favorite aspect of the process is the sheer mental and physical stamina required to get you through the shoot. I found that to be an extraordinary drain, to the point where it actually colors your enthusiasm for what you're doing, which I think is a danger.

Spike Jonze, *Being John Malkovich*

I think the worst part of it probably was watching the assembly a week after we finished production of—it was like this three and a half hour long, really flat, no pacing, not funny, and I was completely depressed. And it was painful.

And the best part is just whenever anything's working. Whether it's an idea you had and you're shooting it, the actor is trying it, or it's an idea that came up, or some accident happened, or something technical where you're trying something with the camera, or watching it with an audience and it's working.

Mel Gibson, *Braveheart*

The hardest part—hmmm—staying a step ahead of everybody else.

I just love the experience. I mean, you can get in critical moments of self-doubt, where you think, "Should I go hang myself now?" which are pretty depressing. But I just don't see the downside. I think I'm incredibly fortunate to be able to do it.

Roman Polanski, *The Pianist*

The worst part is the night call from so-called creative group of studio executives. Everything else about this profession is the best part of it. I love every bit, you know? From the first conception moment to the grading [the color timing of the film—the last thing a director may do—making sure the print has the right colors]. I think we're very lucky people to do this, you know, to have this passion. And I think that there is no one thing that I would like to single out. I like everything about this.

Quentin Tarantino, *Pulp Fiction*

The single worst part of directing, and it's one of the things that when I think about it, I try not to think too early in the process, because it almost makes me wanna not do— it's not the big fights—it's all the little nitpicky questions about this or that or the other, that when you're editing the movie and you're putting it under this microscope, that no movie should be looked at under a microscope. When the producers are watching it, they're making their little notes.

I think the best part is, like, when you've done a good day, when you've, like, you DID IT—you've fuckin' nailed it. And they're better than you could've ever imagined and everyone knows that you're doing good work, you just go home and you just feel so good. And then, when you watch your film with an audience and you've got 'em. You feel the laughter and they're in. Like in my stuff, it's like laugh, laugh, laugh, and then—BOOM—I'm going to stop you from laughing. And then it stops. And then I get you laughing again, and it's like, that's great.

Martin Scorsese, *Gangs of New York*

The best part for me is when something magical sort of happens with the actors and you're there and you're part of it. It becomes a new reality. They take you to a whole other world. It's quite something. And then for me the best also is shooting movement, camera movement. And of course finally for me the best part is in the editing because it reminds me as a kid in a small tenement downtown in New York when I had two hours to myself and I'd make these drawings, nobody'd be talking to me. I could do what I wanted. And the editing reminds me of that. Just myself. Me driving my editor crazy. I've been torturing the woman for twenty-five years.

The thing I hate most is—the damn schedule. Why does it have to be on a schedule? I get it. I know, the money. And of course when they come in—"Do you really need these four pages? Can you do it in two days instead of three?" You'd just like to be left alone and do it. But you can't.

Martin Scorsese, *The Aviator*

Well, for me it's always around the actors and when it's all clicking together with the actors you sort of become part of them. It's just something happens that is absolutely magical. And I sort of become at the same time not only a spectator but like I'm in the movie. And I like the old scale of some of the epic films that have some of those moves across lots of action and lots of extras in the frame. That's very enjoyable to do, especially if you have the time worked out so you're utilizing the time properly. The biggest shots I've ever done—one was in the Olympic stadium for *Raging Bull*—we shot that *Raging Bull* Steadicam shot where he comes out and then he goes up through the whole place and a thousand extras and the Steadicam got on a crane and a boom and then they took him up—in three-quarters of a day. And the same thing with the Copacabana shot in *Goodfellas*. So I enjoy that kind of thing. Yet there's nothing like one or two people just hitting it off in the frame. It's just fantastic.

The hardest stuff I found was the heat and trying to shoot some of the scenes in this picture two hours out of L.A. They tell me, "Marty, dress for it." I say, "Yeah, absolutely." I had a panama hat. I was fine, it looked good. And within a day and a half the heat started to bake my head. I just couldn't think anymore. It was extraordinary. It made me realize, can you imagine [Cecil B.] DeMille [director of *The Ten Commandments* and *The Plainsman*] and [William] Wyler [director of the color *Ben-Hur* and *Best Years of Our Lives*] and [Raoul] Walsh [director of *White Heat* and *High Sierra*]? How about [Erich] von Stroheim [director of *Greed*], the crew members dying in Death Valley? I mean, these were pioneers. Extraordinary. It really made me appreciate even more the legacy we have here in American filmmakers.

Ridley Scott, *Black Hawk Down*

The worst part is committing to something, 'cause you're sure there's gonna be something better around the corner. The worst is being out of work.

Curtis Hanson, *L.A. Confidential*

The best part is being able to do it. I mean to me, to be able to direct a movie is a dream come true. It doesn't even have to be going well. If it's going okay, I just feel so lucky to be able to be there doing it.

The worst part of course is when it's not going okay, and you feel that your dream is turning into shit and there's nothing you can do about it!

Ang Lee, *Crouching Tiger, Hidden Dragon*

I think pressure, you're handling time and also elements. There is gravity, there is a limitation to everything. Your imagination is not. I think among those [pressures], just for my own character, if I pick one—is quick decisions—on the set, every day being asked hundreds of questions. Put together, that's the style of film. But you have to make it quick. Quick is better than nothing. Looks like you know what you're doing. Most of the time you don't. Is pretending, you know, 'cause nobody knows. So that part is the one I hate the most. Sometime I just say I don't know anything or I change my mind. But most of the time I have to function very quickly. That's why homework is good so you prepare for changes or answer questions. That part I really hate.

I think I love the most is if it works. You know, in the theater, see people's face reacting to the reflection of silver screen. Something generated in initially from the back of the head. I think that's pretty cool. I don't like to call "Ang Lee film." That's just me. "Directed by" is very good for me, but I am the pivotal influence on making of the movie, but when I see a group effort or what we're dreaming about when people actually get it and respond, that is the sweetest thing to me.

Robert Zemeckis, *Forrest Gump*

The best part is showing your movie to an audience for the first time. And I also feel it's the worst part!

Mike Newell, *Four Weddings and a Funeral*

The worst is the "focus group" where this indistinct randomly chosen group of thirty people will sit in the first two rows of the theater and you have to then, with the studio, sit one row behind them, as you then have to hear them saying, "I don't really get this."

    I always used to like when they had black-and-white dubs in the dubbing theater [used while mixing the sounds], when they put the color up for the run-through of the reel [after the mix of the sounds], and you would see it with all the sound, suddenly with all the sound and the color as well and how it was going to be. I used to love that.

Sam Mendes, *American Beauty*

My best and worst happened on the same evening. The worst—when the studio saw the film, we went to San Jose or somewhere like that, and I walked in and my heart just sank. I thought—I just had a terrible feeling. I thought they were all much too young; it was rowdy in there, chucking popcorn around. I thought, "My God, they're not going to get this." So I got up and I suddenly became very English, and I said, "Who kind of liked it." And about a third of them put their hands up. And the guy in the front row said, "Ask who really liked it?" And I said, "Well, who really liked it?" And they all put their hands up. And so that was the best.

M. Night Shyamalan, *The Sixth Sense*

What's the worst part of being a director? I guess is at the preview screening with the studio. At the moment when you already know what the audience felt, you came out, you sat with the audience, and you know, yes or no, where it is. "Oh, I need to fix that." But you're waiting for those goddamn numbers that are going to decide your fate. You're helpless there.

    The best is when you're sitting in the audience and your movie's really working and you're like, "Wow."

James Cameron, *Titanic*

Best is when it's done and it's a big hit! But honestly, in terms of the actual process itself, for me it's the moment of discovery on the set with an actor, when an actor creates something that you didn't expect, and it's wonderful, and you're happy to have it in your film.

The worst part for me, I guess, is probably the moment when the lights are going down at the first preview, because that's the moment of truth.

Michael Radford, *Il Postino*

Well, I always used to say that the very best part of being a director is having the idea and imagining yourself nominated for an Oscar—all the rest is a pain.

Alexander Payne, *Sideways*

This was a really harmonious shoot, and the thing I'm proudest of is that many crew people told me by the end, it was one of their happiest, if not very happiest, productions they had ever worked on. And that brought me great, great satisfaction.

Mike Leigh, *Secrets & Lies*

The worst part is that moment when you don't know what you are doing. The best bit is you make a film.

Oliver Stone, *JFK*

I think the pleasure is in the dreaming of it. And the pain is in the destruction of the dream.

Anthony Minghella, *The English Patient*

Every day is filled with pleasure and pain. The best and worst are often holding hands.

•*Appendix A* •

Biographies★

Roberto Benigni, *Life Is Beautiful* **(1999)**

Roberto Benigni is a first-time DGA Feature Film Directorial Award nominee for his film *Life Is Beautiful.* He is one of the world's most acclaimed comic filmmakers and entertainers. In the United States, Roberto is best known for his many memorable comic performances in such films as Jim Jarmusch's *Down by Law* and *Night on Earth*, as well as for his role as the infamous Inspector Clouseau's son in Blake Edwards's *Son of the Pink Panther.* Recently he has appeared in Wim Wender's *Far Away, So Close!* Around the world, Roberto is known as a filmmaker with his own unique style. Among the films he has written, directed, and starred in are *The Little Devil* with Walter Matthau, *The Monster*, and *Johnny Stecchino*, which became the most successful film in the history of Italian cinema. Roberto then appeared in the long-awaited screen version of the popular European comic book *Asterix* with Gerard Depardieu. For *Life Is Beautiful,* he was nominated for Best Picture and Best Screenplay Academy Awards and won the Best Actor Oscar. The film also won the Oscar for Best Foreign Language Film. Benigni's subsequent directorial work included *Pinocchio* and *The Tiger and the Snow.*

James L. Brooks, *As Good As It Gets* **(1998)**

James L. Brooks is the recipient of multiple Academy and Emmy Awards, and a three-time DGA Award nominee. He is responsible for some of film and television's most memorable contributions to contemporary culture. Mr. Brooks has written and created such television classics as *Taxi, The Mary Tyler Moore Show, Rhoda, Lou Grant, Room 222, The Tracey Ullman Show,* and *The Simpsons.* He wrote/produced/directed *Terms of Endearment,* which won the DGA Award for Outstanding Directorial Achievement in 1983 and garnered three Academy Awards, including Best Picture and Best Director. Mr. Brooks's other film credits include

---

★Images of directors adapted from the videos of "Meet the Nominees" Symposia 1992–1995 © Directors Guild of America. All rights reserved.

the Oscar-nominated *Broadcast News, I'll Do Anything*, and *Spanglish*. His film *As Good As It Gets* (1997) received seven Oscar nominations, including one for Best Picture.

James Cameron, *Titanic* (1998)

James Cameron was born in Kapuskasing, Ontario, Canada. In 1971, he moved to California and studied physics at Fullerton College, while working as a machinist and a truck driver. In 1978, Mr. Cameron set his sights on a career in movies and raised money from a consortium of dentists to produce a short film in 35mm. In 1982, he wrote a low-budget, high-impact vehicle called *The Terminator*, which went on to receive international acclaim and made over $80 million worldwide. Mr. Cameron has subsequently written/produced/directed some of the film world's most successful, highest-grossing action and visual-effects adventures, including *The Abyss, Terminator 2: Judgment Day, Aliens, Rambo II, True Lies*, and *Titanic*.

Titanic literally stormed the globe, setting records in every country in which it was released and ultimately grossing more than $600 million at the domestic box office and over $1.2 billion abroad. *Titanic's* worldwide global box office total of $1.8 billion doubled the tally of the previous record holder.

In addition to toppling every established performance record, *Titanic* was recognized and honored by numerous organizations, receiving fourteen Academy Award nominations and winning a record-tying eleven Oscars that included Best Picture, Director, Visual Effects, Music, Song, Cinematography, Sound, and Costume, as well as additional nominations and awards from the Directors Guild of America, Screen Actors Guild, Writers Guild of America, Producers Guild of America, People's Choice Awards, BAFTA, and many others.

Post-*Titanic,* Cameron has begun exploring several new entertainment avenues. In 1998, Cameron formed a television development and production venture with Charles Eglee. Their maiden effort was a one-hour dramatic series for Twentieth Century Fox Television and FBC titled *Dark Angel*. Cameron has also immersed himself in the study of man's potential next great step in the exploration of space: *Mars*. Through his own research, and working closely with experts at NASA and throughout the private sector, Cameron has developed a wholly feasible near-term mission architecture, which could put humans on the Red Planet within the next fifteen years. These central plans provide the spine of two related entertainment projects that Cameron wrote and produced: a five-hour miniseries and a 3D IMAX film (the latter of which Cameron codirected), both focusing on the first manned mission to Mars.

Sofia Coppola, *Lost in Translation* (2004)

A former student of fine art at Cal Arts, Sofia Coppola has worked as a photographer and fashion designer. Her photos have been seen in *Interview, Paris Vogue, Allure* and Tokyo's Parco Gallery. Prior to that, Coppola cowrote and costume designed for the "Life with Zoe" segment of *New York Stories*, directed by her father, Francis Ford Coppola. In 1989, Coppola designed the costumes for the cult classic *The Spirit of '76*, and appeared as Mary Corleone in *The Godfather III* the following year. In 1994, Coppola and friend Zoe Cassavetes created the pop-culture magazine show, *Hi-Octane*, which aired on Comedy Central. Coppola's *Lick the Star*, a short that she wrote and directed, was a popular segment on the Independent Film Channel in 1999.

Sofia made her feature-film debut as director and writer of *The Virgin Suicides*, which was released by Paramount Classics in April 2000 to critical acclaim. The film, which stars James Woods, Kathleen Turner, Kirsten Dunst, and Josh Hartnett, was adapted from Jeffrey Eugenides's best-selling novel about a family of suburban teenage sisters and the boys who were incurably obsessed with them.

Sofia Coppola is a modern auteur whose talents go far beyond directing. With her latest film *Lost in Translation*, which she also wrote and coproduced, Coppola has continued to develop a unique style of balancing story line with an aesthetic that is essentially all her own. Set in modern-day Tokyo, *Lost in Translation* stars Bill Murray, Scarlett Johansson, and Giovanni Ribisi. The critically acclaimed film was awarded the 2004 Golden Globe for Best Picture (Musical or Comedy), Best Screenplay, and Best Actor. Included in over three hundred critics' top-ten lists, the Focus Features release was also nominated for four Academy Awards including Best Picture, Best Director, Best Original Screenplay, and Best Actor. Coppola received the award for best screenplay.

Cameron Crowe, *Jerry Maguire* (1997)

Cameron Crowe was born in Palm Springs, California, and raised in San Diego. He began a career in journalism at the age of fifteen, writing for such publications as *Penthouse*, *Playboy*, *Creem*, and the *Los Angeles Times*. At sixteen, he joined the staff of *Rolling Stone*, where he was a contributing editor and later an associate editor. Crowe profiled such influential music-world figures as Bob Dylan, David Bowie, Neil Young, Eric Clapton, and the members of Led Zeppelin. In 1979, Crowe (then twenty-two) returned to high school to research a book on teen life. *Fast Times at Ridgemont High* became a best seller, and Universal Pictures, which had optioned the book while it was still in galley form, signed Crowe to write the screenplay. Released in the spring of 1982 and directed by Amy Heckerling, *Fast Times at Ridgemont High* became one of the year's biggest hits and launched the careers of such stars as Sean Penn, Jennifer Jason Leigh, Judge Reinhold, Forest Whitaker, Nicolas Cage, and Eric Stoltz. Crowe's screenplay was nominated for a Writers Guild of America Award for Best Screen Adaptation. In 1989, Crowe made his feature-film directorial debut with his original screenplay *Say Anything*. The critically acclaimed film starred John Cusack and Ione Skye. He followed with *Singles* in 1992. Matt Dillon, Bridget Fonda, Kyra Sedgwick, and Campbell Scott starred in this highly praised romantic comedy. In 1996 Cameron directed *Jerry Maguire*, starring Tom Cruise, Renée Zellweger, and Cuba Gooding Jr. In 1997 Crowe received a nomination from the Directors Guild of America for Outstanding Directorial Achievement for a Feature, as well as Academy Award nominations for Best Screenplay Written Directly for the Screen and Best Picture. In November of 1999, Knopf published Crowe's *Conversations with Wilder*, a rare series of interviews conducted with the legendary writer/director Billy Wilder. Since his DGA Award nomination for *Jerry Maguire*, Crowe has directed *Almost Famous* and *Vanilla Sky*. He was nominated for again for a DGA Award for *Almost Famous,* which also won him BAFTA and Academy Award awards for Best Screenplay. His next film was *Elizabethtown*.

Stephen Daldry, *The Hours* (2003)

Stephen Daldry has directed or produced more than a hundred plays at the Royal Court Theatre. For the National Theatre, he directed the multiaward-winning *Machinal* and *An Inspector Calls*, which was also mounted on Broadway where both Stephen and the play received Tony Awards. He has also directed and produced for BBC radio and television, and his first short film, *Eight,* was nominated in 1999 for a BAFTA. Stephen made his feature-film debut in 2000 with *Billy Elliot,* which was nominated for three Academy Awards, including Best Director, Best Supporting Actress (Julie Walters), and Best Screenplay (Lee Hall). It also received twelve BAFTA nominations and won awards for Best Film, Best Actor (Jamie Bell), and Best Supporting Actress (Julie Walters), as well as thirty-two other international awards. *The Hours* is Stephen's second feature film. Since this DGA nomination, Daldry has directed two Caryl Churchill plays, *Far Away* in New York and *A Number* at London's Royal Court Theatre and is working on several feature projects.

Frank Darabont, *The Shawshank Redemption* (1995) and *The Green Mile* (2000)

Frank Darabont's parents fled Hungary during the 1956 uprising. Frank was born three years later in 1959 in Monterbeliard, France, and was brought to America when he was still a baby. He attended Hollywood High School, suffered through the disco era, and began his career in film in 1980 as a production assistant on a low-budget film called *Hell Night.* Frank then spent the next six years working in set construction and as a set dresser, while struggling to be a screenwriter. During this time he also wrote and directed *The Woman in the Room*, a thirty-minute film based on the short story by Stephen King, which aired on PBS. In 1986, people finally started paying him to write, which he has been gratefully doing ever since. Some of his writing credits include feature films *Nightmare on Elm Street 3: Dream Warriors* (1987), *The Blob* (1988), and *The Fly II* (1989). For television, he has written eight episodes of *The Young Indiana Jones Chronicles* and two episodes of the HBO series *Tales from the Crypt*, one of which ("The Ventriloquist's Dummy") was nominated for a Writers Guild Award in 1990. In the same year, Frank directed *Buried Alive*, a highly rated cable-network movie for USA Network.

In 1994 he had his feature-film directorial debut with Castle Rock's 1994 drama *The Shawshank Redemption*, for which he also wrote the screenplay. An adaptation of a Stephen King novella, *The Shawshank Redemption* was nominated for a DGA Award for Outstanding Directorial Achievement in Theatrical Direction as well as seven Academy Awards, including Best Picture. Also, in 1994, Frank cowrote the screenplay for the feature film *Mary Shelley's Frankenstein*.

Darabont returned to the director's chair for the first time in five years following his triumphant big-screen directorial debut *The Shawshank Redemption*. Another Stephen King adaptation, *The Green Mile,* marks Frank's second DGA Award nomination. Starring Tom Hanks, the film was also nominated for four Oscars, including Best Picture.

Andrew Davis, *The Fugitive* (1994)

Andrew Davis is the son of parents who met in the repertory theater. Davis received a degree in journalism from the University of Illinois. He began his work in motion pictures as assistant cameraman to Haskell Wexler on the 1969 classic *Medium Cool.* Wexler's ultrarealistic approach was to have a great influence on Davis, who then became cinematographer on numerous award-winning television commercials and documentaries, as well as on fifteen studio and independent features. In 1976, joined by fellow cinematographers, Andy challenged IATSE's restrictive studio roster system in a landmark class-action suit that forced the industry to open its doors to young technicians in all crafts.

Davis's directorial debut, *Stony Island* (1979), was a critically acclaimed semiautobiographical independent musical that he cowrote and produced. It was followed by the thriller *The Final Terror* (1981), which starred newcomers Daryl Hannah, Joe Pantoliano, Rachel Ward, and Adrian Zmed. Davis then cowrote the screenplay for Harry Belafonte's rap musical *Beat Street* before moving into the director's chair full-time with *Code of Silence* (1985), starring Chuck Norris. Davis directed, co-produced, and cowrote *Above the Law* (1988), which was Steven Seagal's feature debut. Davis then directed *The Package* (1989), starring Gene Hackman and Tommy Lee Jones. In *Under Siege* Davis teamed Steven Seagal with Tommy Lee Jones and Gary Busey, resulting in fall 1992's top-grossing picture.

Davis has an established and enviable reputation for helming intelligent action thrillers, most notably the Academy Award–nominated *The Fugitive* (1992), the fourth highest-grossing picture in Warner Bros. history. Starring Harrison Ford and Tommy Lee Jones, the film garnered seven Academy Award nominations, including Best Picture, and earned Jones an Oscar for Best Supporting Actor. Additionally, *The Fugitive* was nominated for a 1993 Golden Globe and the Directors Guild of America Outstanding Directorial Achievement Award in Theatrical Direction.

Davis's feature *Steal Big, Steal Little* (1995) starred Andy Garcia as rival twin brothers. The 1996 feature *Chain Reaction*, starring Keanu Reeves and Morgan Freeman, brought Davis back to his hometown of Chicago. Since then Davis has directed *A Perfect Murder* (1998), a thriller starring Michael Douglas and Gwyneth Paltrow, *Collateral Damage* (2002), starring Arnold Schwarzenegger, and *Holes* (2003), starring Sigourney Weaver and Jon Voight.

Clint Eastwood, *Unforgiven* (1993), *Mystic River* (2004), and *Million Dollar Baby* (2005)

Clint Eastwood's career spans four decades of moviemaking. Born Clinton Eastwood Jr. on May 31, 1930, in San Francisco, California, he was raised in Oakland, California, after moving from town to town as his father sought work during the Great Depression. His debut in film was as a contract actor for Universal Pictures in 1955 and his first break was on the TV series *Rawhide* (1958), in which he played cowpuncher Rowdy Yates for six years. He has starred in forty-six films (appearing in fifty-seven), directed twenty-five, and produced twenty. Eastwood has simultaneously produced, directed, and starred in thirteen of his own films as well as writing music for ten of them.

Although he has taken on a variety of roles throughout his career, the origins of Eastwood's appeal remain the Western, within which he has created his own subgenre—that of the loner who sees too much and is driven by a hard-edged knowledge of himself. The "spaghetti Western" directed by Sergio Leone, *A Fistful of Dollars* (1967), changed his career forever, illuminating a star on the rise and beginning a sequence of unprecedented hits. *Hang 'Em High* in 1968 brought Universal Pictures its quickest payoff in history. That same year, Eastwood formed his Malpaso Company, allowing him the options of producing and directing as well as starring in his own projects. Malpaso has continued to provide filmmakers with the independent base from which all its projects evolve.

Eastwood's debut as a director was the chilling *Play Misty for Me* (1971), in which he starred with Jessica Walter and Donna Mills. *Dirty Harry* followed the same year and launched several sequels. It was directed by Don Siegel and marked Eastwood's initial association with Warner Bros. as a distributing company. Among his many acting assignments, also adding to Eastwood's diverse list of popular and critical successes, were his directorial projects, which include *High Plains Drifter* (1972), *Breezy* (1973), *The Eiger Sanction* (1974), *The Outlaw Josey Wales* (1976), and *The Gauntlet* (1977), as well as *Bronco Billy* (1980), *Firefox* and *Honkytonk Man* (both 1982), *Sudden Impact* (1983), *Pale River* and "Vanessa in the Garden"—an episode for television's *Amazing Stories* series—(both 1985), *Heartbreak Ridge* (1986), and *Bird* (1988). A tribute to jazz saxophonist Charlie Parker, *Bird* was released to international acclaim and earned Eastwood the Hollywood Foreign Press Association's Best Director Golden Globe award, as well as numerous national and international awards for stars Forest Whitaker and Diane Venora. Subsequent directorial efforts include *White Hunter, Black Heart* (1989), *The Rookie* (1990), *Unforgiven* (1993), *A Perfect World* (1993), *The Bridges of Madison County* (1995), *Absolute Power* (1997), *Midnight in the Garden of Good and Evil* (1997), *True Crime* (1999), *Space Cowboys* (2000), *Blood Work* (2002), *Mystic River* (2003), and *Million Dollar Baby* (2004).

Eastwood's diverse abilities have brought him international stature, box office success, and numerous awards. His revisionist Western *Unforgiven*, released in August 1992, generated $100 million at the box office and has been named on more than two hundred "Ten Best" lists by critics. *Unforgiven* received numerous awards and nominations, including an award for Outstanding Directorial Achievement for Theatrical Direction from the Directors Guild of America and four Oscars for Best Director, Best Picture, Best Supporting Actor, and Best Sound. This also marked the first time in his career that Eastwood received an Oscar nomination for Best Actor. *Unforgiven* was Clint Eastwood's sixteenth feature film as a director and his thirty-sixth in a starring role.

In 2003, Eastwood's critically acclaimed drama, *Mystic River*, debuted at the Cannes Film Festival, earning him a Golden Palm nomination and the Golden Coach Award. *Mystic River* went on to win six Academy Award nominations (Best Picture, Best Director, Best Actor, Best Supporting Actor, Best Supporting Actress, and Best Screenplay) and two Oscars (Best Actor, Sean Penn, and Best Supporting Actor, Tim Robbins).

For *Million Dollar Baby* Eastwood received his third DGA nomination for feature film and second win. The film was nominated for seven Academy Awards, including Eastwood's second Best Actor nomination. The film received four Oscars: Best Picture, Best Director, Best Actress (Hilary Swank), and Best Supporting Actor (Morgan Freeman).

In 1991 Eastwood received Man of the Year Award from Harvard's Hasty Pudding Theatrical Society, the California Governor's Award for the Arts in 1992, awards from both the American Cinema Editors and the Publicists Guild in 1992, a Douglas Sirk Award for Career Achievement, and a Cesar nomination for Best Foreign Film (Meilleur film etranger) for *The Bridges of Madison Country* in 1996.

In 1995, Eastwood was given one of the most highly regarded awards in the motion picture industry, the Irving G. Thalberg Memorial Award from the Academy of Motion Pictures Arts and Sciences. He was also the recipient of the Life Achievement Award from the American Film Institute and the Film Society at Lincoln Center in 1996. In addition, Eastwood received a Cesar Honorary Award (Honneur) from the French Film Society for Career Achievement in 1998 and a Golden Laurel Lifetime Achievement Award from the Producers Guild of America that same year. He was nominated for Favorite All-Time Movie Star in 1999 from the People's Choice Awards (which he won for the Favorite Motion Picture Actor in 1981, 1984, 1985, 1987, and 1998). In January of 2000, Eastwood was presented with a Lifetime Career Achievement Award from New York's National Board of Review. That May he received an honorary doctorate in fine arts from Wesleyan University and in December accepted a Kennedy Center Honors Award. In March of 2003, he accepted a Screen Actors Guild Life Achievement Award, and in August of the same year the Henry Mancini Institute presented Eastwood with the Hank Award, which recognizes distinguished service to American music.

Mr. Eastwood's association with jazz is well documented, as is his assertion that had his acting, directing, or producing careers not been successful, he would have chosen to be a musician. As a young man growing up in Oakland, California, Eastwood performed in small clubs as a pianist. Eastwood's documentary *Piano Blues* concluded Martin Scorsese's 2003 series *The Blues* for PBS.

An avid golfer, Eastwood lives in Carmel, California, where he served as mayor from 1986 through 1988, and where he owns the Mission Ranch Inn and Tehama Golf Club. He is also a partner in the famed Pebble Beach Golf Course and was named commissioner to the California State Board of Parks and Recreation in June 2002. Eastwood serves as a commissioner on the California Film Commission, appointed by Governor Arnold Schwarzenegger, and has been named, for the second time, to serve as the national spokesperson for Take Pride in America.

Clint Eastwood is, perhaps, the most conscientious filmmaker who ever got behind a camera. He has no patience for waste, be it time or money. He makes movies, loves the process, and start to finish, each day and each dollar belongs to him. When not in production, he lives quietly with his wife, Dina Ruiz Eastwood (married March 31, 1996), and their daughter, Morgan (born December 12, 1996), in Carmel.

Marc Forster, *Finding Neverland* (2005)

Born in Germany and raised in Switzerland, Marc Forster came to the United States in 1990 to attend NYU Film School, graduating in 1993. After completing two documentaries for European television, Forster moved to Los Angeles, where he soon made a name for himself based on the offbeat appeal and popularity of his first film *Loungers*. An absurdist musical about four wannabe lounge singers, *Loungers* won the Audience Award at the 1996 Slamdance International Film Festival.

The seeds of Forster's moody, reflective aesthetic were sown in his second film, *Everything Put Together*, which he also cowrote. A creeping, subversive piece of psychological horror about a woman (*High Art's* Radha Mitchell) who finds herself alienated and haunted after her newborn baby dies of sudden infant death syndrome, *Everything Put Together* premiered at the 2000 Sundance Film Festival before earning Forster the Movado Someone to Watch/Independent Spirit Award.

It was Marc Forster's unique creative vision that led him to be tapped to direct Lions Gate's award-winning *Monster's Ball*, which over the years had become infamous as one of the best scripts floating through Hollywood. Though only his third feature, *Monster's Ball* received two Oscar nominations, with Halle Berry winning for Best Actress. Teeming with raw emotion and quiet intensity, *Monster's Ball* offered a powerful glimpse into the encumbering legacies of family and race, loss and redemption, as well as commanding performances by Berry, Billy Bob Thornton, Heath Ledger, Peter Boyle, and Sean Combs. In the delicate balance of narrative economy and visual lyricism, Forster rendered a film of unflinching honesty, full of characters struggling to transcend the compromises of their condition.

With the critical and commercial success of *Monster's Ball* in 2001, Forster solidified himself as a director at ease with the metaphorical and lyrical language of cinema. In *Finding Neverland*, Forster re-creates turn-of-the-century London, crafting a magical story about the friendship between J. M. Barrie, author of *Peter Pan*, and the four young boys and single mother who live next door to him. Starring Johnny Depp, Kate Winslet, Dustin Hoffman, and Julie Christie, *Neverland* gained high regards from critics, was named Best Picture by the National Board of Review, and earned nominations for Best Picture and Best Director at the Golden Globes. The film was also nominated for seven Academy Awards, including Best Picture.

Forster currently resides in Los Angeles.

Mel Gibson, *Braveheart* (1996)

Mel Gibson was born in upstate New York and moved with his family to Australia when he was twelve years old. Gibson attended the National Institute of Dramatic Arts at the University of South Wales in Sydney. His stage appearances include *Death of a Salesman.* Gibson was eventually brought to the attention of director George Miller, who cast him in *Mad Max,* the film that first brought him worldwide recognition. This was followed by the title role in *Tim.* Gibson's portrayal of a handicapped young man won him an Australian Film Institute Best Actor Award. He was further established as an international star by the two hit sequels to *Mad Max*—*The Road Warrior* and *Mad Max beyond Thunderdome*—along with Peter Weir's *Gallipoli,* which brought Gibson a second Australian Best Actor Award. A few years later, Weir and Gibson again collaborated on *The Year of Living Dangerously.* Gibson made his American film debut in *The River.* He starred in another popular series of films with the high-grossing *Lethal Weapon* series. Gibson's other films include *The Bounty, Mrs. Soffel, Tequila Sunrise, Bird on a Wire, Air America,* and *Hamlet.*

When Gibson starred in *Hamlet,* directed by Franco Zeffirelli, the film was the first to be produced by Gibson's production company, Icon Pictures. The role brought him the William Shakespeare Award from the Folger Theatre in Washington, D.C. Icon also produced *Forever Young* and *Maverick,* with Mel starring in both films. Gibson made his directorial debut and starred in *The Man without a Face,* another Icon production.

In 1995 Gibson produced, directed, and starred in the critical and box office success *Braveheart,* which received ten Academy Award nominations. The film won Best Picture and Best Director, and Gibson also won a Golden Globe Award for Best Director. He received a Special Achievement in Filmmaking Award given by the National Board of Review and was honored as the 1996 NATO/ShoWest Director of the Year, as well as being the recipient of the Best Director Award given by the Broadcast Film Critics Association. In 1996, Gibson starred in *Ransom,* directed by Ron Howard, for Disney's Touchstone pictures. This film is a remake of the 1956 MGM film telling the story of a New York millionaire who must employ daring tactics to retrieve his kidnapped son. He received a Golden Globe nomination for Best Actor in a Motion Picture (Drama), as well as winning the People's Choice Award for Favorite Motion Picture Actor and the Blockbuster Entertainment Award for Favorite Male (Suspense).

In 1997, Gibson starred in the romantic thriller *Conspiracy Theory,* costarring Julia Roberts and directed by Richard Donner, for Warner Bros. In 1998, Gibson starred in *Lethal Weapon* 4, which grossed close to $300 million worldwide. In 1999, he starred in *Payback,* an Icon production marking the directorial debut of Brian Helgeland, who wrote the screenplay for this hard-edged thriller based on Donald F. Westlake's (writing as Richard Stark) novel *The Hunter.* More recently, Gibson directed and produced *The Passion of the Christ.*

Taylor Hackford, *Ray* (2005)

Taylor Hackford began his entertainment career at KCET, the Los Angeles public-television affiliate, where he pioneered the presentation of uninterrupted rock and roll performances on American television. In addition to creating several award-winning documentaries for the station's cultural department, he also served as an investigative reporter in their news division, where he received an Associated Press Award and two Emmy awards for his journalism.

In 1979, Taylor won an Academy Award in the category of Best Live-Action Short Film for his first dramatic effort, *Teenage Father*. He proceeded to make his feature directorial debut in 1980 with *The Idolmaker*, starring Ray Sharkey and Peter Gallagher. *An Officer and a Gentleman*, starring Richard Gere and Debra Winger, Taylor's second film, was a commercial and critical hit in 1982. It received five Academy Award nominations and brought home Oscars for Louis Gossett Jr. as Best Supporting Actor and Best Original Song ("Up Where We Belong"). In addition, Taylor was nominated by the Directors Guild of America for his outstanding achievement.

On all his subsequent films, Taylor has functioned as both director and producer. His credits include *Against All Odds,* starring Jeff Bridges, Rachel Ward, and James Woods; *White Nights,* starring Mikhail Baryshnikov, Gregory Hines, Helen Mirren, and Isabella Rossellini; *Everybody's All-American,* starring Dennis Quaid, Jessica Lange, and John Goodman; and the acclaimed documentary *Chuck Berry: Hail! Hail! Rock n' Roll,* featuring Chuck Berry and Keith Richards.

Taylor, who has been fascinated by all things Latino since his stint as a Peace Corp volunteer in South America (1968–1969), developed and produced *La Bamba*, the Ritchie Valens biography which launched Lou Diamond Phillips's career. Written and directed by Luis Valdez, *La Bamba* became a sleeper success, breaking new ground for Hispanic artists in Hollywood. It is still the most successful Latin-themed feature film in history.

Taylor formed New Visions Pictures to produce modestly budgeted movies with other directors. Some of his producing credits include the much lauded *The Long Walk Home*, directed by Richard Pearce and starring Sissy Spacek and Whoopi Goldberg; *Mortal Thoughts*, directed by Alan Rudolph and starring Demi Moore, Glenn Headley, and Bruce Willis; *Defenseless*, directed by Martin Campbell and starring Barbara Hershey, Mary Beth Hurt, and Sam Shepard; and *Queens Logic*, directed by Steve Rash and featuring an ensemble cast which included John Malkovich, Kevin Bacon, Joe Mantegna, Jamie Lee Curtis, and Linda Fiorentino.

He returned to directing after five years to helm the epic drama of East L.A., *Blood In, Blood Out (Bound by Honor)*. This film earned Taylor a trophy as Best Director at the 1993 Tokyo Film Festival. His next film, *Dolores Claiborne*, released by Castle Rock Entertainment and Columbia Pictures, starred Kathy Bates and Jennifer Jason Leigh. *Dolores* was selected for screening at the 1995 Venice, Deauville, and Tokyo Film Festivals.

In 1996 Taylor discovered some unreleased documentary footage of the legendary Muhammad Ali/George Foreman title fight in Zaire, Africa. Taylor restructured this footage shot originally in 1974 by Leon Gast, conducted present-day interviews with Norman Mailer, George Plimpton, and Spike Lee, and added footage of the original fight to create a feature-length documentary that revealed the hype, politics, and personalities that made up this larger-than-life event. The completed film, *When We Were Kings*, was a hit at the 1996 Sundance Film Festival and won the 1997 Academy Award for Best Documentary Feature.

In 1998 Hackford directed the critically acclaimed worldwide hit *The Devil's Advocate*, a contemporary morality tale set in the world of New York's powerful legal profession, starring Al Pacino and Keanu Reeves. This film also introduced newcomers Charlize Theron and Connie Nielsen. Then in 2001 he delivered the riveting *Proof of Life*, with Meg Ryan, Russell Crowe, and David Morse, based on William Prochnau's *Vanity Fair* article "Adventures in the Ransom Trade," about the real-life kidnapping of American businessman Thomas Hargrove.

Taylor's *Ray,* a dramatic film portrait of American musical icon Ray Charles, stars Jamie Foxx. Hackford struggled for nearly fifteen years to make this film but finally found someone who believed in the power of Ray's incredible life as much as he did: financier Phil Anschutz. Anschutz and Howard Baldwin's Crusader Entertainment financed the film in 2003, and Universal Pictures released it nationally on October 29, 2004. Hackford was nominated for a DGA Award and an Academy Award for Best Achievement in directing for *Ray.*

Curtis Hanson, *L.A. Confidential* (1998)

Curtis Hanson is a writer, director, and producer. He edited and did the photography for *Cinema* magazine before turning to screenwriting and directing. In 1978 Hanson wrote the multiple-award-winning Canadian feature *The Silent Partner.* In 1982, he cowrote with director Samuel Fuller the screenplay for *White Dog,* and one year later cowrote the screenplay for Carroll Ballard's *Never Cry Wolf.* His directing credits include the 1987 thriller *The Bedroom Window* (which he also wrote), starring Steve Guttenberg, Elizabeth McGovern, and Isabelle Huppert; *Bad Influence* (1990), starring Rob Lowe and James Spader; *The Hand That Rocks the Cradle* (1992), starring Rebecca De Mornay and Annabella Sciorra; and *The River Wild* (1994), starring Meryl Streep, Kevin Bacon, and David Strathairn. Hanson also directed, produced, and cowrote (with Brian Helgeland) the screenplay for *L.A. Confidential.* In addition to winning 1997 Academy Awards for Best Adapted Screenplay and Best Supporting Actress (Kim Basinger), the film won the Best Adapted Screenplay award from the Writers Guild of America and was the first picture ever to win Best Picture and Best Director from every major critics' organization. Hanson then made *Wonder Boys,* which stars Michael Douglas, Tobey Maguire, Frances McDormand, Katie Holmes, and Robert Downey Jr.

Since this DGA Award nomination, Hanson has gone on to direct *8 Mile,* starring Eminem and Kim Basinger, *In Her Shoes,* and *Lucky You.*

Scott Hicks, *Shine* (1997)

Scott Hicks was born and raised in East Africa and is an Emmy Award–winning director whose work encompasses films, television drama, and documentaries, as well as commercials and music videos. Hicks's film *Sebastian and the Sparrow,* which he also wrote and produced, is a story of a rich boy and a street kid who team up to find the latter's mother. The film was a winner in three international film festival competitions, including Frankfurt, where it was awarded the Lucas Prize as Best Film (1990). Following a successful cinema season and television release in Australia, the film was invited to participate in numerous other international festivals. Hicks also directed and cowrote the acclaimed documentary series *The Great Wall of Iron,* an in-depth portrait of the People's Liberation of China, and the four-hour series *Submarines: Sharks of Steel.* Both were recognized as award winners in various groups and became two of the highest-rated programs to air on America's The Discovery Channel. Hick's directed a telefilm, *Call Me Mr. Brown,* in 1985 and the Australian miniseries *Finders Keepers* in 1991. Hicks wrote and directed *The Space Shuttle* in 1994 and *The Ultimate Athlete*, a documentary project, in 1996.

He is best known for his internationally acclaimed film *Shine*, which received seven Oscar nominations in 1997, including two for Hicks personally, in the Best Director and Best Original Screenplay categories, as well as a nomination from the Directors Guild of America for Outstanding Directorial Achievement in Theatrical Direction in 1997. He also received a Golden Globe nomination and nominations from the Writers Guild of America and BAFTA.

Since this DGA Award nomination, Hicks has directed *Snow Falling on Cedars*, produced by Kathleen Kennedy and Frank Marshall and released by Universal Pictures, and *Hearts in Atlantis*, based on the Stephen King book, starring Anthony Hopkins and Hope Davis.

Scott lives with his wife, Kerry Heysen (who served as creative consultant on *Shine* and associate producer *on Snow Falling on Cedars*), and their two sons in Adelaide, South Australia.

Ron Howard, *A Beautiful Mind* (2002)

The Academy Award-winning filmmaker Ron Howard is one of his generation's most popular directors. From the critically acclaimed dramas *A Beautiful Mind* and *Apollo 13* to the hit comedies *Parenthood* and *Splash*, he has created some of Hollywood's most memorable films. He earned an Oscar for Best Director for *A Beautiful Mind*, which also won awards for Best Picture, Best Screenplay, and Best Supporting Actress. The film garnered four Golden Globes as well, including the award for Best Motion Picture Drama, and Howard won Best Director of the Year from the Directors Guild of America. Howard and producer Brian Grazer received the first annual Awareness Award from the National Mental Health Awareness Campaign for their work on the film.

Howard's skill as a director has long been recognized. In 1995, he received his first Best Director of the Year award from the DGA for *Apollo 13*. The true-life drama also garnered nine Academy Award nominations, winning Oscars for Best Film Editing and Best Sound. It also received Best Cast and Best Supporting Actor awards from the Screen Actors Guild. Many of Howard's past films have also received Academy Award nods, including the popular hits *Backdraft*, *Parenthood*, and *Cocoon*, the last of which took home two Oscars. Howard has served as an executive producer as well on a number of award-winning films and television shows, such as the HBO miniseries *From the Earth to the Moon*.

Howard's portfolio includes some of the most popular films of the past twenty years. In 1991, Howard created the acclaimed drama *Backdraft*, starring Robert De Niro, Kurt Russell, and William Baldwin. He followed it with the historical epic *Far and Away*, starring Tom Cruise and Nicole Kidman. Howard directed Mel Gibson, Rene Russo, Gary Sinise, and Delroy Lindo in the 1996 suspense thriller *Ransom*. Howard worked with Tom Hanks, Kevin Bacon, Ed Harris, Bill Paxton, Gary Sinise, and Kathleen Quinlan on *Apollo 13*, which was rereleased recently in the IMAX format. Howard's other films include the blockbuster *Dr. Seuss' How the Grinch Stole Christmas*, starring Jim Carrey; *Parenthood*, starring Steve Martin; the fantasy epic *Willow*; and *Night Shift*, starring Henry Winkler, Michael Keaton, and Shelley Long. Most recently, Howard directed Oscar winners Cate Blanchett and Tommy Lee Jones in the suspenseful Western *The Missing* and *Cinderella Man* with Russell Crowe and Renée Zellweger.

Howard and longtime producing partner Brian Grazer first collaborated on the hit comedies *Night Shift* and *Splash*. The pair cofounded Imagine Entertainment in 1986 to create independently produced feature films. The company has since produced a variety of popular hits including *The Nutty Professor*, *Nutty Professor II: The Klumps*, *Bowfinger*, *The Paper*, *Inventing the Abbotts*, and *Liar, Liar*.

Howard made his directorial debut in 1978 with the comedy *Grand Theft Auto*. He began his career in film, though, as an actor. He first appeared in *The Journey* and *The Music Man*, then as Opie on the long-running television series *The Andy Griffith Show*. During the 1970s, Howard starred in the popular series *Happy Days* and drew favorable reviews for his performances in *American Graffiti* and *The Shootist*.

Peter Jackson, *The Lord of the Rings: The Fellowship of the Ring* (2002), *The Lord of the Rings: The Two Towers* (2003), and *The Lord of the Rings: The Return of the King* (2004)

Born in New Zealand on Halloween in 1961, Peter Jackson began at an early age making movies with his parents' Super 8 camera. At seventeen he left school and, failing to get a job in the New Zealand film industry as he had hoped, started work as a photoengraving apprentice. After purchasing a 16mm camera, Jackson began shooting a science fiction comedy short, which, three years later, had grown to a seventy-five-minute feature called *Bad Taste*, funded entirely from his own wages. The New Zealand Film Commission eventually gave Jackson money to complete the film, which has become a cult classic.

Jackson received widespread acclaim for his 1994 feature *Heavenly Creatures*, which was awarded a Silver Lion at the Venice Film Festival and an Oscar nomination for Best Screenplay. Written by Jackson and his collaborator, Fran Walsh, the film is based on an infamous New Zealand murder of the 1950s, and the story of two intelligent and imaginative young girls whose obsessive friendship leads them to murder one of their mothers.

Other film credits include *The Frighteners* starring Michael J. Fox, the adult puppet feature *Meet the Feebles*, and *Braindead*, which Jackson cowrote. *Braindead* played at festivals around the world winning sixteen international science fiction awards including the prestigious Saturn. Jackson also codirected the television documentary *Forgotten Silver* which also hit the film-festival circuit.

A longtime J. R. R. Tolkien fan, Peter made history with *The Lord of The Rings* trilogy, becoming the first to direct three major feature films simultaneously. *The Lord of the Rings: The Fellowship of the Ring* was nominated for thirteen Academy Awards (including Best Director) and won four. The film also received the American Film Institute's prestigious Film Award and was nominated for twelve awards from the British Academy of Film and Television Arts (BAFTA), winning awards for Best Film and garnering Jackson the David Lean Award for direction. In addition to four Golden Globe nominations, the film also received numerous distinctions and awards around the world.

The Lord of the Rings: The Two Towers was nominated for six Academy Awards and won two. The third and final installment, *The Lord of the Rings: The Return of the King*, released in 2003, earned four Golden Globe Awards, including one for Peter as Best Director. It won all eleven Academy Awards for which it was nominated, including Peter's second nomination for Best Director. That year he would win or share Oscars in three categories: Best Director, Best Picture, and Best Screenplay Based on Material Previously Produced or Published. The film also garnered Jackson his Directors Guild of America Award.

Jackson's followed these films with a remake of the 1933 classic *King Kong*.

Spike Jonze, *Being John Malkovich* (2000)

Being John Malkovich is Spike Jonze's feature-length directorial debut and his first DGA Award nomination. For three consecutive years, his work has been featured at the Sundance Film Festival. First came his 1996 on-screen appearance in Francine McDougall's *Pig*, followed by his own film *How They Get There* in 1997, and in 1998 by his documentary short *Amarillo by Morning*. Spike's pairing of interesting visuals and contemporary music in his early work formed the genesis of what would become a successful career in music videos and commercials. His music-video work with such artists as Puff Daddy and R.E.M. has resulted in annual MTV Video Music Award nominations, and Spike's commercial work has garnered him the coveted Palme d'Or at the Cannes International Advertising Film Festival. Since his DGA Award nomination, he has directed *Adaptation*, which won the Silver Bear Jury Grand Prix at the 2002 Berlin International Film Festival.

Neil Jordan, *The Crying Game* (1993)

Born in Sligo, in northwest Ireland, Jordan began his career as a novelist. In 1974 he founded the Irish Writers Cooperative, and in 1979, his collection of stories, *Night in Tunisia*, won the *Guardian* newspaper's fiction prize. He has also published two novels, *The Past* and *The Dream of the Beast*. Jordan began his film career as a creative consultant on *Excalibur*, directed by John Boorman, in 1981. *Angel* (aka *Danny Boy*), Jordan's debut film, which he wrote and directed, won the *London Evening Standard*'s Most Promising Newcomer Award in 1982. His next film, *The Company of Wolves* (1984), adapted from a story by Angela Carter, starred Angela Lansbury, and was honored with Best Film and Best Director Awards by the London Critics' Circle, and a Golden Scroll for Outstanding Achievement from the Academy of Science Fiction and Horror Films. Jordan's third film, *Mona Lisa* (1986), starred Bob Hoskins, Michael Caine, and Cathy Tyson and was selected for competition at the Cannes Film Festival. The Cannes jury subsequently awarded Hoskins Best Actor. He also received a Best Actor Award from the National Society of Film Critics and an Academy Award nomination. *Mona Lisa* won a Golden Globe Award, a Los Angeles Film Critics Award, and a Best Screenplay nomination from the Writers Guild of America. It was also nominated in the categories Best Film, Best Achievement in Direction, and Best Original Screenplay at the 1986 BAFTA Awards. In 1988, Jordan directed the comedy *High Spirits,* starring Peter O'Toole, Daryl Hannah, and Steve Guttenberg, followed by the next year's *We're No Angels*, which starred Robert De Niro and Sean Penn and was Jordan's first entirely American production. *The Miracle* (1990), the second film that Jordan shot in his native Ireland and the first made in his hometown of Bray, starred Beverly D'Angelo and Donal McCann and won the *London Evening Standard*'s Best Screenplay Award in 1991. *The Crying Game*, written and directed by Jordan, was his seventh film and his fifth collaboration with Stephen Woolley and Palace Pictures. Part love story, part confrontation of one's own destiny, according to the director, the film deals with real life-or-death issues, with people at the most extreme edges of a political situation. *The Crying Game* (1992) earned six Oscar nominations and included a win for Best Screenplay by Jordan, as well as a nomination for Outstanding Directorial Achievement in Theatrical Direction from the Directors Guild of America in 1993. In 1993 Jordan landed the plum, if daunting, assignment of adapting Anne Rice's tricky best seller *Interview with the Vampire* to the screen. In 1996, Jordan returned to Ireland to shoot his next film, *Michael*

Collins, a cherished project for which he had spent more than a decade developing the script. This biopic of the still-controversial Irish hero told a story that had taken nearly four decades to get to the screen. In 1999 Jordan directed the psychological thriller *In Dreams*, starring Annette Bening. Recent projects include *The End of the Affair* (1999), which won a BAFTA Best Adapted Screenplay Award, *The Good Thief* (2002), and *Breakfast on Pluto*, with Liam Neeson, Cillian Murphy, Stephen Rea, and Brendan Gleeson.

Ang Lee, *Crouching Tiger, Hidden Dragon* (2001)

Ang Lee was born in Taiwan in 1954 and moved to the United States in 1978, where he received his BFA in theater from the University of Illinois and his MFA in film production from New York University. *Pushing Hands*, Ang's first feature, screened in the Panorama section of the 1992 Berlin Film Festival and won Best Film in the Asian-Pacific Film Festival. It was also nominated for nine Golden Horse Awards (the Taiwanese Academy Award) and won three, including a Special Jury Prize for Ang's direction. In 1994, *The Wedding Banquet* premiered at the Berlin Film Festival and was awarded top prize for direction. The film was nominated for the Academy and Golden Globe Awards for Best Foreign Language Film and six Independent Spirit Awards. In Taiwan, *The Wedding Banquet* received five Golden Horse Awards, including awards for Best Film and Best Director. *Eat Drink Man Woman*, the third film in Ang's *Father Knows Best* trilogy, premiered as the Director's Fortnight at the Cannes Film Festival in 1994. It was nominated for Academy and Golden Globe Awards and was voted Best Foreign Language Film by the National Board of Review. In 1995, Ang directed *Sense and Sensibility* starring Emma Thompson, Hugh Grant, and Kate Winslet. The film was nominated for seven Academy Awards, including Best Picture, and won the Oscar for Best Screenplay Adaptation. In addition, the film received the Golden Bear Award at the Berlin Film Festival, as well as Golden Globes for Best Screenplay and Best Film. One of the most critically acclaimed films of the year, *Sense and Sensibility* was featured in over 100 ten-best-films lists. In 1996, Ang completed his first feature on an entirely American subject, *The Ice Storm*, which was adapted from the acclaimed novel by Rick Moody and stars Kevin Kline, Sigourney Weaver, and Joan Allen. The film was selected for competition at the Fiftieth International Film Festival in Cannes and won the award for Best Screenplay Adaptation. In 1999, Ang directed *Ride with the Devil*, a Civil War-era Western adapted from Daniel Woodrell's novel *Woe to Live On*, starring Skeet Ulrich, Tobey Maguire, and Jewel. *Crouching Tiger, Hidden Dragon* marks Ang's second Directors Guild nomination in the Feature Film category. He was previously nominated in 1995 for *Sense and Sensibility*.

Mike Leigh, *Secrets & Lies* (1997)

Mike Leigh, writer and film director, was born in 1943 in Salford, Lancashire. He trained at the Royal Academy of Dramatic Art, at Camberwell and Central Art Schools, and at the London Film School.

His style, in which the commonplace is often tinged with the extraordinary, has been dubbed "social surrealism," or as Leigh prefers to call it, "heightened realism." A creative force in London's experimental fringe theater since the 1960s, Leigh has written and directed more than twenty stage plays.

His first feature film was *Bleak Moments* (1971), which won the Grande Prix at Chicago and Locarno Film Festivals. This was followed by the full-length television films *Hard Labor* (1973), *Nuts in May* (1975), *The Kiss of Death* (1976), *Who's Who* (1978), *Grown-ups* (1980) *Home Sweet Home* (1982), *Meantime* (1983), *and Four Days in July* (1984), which was shot entirely on location in Belfast.

His later feature films, *High Hopes* (1988), *Life Is Sweet* (1990), and *Naked* (1992), were highly successful internationally, all winning numerous prestigious awards, including Best Director for *Naked* at the 1993 Cannes Film Festival.

In 1995 he made the film *Secrets & Lies*, which in May 1996 won the Palme d'Or. The film went on to receive international acclaim, winning, among many other awards, the L.A. Critics Awards for Best Film and Director, BAFTA Awards for Best Original Screenplay, and the Alexander Korda Award for Best British Film. The film also received five Oscar nominations, as well as a nomination from the Directors Guild of America for Outstanding Directorial Achievement for Theatrical Direction. Since this DGA Award nomination, Leigh has directed *Career Girls, Topsy-Turvy, All or Nothing*, and *Vera Drake*, which won the BAFTA David Lean Award for Direction and was nominated for Best Directing and Best Writing Academy Awards.

Mike Leigh formed Thin Man Films with producer Simon Channing-Williams in 1988.

Barry Levinson, *Bugsy* (1992)

Academy Award–winning director-screenwriter-producer Barry Levinson has crafted an enviable reputation in the film industry as a director who blends literate and intelligent visions into films.

In 1987, he directed Robin Williams in the comedy *Good Morning, Vietnam*, which went on to become one of the year's most acclaimed and popular movies. Levinson was awarded the 1988 Best Director Oscar for the multiple-award-winning *Rain Man*, starring Dustin Hoffman and Tom Cruise. In 1991 *Bugsy*, which was directed and produced by Barry Levinson, was nominated for ten Academy Awards, including Best Picture and Best Director.

Born and raised in Baltimore, Levinson has used his hometown as the setting for three widely praised features: *Diner*, the semiautobiographical comedy-drama that marked his directorial debut; *Tin Men*, starring Danny DeVito and Richard Dreyfuss as warring aluminum siding salesmen; and *Avalon*, in which his native city takes center stage through the recollections of an immigrant family.

After attending American University in Washington, D.C., Levinson moved to Los Angeles, where he began acting as well as writing and performing comedy routines. He then went on to write for several television variety shows, including *The Marty Feldman Comedy Machine*, which originated in England, *The Lohman and Barkley Show, The Tim Conway Show*, and *The Carol Burnett Show*. A meeting with Mel Brooks led Levinson to collaborate with the veteran comedian on the features *Silent Movie* and *High Anxiety*, the latter additionally notable for his film-acting debut.

As a screenwriter, Levinson has received three Academy Award nominations for *And Justice for All, Diner*, and *Avalon*. Levinson's other directorial credits include *The Natural, Young Sherlock Holmes, Toys, Jimmy Hollywood, Disclosure,* and *Sleepers*.

Barry returned to Baltimore to film the *Homicide: Life on the Street* television series. His work on this critically acclaimed drama earned him an Emmy for Best Individual Director of a Drama Series. The series has also received three Peabody Awards, two Writers Guild Awards, and an Excellence in Quality Television Founders Award for the 1994 and 1995 seasons. In 1996 the series won the Nancy Susan Reynolds Award for outstanding portrayal of sexual responsibility in a dramatic series as well as a PRISM Commendation. In 1998 the series garnered a TCA Award for the program of the year and drama of the year.

Barry's feature *Sleepers* (1996), a film based on the best-selling book by Lorenzo Carcaterra, starring Robert De Niro, Brad Pitt, Jason Patric, Kevin Bacon, and Dustin Hoffman, garnered critical acclaim and box office success. The close of 1997 saw Barry at his most prolific, releasing two films nearly back-to-back, *Wag the Dog* and *Sphere*. *Wag the Dog*, a political satire written by Hilary Henkin and David Mamet (from the Larry Beinhart novel *American Hero*), was nominated for two Academy Awards. *Sphere* (1998), a science fiction film adapted from the Michael Crichton novel, stars Sharon Stone and Samuel L. Jackson and marks the fourth collaboration with Dustin Hoffman (*Rain Man, Sleepers, Wag the Dog*).

Until 1998 Levinson produced films through his production company Baltimore Pictures, Inc. Critically acclaimed releases include *Quiz Show, Donnie Brasco*, and *The Second Civil War* (HBO). At the beginning of 1998 Barry Levinson partnered with Paula Weinstein, forming Baltimore/Spring Creek Pictures. Together they produced *Analyze This* (1999), a comedy starring Robert De Niro and Billy Crystal, which opened to instant box office success, and the sequel *Analyze That* (2002). Barry became one of *Variety*'s Billion Dollar Directors as well as ShoWest's Director of the Year in 1998.

Barry was honored in February 1999 with a Creative Achievement Award by the Thirteenth Annual American Comedy Awards. In May 1999, American University of Washington, D.C., conferred upon Barry the degree of Doctor of Fine Arts, honoris causa, for his distinguished work in the field of communications and his defining impact on the motion picture and television industry. Barry was honored for his commitment to the craft of filmmaking, his dedication to telling insightful stories, his exquisite sensitivity to the details of life as we live it, and his gifts and accomplishments as a director. Barry and Baltimore Pictures received the 1999 Humanitas award for *Homicide: Life on the Street*'s "Shades of Grey" episode.

Barry's fourth Baltimore feature, *Liberty Heights*, was released in November 1999 to wide critical acclaim, praised as possibly the best of his Baltimore series. This humorous, touching drama captures the spirit of change in Baltimore circa 1954, addressing issues of race, class, and religion. His most recent directing credits include *An Everlasting Piece, Bandits,* and *Envy*.

Baz Luhrmann, *Moulin Rouge* (2002)

Writer/producer/director Baz Luhrmann is the cofounder and director of Bazmark Inq. (and its subsidiaries Bazmark Live and Bazmark Music), which produces films, opera, theater, music, multimedia, and events worldwide.

Luhrmann studied at National Institute of Dramatic Arts in Sydney, Australia, where he conceived, staged, and directed the thirty-minute play, *Strictly Ballroom*. This production won Best Production and Best Director at the World Youth Theatre Festival in Czechoslovakia and was later brought to the screen by Luhrmann, winning three BAFTAs, eight Australian Film Institute Awards, and a Golden Globe nomination for Best Picture Musical or Comedy.

Luhrmann has mounted numerous operas, most notably two award-winning productions for the Australian Opera: Puccini's *La Bohème* and his Hindi interpretation of Britten's *A Midsummer Night's Dream*. In 2002 Luhrmann reworked his original production of *La Bohème* for a six-month run on Broadway. It was nominated for six Tony Awards (including Best Revival and Best Director), winning for the ensemble cast, set design, and lighting, and later had a successful tour to the Ahmanson Theatre in Los Angeles.

Luhrmann developed, cowrote, produced, and directed *William Shakespeare's Romeo + Juliet*, which opened at number one in the United States, grossed over $140 million worldwide, and earned four BAFTAs (including Best Direction and Best Adapted Screenplay for Luhrmann), and four Berlin Film Festival Awards (including Alfred Bauer Award for Most Innovative Direction). The two sound-track albums surpassed triple platinum sales in the United States.

In 1997 Luhrmann married production and costume designer Catherine Martin and together they set up their production company Bazmark Inq. Later that year Bazmark produced the concept album, *Something for Everybody*, which went platinum in Australia and gold in the United States, and featured the number one hit "Everybody's Free (To Wear Sunscreen)."

Luhrmann developed, cowrote, produced, and directed *Moulin Rouge*, garnering him BAFTA nominations for Best Director and Best Screenplay, and a Golden Globe nomination for Best Director. The film's sales surpassed $170 million and it won a Golden Globe for Best Musical or Comedy, National Board of Review and Producers Guild of America Film of the Year Awards, Academy Awards for Art Direction and Costumes, and six other nominations including Best Picture. The two soundtrack albums went multiplatinum, selling over 6 million copies worldwide.

In 2004 Luhrmann conceived, produced, and directed a worldwide television and cinema campaign for the House of Chanel's *Chanel No. 5* perfume featuring Nicole Kidman. After having completed his Red Curtain Trilogy works, Luhrmann has worked on a trio of epics: one ancient, one Australian, and one European.

John Madden, *Shakespeare in Love* (1999)

John Madden was born in Portsmouth and educated at Clifton College and Cambridge. He began his career as Artistic Director of the Oxford and Cambridge Shakespeare Company, moving later to the BBC to work in television and radio drama.

He moved to America in 1975 to develop radio drama with Earplay, the National Public Radio drama project. Winning the Prix Italia with Arthur Kopit's *Wings,* he subsequently directed the play for the stage at Yale.

Further stage work included the premieres of Jules Feiffer's *Grown-ups*, Christopher Durang's *Beyond Therapy*, and Arnold Wesker's *Caritas*. During the time he taught in the acting and playwriting programs at the Yale School of Drama.

In 1984 he began to work extensively in film, directing for the BBC and for commercial television. His films included *Poppyland*, *After the War*, a series of films by Frederic Raphael, *The Widow-maker*, and several films in the Inspector Morse series.

He returned to America in 1990 to make his first feature film, *Ethan Frome*, adapted by Richard Nelson from Edith Wharton's novella, starring Liam Neeson and Patricia Arquette, followed by *Golden Gate*, a story of cultural collision in Chinatown, San Francisco, in the 1950s and 1960s. The film was written by David Hwang and stars Matt Dillon and Joan Chen. *Prime Suspect—The Lost Child* received a BAFTA nomination for Best Series, and his BBC film *Truth or Dare*, starring John Hannah and Helen Baxendale, won the Scottish BAFTA for Best Single Drama.

His film *Mrs. Brown* (screenplay by Jeremy Brock), starring Dame Judi Dench and Billy Connolly, received two Oscar and eight BAFTA nominations, including Best Film.

His film, *Shakespeare in Love*, with screenplay by Tom Stoppard and Marc Norman, stars Joseph Fiennes and Gwyneth Paltrow. It received three Golden Globe Awards, including Best Picture, and received seven Academy Awards, including Best Picture.

Since this nomination, John Madden has directed *Captain Corelli's Mandolin* and *Proof,* starring Gwyneth Paltrow and Anthony Hopkins.

John Madden is married and lives in London with his wife and two children.

Michael Mann, *The Insider* (2000)

Michael Mann has earned numerous honors for his work as a director, writer, and producer, including four Academy Award nominations for *The Insider* and for producing *The Aviator*. A Chicago native, Mann is recognized for his groundbreaking and cinematically captivating dramas, including *Thief, Manhunter, The Last of the Mohicans, Heat, The Insider, Ali,* and *Collateral*, and producing the critically acclaimed box office hit *The Aviator*.

In the mid-1970s, Mann began a career as a television writer, working on *Police Story*, the first episodes of *Starsky & Hutch*, and the series *Vega$*. In 1979, he directed and cowrote his first drama, movie of the week *The Jericho Mile*, starring Peter Strauss. It garnered four Emmys and a Directors Guild Award for Best Director.

In 1981, Mann made his theatrical-film debut with *The Thief*, a modernist crime story starring James Caan, Tuesday Weld, Willie Nelson, and Jim Belushi that was nominated for the Golden Palm Award at Cannes. He followed this in 1983 with the gothic horror film *The Keep*, starring Gabriel Byrne, Scott Glenn, and Ian McKellen. In 1986, he directed *Manhunter*, a psychological thriller based upon the first of Thomas Harris's Hannibal Lecter books, *Red Dragon*, featuring William Petersen and Brian Cox as Lecter.

Throughout the 1980s, Mann continued to work in television with the revolutionary *Miami Vice* and the acclaimed Chicago and Las Vegas drama *Crime Story*, starring Dennis Farina. In addition to these efforts, he produced the 1990 Emmy-winning miniseries *Drug Wars: The Camarena Story* and executive produced the 1992 Emmy-nominated sequel *Drug Wars: The Cocaine Cartel*.

In 1992, Mann directed, cowrote, and produced *The Last of the Mohicans*, starring Daniel Day-Lewis and Madeleine Stowe. Following this success, in 1995, he directed *Heat* from his own original screenplay about the taut relationship between an obsessive detective and a professional thief. It starred Al Pacino and Robert De Niro, as well as Jon Voight, Val Kilmer, and Tom Sizemore. Additionally, Ashley Judd and Amy Brenneman each had their first major roles in *Heat*.

In 1999, Mann earned Oscar nominations cowriting, directing, and producing *The Insider*, starring Russell Crowe and Al Pacino. Based upon Marie Brenner's *Vanity Fair* article "The Man Who Knew Too Much," the film tells the true story of Jeffrey Wigand, a tobacco-industry executive who blew the whistle on the industry's cover-up of cigarettes' known health risks.

In 2001, Mann took audiences into the heart and life of legendary boxer Muhammad Ali in *Ali,* starring Will Smith and Jon Voight, both of whom received Oscar nominations. Additionally, in 2002, Mann produced *Robbery: Homicide Division* for CBS, starring Tom Sizemore. In 2004, Mann directed the psychological thriller *Collateral*, starring Academy Award nominee Tom Cruise and Oscar winner Jamie Foxx. Mann earned numerous awards and nominations for this film, including a David Lean Award for Directing nomination at the 2004 BAFTAs. Also in 2004, Mann produced the Howard Hughes biopic, *The Aviator*, starring Leonardo DiCaprio and Cate Blanchett. This film led the 2004 Academy Awards contenders with eleven Oscar nominations, including Best Picture.

Mann went on to a big-screen version of *Miami Vice*, a harder-hitting, racier, and darker successor to the memorable, groundbreaking television series. This film stars Colin Farrell, Jamie Foxx, and Chinese actress Gong Li.

Rob Marshall, *Chicago* (2003)

The first feature film Mr. Marshall directed and choreographed was the Academy Award–winning film *Chicago* (winner of six Oscars, including Best Picture). For his work on that film he received the Director's Guild Award, an Oscar nomination, a Golden Globe Award nomination, a BAFTA nomination, the New York Film Critics and National Board of Review Awards for Best Directorial Debut, and the American Choreography Award for Achievement in Film. Prior to that, Mr. Marshall directed and choreographed Disney/ABC's critically acclaimed movie musical *Annie*, which received twelve Emmy nominations and won the prestigious Peabody Award. For his work on that film he received an Emmy Award, a Director's Guild Award nomination, and an American Choreography Award. A six-time Tony Award nominee, Mr. Marshall codirected and choreographed the worldwide award-winning production of *Cabaret* and directed and choreographed the Broadway revival of *Little Me*, starring Martin Short. He made his Broadway choreographic debut with *Kiss of the Spider Woman*, directed by Hal Prince, which also played London's West End, Vienna, Argentina, and Japan. He followed that with productions of *She Loves Me* (Broadway, London), *Damn Yankees* (Broadway, National Tour, London), Blake Edwards's *Victor/Victoria* (Broadway), *A Funny Thing Happened on the Way to the Forum* (Broadway), *Company* (Broadway), and *The Petrified Prince* (Public Theater). Mr. Marshall directed *Promises, Promises* for the City Center Encores! series, as well as regional productions of *Chess* and *Chicago* and national tours of *Camelot* and *Brigadoon*. Additional choreography credits include the feature film *The Cradle Will Rock*, the Disney/ABC movie musical *Cinderella*, the CBS movie musical *Mrs. Santa Claus*, and The Kennedy Center Honors (Kander & Ebb and Chita Rivera tributes). In addition to the above-mentioned awards, Mr. Marshall has been the recipient of the Outer Critics Circle Award, the L.A. Drama Critics Circle Award, and the Civil Rights Award, as well as nominations for the Emmy Award, the Olivier Award, and the Drama Desk Award. Mr. Marshall's next project after *Chicago* is the film of the best-selling novel by Arthur Golden, *Memoirs of a Geisha*, for Columbia/Dreamworks.

Mr. Marshall is a graduate of Carnegie Mellon University.

Sam Mendes, *American Beauty* (2000)

In 1992, Sam Mendes founded and ran the Donmar Warehouse in London until 2002; Donmar productions included *Assassins, Translations, Cabaret, Glengarry Glen Ross, The Glass Menagerie, Company, Habeas Corpus, The Front Page, The Blue Room, To the Green Fields Beyond, Uncle Vanya*, and *Twelfth Night*, which transferred to the Brooklyn Academy of Music in 2004. He has also produced—in tandem with his associate Caro Newling—over sixty plays, many of which have transferred to New York, including *Electra, True West, Juno and the Paycock*, and the Tony Award–winning *The Real Thing*. He recently directed *Gypsy* with Bernadette Peters on Broadway.

His work for the Royal Shakespeare Company includes *Troilus and Cressida, The Alchemist, The Tempest*, and *Richard III*. For the National Theatre, he directed *The Sea, The Rise and Fall of Little Voice, The Birthday Party*, and *Othello*. In the West End, he directed *The Cherry Orchard, The Plough and the Stars, Kean, London Assurance*, and *Oliver!* He also directed the Broadway productions of *Cabaret,* which received four Tony Awards including Best Musical, and David Hare's *The Blue Room*, which starred Nicole Kidman.

In 1999, Mendes made his film directorial debut on *American Beauty*, for which he received a Golden Globe Award and the DGA Award for Outstanding Director. The film garnered five Academy Awards including Best Picture and Mendes received the award for Best Director. In 2002, Mendes brought to life Max Collins's graphic novel, *Road to Perdition*, starring Tom Hanks and Paul Newman. The film earned seven Academy Award nominations and was a big international hit.

Mendes went on to an adaptation of Anthony Swofford's Gulf War memoir, *Jarhead*, starring Jake Gyllenhaal and Jamie Foxx.

Anthony Minghella, *The English Patient* (1997)

Born of Italian parents in 1954 on the Isle of Wight, Anthony Minghella lectured at the University of Hull until 1981, when he began his playwriting career. In 1984 he was named the most promising playwright of the year by the London Theatre Critics for three plays, *A Little Like Drawing*, *Love Bites*, and *Two Planks and a Passion*. Two years later the London critics honored *Made in Bangkok* as Best Play of the Year. Minghella's radio play *Hang Up* won the Prix D'Italia in 1988. Another radio play, *Cigarettes and Chocolate*, was a finalist for the Prix D'Italia in 1989 and won several other honors. Anthony Minghella wrote the pilot script and regularly contributed to British television's award-winning series *Inspector Morse*, and his television trilogy, *What If It's Raining?*, was highly acclaimed throughout Europe. Minghella wrote all nine of the short television films in the Emmy Award–winning *Storyteller* series for Jim Henson and NBC. He also wrote another film for the same team, *Living with Dinosaurs*, which won an international Emmy in 1990.

Minghella made an auspicious feature-film debut in 1991 with *Truly, Madly, Deeply*, which he wrote as well as directed after a decade of writing for theater and television. The film won numerous accolades, including awards for Minghella from the British Film and Television Academy (BAFTA) and the Writer's Guild of Great Britain. In 1993, Minghella directed his second film, *Mr. Wonderful*, starring Matt Dillon and Mary Louise Parker.

The English Patient, starring Ralph Fiennes, Kristin Scott Thomas, and Juliette Binoche, won nine Academy Awards, including Best Director and Best Picture, as well as an award for Outstanding Directorial Achievement from the Directors Guild of America. Among Minghella's more recent projects are *The Talented Mr. Ripley*, which he also wrote and for which he received a Best Screenplay Academy Award nomination, *Cold Mountain*, which also received a Best Adapted Screenplay BAFTA nomination for screen writing, and *Breaking and Entering*, which he also wrote and directed.

Mike Newell, *Four Weddings and Funeral* (1995)

Mike Newell joined Granada Television as a production trainee in 1963 after graduating in English from Cambridge University. While at Granada he directed numerous television plays, including *Them Down There, Ready When You Are Mr. McGill, Destiny,* and *The Melancholy Hussar,* before moving into the world of films. His feature credits include *The Man in the Iron Mask* (1976), *The Awakening* (1977), *Bad Blood* (1980), *Dance with a Stranger* (1984), which was awarded the Prix Italia, *Amazing Grace and Chuck* (1986), *Soursweet* (1987), *Enchanted April* (1991), which received three Oscar nominations, and *Into the West* (1992). His 1994 release *Four Weddings and a Funeral* was nominated for a DGA Award, an Academy Award for Best Picture, and a BAFTA Award for Best Film and Achievement in Direction. The film won British Film of the Year, British Director of the Year, and a Cesar Award for Best Foreign Language Film. In 1995, Mike released *An Awfully Big Adventure,* which, like *Four Weddings,* screened at the Sundance Film Festival. In 1997, Newell directed *Donnie Brasco,* starring Al Pacino and Johnny Depp, which tells the story of an FBI agent who infiltrates the mob and then finds he identifies more with the Mafia life than his own life. In 1999 he directed *Pushing Tin,* starring John Cusack, Billy Bob Thornton, Cate Blanchett, and Angelina Jolie. In 2003, he directed *Mona Lisa Smile* starring Julia Roberts, Kirsten Dunst, Maggie Gyllenhaal, and Julia Stiles, and in 2005 he directed *Harry Potter and the Goblet of Fire.*

Christopher Nolan, *Memento* (2002)

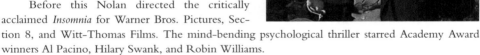

Batman Begins is Christopher Nolan's 2005 directorial endeavor. The film chronicles the early life of the "Caped Crusader" and stars Christian Bale in the title role with a stellar cast that includes Michael Caine, Liam Neeson, Katie Holmes, Gary Oldman, Cillian Murphy, Ken Watanabe, and Morgan Freeman.

Before this Nolan directed the critically acclaimed *Insomnia* for Warner Bros. Pictures, Section 8, and Witt-Thomas Films. The mind-bending psychological thriller starred Academy Award winners Al Pacino, Hilary Swank, and Robin Williams.

Nolan's second film, *Memento,* was adapted from a short story by his brother Jonathan Nolan about a man who struggles to find himself within the remnants of his hazy past. Starring Guy Pearce, Carrie-Anne Moss, and Joe Pantoliano, the small-budget independent film was named best of the year by the Broadcast Film Critics and went on to gross over $25 million and garnered accolades for Nolan, including a DGA Award nomination. In addition, Nolan's screenplay garnered an Academy Award nomination for Best Screenplay and a Golden Globe nomination and was honored by the Los Angeles Film Critics and Broadcast Film Critics, as well as winning the Waldo Salt Screenwriting Award at the 2001 Sundance Film Festival.

Filmmaking has truly been a lifelong pursuit for Nolan, who began making movies at the age of seven using his father's Super 8 camera. While studying English literature at University College London, Nolan shot 16mm films at the school's film society, before applying the same guerrilla-style production techniques to his feature-length script, *Following.* The no-budget noir film, which *The New Yorker*'s Bruce Diones hailed as "leaner and meaner" than the thrillers of Hitchcock, enjoyed great success at numerous international film festivals (including Toronto, Rotterdam, Slam Dance, and

Hong Kong) prior to being released theatrically in the United States (Zeitgeist), United Kingdom (Alliance), France (CCI), and various other territories.

Alexander Payne, *Sideways* (2005)

Director/coscreenwriter Alexander Payne's *Sideways* was one of the most lauded films of 2004, having earned a total of seven Golden Globe nominations including Best Picture/Comedy or Musical, Best Director, and Best Screenplay; four Critics' Choice Awards including Best Picture and Best Screenplay; a Directors Guild of America nomination; a Writers Guild of America nomination for Best Adapted Screenplay; a Producers Guild nomination for Best Picture; four Screen Actors Guild nominations; and six Independent Spirit Award nominations including Best Feature, Best Director, and Best Screenplay. The film earned Best Picture honors from the Los Angeles, New York Film Critics Circle, Chicago, London Critics Circle, Toronto, San Francisco, New York Online, Washington Area, and Boston critics groups and was named to the top-ten lists of more than 350 critics lists including the American Film Institute, National Board of Review, *Rolling Stone*, and *Newsweek* amongst others. The film received five Academy Award nominations, including Best Picture and Best Director, and received the Best Adapted Screenplay Oscar for Payne and Taylor.

Payne made his feature-film debut with the critically acclaimed *Citizen Ruth*, a provocative satire about the abortion-rights war. He followed that up in 1999 with the much lauded *Election*, which led the year's critics' top-ten lists, earned Best Director and Best Film Independent Spirit Awards, and, for Payne and cowriter Jim Taylor, won a number of Best Screenplay awards including the Writers Guild of America, the New York Film Critics Circle, and the Independent Spirit Award, as well as an Oscar nomination for Best Adapted Screenplay.

Payne followed with *About Schmidt*, starring Jack Nicholson and Kathy Bates. The film earned two Golden Globes (Best Adapted Screenplay and Best Director) and was voted Best Film of 2002 by the Los Angeles and London Film Critics Circles. Additionally, he executive produced the film *The Assassination of Richard Nixon*.

Born and raised in Omaha, Nebraska, Payne holds BA degrees in history and Spanish literature from Stanford University and an MFA in filmmaking from UCLA. His thesis film, *The Passion of Martin*, which he wrote, directed, and produced, screened at the 1991 Sundance Film Festival.

Roman Polanski, *The Pianist* (2003)

Roman Polanski's feature directorial debut was *Knife in the Water,* winning the Critics' Prize at the Venice Film Festival and an Oscar nomination as Best Foreign Language Film. Roman's first English-language features, *Repulsion* and *Cul de Sac* won a Silver Bear and a Golden Bear at the Berlin Film Festival. He made his American film debut with *Rosemary's Baby,* which garnered an Oscar nomination for Best Adapted Screenplay and earned an Oscar for Best Supporting Actress (Ruth Gordon). *Chinatown* won the 1974 Golden Globe for Best Picture and was nominated for eleven Oscars, including Best Picture and Best Director, winning Best

Original Screenplay (Robert Towne). Roman next directed *The Tenant* and *Tess*, which earned six Oscar nominations including one for Best Director, and won Oscars for Cinematography, Art Direction, and Costume Design. He is a member of the Institute de France Académie des Beaux-Arts, and received the 2002 Golden Scepter Award from the Foundation of Polish Culture. Roman has appeared as an actor in many films and his most recent directing is a version of *Oliver Twist*.

Michael Radford, *Il Postino* (1996)

Michael Radford was born on February 24, 1946, in New Delhi, India, to an English father and an Austrian mother. He grew up mainly in the Middle East, where his father served in the British army. He was educated at Bedford School and at Worcester College, Oxford. At the age of twenty-five, having been a teacher for a number of years in Edinburgh, he went to the National Film School and was one of the first twenty-five students in its inaugural year.

Upon graduating from the National Film School in 1974, he embarked on a series of documentaries, mainly for the BBC, including *The Madonna* and *The Volcano* (Grand Prix Nyon 1976) and the *Last Stronghold of the Pure Gospel*. In 1980, he wrote and directed his first feature film for BBC Scotland, entitled *The White Bird Passes,* adapted from the novel by Jessie Kesson. It was the success of this collaboration that led to the writing and making of *Another Time, Another Place*, one of the first films commissioned by Channel 4 for the cinema, selected for the Quinzaine des Realisateurs at Cannes in 1983 and winner of fifteen major prizes at festivals around the world. The critical success of this film launched his career in feature films. Radford's second film, the following year (1984), was the cinematic adaptation of George Orwell's *1984* starring Richard Burton and John Hurt. The film won the British Film Award for Best Film and Best Actor, as well as numerous other international prizes.

White Mischief, starring Greta Scacchi and Joss Ackland, followed this in 1987. Although the film has now become somewhat of a cult film in the United States, it was a commercial failure and Radford did not make another film for more than six years. During this period he left England and went to live first in France and later in Italy, writing screenplays and directing commercials. It was his longstanding friendship with the Italian actor Massimo Troisi that led to the writing and making of *Il Postino*, the first Italian film ever made by an Englishman. The film became the highest-grossing foreign-language film in the history of cinema and was nominated for five Academy Awards, including Best Director and Best Screenplay. The film won more than thirty-five international awards, including BAFTAs for Best Director and Best Foreign Film. It was a film made under the most tragic of circumstances, as the star of the film was dying during the making of it and was not to live to enjoy its success.

Since *Il Postino*, Radford has cowritten and directed *B Monkey*, his first film in Britain in eight years, and *The Merchant of Venice,* starring Al Pacino, Jeremy Irons, and Joseph Fiennes. Radford speaks four languages and has two children.

Rob Reiner, *A Few Good Men* (1993)

A Few Good Men's producer/director Rob Reiner has established himself as one of Hollywood's top directors, creating films that win both audience enthusiasm and critical acclaim. His first film, 1984's *This Is Spinal Tap*, a "rockumentary" on the ups and downs of a fictitious British rock band, received wide acclaim and established Reiner's reputation as a filmmaker of unique vision and sparkling satiric wit. His other credits include *The Sure Thing* (1985), a hate-turned-to-love story about two collegians, and *Stand By Me* (1986), which depicted four boys coming of age in the 1950s and received an Academy Award nomination for Best Adapted Screenplay, while Reiner garnered Best Director nominations from the Directors Guild of America and the Hollywood Foreign Press Association. Following was the much-loved fantasy *The Princess Bride* (1987) and 1989's *When Harry Met Sally*, the hit romantic comedy that received an Oscar nomination for Best Original Screenplay, five Golden Globe Awards, and a Directors Guild nomination. In 1990 came his film *Misery,* for which Kathy Bates garnered an Oscar for her portrayal of deranged fan Annie Wilkes. The year 1992 brought the mega box office hit *A Few Good Men*, starring Tom Cruise, Jack Nicholson, and Demi Moore, which garnered another DGA Best Director nomination as well as four Academy Award nominations, including Best Picture. *North* was released in 1994 and starred Elijah Wood, Bruce Willis, Jon Lovitz, Jason Alexander, and Julia Louis-Dreyfus. Reiner directed the hit comedy *The American President* in 1995, which starred Michael Douglas and Annette Bening. *Ghosts of Mississippi* followed in 1996 and was the true story of the reprosecution of Byron De La Beckwith, the racist murderer of civil rights leader Medgar Evers, starring Alec Baldwin, Whoopi Goldberg, and James Woods. Next came *The Story of Us*, starring Bruce Willis and Michelle Pfeiffer, a romantic comedy exploring the question, "Can a marriage survive fifteen years of marriage?" Reiner has directed *Alex & Emma* and *Rumor Has It*, with Jennifer Aniston, Mark Ruffalo, Shirley MacLaine, and Kevin Costner.

Prior to his directorial debut, Reiner, son of comedian Carl Reiner, acted in many television and feature films and wrote for *The Smothers Brothers Comedy Hour*. It was, however, his award-winning portrayal of Michael Stivic, Archie Bunker's son-in-law in the phenomenal hit series *All in the Family*, that made him a household name.

In 1997 Rob Reiner and his wife joined forces on a national public awareness and engagement campaign to communicate the importance of the prenatal period through the first three years of life. As a result of Reiner's work with the National Governor's Association, in February of that year a ten-governor, bipartisan task force was assigned to develop state policies for very young children. Then in April, a White House summit on early brain development, hosted by President Clinton and the First Lady, was the launch point for the "I Am Your Child" campaign. An hour-long prime-time special followed on ABC-TV, which Reiner coproduced, cowrote, and directed. The "I Am Your Child" campaign has made parenting information available on the Internet through the www.imyourchild .org website.

Rob Reiner is a principal and cofounder of Castle Rock Entertainment. In addition to directing feature films, he is involved in all phases of Castle Rock's creative activities. Rob Reiner is married to Michele Singer Reiner, a professional photographer. They have three children.

Gary Ross, *Seabiscuit* (2004)

A four-time Academy Award nominee, Gary Ross is a filmmaker who delves into America's favorite pastimes and lauded institutions to create some of the most beloved films in recent history. A true Renaissance man, Ross's career includes directing and producing, in addition to his first calling as a gifted screenwriter. Ross exploded onto the film scene with his first produced screenplay, *Big*. The 1988 blockbuster comedy, starring Tom Hanks as a child whose wish to be a grown-up is granted, grossed more than $100 million in domestic box office receipts and garnered two Oscar nominations (for Gary Ross and Anne Spielberg's original screenplay and Tom Hanks's performance). Ross also co-produced the motion picture, which was directed by Penny Marshall. Ross drew on his knowledge and love of the American political process for his screenplay of the Capra-esque comedy hit *Dave*. Starring Kevin Kline as an ordinary guy recruited to stand in for the president of the United States, the film also starred Sigourney Weaver and was directed by Ivan Reitman. Ross received his second Academy Award nomination for his original screenplay for *Dave*. He also won the Writers Guild Paul Selvin Award for a screenplay that "embodies the spirit of the constitutional and civil rights and liberties which are indispensable to the survival of free writers everywhere." In 1998, Ross decided it was time to direct one of his scripts. The result was the Oscar-nominated *Pleasantville*. A social comedy with equal parts heart and mind, *Pleasantville* tells the story of two teens (played by Tobey Maguire and Reese Witherspoon) who are inexplicably transported to the black-and-white world of a fictional 1950s television town. Their presence there ripples through the fairy-tale community, whose residents are consequently granted the chance to experience the wonders, comedies, and dangers of "real" life. Later that year, Ross's production company, Larger than Life, found a new home at Universal. *Seabiscuit* received seven Academy Award nominations, including Best Picture and Best Adapted Screenplay for Ross.

Throughout Ross's career, he has remained active in local and national politics. During his college years, Ross spent his summers working on Capitol Hill as an intern. In addition to exploring the fictional political world in *Dave*, he keeps his feet firmly planted in real politics, having written numerous speeches for such political luminaries as President Clinton. He has also attended the Democratic National Convention as a delegate. Ross also remains active in civic and charitable work. During his tenure as president of the Los Angeles Library, Ross established mentoring programs for inner-city youth and expanded teenage and youth-at-risk services throughout the Los Angeles library system. For his service, he was awarded the 1999 Light of Learning Award by the Los Angeles Public Library. In 2000, Ross gave the keynote address for the American Library Association in Chicago. He also received the ACLU's Bill of Rights Award for 2000.

Martin Scorsese, *Gangs of New York* (2003) and *The Aviator* (2005)

Martin Scorsese was born in 1942 in New York City, and was raised in the downtown neighborhood of Little Italy, which later provided the inspiration for several of his films. Scorsese earned a BS degree in film communications in 1964, followed by an MA in the same field in 1966 at New York University's School of Film. During this time, he made numerous prizewinning short films, including *The Big*

Shave. His first feature, *Who's That Knocking at My Door?*, caught the attention of Roger Corman, who asked him to direct *Boxcar Bertha*. He also served as assistant director and an editor of the documentary *Woodstock* in 1970 and won critical and popular acclaim for his 1973 film *Mean Streets*. In 1976, Scorsese's *Taxi Driver* was awarded the Palme d'Or at the Cannes Film Festival. He followed with *New York, New York* in 1977, *The Last Waltz* in 1978, and *Raging Bull* in 1980, which received eight Academy Award nominations including Best Film and Best Director. His filmmaking career also includes *Alice Doesn't Live Here Anymore, The King of Comedy, After Hours, The Color of Money, The Last Temptation of Christ, Goodfellas* (six Academy Award nominations, including Best Picture and Best Director), *Cape Fear, The Age of Innocence, Casino, Kundun,* and *Bringing Out the Dead*.

Scorsese's long-cherished project, *Gangs of New York*, was released in 2002, earning numerous critical honors including a Golden Globe Award for Best Director. The film received ten Academy Award nominations, including Best Picture and Best Director. His next feature film, *The Aviator*, received the most Academy Award nominations of any Scorsese film (eleven), including those for Best Picture and Director. The film won five Oscars, including Best Supporting Actress (Cate Blanchett). Marty has also sponsored other filmmakers, coproducing Matthew Harrison's *Kicked in the Head* and Stephen Frears's *The Hi-Lo Country*, and he was executive producer on Kenneth Lonergan's *You Can Count On Me*. He codirected and cowrote (with Michael Henry Wilson) the British Film Institute/Channel 4 documentary *A Personal Journey with Martin Scorsese through American Movies* and directed *Italianamerican*, a documentary about his parents. More recent productions include *The Departed* and *No Direction Home: Bob Dylan*. He is a founder of the Film Foundation and in 1992 launched Martin Scorsese Presents, a company dedicated to the restoration and distribution of film classics.

In 1996, Scorsese completed a four-hour documentary, *A Personal Journey with Martin Scorsese through American Movies*, codirected by Michael Henry Wilson. The documentary was commissioned by the British Film Institute to celebrate the one hundredth anniversary of the birth of cinema. In 2001, Scorsese released *Il mio viaggio in Italia*, an epic documentary that affectionately chronicles his love for Italian cinema. In 2003, PBS broadcast the seven-film documentary series *Martin Scorsese Presents: The Blues*. Scorsese is the founder and chair of the Film Foundation, a nonprofit organization dedicated to the preservation and protection of motion picture history. He is also a cochair of the Tribeca Film Festival. His many awards and honors include the Golden Lion from the Venice Film Festival (1995), the AFI Life Achievement Award (1997), the Honoree at the Film Society of Lincoln Center's Twenty-fifth Gala Tribute (1998), and the DGA Lifetime Achievement Award (2003).

Ridley Scott, *Black Hawk Down* (2002)

Ridley Scott began his feature-directing career with *The Duellists*, which brought him the Jury Prize at the 1978 Cannes Film Festival. His second film was the breakthrough hit *Alien*, which won an Academy Award for Special Effects, followed by the landmark science fiction film *Blade Runner,* as well as *Legend, Someone to Watch Over Me,* and *Black Rain*. Ridley directed and produced the Academy Award–winning *Thelma and Louise* and *1492: Conquest of Paradise*. With his brother Tony, Ridley formed Scott Free Productions, which produced *White Squall* and *G.I. Jane*, both directed by Ridley. He was a producer on *Clay Pigeons, Where the Money Is, The Browning Version*, and the Cable Ace Award–winning Showtime anthology series *The Hunger*. Ridley also produced the Emmy and Golden Globe Award–winning HBO feature *RKO 281*. Prior to this nomination, he directed *Gladiator*, which won five Oscars including Best Picture, and *Hannibal*, based on Thomas Harris's sequel to *The Silence of the Lambs*. Since his DGA Award and Best Director Oscar nominations, Sir Ridley (knighted in 2003) has directed *Matchstick Men* and *Kingdom of Heaven*.

M. Night Shyamalan, *The Sixth Sense* (2000)

M. Night Shyamalan began making films at the age of ten in his hometown of Philadelphia. At sixteen, he had completed his forty-fifth short film. Following his stint at New York University's Tisch School of the Arts, Night found himself on a plane to India with the funding to make his first low-budget feature film, *Praying with Anger*, on which he served as director, writer, producer, and star. Twentieth Century Fox subsequently purchased his original screenplay *Labor of Love*, and in 1995 he was asked by Columbia Pictures to write the fantasy screen adaptation of *Stuart Little*, based on E. B. White's beloved children's classic. Night's second feature, *Wide Awake*, was released theatrically in 1997. *The Sixth Sense* marks Night's first DGA Award nomination. The film was also nominated for six Academy Awards, including Best Director and Best Picture. Since this DGA Award nomination, Shyamalan has gone on to direct *Unbreakable, Signs*, and *The Village*.

Steven Soderbergh, *Erin Brockovich* (2001) and *Traffic* (2001)

Steven Soderbergh was born in Georgia and raised primarily in Baton Rouge, Louisiana. He began making short films at age thirteen. After graduating from high school, he traveled to Los Angeles and worked as a freelance editor, before returning to Baton Rouge to continue making short films and writing screenplays. After shooting a documentary profiling the rock group Yes, he was asked to direct a full-length concert film for the band. The result was *9012LIVE*, which received a Grammy Award nomination in 1986 for Best Long-Form Music Video. Steven spent two more years writing screenplays, both on spec and for hire, and completed the script for *sex, lies, and videotape*. He shot the film, his feature directorial debut, in Baton Rouge with James Spader, Andie MacDowell, Peter Gallagher, and Laura San Giacomo playing the four lead roles. The film world premiered at the Sundance Film Festival in January 1989 and four months later won the Palme d'Or at the Cannes International Film Festival. His second film, *Kafka* (1991), was a black-and-white mystery/suspense film set in post-WWI Prague starring Jeremy Irons in the title role. The memoirs of author A. E. Hotchner provided the basis for his third film, *King of the Hill* (1993), which detailed the attempts of an imaginative twelve-year old boy to keep his family together during the Great Depression. *The Underneath* (1995) was a dark tale of obsession and betrayal set in present-day Austin, Texas. In 1997, Steven released both *Schizopolis*, an experimental low-budget comedy, and *Gray's Anatomy*, in which Spalding Gray describes his medical experiences after being diagnosed with a rare eye disease. *Out of Sight*, starring George Clooney and Jennifer Lopez, opened in 1998 and was based on the Elmore Leonard novel of the same name. The National Society of Film Critics awarded *Out of Sight* its top three awards: Best Director, Best Picture, and Best Screenplay. In addition, the film received Oscar noms for Best Adapted Screenplay and Best Film Editing. *The Limey* (1999) earned five Independent Spirit Award nominations for Best Picture, Best Actor, Best Supporting Actor, Best Director, and Best Screenplay.

Steven is only the second director to receive two DGA Feature Film nominations in the same year since the current method of selecting five nominees from which one winner is chosen began in

1970. In 1974, Francis Ford Coppola was nominated for both *The Godfather Part II* and *The Conversation* and received that year's DGA Feature Film Award for *The Godfather*. *Traffic* and *Erin Brockovich* are Steven's first DGA nominations in the Feature Film category. Steven also competed against himself in the Oscar race, receiving Best Director nomination for both films. He won the Oscar for *Traffic*. Since then, he's directed *Ocean's Eleven*, *Solaris*, and *Ocean's Twelve* as well as the television projects *Unscripted* and *K Street*.

Steven Spielberg, *Amistad* (1997) and *Saving Private Ryan* (1999)

Steven Spielberg is a nine-time DGA Award nominee and three-time winner, having won previously for *The Color Purple* and *Schindler's List*, which also garnered Oscars for Best Picture and Best Director. His other DGA Award–nominated films are *E.T.: The Extra-Terrestrial*, *Raiders of the Lost Ark*, *Close Encounters of the Third Kind*, *Empire of the Sun*, *Jaws*, and *Amistad*. Steven has directed, produced, or executive produced seven of the top-grossing films of all time. He is the recipient of the Lifetime Achievement Award from the American Film Institute and the prestigious Irving G. Thalberg Award from the Academy of Motion Picture Arts and Sciences.

Spielberg's 1998 film *Saving Private Ryan* was nominated for eleven Academy Awards and won five, including Best Director. *Saving Private Ryan* also won two Golden Globe Awards for Best Picture and Best Director, in addition to the Best Picture Award from the New York Film Critics Circle, and Best Picture and Best Director Awards from the Los Angeles Film Critics Association and the Broadcast Film Critics.

Since this nomination, Spielberg has directed *AI: Artificial Intelligence*, *Minority Report*, *Catch Me If You Can*, *The Terminal*, and *War of the Worlds*.

Oliver Stone, *JFK* (1992)

Director-writer Oliver Stone was born in New York City in 1946. He served in Vietnam from 1967 to 1968 and also worked as a teacher and merchant seaman in Southeast Asia from 1965 to 1966. He graduated from the New York University Film School in 1971.

Oliver Stone explores perhaps America's most important and controversial event of the twentieth century with *JFK*, a look at the conspiracy behind the assassination of President Kennedy. Stone's *JFK* (1991), starring Kevin Costner, Tommy Lee Jones, and Gary Oldman, chronicles New Orleans District Attorney Jim Garrison's investigation into the assassination of President Kennedy. The film takes a fresh look at all the credible assassination theories in a gripping thriller that raises the nation's persistent questions, doubts, and suspicions. Filmed on location in Dallas, New Orleans, and Washington, D.C., *JFK* also features an extensive gallery of appearances by acclaimed actors, including Edward Asner, Walter Matthau, Jack Lemmon, and Donald Sutherland. The film received three Academy Award nominations in 1992 for Best Picture, Best Director, and Best Writing, Screenplay Based on Material from Another Medium, as well as a nomination from the Directors Guild of America for Outstanding Directorial Achievement in Theatrical Direction.

Stone, a three-time Academy Award winner, directed and cowrote *The Doors*, which starred Val Kilmer as Jim Morrison and chronicled the rise and fall of one of the great rock bands of the 1960s. In 1990, Stone received an Academy Award for his direction of *Born on the Fourth of July*, which received a total of seven nominations. Additionally, Stone received the Directors Guild of America Award and was nominated for his screenplay (with Rob Kovic) by the Writers Guild of America. In 1986, Stone directed and wrote *Platoon*, which was nominated for eight Academy Awards, winning four, including Best Picture and Best Director. Stone also received the Directors Guild of America Award and a British Academy award for his direction as well as a nomination for his screenplay from the Writers Guild of America. In 1987, Stone cowrote (with Stanley Weiser) and directed *Wall Street*, which earned Michael Douglas an Academy Award for Best Actor. In 1988, Stone directed and co-wrote (with Eric Bogosian) *Talk Radio*. Stone also wrote and directed *The Hand* (1981) and *The Seizure* (1973) and wrote screenplays for several motion pictures, including *Conan the Barbarian*, *Scarface*, *Year of the Dragon* (with Michael Cimino), and *Midnight Express*, for which he received an Academy Award and the Writers Guild of America Award. He also produced *Zebrahead* and *South Central* and, with Ed Pressman, coproduced *Blue Steel* and *Reversal of Fortune*.

Additional directing credits include *Heaven and Earth* (1993), *Natural Born Killers* (1994), and *Nixon* (1995), which Stone also cowrote and which was nominated for an Academy Award for Best Screenplay Written Directly for the Screen in 1996.

Following in 1997 was *U-Turn*. In 1999 he cowrote and directed *Any Given Sunday* starring Al Pacino, Dennis Quaid, James Woods, and Ed Burns. In 2004, he produced, directed, and wrote *Alexander*.

Barbra Streisand, *The Prince of Tides* (1992)

The Prince of Tides, which Barbra Streisand directed, produced, and starred in, earned her a nomination for Best Director by the Directors Guild of America and was yet another bold mark in a career highlighted by a series of "firsts." For her very first Broadway appearance in *I Can Get It for You Wholesale*, she won the New York Drama Critics Circle Award and received a Tony nomination. For her very first record album, *The Barbra Streisand Album*, she won two 1963 Grammy Awards, the youngest person, age twenty-two, to win for Best Female Vocal Performance and Album of the Year. She was honored with an Emmy Award for her first television special, *My Name is Barbra*, in 1965. For her motion picture debut, in *Funny Girl*, she won the 1968 Academy Award as Best Actress. She is the first female composer ever to win an Academy Award for her song "Evergreen," the love theme from her hit film *A Star Is Born*. Forty-two of her albums have become gold (Elvis Presley is the only artist that exceeds that), twenty-five have reached platinum status, and thirteen have gone multiplatinum, the most for any female artist in all categories. She has been honored with eight Grammy Awards. The Recording Industry Association of America recently designated Barbra Streisand as Female Artist of the Century. She has received ten Golden Globes, the most for any artist.

Undertaking the challenge of making the motion picture *Yentl,* Streisand is recorded as the first woman ever to produce, direct, write, and star in a major film.

The filmmaker entertainer was born April 24 in Brooklyn to Diana and Emanuel Streisand. Her father, who passed away when Barbra was fifteen months old, was a teacher and a scholar. An honor student at Erasmus Hall High School in Brooklyn, the teenage Streisand plunged, unassisted and without encouragement, into show business by winning a singing contest at a small Manhattan club. Soon she was attracting music industry attention at such spots as the Bon Soir and the Blue Angel. Streisand signed a contract with Columbia Records in 1962, and her debut album quickly became the nation's top-selling record by a female vocalist. She was then signed to play the great comedienne Fanny Brice in the Broadway production of *Funny Girl*, and her distinctly original musical-comedy performance won her a second Tony nomination. When she signed a ten-year contract with CBS Television to produce and star in TV specials, the contract gave her complete artistic control, an unheard-of concession to an artist so young and inexperienced. The first special, *My Name is Barbra*, earned five Emmy Awards, and the following four shows, including the memorable *Color Me Barbra*, earned the highest critical praise and audience ratings. Few movie debuts have been as auspicious as Streisand's in *Funny Girl*. In addition to winning the 1968 Academy Award, she won the Golden Globe and was named Star of the Year by the National Association of Theatre Owners. After appearing in the films *Hello Dolly!*, *On a Clear Day You Can See Forever*, *The Owl and the Pussycat*, and *What's Up, Doc?*, in 1972 she starred in *Up the Sandbox*, one of the first American films to deal with the growing women's movement. It was the premiere picture for her own production company, Barwood Films. In 1973, *The Way We Were* brought her an Academy Award nomination as Best Actress. *A Star Is Born*, released in 1976, was the first movie to benefit from her energy and insight as a producer.

When Streisand completed her first movie, she had read a short story titled "Yentl, the Yeshiva Boy" and hoped to make it her second film. However, it took fourteen years of development before the dream came true. *Yentl*, a romantic drama with music, is a movie that celebrates women trying to be all that they can be. Streisand's directorial debut received four 1984 Academy Award nominations (including a Best Supporting Actress nomination for Amy Irving), and Streisand received Golden Globe Awards as both Best Director (becoming the first woman to win that honor) and Producer of the Best Picture (Musical or Comedy) of 1984. The awards represent two of the ten Golden Globes she received throughout her career. She was accorded the Hollywood Foreign Press Association's Year 2000 Cecil B. DeMille Award for Lifetime Achievement. Through her Barwood Films, she also produced and starred in *Nuts*, the unusual story of a smart woman shaped into an angry, antisocial character by peculiar circumstances, a difficult role judged to be one of her finest performances. She also wrote the music for the powerful drama released in 1987.

Streisand's *The Prince of Tides*, based on Pat Conroy's best-selling novel, is an emotional masterpiece, and the performances of Nick Nolte, Blythe Danner, and Kate Nelligan are powerful and profoundly poignant. *The Prince of Tides* was the first motion picture directed by its star ever to receive a nomination from the Directors Guild of America for Outstanding Directorial Achievement in Theatrical Direction, as well as seven Academy Award nominations, including a Best Actor nomination for Nick Nolte. Barbra Streisand produced the heralded drama in addition to directing and starring in it.

After working with her for two weeks, the book's author, Pat Conroy, gave Streisand a copy of his novel with the inscription: "To Barbra Streisand: The Queen of Tides . . . you are many things, Barbra, but you're also a great teacher . . . one of the greatest to come into my life. I honor the great teachers and they live in my work and they dance invisibly in the margins of my prose. You've honored me by taking care of it with such great seriousness and love. Great thanks, and I'll never forget that you gave *The Prince of Tides* back to me as a gift. Pat Conroy."

Recipient in 1995 of an honorary doctorate in arts from Brandeis University, Barbra Streisand is perhaps the only artist to earn Oscar, Tony, Emmy, Grammy, Golden Globe, Cable Ace, and Peabody Awards. Her most recent motion picture directorial effort, the TriStar Pictures' *The Mirror Has Two Faces*, continued the tradition of each Streisand-directed film being accorded Academy Award nominations, including her second Best Song nomination for cowriting the music to "I Finally Found Someone." The romantic comedy, her third triple effort as director/producer/star, received two Oscar nominations in 1997 and led, as well, to Lauren Bacall winning the Golden Globe's Best Supporting Actress and earning an Academy Award nomination. It is noteworthy that each of the films directed by Ms. Streisand resulted in an acting Academy Award nomination.

Barbra Streisand's Barwood Films has placed great emphasis on bringing to television dramatic explorations of pressing social, historic, and political issues, which would not otherwise be addressed in more widely viewed television movies. *The Rescuers*, a series of six dramas broadcast on Showtime, pays tribute to non-Jews who heroically saved Jews from the Holocaust. Through Barwood, Ms. Streisand helped bring to millions of television viewers a drama investigating military harassment of and repression of the civil rights of gays. It was acknowledged that the critically praised *Serving in Silence: The Margarethe Cammermeyer Story* would never have been realized on network television had not Barbra Streisand put her executive producing talents and considerable artistic and social-issue influence behind it. It had great impact in conveying its urgent civil rights issue and earned three Emmys, six Emmy nominations, and the Peabody Award in the process. Barwood's CBS movie of the week, *The Long Island Incident: The Carolyn McCarthy Story*, inspired a national debate on gun control with its true story of a wife and mother who surmounted tragedy to win a seat in Congress after initiating a crusade to achieve sensible controls on guns. Similarly, Barwood prepared for Showtime a film supporting the Middle East peace process. *Two Hands That Shook the World* parallels the lives of Yitzhak Rabin and Yasser Arafat up to their historic handshake at the White House.

And like the true Renaissance woman she is, her life and her art are dedicated to the humanities as reflected by the Streisand Foundation, which is committed to gaining women's equality, the protection of both human rights and civil rights and liberties, the needs of children at risk in society, and the preservation of the environment. Through the Streisand Foundation, she directed the United States Environmental Defense Fund's research for and participation in the recent global warming world summit conference in Kyoto. Her environmental dedication is reflected also in her donation to the Santa Monica Mountains Conservancy of the five-home, twenty-four-acre Malibu estate on which her One Voice concert had been performed. The site has been dedicated as a center for ecological studies. Ms. Streisand is a leading spokesperson and fund-raiser for social causes close to her heart, including AIDS. During the twenty-seven years that preceded her limited 1994 tour and the Las Vegas New Year's appearances, she had devoted her live concert performances exclusively to the benefit of those causes she supports. Her concern with social issues is reflected not only in the dedications of her personal life, but in the subject matter of the films she has initiated, each of which has addressed some social consideration.

Recent honors reflecting the range of her involvement in charitable and social causes include the 1992 Commitment to Life Award from AIDS Project Los Angeles for her dedication to helping people living with that disease and the ACLU Bill of Rights Award for her ongoing defense of constitutional rights. Ms. Streisand's feelings about the rights and obligations of artists to participate in the political process were brought into sharp focus by her early 1995 speech at Harvard University under the sponsorship of the John F. Kennedy School of Government. The address won unprecedented reportage and reproduction in such print media as the *New York Times* and the *Washington Post*. It was carried a record number of times on C-Span. Her speech at Harvard's Kennedy School of Government on "The Artist as Citizen" was reprinted in Senator Robert Torricelli's book *In Our Own Words*, a collection of the greatest speeches of the twentieth century.

Prior to the 1986 elections, she performed her first full-length concert in twenty years, raising money for the Hollywood Women's Political Committee to disburse to liberal candidates. The money raised that night helped elect five Democratic Senators, which restored a Democratic majority in the Senate. To date, more than $10 million, including $7 million in profits from "Barbra Streisand: One Voice," has been channeled to charities through the Streisand Foundation, which continues to occupy much of the star's energy and resources. Her passionate political activism continues.

On July 1, 1998, Barbra married actor/director James Brolin.

Quentin Tarantino, *Pulp Fiction* (1995)

Hollywood history has its share of artistic rebels and writer/director Quentin Tarantino has already established himself as one of the most unique and talented filmmakers of his generation. Not bad for this former video store rental clerk whose biggest professional credit a couple of years ago was an appearance as an Elvis impersonator on *The Golden Girls.*

Tarantino wrote, directed, and starred in *Pulp Fiction*, which won the prestigious Palme d'Or at the 1994 Cannes Film Festival, numerous critics' awards, and a Golden Globe for Best Screenplay, was nominated for seven Academy Awards, including Best Picture and Best Director, and received an Academy Award for Best Screenplay. A trilogy of interrelated stories about seedy criminals in contemporary Hollywood, the film stars John Travolta, Bruce Willis, Uma Thurman, Samuel L. Jackson, Eric Stoltz, Harvey Keitel, Tim Roth, Maria de Medeiros, Amanda Plummer, and Christopher Walken. The film has also made over $100 million in the U.S. box office alone.

While still working at a Southern California video store, Tarantino passed his time writing screenplays. Tarantino's first produced project was *Reservoir Dogs.* Made on a shoestring budget with a cadre of impressive talent (including Harvey Keitel, Tim Roth, and Michael Madsen), Tarantino's twisted tale of cops and robbers made an immediate impact on audiences and critics all over the world. Released by Miramax, the film continued to draw audiences in Europe and midnight screenings in the United States nearly three years after it first hit the festival circuit.

Hollywood was obviously enamored of Tarantino's harrowing vision of contemporary life, where torture, violence, and humiliation are turned on their head as Tarantino's memorably malevolent characters take a walk on the seedier side of life. Clamoring for more Tarantino material, Hollywood bought up some of the properties Tarantino had written as an unknown. *True Romance* was made into a critically successful film by Tony Scott and starred Christian Slater and Patricia Arquette and featured a host of cameos from actors like Brad Pitt and Gary Oldman. Oliver Stone turned Tarantino's *Natural Born Killers* into a feature starring Woody Harrelson and Juliette Lewis as serial killers on the run.

With his production partner Lawrence Bender (through their company A Band Apart Productions), he served as executive producer on October Films' *Killing Zoe*, directed by Roger Avary and starring Jean-Hugues Anglade, Julie Delpy, and Eric Stoltz.

His acting roles include *Destiny Turns on the Radio*, in which he plays Johnny Destiny, directed by Jack Baran, and a role in *Desperado*, which was Robert Rodriguez's follow-up to *El Mariachi.*

In 1995 Tarantino also completed the omnibus feature *Four Rooms*, produced by Lawrence Bender, in which he wrote, directed, and starred in a segment, as well as executive producing. Set in a Hollywood hotel on New Year's Eve night, the film follows the adventures of a bellboy as he witnesses the goings-on in four different hotel rooms, directed by Allison Anders, Alexandre Rockwell, Robert Rodriguez, and Tarantino and released in 1995 by Miramax.

Not content to stay idle, Tarantino turned his attention toward the small screen with a cameo on an episode of Margaret Cho's *All-American Girl* entitled "Pulp Sitcom." This was followed by his television directorial debut with an episode of the hit drama *ER* entitled "Motherhood." Renowned for his gritty, realistic style of writing, he also performed a dialogue polish on the hit film *Crimson Tide.*

Tarantino executive produced and starred in *From Dusk till Dawn* from his own script, featuring George Clooney, Harvey Keitel, and Juliette Lewis. Directed by Robert Rodriguez, *From Dusk till Dawn* was released by Miramax in 1996. He also executive produced *Curdled*, featuring Billy Baldwin and Angela Jones for Miramax. Their confidence in Tarantino led to the formation of his own independent distribution arm, Rolling Thunder. Created to provide a showcase for unique films that would not otherwise receive distribution, 25 percent of all profits from Rolling Thunder will be donated towards film preservation. Rolling Thunder's first release was Wong Kar-Wai's *Chungking Express*. This was followed by a rerelease of Jack Hill's cult classic *Switchblade Sisters*.

Tarantino wrote, directed, and produced *Jackie Brown*, a comic crime caper loosely based on Elmore Leonard's novel *Rum Punch*, starring black action goddess Pam Grier, veteran actor Robert Forster, Samuel L. Jackson, Robert De Niro, Bridget Fonda, and Michael Keaton, and was released by Miramax in December of 1997.

Tarantino then took a turn for the theater, taking a lead role in the dramatic thriller *Wait until Dark*, starring against Marisa Tomei in his Broadway debut.

Tarantino's next big-screen directorial endeavors were *Kill Bill: Vol 1* and *Kill Bill: Vol 2*.

Gus Van Sant, *Good Will Hunting* (1998)

Gus Van Sant has been winning over critics and audiences alike since bursting on the scene with his widely acclaimed feature *Mala Noche,* which won the Los Angeles Film Critics Award for Best Independent/ Experimental Feature of 1987. He has also directed other award-winning features, including *Drugstore Cowboy, My Own Private Idaho, To Die For,* and *Even Cowgirls Get the Blues.* Mr. Van Sant's direction of Nicole Kidman in the black comedy *To Die For* won her a Golden Globe Award, and the film was screened at the 1995 Cannes and Toronto Film Festivals.

Throughout his career Mr. Van Sant has continued to make evocative short films that have been winning awards in film festivals around the world. In 1996 Van Sant directed Allen Ginsberg reading his poem "Ballad of the Skeletons" to the music of Paul McCartney and Philip Glass, which premiered at the 1997 Sundance Film Festival. A longtime musician, he has also directed music videos for such artists as David Bowie, Elton John, Tracy Chapman, The Red Hot Chili Peppers, and Hanson.

Van Sant was nominated for an Academy Award for Best Director in 1998 for *Good Will Hunting*, which received a total of nine Academy Award nominations and went on to gross $250 million worldwide. Van Sant's highly controversial remake of the Alfred Hitchcock classic *Psycho* was the first shot-for-shot recreation of a classic film.

Since his DGA Award nomination, Van Sant has continued to win awards for films he's directed, including *Gerry, Elephant, Finding Forrester* (which starred Sean Connery and Rob Brown), and *Last Days.*

Peter Weir, *The Truman Show* (1999) and *Master and Commander: The Far Side of the World* (2004)

Born in Sydney, Australia, Peter Weir briefly attended Sydney University, dropped out to join his father's real estate business, and, with money saved, left for Europe on a working holiday in 1965. Returning to Sydney in 1966, he took a job as a stagehand at a TV station. Peter then began working on a variety of short films as writer, director, and performer. In 1969 he signed on with the Commonwealth Film Unit (now FILM AUSTRALIA) as a production assistant, which lead to opportunities to direct a number of prizewinning short films and eventually features. He remained with the "Unit" until 1973 when he left to make his first feature-length film, *The Cars That Ate Paris*, an offbeat comedy-horror film based on his own short story. His first international motion picture success came in 1975 with *Picnic at Hanging Rock,* which brought him widespread attention and became the most successful Australian film of the 1970s.

Weir's contribution to the Australian film renaissance of the late 1970s lay in his ability to portray the imminent disruption of the rational world by irrational forces hovering just beyond our mundane lives. His reputation as the most stylish of the new Australian directors was built on his charting of that country's landscape and cultural oddities with a sense of wonder. In 1977, he directed *The Last Wave*, starring Richard Chamberlain as a lawyer haunted by recurring dreams. He then wrote and directed *The Plumber* (1978), an unusual black comedy made for television that won the Australian Sammy Award for Best Writer (Television Plays) and Best Television Play.

Weir's next film, *Gallipoli*, the story of two Australian youths caught up in the idealistic fervor of World War I, swept the Australian Film Institute Awards and became a worldwide box office success. In 1983, Weir reunited with his *Gallipoli* star Mel Gibson for *The Year of Living Dangerously*, which also starred Sigourney Weaver and Linda Hunt. Hunt won an Academy Award for Best Supporting Actress for her memorable work in the film.

In 1985, Weir directed Harrison Ford in *Witness*, the haunting thriller in which a young Amish boy witnesses a murder, sparking a clash of cultures within his community. The film received eight Academy Award nominations, including Best Picture and a Best Direction nomination for Weir. In 1986, Weir directed *The Mosquito Coast*, again starring Harrison Ford.

Weir received an Oscar nomination in 1991 for the screenplay of his romantic comedy *Green Card*, starring Gerard Depardieu and Andie MacDowell. In 1990 he directed *Dead Poets Society*, which earned him an Oscar nomination for Best Director, as well as the BAFTA Award for Best Picture and Italy's Donatello Award for Best Direction. In 1993, he directed *Fearless*, a drama about people's varying reactions to tragedy and loss, which starred Jeff Bridges, Rosie Perez, Isabella Rossellini, and John Turturro.

In 1998 Weir directed *The Truman Show*, which starred Jim Carrey as Truman Burbank, the unwitting star of the longest-running, most popular documentary–soap opera in history. The critically acclaimed film was nominated for three Academy Awards, including one for Weir as Best Director, Ed Harris as Best Actor in a Supporting Role, and Andrew Niccol for Best Screenplay Written Directly for the Screen. *The Truman Show* also earned six Golden Globe nominations, including a Best Director nomination for Weir and a Golden Globe win for Jim Carrey, as Best Actor in a Motion Picture Drama. In addition, Weir was honored by BAFTA with the David Lean Award for Direction for the film and received a nomination of Outstanding Directorial Achievement in Theatrical Direction from the Directors Guild of America.

Since this nomination, Weir has directed *Master and Commander: The Far Side of the World*, which was nominated for ten Academy Awards, including Best Picture and Best Director. For this film, Weir won the BAFTA David Lean Award for Direction and received another nomination from the Directors Guild of America.

Robert Zemeckis, *Forrest Gump* (1995)

Robert Zemeckis was born and raised on the south side of Chicago, and began making films with an 8mm camera while in high school. He attended Northern Illinois University before transferring to the University of Southern California School of Cinema. After winning a Student Academy award for his film *Field of Honor*, Robert showed the film to directors Steven Spielberg and John Milius. Later the filmmakers made it possible for Robert and his USC writing partner Bob Gale to get a development deal for their original screenplay *1941*, which Spielberg chose to direct. Robert made his directorial debut in 1978 with a screenplay he cowrote with Bob Gale, *I Wanna Hold Your Hand*. The two teamed again to write *Used Cars*, which Robert also directed. He has also directed several projects for small screen, including an episode of Steven Spielberg's *Amazing Stories* and an episode for HBO's *Tales from the Crypt*, on which he also serves as an executive producer. He executively produced and directed a pilot episode of the CBS series *Johnny Bago*, a series he helped create. Robert's third feature film was *Romancing the Stone*, followed by *Back to the Future*, *Who Framed Roger Rabbit?* (for which he received a DGA Award nomination), *Back to the Future Part II*, *Back to the Future Part III*, *Death Becomes Her*, and the sci-fi drama *Contact*, which all achieved worldwide grosses in excess of $2 billion.

Forrest Gump (1994) won the DGA Award for Outstanding Directorial Achievement, as well as garnering the Academy Awards for Best Picture and Best Actor, and NATO ShoWest Director of the Year. The film earned in excess of $600 million worldwide. Zemeckis utilized the latest technological wizardry, as he had done with his earlier films, to tell the story of the amiable *Forrest Gump* as his life crisscrosses in and out of some of the nation's most significant events and he interacts with some of the most significant people.

Zemeckis took a turn directing for the small screen again, when he executive produced and directed *The Pursuit of Happiness*, a feature-length documentary on the influence and effect of drugs and alcohol on society in the twentieth century, for Showtime.

More recent productions for Zemeckis have included *Cast Away* and *The Polar Express*.

An obvious proponent of using technology to enhance the creative aspects of films, Zemeckis is also extremely concerned with how the current development of new technologies will affect artists in the coming years. Because of this concern, Zemeckis was an avid supporter of the Artists Rights Foundation.

The Directors Guild of America
Nominees and Winners

*E*ach year since 1948, the members of the Directors Guild of America have bestowed an award on the film director whose theatrical feature has been judged as the most distinguished of that year. In the following listing, both winners and nominees are cited, with this exception: from 1948–1952, quarterly as well as annual winners were announced; for these years only, the nominees in each quarter are not included. Actual winners are indicated in bold.

1948–49 Quarter	Howard Hawks	Red River
1948–49 Quarter	Anatole Litvak	The Snake Pit
1948–49 Quarter	Fred Zinnemann	The Search
1948–49 Winner	**Joseph L. Mankiewicz**	**A Letter to Three Wives**
1949–50 Quarter	Carol Reed	The Third Man
1949–50 Quarter	Mark Robson	Champion
1949–50 Quarter	Alfred Werker	Lost Boundaries
1949–50 Winner	**Robert Rossen**	**All the King's Men**
1950–51 Quarter	John Huston	The Asphalt Jungle
1950–51 Quarter	Vincente Minnelli	Father's Little Dividend
1950–51 Quarter	Billy Wilder	Sunset Boulevard
1950–51 Winner	**Joseph L. Mankiewicz**	**All About Eve**
1951 Quarter	Alfred Hitchcock	Strangers on a Train
1951 Quarter	Vincente Minnelli	An American in Paris
1951 Winner	**George Stevens**	**A Place in the Sun**
1951	László Benedek	Death of a Salesman
1951	Michael Gordon	Cyrano de Bergerac
1951	Elia Kazan	A Streetcar Named Desire
1951	Henry King	David and Bathsheba
1951	Mervyn LeRoy	Quo Vadis
1951	Anatole Litvak	Decision before Dawn
1951	George Sidney	Showboat
1951	Richard Thorpe	The Great Caruso
1951	William Wyler	Detective Story
1952 Quarter	Charles Crichton	The Lavender Hill Mob
1952 Quarter	Joseph L. Mankiewicz	Five Fingers
1952 Quarter	Fred Zinnemann	High Noon

1952 Winner	**John Ford**	**The Quiet Man**
1952	George Cukor	Pat and Mike
1952	Michael Curtiz	I'll See You in My Dreams
1952	Cecil B. DeMille	The Greatest Show on Earth
1952	Stanley Donen	Singin' in the Rain (Codirector)
1952	Gene Kelly	Singin' in the Rain (Codirector)
1952	Hugo Fregonese	My Six Convicts
1952	Howard Hawks	The Big Sky
1952	Elia Kazan	Viva Zapata!
1952	Henry King	The Snows of Kilimanjaro
1952	Akira Kurosawa	Rashômon
1952	Albert Lewin	Pandora and the Flying Dutchman
1952	Vincente Minnelli	The Bad and the Beautiful
1952	George Sidney	Scaramouche
1952	Richard Thorpe	Ivanhoe
1952	Charles Vidor	Hans Christian Andersen
1953 Finalist	George Stevens	Shane
1953 Finalist	Charles Walters	Lili
1953 Finalist	Billy Wilder	Stalag 17
1953 Finalist	William Wyler	Roman Holiday
1953 Winner	**Fred Zinnemann**	**From Here to Eternity**
1953	Melvin Frank	Above and Beyond (Codirector)
1953	Norman Panama	Above and Beyond (Codirector)
1953	Henry Koster	The Robe
1953	Walter Lang	Call Me Madam
1953	Joseph L. Mankiewicz	Julius Caesar
1953	Daniel Mann	Come Back, Little Sheba
1953	Jean Negulesco	Titanic
1953	George Sidney	Young Bess
1954 Finalist	Alfred Hitchcock	Rear Window
1954 Finalist	George Seaton	The Country Girl
1954 Finalist	William Wellman	The High and the Mighty
1954 Finalist	Billy Wilder	Sabrina
1954 Winner	**Elia Kazan**	**On the Waterfront**
1954	George Cukor	A Star Is Born
1954	Edward Dmytryk	The Caine Mutiny
1954	Stanley Donen	Seven Brides for Seven Brothers
1954	Melvin Frank	Knock on Wood (Codirector)
1954	Norman Panama	Knock on Wood (Codirector)
1954	Samuel Fuller	Hell and High Water
1954	Alfred Hitchcock	Dial M for Murder
1954	Henry King	King of the Khyber Rifles
1954	Anthony Mann	The Glenn Miller Story
1954	Jean Negulesco	Three Coins in the Fountain
1954	Don Siegel	Riot in Cell Block 11
1954	Robert E. Wise	Executive Suite
1955 Finalist	John Ford	Mister Roberts (Codirector)

1955 Finalist	Mervyn LeRoy	Mister Roberts (Codirector)
1955 Finalist	Elia Kazan	East of Eden
1955 Finalist	Joshua Logan	Picnic
1955 Finalist	John Sturges	Bad Day at Black Rock
1955 Winner	**Delbert Mann**	**Marty**
1955	Richard Brooks	The Blackboard Jungle
1955	John Ford	The Long Gray Line
1955	Henry Koster	A Man Called Peter
1955	Daniel Mann	The Rose Tattoo
1955	Mark Robson	The Bridges of Toko-Ri
1955	Charles Vidor	Love Me or Leave Me
1955	Billy Wilder	The Seven Year Itch
1956 Finalist	John Ford	The Searchers
1956 Finalist	Alfred Hitchcock	The Man Who Knew Too Much
1956 Finalist	Alfred Hitchcock	The Trouble with Harry
1956 Finalist	Nunnally Johnson	The Man in the Gray Flannel Suit
1956 Finalist	Henry King	Carousel
1956 Finalist	Walter Lang	The King and I
1956 Finalist	Carol Reed	Trapeze
1956 Finalist	Robert Rossen	Alexander the Great
1956 Finalist	Roy Rowland	Meet Me in Las Vegas
1956 Finalist	George Sidney	The Eddy Duchin Story
1956 Winner	**George Stevens**	**Giant**
1956	Michael Anderson	Around the World in 80 Days
1956	John Huston	Moby Dick
1956	Joshua Logan	Bus Stop
1956	Daniel Mann	Teahouse of the August Moon
1956	King Vidor	War and Peace
1956	Robert E. Wise	Somebody Up There Likes Me
1956	William Wyler	Friendly Persuasion
1957 Finalist	Joshua Logan	Sayonara
1957 Finalist	Sidney Lumet	Twelve Angry Men
1957 Finalist	Mark Robson	Peyton Place
1957 Finalist	Billy Wilder	Witness for the Prosecution
1957 Winner	**David Lean**	**The Bridge on the River Kwai**
1957	George Cukor	Les Girls
1957	Stanley Donen	Funny Face
1957	José Ferrer	The Great Man
1957	John Huston	Heaven Knows, Mr. Allison
1957	Elia Kazan	A Face in the Crowd
1957	Stanley Kramer	The Pride and the Passion
1957	Anthony Mann	Men in War
1957	Leo McCarey	An Affair to Remember
1957	Robert Mulligan	Fear Strikes Out
1957	John Sturges	Gunfight at the O.K. Corral
1957	Billy Wilder	Love in the Afternoon
1957	Fred Zinnemann	A Hatful of Rain

1958 Finalist	Richard Brooks	Cat on a Hot Tin Roof
1958 Finalist	Stanley Kramer	The Defiant Ones
1958 Finalist	Mark Robson	The Inn of the Sixth Happiness
1958 Finalist	Robert E. Wise	I Want to Live!
1958 Winner	**Vincente Minnelli**	**Gigi**
1958	Stanley Donen	Damn Yankees (Codirector)
1958	George Abbott	Damn Yankees (Codirector)
1958	Richard Brooks	The Brothers Karamazov
1958	Delmer Daves	Cowboy
1958	Edward Dmytryk	The Young Lions
1958	Richard Fleischer	The Vikings
1958	Alfred Hitchcock	Vertigo
1958	Martin Ritt	The Long Hot Summer
1958	George Seaton	Teacher's Pet
1958	William Wyler	The Big Country
1959 Finalist	Otto Preminger	Anatomy of a Murder
1959 Finalist	George Stevens	The Diary of Anne Frank
1959 Finalist	Billy Wilder	Some Like It Hot
1959 Finalist	Fred Zinnemann	The Nun's Story
1959 Winner	**William Wyler**	**Ben-Hur**
1959	Charles Barton	The Shaggy Dog
1959	Frank Capra	A Hole in the Head
1959	Richard Fleischer	Compulsion
1959	John Ford	The Horse Soldiers
1959	Howard Hawks	Rio Bravo
1959	Alfred Hitchcock	North by Northwest
1959	Leo McCarey	Rally Round the Flag, Boys!
1959	Douglas Sirk	Imitation of Life
1960 Finalist	Jack Cardiff	Sons and Lovers
1960 Finalist	Alfred Hitchcock	Psycho
1960 Finalist	Vincente Minnelli	The Bells Are Ringing
1960 Finalist	Fred Zinnemann	The Sundowners
1960 Winner	**Billy Wilder**	**The Apartment**
1960	Richard Brooks	Elmer Gantry
1960	Vincent J. Donehue	Sunrise at Campobello
1960	Lewis Gilbert	Sink the Bismarck!
1960	Walter Lang	Can-Can
1960	Delbert Mann	The Dark at the Top of the Stairs
1960	Vincente Minnelli	Home from the Hill
1960	Carol Reed	Our Man in Havana
1960	Alain Resnais	Hiroshima, Mon Amour
1960	Charles Walters	Please Don't Eat the Daisies
1961 Finalist	Blake Edwards	Breakfast at Tiffany's
1961 Finalist	Stanley Kramer	Judgment at Nuremberg
1961 Finalist	Robert Rossen	The Hustler
1961 Finalist	J. Lee Thompson	The Guns of Navarone
1961 Winner	**Jerome Robbins**	**West Side Story (Codirector)**

1961 Winner	**Robert E. Wise**	**West Side Story (Codirector)**
1961	Marlon Brando	One-Eyed Jacks
1961	Frank Capra	Pocketful of Miracles
1961	Jack Clayton	The Innocents
1961	Peter Glenville	Summer and Smoke
1961	John Huston	The Misfits
1961	Elia Kazan	Splendor in the Grass
1961	Henry Koster	Flower Drum Song
1961	Mervyn LeRoy	A Majority of One
1961	Philip Leacock	Hand in Hand
1961	Joshua Logan	Fanny
1961	Anthony Mann	El Cid
1961	Robert Mulligan	The Great Imposter
1961	Daniel Petrie	A Raisin in the Sun
1961	Robert Stevenson	The Absent-Minded Professor
1961	Peter Ustinov	Romanoff and Juliet
1961	William Wyler	The Children's Hour
1962 Finalist	Bernhard Wicki	The Longest Day (Codirector)
1962 Finalist	Ken Annakin	The Longest Day (Codirector)
1962 Finalist	Andrew Marton	The Longest Day (Codirector)
1962 Finalist	John Frankenheimer	The Manchurian Candidate
1962 Finalist	Pietro Germi	Divorce, Italian Style
1962 Finalist	John Huston	Freud
1962 Finalist	Stanley Kubrick	Lolita
1962 Finalist	Sidney Lumet	Long Day's Journey into Night
1962 Finalist	Peter Ustinov	Billy Budd
1962 Winner	**David Lean**	**Lawrence of Arabia**
1962	Robert Aldrich	Whatever Happened to Baby Jane?
1962	Morton DaCosta	The Music Man
1962	John Frankenheimer	Birdman of Alcatraz
1962	Lewis Milestone	Mutiny on the Bounty
1962	Robert Mulligan	To Kill a Mockingbird
1962	Ralph Nelson	Requiem for a Heavyweight
1962	Arthur Penn	The Miracle Worker
1962	Tony Richardson	A Taste of Honey
1963 Winner	**Tony Richardson**	**Tom Jones**
1963	Federico Fellini	Fellini's 8½
1963	Elia Kazan	America, America
1963	Ralph Nelson	Lilies of the Field
1963	Martin Ritt	Hud
1964 Winner	**George Cukor**	**My Fair Lady**
1964	Peter Glenville	Becket
1964	John Huston	Night of the Iguana
1964	Stanley Kubrick	Dr. Strangelove
1964	Robert Stevenson	Mary Poppins
1965 Winner	**Robert E. Wise**	**The Sound of Music**
1965	Sidney Furie	The Ipcress File

1965	Sidney Lumet	The Pawnbroker
1965	John Schlesinger	Darling
1965	Elliot Silverstein	Cat Ballou
1966 Winner	**Fred Zinnemann**	**A Man for All Seasons**
1966	Richard Brooks	The Professionals
1966	John Frankenheimer	Grand Prix
1966	Lewis Gilbert	Alfie
1966	James Hill	Born Free
1966	Norman Jewison	The Russians Are Coming, The Russians Are Coming
1966	Claude Lelouch	A Man and a Woman
1966	Silvio Narizzano	Georgy Girl
1966	Mike Nichols	Who's Afraid of Virginia Woolf?
1966	Robert E. Wise	The Sand Pebbles
1967 Finalist	Richard Brooks	In Cold Blood
1967 Finalist	Norman Jewison	In the Heat of the Night
1967 Finalist	Stanley Kramer	Guess Who's Coming to Dinner
1967 Finalist	Arthur Penn	Bonnie and Clyde
1967 Winner	**Mike Nichols**	**The Graduate**
1967	Robert Aldrich	The Dirty Dozen
1967	James Clavell	To Sir with Love
1967	Stanley Donen	Two for the Road
1967	Stuart Rosenberg	Cool Hand Luke
1967	Joseph Strick	Ulysses
1968 Finalist	Stanley Kubrick	2001: A Space Odyssey
1968 Finalist	Paul Newman	Rachel, Rachel
1968 Finalist	William Wyler	Funny Girl
1968	Carol Reed	Oliver!
1968 Winner	**Anthony Harvey**	**The Lion in Winter**
1968	Paul Almond	Isabel
1968	Jirí Menzel	Closely Watched Trains
1968	Roman Polanski	Rosemary's Baby
1968	Gene Saks	The Odd Couple
1968	Franco Zeffirelli	Romeo and Juliet
1969 Finalist	Costa Gravas	Z
1969 Finalist	George Roy Hill	Butch Cassidy and the Sundance Kid
1969 Finalist	Dennis Hopper	Easy Rider
1969 Finalist	Sydney Pollack	They Shoot Horses, Don't They?
1969 Winner	**John Schlesinger**	**Midnight Cowboy**
1969	Richard Attenborough	Oh, What a Lovely War
1969	Gene Kelly	Hello, Dolly
1969	Sam Peckinpah	The Wild Bunch
1969	Larry Peerce	Goodbye, Columbus
1969	Haskell Wexler	Medium Cool
1970 Winner	**Franklin Schaffner**	**Patton**
1970	Robert Altman	M★A★S★H
1970	Arthur Hiller	Love Story

1970	David Lean	Ryan's Daughter
1970	Bob Rafelson	Five Easy Pieces
1971 Winner	**William Friedkin**	**The French Connection**
1971	Peter Bogdanovich	The Last Picture Show
1971	Stanley Kubrick	A Clockwork Orange
1971	Robert Mulligan	Summer of '42
1971	John Schlesinger	Sunday, Bloody Sunday
1972	Bob Fosse	Cabaret
1972 Winner	**Francis Ford Coppola**	**The Godfather**
1972	John Boorman	Deliverance
1972	George Roy Hill	Slaughterhouse Five
1972	Martin Ritt	Sounder
1973 Winner	**George Roy Hill**	**The Sting**
1973	Bernardo Bertolucci	Last Tango in Paris
1973	William Friedkin	The Exorcist
1973	George Lucas	American Graffiti
1973	Sidney Lumet	Serpico
1974 Winner	**Francis Ford Coppola**	**The Godfather Part II**
1974	Francis Ford Coppola	The Conversation
1974	Bob Fosse	Lenny
1974	Sidney Lumet	Murder on the Orient Express
1974	Roman Polanski	Chinatown
1975 Winner	**Milos Forman**	**One Flew over the Cuckoo's Nest**
1975	Robert Altman	Nashville
1975	Stanley Kubrick	Barry Lyndon
1975	Sidney Lumet	Dog Day Afternoon
1975	Steven Spielberg	Jaws
1976 Winner	**John G. Avildsen**	**Rocky**
1976	Sidney Lumet	Network
1976	Alan J. Pakula	All the President's Men
1976	Martin Scorsese	Taxi Driver
1976	Lina Wertmuller	Seven Beauties
1977 Winner	**Woody Allen**	**Annie Hall**
1977	George Lucas	Star Wars
1977	Herbert Ross	The Turning Point
1977	Steven Spielberg	Close Encounters of the Third Kind
1977	Fred Zinnemann	Julia
1978 Winner	**Michael Cimino**	**The Deer Hunter**
1978	Hal Ashby	Coming Home
1978	Warren Beatty	Heaven Can Wait (Codirector)
1978	Buck Henry	Heaven Can Wait (Codirector)
1978	Paul Mazursky	An Unmarried Woman
1978	Alan Parker	Midnight Express
1979 Winner	**Robert Benton**	**Kramer vs. Kramer**
1979	Woody Allen	Manhattan
1979	James Bridges	The China Syndrome
1979	Francis Ford Coppola	Apocalypse Now

1979	Peter Yates	Breaking Away
1980 Winner	**Robert Redford**	**Ordinary People**
1980	Michael Apted	Coal Miner's Daughter
1980	David Lynch	The Elephant Man
1980	Richard Rush	The Stunt Man
1980	Martin Scorsese	Raging Bull
1981 Winner	**Warren Beatty**	**Reds**
1981	Hugh Hudson	Chariots of Fire
1981	Louis Malle	Atlantic City
1981	Mark Rydell	On Golden Pond
1981	Steven Spielberg	Raiders of the Lost Ark
1982 Winner	**Richard Attenborough**	**Gandhi**
1982	Taylor Hackford	An Officer and a Gentleman
1982	Wolfgang Petersen	Das Boot
1982	Sydney Pollack	Tootsie
1982	Steven Spielberg	E.T.: The Extra-Terrestrial
1983 Winner	**James L. Brooks**	**Terms of Endearment**
1983	Bruce Beresford	Tender Mercies
1983	Ingmar Bergman	Fanny and Alexander
1983	Lawrence Kasdan	The Big Chill
1983	Philip Kaufman	The Right Stuff
1984 Winner	**Milos Forman**	**Amadeus**
1984	Robert Benton	Places in the Heart
1984	Norman Jewison	A Soldier's Story
1984	Roland Joffé	The Killing Fields
1984	David Lean	A Passage to India
1985	Sydney Pollack	Out of Africa
1985 Winner	**Steven Spielberg**	**The Color Purple**
1985	Ron Howard	Cocoon
1985	John Huston	Prizzi's Honor
1985	Peter Weir	Witness
1986 Winner	**Oliver Stone**	**Platoon**
1986	Woody Allen	Hannah and Her Sisters
1986	Randa Haines	Children of a Lesser God
1986	James Ivory	A Room with a View
1986	Rob Reiner	Stand by Me
1987 Winner	**Bernardo Bertolucci**	**The Last Emperor**
1987	James L. Brooks	Broadcast News
1987	Lasse Hallström	My Life As a Dog
1987	Adrian Lyne	Fatal Attraction
1987	Steven Spielberg	Empire of the Sun
1988 Winner	**Barry Levinson**	**Rain Man**
1988	Charles Crichton	A Fish Called Wanda
1988	Mike Nichols	Working Girl
1988	Alan Parker	Mississippi Burning
1988	Robert Zemeckis	Who Framed Roger Rabbit?
1989 Winner	**Oliver Stone**	**Born on the Fourth of July**

1989	Woody Allen	Crimes and Misdemeanors
1989	Rob Reiner	When Harry Met Sally . . .
1989	Phil Alden Robinson	Field of Dreams
1989	Peter Weir	Dead Poets Society
1990 Winner	**Kevin Costner**	**Dances with Wolves**
1990	Francis Ford Coppola	The Godfather Part III
1990	Barry Levinson	Avalon
1990	Martin Scorsese	Goodfellas
1990	Giuseppe Tornatore	Cinema Paradiso
1991 Winner	**Jonathan Demme**	**The Silence of the Lambs**
1991	Barry Levinson	Bugsy
1991	Ridley Scott	Thelma and Louise
1991	Oliver Stone	JFK
1991	Barbra Streisand	The Prince of Tides
1992 Winner	**Clint Eastwood**	**Unforgiven**
1992	Robert Altman	The Player
1992	James Ivory	Howards End
1992	Neil Jordan	The Crying Game
1992	Rob Reiner	A Few Good Men
1993 Winner	**Steven Spielberg**	**Schindler's List**
1993	Jane Campion	The Piano
1993	Andrew Davis	The Fugitive
1993	James Ivory	The Remains of the Day
1993	Martin Scorsese	The Age of Innocence
1994 Winner	**Robert Zemeckis**	**Forrest Gump**
1994	Frank Darabont	The Shawshank Redemption
1994	Mike Newell	Four Weddings and a Funeral
1994	Robert Redford	Quiz Show
1994	Quentin Tarantino	Pulp Fiction
1995	Mel Gibson	Braveheart
1995 Winner	**Ron Howard**	**Apollo 13**
1995	Mike Figgis	Leaving Las Vegas
1995	Ang Lee	Sense and Sensibility
1995	Michael Radford	Il Postino
1996 Winner	**Anthony Minghella**	**The English Patient**
1996	Joel Coen	Fargo
1996	Cameron Crowe	Jerry Maguire
1996	Scott Hicks	Shine
1996	Mike Leigh	Secrets & Lies
1997 Winner	**James Cameron**	**Titanic**
1997	James L. Brooks	As Good As It Gets
1997	Curtis Hanson	L.A. Confidential
1997	Steven Spielberg	Amistad
1997	Gus Van Sant	Good Will Hunting
1998 Winner	**Steven Spielberg**	**Saving Private Ryan**
1998	John Madden	Shakespeare in Love
1998	Peter Weir	The Truman Show

1998	Roberto Benigni	Life Is Beautiful
1998	Terrence Malick	The Thin Red Line
1999	Frank Darabont	The Green Mile
1999	Spike Jonze	Being John Malkovich
1999	Michael Mann	The Insider
1999 Winner	**Sam Mendes**	**American Beauty**
1999	M. Night Shyamalan	The Sixth Sense
2000	Cameron Crowe	Almost Famous
2000 Winner	**Ang Lee**	**Crouching Tiger, Hidden Dragon**
2000	Ridley Scott	Gladiator
2000	Steven Soderbergh	Erin Brockovich
2000	Steven Soderbergh	Traffic
2001 Winner	**Ron Howard**	**A Beautiful Mind**
2001	Peter Jackson	The Lord of the Rings: The Fellowship of the Ring
2001	Baz Luhrmann	Moulin Rouge
2001	Christopher Nolan	Memento
2001	Ridley Scott	Black Hawk Down
2002	Stephen Daldry	The Hours
2002	Peter Jackson	The Lord of the Rings: The Two Towers
2002 Winner	**Rob Marshall**	**Chicago**
2002	Roman Polanski	The Pianist
2002	Martin Scorsese	Gangs of New York
2003	Sofia Coppola	Lost in Translation
2003	Clint Eastwood	Mystic River
2003 Winner	**Peter Jackson**	**The Lord of the Rings: The Return of the King**
2003	Gary Ross	Seabiscuit
2003	Peter Weir	Master and Commander: The Far Side of the World
2004 Winner	**Clint Eastwood**	**Million Dollar Baby**
2004	Marc Forster	Finding Neverland
2004	Taylor Hackford	Ray
2004	Alexander Payne	Sideways
2004	Martin Scorsese	The Aviator

Elia Kazan: On What Makes a Director

$\mathcal{S}$ome of you may have heard of the auteur theory. That concept is partly a critic's plaything. Something for them to spat over and use to fill a column. But it has its point, and that point is simply that the director is the true author of the film. The director TELLS the film, using a vocabulary the lesser part of which is an arrangement of words.

A screenplay's worth has to be measured less by its language than by its architecture and how that dramatizes the theme. A screenplay, we directors soon enough learn, is not a piece of writing as much as it is a construction. We learn to feel for the skeleton under the skin of words.

Meyerhold, the great Russian stage director, said that words were the decoration on the skirts of action. He was talking about theater, but I've always thought his observations applied more aptly to film.

It occurred to me when I was considering what to say here that since you all don't see directors—it's unique for Wesleyan to have a filmmaker standing where I am after a showing of work, while you have novelists, historians, poets, and writers of various kinds of studies living among you—that it might be fun if I were to try to list for you and for my own sport what a film director needs to know and what personal characteristics and attributes he might advantageously possess.

How must he educate himself?

Of what skills is his craft made?

What kind of a man must he be?

Of course, I'm talking about a book-length subject. Stay easy, I'm not going to read a book to you tonight. I will merely try to list the fields of knowledge necessary to him, and later those personal qualities he might happily possess, give them to you as one might give chapter headings, section leads, first sentences of paragraphs, without elaboration.

Here we go.

Literature. Of course. All periods, all languages, all forms. Naturally a film director is better equipped if he's well read. Jack Ford, who introduced himself with the words, "I make Westerns," was an extremely well- and widely read man.

The literature of the theater. For one thing, so the film director will appreciate the difference from film, he should also study the classic theater literature for construction, for exposition of theme, for the means of characterization, for dramatic poetry, for the elements of unity, especially that unity created by pointing to climax and then for climax as the essential and final embodiment of the theme.

The craft of screen dramaturgy. Every director, even in those rare instances when he doesn't work with a writer or two—Fellini works with a squadron—must take responsibility for the screenplay. He has not only to guide rewriting but to eliminate what's unnecessary, cover faults, appreciate nonverbal possibilities, ensure correct structure, have a sense of screen time, how much will elapse, in what places, for what purposes. Robert Frost's "Tell Everything a Little Faster" applies to all expositional parts. In the climaxes, time is unrealistically extended, "stretched," usually by close-ups.

The film director knows that beneath the surface of his screenplay there is a subtext, a calendar of intentions and feelings and inner events. What appears to be happening, he soon learns, is rarely what is happening. This subtext is one of the film director's most valuable tools. It is what he directs. You will rarely see a veteran director holding a script as he works—or even looking at it. Beginners, yes.

Most directors' goal today is to write their own scripts. But that is our oldest tradition. Chaplin would hear that Griffith Park had been flooded by a heavy rainfall. Packing his crew, his standby actors, and his equipment in a few cars, he would rush there, making up the story of the two-reel comedy en route, the details on the spot.

The director of films should know comedy as well as drama. Jack Ford used to call most parts "comics." He meant, I suppose, a way of looking at people without false sentiment, through an objectivity that deflated false heroics and undercut self-favoring and finally revealed a saving humor in the most tense moments. "The Human Comedy," another Frenchman called it. The fact that Billy Wilder is always amusing doesn't make his films less serious.

Quite simply, the screen director must know either by training or by instinct how to feed a joke and how to score with it, how to anticipate and protect laughs. He might well study Chaplin and the other great two-reel-comedy makers for what are called sight gags, nonverbal laughs, amusement derived from "business," stunts and moves, and simply from funny faces and odd bodies. This vulgar foundation—the banana peel and the custard pie—are basic to our craft and part of its health. Wyler and Stevens began by making two-reel comedies, and I seem to remember Capra did too.

American film directors would do well to know our vaudeville traditions. Just as Fellini adored the clowns, music hall performers, and the circuses of his country and paid them homage again and again in his work, our filmmaker would do well to study magic. I believe some of the wonderful cuts in *Citizen Kane* came from the fact that Welles was a practicing magician and so understood the drama of sudden unexpected appearances and the startling change. Think too of Bergman, how often he uses magicians and sleight of hand.

The director should know opera, its effects and its absurdities, a subject in which Bernardo Bertolucci is schooled. He should know the American musical stage and its tradition, but, even more important, the great American musical films. He must not look down on these; we love them for very good reasons.

Our man should know acrobatics, the art of juggling and tumbling, the techniques of the wry comic song. The techniques of the Commedia dell'arte are used, it seems to me, in a film called *O Lucky Man!* Lindsay Anderson's master. Bertolt Brecht adored the Berlin satirical cabaret of his time and adapted their techniques.

Let's move faster because it's endless.

Painting and sculpture; their history, their revolutions and counterrevolutions.

The painters of the Italian Renaissance used their mistresses as models for the Madonna, so who can blame a film director for using his girlfriend in a leading role—unless she does a bad job.

Many painters have worked in the theater. Bakst, Picasso, Aronson, and Matisse come to mind. More will. Here, we are still with Disney.

Which brings us to dance. In my opinion, it's a considerable asset if the director's knowledge here is not only theoretical but practical and personal. Dance is an essential part of a screen director's education. It's a great advantage for him if he can "move." It will help him not only to move actors but move the camera. The film director, ideally, should be as able as a choreographer, quite literally so. I don't mean the tango in Bertolucci's *Last* or the high school gym dance in *American Graffiti* as much as I do the baffle scenes in D. W. Griffith's *Birth of a Nation*, which are pure choreography and very beautiful. Look at Ford's cavalry charges that way. Or Jim Cagney's dance of death on the long steps in *The Roaring Twenties*.

The film director must know music, classic, so-called—too much of an umbrella word, that! Let us say of all periods. And as with sculpture and painting, he must know what social situations and currents the music came out of.

Of course he must be particularly INTO the music of his own day—acid rock, Latin rock, blues and jazz, pop, Tin Pan Alley, barbershop, corn, country, Chicago, New Orleans, Nashville.

The film director should know the history of stage scenery, its development from background to environment and so to the settings INSIDE WHICH films are played out. Notice I stress INSIDE WHICH as opposed to IN FRONT OF. The construction of scenery for filmmaking was traditionally the work of architects. The film director must study, from life, from newspaper clippings, and from his own photographs, dramatic environments and particularly how they affect behavior.

I recommend to every young director that he start his own collection of clippings and photographs and, if he's able, his own sketches.

The film director must know costuming, its history through all periods, its techniques, and what it can be as expression. Again, life is a prime source. We learn to study, as we enter each place, each room, how the people there have chosen to present themselves. "How he comes on," we say.

Costuming in films is so expressive a means that it is inevitably the basic choice of the director. Visconti is brilliant here. So is Bergman in a more modest vein. The best way to study this again is to notice how people dress as an expression of what they wish to gain from any occasion, what their intention is. Study your husband, study your wife, how their attire is an expression of each day's mood and hope, their good days, their days of low confidence, their time of stress and how it shows in clothing.

Lighting. Of course. The various natural effects, the cross light of morning, the heavy flat top light of midday—avoid it except for an effect—the magic hour, so called by cameramen, dusk. How do they affect mood? Obvious. We know it in life. How do they affect behavior? Study that. Five o'clock is a low time; let's have a drink! Directors choose the time of day for certain scenes with these expressive values in mind. The master here is Jack Ford, who used to plan his shots within a sequence to best use certain natural effects that he could not create but could very advantageously wait for.

Colors? Their psychological effect. So obvious I will not expand. Favorite colors. Faded colors. The living grays. In *Baby Doll* you saw a master cameraman, Boris Kaufman, making great use of white on white, to help describe the washed out Southern whites.

And of course, there are the instruments which catch all and should dramatize all; the tools the director speaks through, the CAMERA and the TAPE RECORDER. The film director obviously must know the camera and its lenses, which lens creates which effect, which one lies, which one tells the cruel truth. Which filters bring out the clouds. The director must know the various speeds at which the camera can roll and especially the effects of small variations in speed.

He must also know the various camera mountings, the cranes and the dollies and the possible moves he can make, the configurations in space through which he can pass this instrument. He must know the zoom well enough so he won't use it or almost never.

He should be intimately acquainted with the tape recorder. Andy Warhol carries one everywhere he goes. Practice "bugging" yourself and your friends. Notice how often speech overlaps.

The film director must understand the weather, how it's made and where, how it moves, its warning signs, its crises, the kind of clouds and what they mean. Remember the clouds in *Shane*. He must know weather as dramatic expression, be on the alert to capitalize on changes in weather as one of his means. He must study how heat and cold, rain and snow, a soft breeze, a driving wind affect people and whether it's true that there are more expressions of group rage during a long hot summer and why.

The film director should know the city, ancient and modern, but particularly his city, the one he loves like De Seta loves Naples; Fellini, Rimini; Bergman, his island; Ray, Calcutta; Renoir, the French countryside; Clair, the city of Paris. His city, its features, its operation, its substructure, its scenes behind the scenes, its functionaries, its police, firefighters, garbage collectors, post office workers, commuters and what they ride, its cathedrals, and its whorehouses.

The film directors must know the country—no, that's too general a term. He must know the mountains and the plains, the deserts of our great Southwest, the heavy, oily bottom soil of the Delta, the hills of New England. He must know the water off Marblehead and Old Orchard Beach, too cold for lingering, and the water off the Florida Keys, which invites dawdling. Again, these are means of expression that he has and among them he must make his choices. He must know how a breeze from a fan can animate a dead-looking set by stirring a curtain.

He must know the sea, firsthand, chance a shipwreck so he'll appreciate its power. He must know under the surface of the sea; it may occur to him, if he does, to play a scene there. He must have crossed our rivers and know the strength of their currents. He must have swum in our lakes and caught fish in our streams. You think I'm exaggerating. Why did old man Flaherty and his Missus spend at least a year in an environment before they exposed a foot of negative? While you're young, you aspiring directors, hitchhike our country!

And topography, the various trees, flowers, ground cover, grasses. And the subsurface, shale, sand, gravel, New England ledge, six feet of old riverbottom? What kind of man works each and how does it affect him?

Animals too. How they resemble human beings. How to direct a chicken to enter a room on cue. I had that problem once and I'm ashamed to tell you how I did it. What a cat might mean to a love scene. The symbolism of horses. The family life of the lion, how tender! The patience of a cow.

Of course, the film director should know acting, its history and its techniques. The more he knows about acting, the more at ease he will be with actors. At one period of his growth, he should force himself onstage or before the camera so he knows this experientially too. Some directors, and very famous ones, still fear actors instead of embracing them as comrades in a task. But by contrast, there is the great Jean Renoir, see him in *Rules of the Game*. And his follower and lover, Truffaut in *The Wild Child*, now in *Day for Night*.

The director must know how to stimulate, even inspire the actor. Needless to say, he must also know how to make an actor seem NOT to act. How to put him or her at their ease, bring them to that state of relaxation where their creative faculties are released.

The film director must understand the instrument known as the VOICE. He must also know SPEECH. And that they are not the same, as different as resonance and phrasing. He should also know the various regional accents of his country and what they tell about character.

All in all he must know enough in all these areas so his actors trust him completely. This is often achieved by giving the impression that any task he asks of them, he can perform, perhaps even better than they can. This may not be true, but it's not a bad impression to create.

The film director, of course, must be up on the psychology of behavior, "normal" and abnormal. He must know that they are linked, that one is often the extension or intensification of the other and that under certain stresses which the director will create within a scene as it's acted out, one kind of behavior can be seen becoming the other. And that is drama.

The film director must be prepared by knowledge and training to handle neurotics. Why? Because most actors are. Perhaps all. What makes it doubly interesting is that the film director often is. Stanley Kubrick won't get on a plane—well, maybe that isn't so neurotic. But we are all delicately balanced—isn't that a nice way to put it? Answer this: How many interesting people have you met who are not—a little?

Of course we work with the psychology of the audience. We know it differs from that of its individual members. In cutting films great comedy directors like Hawks and Preston Sturges allow for the group reactions they expect from the audience; they play on these. Hitchcock has made this his art.

The film director must be learned in the erotic arts. The best way here is through personal experience. But there is a history here, an artistic technique. Pornography is not looked down upon. The film director will admit to a natural interest in how other people do it. Boredom, cruelty, banality are the only sins. Our man, for instance, might study the Chinese erotic prints and those scenes on Greek vases of the Golden Age which museum curators hide.

Of course, the film director must be an authority, even an expert on the various attitudes of lovemaking, the postures and intertwining of the parts of the body, the expressive parts and those generally considered less expressive. He may well have, like Buñuel with feet, special fetishes. He is not concerned to hide these; rather he will probably express his inclinations with relish.

The director, here, may come to believe that suggestion is more erotic than show. Then study how to go about it.

Then there is war. Its weapons, its techniques, its machinery, its tactics, its history—oh my—

Where is the time to learn all this?

Do not think, as you were brought up to think, that education starts at six and stops at twenty-one, that we learn only from teachers, books, and classes. For us that is the least of it. The life of a film director is a totality and he learns as he lives. Everything is pertinent; there is nothing irrelevant or trivial. O Lucky Man, to have such a profession! Every experience leaves its residue of knowledge behind. Every book we read applies to us. Everything we see and hear, if we like it, we steal it. Nothing is irrelevant. It all belongs to us.

So history becomes a living subject, full of dramatic characters, not a bore about treaties and battles. Religion is fascinating as a kind of poetry expressing fear and loneliness and hope. The film director reads *The Golden Bough* because sympathetic magic and superstition interest him; these beliefs of the ancients and the savages parallel those of his own time's people. He studies ritual because ritual as a source of stage and screen mise-en-scene is an increasingly important source.

Economics a bore? Not to us. Consider the demoralization of people in a labor pool, the panic in currency, the reliance of a nation on imports and the leverage this gives the country supplying the needed imports. All these affect or can affect the characters and milieus with which our film is concerned. Consider the facts behind the drama of *On the Waterfront*. Wonder how we could have shown more of them.

The film director doesn't just eat. He studies food. He knows the meals of all nations and how they're served, how consumed, what the variations of taste are, the effect of the food, food as a soporific, food as an aphrodisiac, as a means of expression of character. Remember the scene in *Tom Jones*? *La Grande Bouffe*?

And of course, the film director tries to keep up with the flow of life around him, the contemporary issues, who's pressuring whom, who's winning, who's losing, how pressure shows in the politician's body and face and gestures. Inevitably, the director will be a visitor at night court. And he will not duck jury duty. He studies advertising and goes to "product meetings" and spies on those who make the ads that influence people. He watches talk shows and marvels how Jackie Susann peddles it. He keeps up on the moves, as near as he can read them, of the secret underground societies. And skyjacking, what's the solution? He talks to pilots. It's the perfect drama—that situation—no exit.

Travel. Yes. As much as he can. Let's not get into that.

Sports? The best directed shows on TV today are the professional football games. Why? Study them. You are shown not only the game from far and middle distance and close-up; you are shown the bench, the way the two coaches sweat it out, the rejected sub, Craig Morton, waiting for Staubach to be hurt and Woodall, does he really like Namath? Johnson, Snead? Watch the spectators too. Think how you might direct certain scenes playing with a ball, or swimming or sailing—even though that is nowhere indicated in the script. Or watch a ball game like Hepburn and Tracy in George Steven's film, *Woman of the Year!*

I've undoubtedly left out a great number of things and what I've left out is significant, no doubt, and describes some of my own shortcomings.

Oh! Of course, I've left out the most important thing. The subject the film director must know most about, know best of all, see in the greatest detail and in the most pitiless light with the greatest appreciation of the ambivalences at play is—what?

Right. Himself.

There is something of himself, after all, in every character he properly creates. He understands people truly through understanding himself truly.

The silent confessions he makes to himself are the greatest source of wisdom he has. And of tolerance for others. And for love, even that. There is the admission of hatred to awareness and its relief through understanding and a kind of resolution in brotherhood.

What kind of person must a film director train himself to be?

What qualities does he need? Here are a few. Those of—

A white hunter leading a safari into dangerous and unknown country;

A construction gang foreman, who knows his physical problems and their solutions and is ready, therefore, to insist on these solutions;

A psychoanalyst who keeps a patient functioning despite intolerable tensions and stresses, both professional and personal;

A hypnotist who works with the unconscious to achieve his ends;

A poet, a poet of the camera, able both to capture the decisive moment of Cartier Bresson or to wait all day like Paul Strand for a single shot which he makes with a bulky camera fixed on a tripod;

An outfielder for his legs. The director stands much of the day, dares not get tired, so he has strong legs. Think back and remember how the old-time directors dramatized themselves. By puttees, right.

The cunning of a trader in a Baghdad bazaar.

The firmness of an animal trainer. Obvious. Tigers!

A great host. At a sign from him fine food and heartwarming drink appear.

The kindness of an old-fashioned mother who forgives all.

The authority and sternness of her husband, the father, who forgives nothing, expects obedience without question, brooks no nonsense.

These alternatively.

The illusiveness of a jewel thief—no explanation, take my word for this one.

The blarney of a PR man, especially useful when the director is out in a strange and hostile location as I have many times been.

A very thick skin.

A very sensitive soul.

Simultaneously.

The patience, the persistence, the fortitude of a saint, the appreciation of pain, a taste for self-sacrifice, everything for the cause.

Cheeriness, jokes, playfulness, alternating with sternness, unwavering firmness. Pure doggedness.

An unwavering refusal to take less than he thinks right out of a scene, a performer, a co-worker, a member of his staff, himself.

Direction, finally, is the exertion of your will over other people, disguise it, gentle it, but that is the hard fact.

Above all: COURAGE. Courage, said Winston Churchill, is the greatest virtue; it makes all the others possible.

One final thing. The ability to say, "I am wrong," or "I was wrong." Not as easy as it sounds. But in many situations, these three words, honestly spoken, will save the day. They are the words, very often, that the actors struggling to give the director what he wants most need to hear from him. Those words, "I was wrong; let's try it another way," the ability to say them can be a lifesaver.

The director must accept the blame for everything. If the script stinks, he should have worked harder with the writers or himself before shooting. If the actor fails, the director failed him! Or made a mistake in choosing him. If the camera work is uninspired, whose idea was it to engage that cameraman? Or choose those setups? Even a costume after all—the director passed on it. The settings. The music, even the goddamn ads, why didn't he yell louder if he didn't like them? The director was there, wasn't he? Yes, he was there! He's always there!

That's why he gets all that money, to stand there, on that mound, unprotected, letting everybody shoot at him and deflecting the mortal fire from all the others who work with him.

The other people who work on a film can hide.

They have the director to hide behind.

And people deny the auteur theory!

After listening to me so patiently you have a perfect right now to ask, "Oh, come on, aren't you exaggerating to make some kind of point?"

Of course I'm exaggerating and it is to make a point.

But only a little exaggerating.

The fact is that a director from the moment a phone call gets him out of bed in the morning ("Rain today. What scene do you want to shoot?") until he escapes into the dark at the end of shooting to face, alone, the next day's problems, is called upon to answer an unrelenting string of questions, to make decision after decision in one after another of the fields I've listed. That's what a director is, the man with the answers.

Watch Truffaut playing Truffaut in *Day for Night*, watch him as he patiently, carefully, sometimes thoughtfully, other times very quickly, answers questions. You will see better than I can tell you how these answers keep his film going. Truffaut has caught our life on the set perfectly.

Do things get easier and simpler as you get older and have accumulated some or all of this savvy?

Not at all. The opposite. The more a director knows, the more he's aware how many different ways there are to do every film, every scene.

And the more he has to face that final awful limitation, not of knowledge but of character. Which is what? The final limitation and the most terrible one is the limitations of his own talent. You find, for instance, that you truly do have the faults of your virtues. And that limitation, you can't do much about. Even if you have the time.

One last postscript. The director, that miserable son of a bitch, as often as not these days has to get out and promote the dollars and the pounds, scrounge for the liras, francs, and marks, hock his family's home, his wife's jewels, and his own future so he can make his film. This process of raising the wherewithal inevitably takes ten to a hundred times longer than making the film itself. But the director does it because he has to. Who else will? Who else loves the film that much?

So, my friends, you've seen how much you have to know and what kind of a bastard you have to be. How hard you have to train yourself and in how many different ways. All of which I did. I've never stopped trying to educate myself and to improve myself.

Elia Kazan (1909–2003) had a distinguished career in theater and films. He received six Tony nominations for Best Director and won three times (for *All My Sons*, 1947; *Death of a Salesman*, 1949; and *J.B.*, 1959). Among his notable films are *A Streetcar Named Desire* (1951), *Viva Zapata!* (1952), *East of Eden* (1955), *A Face in the Crowd* (1957), *Splendor in the Grass* (1961) and *America, America* (1963), all of which received nominations for Best Direction from the Directors Guild of America. He received five Academy Award nominations for Best Director, and two of his films, *Gentleman's Agreement* (1947) and *On the Waterfront* (1954), received Oscars for Best Picture and Best Director. The latter film also won Kazan the DGA Award for Best Direction. He was a Kennedy Center Honoree in 1983 and received an Honorary Oscar in 1999. His autobiography, *A Life*, was published in 1988.

Index

About the Moderator and Editor

Jeremy Kagan works as a director, writer, and producer in feature films and television. After graduating Harvard where he wrote a thesis on filmmaker Sergei Eisenstein, Jeremy attended graduate film school at NYU and then joined the first group of fellows at the American Film Institute in Los Angeles, where he started his professional career directing series, which led to many television movies (his favorite being one he wrote as well—*Katherine: A Portrait of an American Revolutionary,* starring Sissy Spacek). His first theatrical movie was the box office hit *Heroes.* Among some of his other features as a director are *The Big Fix, The Chosen* (Grand Prix at the Montreal World Film Festival and Christopher Award in 1982), and *The Journey of Natty Gann* (the first American film to win a Gold Prize at the Moscow Film Festival in 1987). He has produced and directed and written a number of cable movies, including *Conspiracy: The Trial of the Chicago 8* (HBO, 1988 ACE Awards for Best Special Dramatic Special), *Descending Angel, Courage,* and *Roswell: The UFO Cover-up* (nominated for a 1994 Golden Globe). Jeremy won the 1996 Emmy for Outstanding Direction of a Drama Series (*Chicago Hope*) and his recent works include *Bobbie's Girl,* the Emmy-awarded *Steven Spielberg Presents "Taken,"* and *Crown Height,* which won the Humanitas Award and was nominated for a Directors Guild Award in 2004.

Jeremy has also worked in animation, documentaries, music videos, and multimedia. He is a tenured full professor at USC and has served as the Artistic Director of the Sundance Institute. He is chairperson of the Directors Guild's Special Projects Committee and was awarded the Robert Aldrich Award for "extraordinary service to the guild." Since 1992 he has moderated all the "Meet the Nominees" symposia on which this book is based.